Public Management in the United Kingdom

Public Management in the United Kingdom

A New Introduction

June Burnham

and

Sylvia Horton

palgrave
macmillan

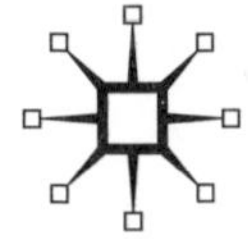

First published 2013 by
PALGRAVE MACMILLAN

Palgrave Macmillan in the UK is an imprint of Macmillan Publishers Limited, registered in England, company number 785998, of Houndmills, Basingstoke, Hampshire RG21 6XS.

Palgrave Macmillan in the US is a division of St Martin's Press LLC, 175 Fifth Avenue, New York, NY 10010.

Palgrave Macmillan is the global academic imprint of the above companies and has companies and representatives throughout the world.

Palgrave® and Macmillan® are registered trademarks in the United States, the United Kingdom, Europe and other countries

ISBN 978–0–230–57628–5 hardback
ISBN 978–0–230–57629–2 paperback

This book is printed on paper suitable for recycling and made from fully managed and sustained forest sources. Logging, pulping and manufacturing processes are expected to conform to the environmental regulations of the country of origin.

A catalogue record for this book is available from the British Library.

A catalog record for this book is available from the Library of Congress.

10 9 8 7 6 5 4 3 2 1
22 21 20 19 18 17 16 15 14 13

Printed in China

Contents

List of Illustrative Materials

Boxes

Figures

Tables

List of Abbreviations

AA	Administrative Assistant
ACPO	Association of Chief Police Officers
AHP	Allied Health Professionals
AI	Additional Inspector of schools
AME	Annually Managed Expenditure
AO	Administrative Officer
BA	British Airways
BBC	British Broadcasting Corporation
BEM	Business Excellence Model
BERR	Department for Business, Enterprise and Regulatory Reform
BID	Business Improvement District
C&AG	Comptroller and Auditor General
CAA	Comprehensive Area Assessment
CAF	Common Assessment Framework
CCT	Compulsory Competitive Tendering
CIPD	Chartered Institute of Personnel and Development
CIPFA	Chartered Institute of Public Finance and Accountancy
CLSP	Community Legal Service Partnership
COSLA	Convention of Scottish Local Authorities
CP	Connexions Partnership
CPA	Comprehensive Performance Assessment
CPD	Continuing professional development
CSA	Child Support Agency
CSC	Civil Service Commissioners
CSCI	Commission for Social Care Inspection
CSIW	Care Standards Inspectorate for Wales
CSR	Comprehensive Spending Review
CSSIW	Care and Social Services Inspectorate for Wales
CTC	City Technology College
DA	Delivery Agreement
DCLG	Department for Communities and Local Government
DEFRA	Department for Environment, Food and Rural Affairs
DEL	Departmental Expenditure Limit
DERA	Defence Evaluation and Research Agency
DETR	Department for the Environment, Transport and the Regions
DfE	Department for Education
DfES	Department for Education and Skills
DfT	Department for Transport

DG	Director General
DH	Department of Health
DHA	District Health Authority
DWP	Department for Work and Pensions
EAZ	Education Action Zone
ECHR	European Court of Human Rights
ECJ	European Court of Justice
EFQM	European Foundation for Quality Management
ENA	Ecole Nationale d'Administration
EO	Executive Officer
ERG	Efficiency and Reform Group
EU	European Union
FHSA	Family Health Service Authorities
FMI	Financial Management Initiative
FTE	Full-Time Equivalent
GCHQ	Government Communications Headquarters
GCSE	General Certificate of Secondary Education
GDP	Gross Domestic Product
GLA	Greater London Authority
GLC	Greater London Council
GMS	Grant Maintained Status
GP	General Practitioner
HAZ	Health Action Zone
HEO	Higher Executive Officer
HMIC	Her Majesty's Inspectorate of Constabulary
HMIP	Her Majesty's Inspectorate of Prisons
HMIS	Her Majesty's Inspectorate of Schools
HMRC	Her Majesty's Revenue & Customs
HR	Human Resources
HRA	Housing Revenue Account
HRM	Human Resource Management
ICT	Information and Communications Technology
ITU	International Telecommunications Union
JP	Justice of the Peace
KSF	Knowledge and Skills Framework
LA	Local Authority
LAA	Local Area Agreement
LEA	Local Education Authority
LEP	Local Enterprise Partnership
LGA	Local Government Association
LSC	Legal Services Commission
LSP	Local Strategic Partnership
MP	Member of Parliament
MPC	Monetary Policy Committee

NAO	National Audit Office
NATS	National Air Traffic Services
NDCP	New Deal for Communities Partnership
NDPB	Non-Departmental Public Body
NHS	National Health Service
NICE	National Institute for Health and Clinical Excellence
NICs	National Insurance Contributions
NICS	Northern Ireland Civil Service
NJC	National Joint Council
NLC	National Leadership Council
NPM	New Public Management
O&M	Organization and Methods
OBR	Office for Budget Responsibility
OCPA	Office of the Commissioner for Public Appointments
ODPM	Office of the Deputy Prime Minister
OECD	Organisation for Economic Co-operation and Development
Ofcom	Office of Communications
Ofgem	Office of Gas and Electricity Markets
OFSTED	Office for Standards in Education, Children's Services and Skills
Oftel	Office of Telecommunications
OPSR	Office of Public Services Reform
ORR	Office of Rail Regulation
PAC	Public Accounts Committee
PASC	Public Administration Select Committee
PCG	Primary Care Group
PCS	Public and Commercial Services Union
PCT	Primary Care Trust
PESC	Public Expenditure Survey Committee
PESTLE	Political, Economic, Social, Technological, Legal Environmental contexts
PFI	Private Finance Initiative
PI	Performance Indicator
PMDU	Prime Minister's Delivery Unit
PMSU	Prime Minister's Strategy Unit
POSDCORB	Planning, Organizing, Staffing, Directing, COordinating, Reporting, Budgeting
PPBS	Planned Programme Budgeting System
PPP	Public–Private Partnership
PRP	Performance-Related Pay
PSA	Public Service Agreement
PSG	Professional Skills for Government
RDA	Regional Development Agency
RHA	Regional Health Authority

RISP	Regional Inspection Servicc Provider
SAT	Standard Attainment Test
SCS	Senior Civil Service
SEF	Self Evaluation Form
SEO	Senior Executive Officer
SHA	Strategic Health Authority
SMART	Specific, Measurable, Achievable, Realistic and Time-bound
SNP	Scottish National Party
SOA	Single Outcome Agreement
SPA	Strategic Partnership Agreement
SRA	Strategic Rail Authority
SSI	Social Services Inspectorate
SSIW	Social Services Inspectorate for Wales
SSRB	Senior Salaries Review Body
SWOT	Strengths, Weaknesses, Opportunities, Threats
TfL	Transport for London
TME	Total Managed Expenditure
TPM	Traditional Personnel Management
TQM	Total Quality Management
TUPE	Transfer of Undertakings (Protection of Employment) Regulations
UK	United Kingdom
USA	United States of America
VAT	Value-Added Tax
VfM	Value for Money
VSM	Very Senior Managers
WAG	Welsh Assembly Government
WAO	Wales Audit Office
WIRS	Workplace Industrial Relations Survey

Acknowledgements

We are grateful to Palgrave Macmillan for agreeing to publish this book and our special thanks to Steven Kennedy, who commissioned the book, for his patience and belief that it would eventually arrive. We are also thankful to those reviewers who thought it was worthy of publication. Finally, our thanks to all those involved in getting the book ready for publication on time. As co-authors, however, we remain responsible for the final product.

JUNE BURNHAM
SYLVIA HORTON

Chapter 1

Public Management: Change or Continuity?

What's in a name? That was the question in the 1980s when public management started to replace public administration. Was it a new label for an old practice or a new practice replacing an old one? Old wine in new bottles or new wine and new bottles? The label 'new public management' (NPM) emphasized the newness. Gunn (1988) suggested it was rooted in the movement to introduce private-sector management into public organizations and was about making the public more like the private. Perry and Kraemer (1983), however, thought it was a new approach to managing public organizations – and was a merger between traditional public administration and private-sector general management; in other words, it was *sui generis* and unique. Pollitt (1990) saw it as an ideology of managerialism based upon a belief in the superiority of the market. Yet a few decades later, Lynn (2006) was rather sceptical that a clear distinction could be found between public administration and public management. These debates are examined and developed further in the early chapters of the book.

The name NPM took hold and Hood (1991) provided a now classic account of this new 'set of doctrines' in public administration. Hood's paper was followed by another classic, Osborne and Gaebler (1992), highlighting the changing role of government and the effect it was having on the way public services were provided and on the relationships between governments, public service providers and the public. Hood (1991) saw NPM as an international as much as a British phenomenon: it was characterized by a slowing-down in the growth of public expenditure, of the size of the public sector and in the number of people employed, and by a trend towards privatization and quasi-privatization: together they were changing the role of the state from provider to enabler. An information technology (IT) revolution was facilitating these changes, and governments across the world were adopting common agendas, including a concern for the 3Es of economy, efficiency and effectiveness, value for money and high quality public services. Hood (2000), while continuing to observe the commonality in the reforms across many different countries, now focused rather on the substantial diversity of national approaches to managerial reform in content, speed and extent. Rather than a 'global paradigm', there were varied responses to the proposals being made by the champions of reform; and this variation continues today.

Public management has a different focus from that of public administration. Public management is concerned essentially with the way resources are used and managed to achieve the political objectives of government: public administration is more concerned with the way that laws and policies are implemented according to rules and correct procedures. Both involve systems of accountability and control but the former is judged by results, outputs and outcomes, the latter by compliance, process and mistake avoidance. However, both sets of practices have to be examined within the contexts of their historical, cultural, political, social, economic and administrative subsystems, not forgetting the impact of ideology and new ideas upon decision makers. This framework was used by Pollitt and Bouckaert (2004) to compare different countries, and helped to explain the radical nature of the British reforms.

The public sector is not fixed because the boundaries of the state are politically determined as we show in the book. A once small public sector has expanded, and is still large. Public management today is still the management of more than half the economy but the institutional composition is more complex than three decades ago. The core, consisting of central and local government departments and agencies within a semi-federal system, is now surrounded by a penumbra of private businesses, social enterprises and voluntary organizations working in partnerships and hybrid relationships within a system of governance. These organizations and networks must work collaboratively to meet the needs and expectations of the public they are there to serve.

In the following chapters we explain these new ways of organizing the public sector in the United Kingdom (UK). We trace the changes in public management and the public sector itself over the last thirty or so years. It is not possible to understand today's practices unless we can see them in the context of what has gone before and how the historical and cultural context fashions the ways we do things now. It demonstrates that there are legacies of the past overlapping with new ideas: continuity mingles with change. There are different trajectories of public management reform, which reflect different perceptions of the nature of the problems faced by governments: first, the size and role of the state; second, the structure of government; third, inefficiency in the public sector; fourth, the delivery of services that people want; and fifth, the lack of involvement of the public and communities in conceiving and delivering public services. Each of these trajectories has called for different responses, including privatization, structural re-engineering and agencification, performance management, total quality management, decentralization, democratization and now community empowerment and 'the Big Society'.

The following chapters naturally emphasize these innovations in public management, setting each within its particular contexts of evolutionary inheritance and contemporary pressures for change. Before introducing those chapters in more detail, we outline here the more general background that stretches across chapters, in which the key features are: first, the constitutional and institutional development of the four-nation division that shows we cannot assume there is one 'public management in the UK'; second, the general approach (or approaches) in the UK to the scope and delivery of public services; and third, the UK's involvement in international networks that both constrain and support its public management style.

It is impossible to introduce *Public Management in the United Kingdom* today without reference to its international, national and sub-national environments. The international context is overwhelmingly that of a financial crisis, which is having an acute effect on public budgets, staffing and services in the UK as in many other countries. Yet this critical phase is only one moment in the UK's steady integration into the European and global political economy that is modifying many aspects of domestic public management.

At UK level, the advent in 2010 of the Coalition Government of Conservatives and Liberal Democrats, and the scale of change it decided to impose on the public sector, were both unprecedented in recent times. Nevertheless, there is much that is evolutionary rather than revolutionary: Prime Minister David Cameron's orientation towards a wider range of service providers in 'the Big Society' is an incremental development from Labour's 'third sector', which itself built on the historic participation of voluntary organizations in collective services; and many of the Coalition's initial, more radical, proposals were substantially moderated before or during implementation. Even the Coalition's drastic cutbacks were made credible by the recent history of reform to public financial and performance management: there is now a well-established expectation that public services will be managed economically in good times or bad.

The devolution of political power to 'sub-national' governments in Scotland, Wales and Northern Ireland – and more devolution is under way – was a highly radical departure from the recent practices of centralizing governments in London. However, these reforms amplified an existing diversity of administrative provisions that originated in the construction of the UK from distinct nations and provinces. At each territorial level, therefore, prominent or arresting decisions in the domain of public management are being made within a broader political, economic, cultural and historic environment that sets the boundaries for the choices made today.

The development of four-nation governance

The Coalition Government granted additional powers to Scotland, Wales and Northern Ireland, further deepening the 'asymmetric' system of governance across the four parts of the UK. The Labour Government in 1999 had already devolved law-making competence and taxation powers to a new Scottish

Parliament and given the new Welsh Assembly secondary, regulation-making powers. Since 1999, most domestic policy-making functions have been restored to Northern Ireland, which had been substantially autonomous until 1972. England is the largest part of the UK but neither the nation nor its regions have separate political institutions. Labour proposed to create regional assemblies but in practice they emerged only in London. Devolution has, paradoxically, made it much clearer that distinctions already existed between the ways in which public services in the component parts of the UK were managed, deriving from their different historical development (Mitchell 2009).

England (and the UK from 1707)

England has long been the dominant part of the UK, partly because of its greater wealth and size (currently more than three-quarters of the UK population), partly because it was the first to become an organized sovereign state. Yet it was slow to develop a public bureaucracy or a universal system of local government services. From the thirteenth century the sovereign appointed a Justice of the Peace (JP) to each area of the country to settle local legal cases. They accrued responsibilities for some limited local service provision (justice, prisons, highways, rudimentary social welfare) at county level until the end of the nineteenth century, while prosperous market towns were granted the status of self-government as borough corporations (burghs in Scotland). Growing parliamentary and judicial authority in the seventeenth century followed by civil war between parliamentarians and royalists ended with a limited monarchy in which the sovereign ruled with the advice of a Cabinet of ministers, whose advice he or she increasingly had to take. At national level, the separate departments of state (diplomacy, trade, education, agriculture, public health) started to emerge as committees advising ministers; but they remained very slow to develop policy functions and a bureaucratic organization until well into the nineteenth century.

Electoral reform from 1832 encouraged ministers and other leading politicians to develop party machinery to organize voter support, and then party discipline to control parliament. The remaining royal powers, such as appointing ministers to the various departments and recruiting and managing a civil service, were exercised by the prime minister. By the 1890s, a government with a single-party majority had the power that is a strong feature of British governments and which could have enabled them to implement public management reforms. However, in the nineteenth century, both major parties, the Conservatives and the Liberals, were against public intervention. Despite the growing social needs stemming from mass industrialization and urbanization, they were reluctant to install a nation-wide system of funded local government or a centrally organized public bureaucracy capable of dealing with these problems. Conservatives traditionally resisted the introduction of new institutions, partly to keep down property taxes but also because they followed the precepts of the political philosopher Edmund Burke, who argued that long-established ways were better because their survival had proved their value ('what matters is what works', as the Blair Government said). Nevertheless, 'to avert the risk of more drastic change' (Ellis and Treasure 2005: 173), a Conservative government introduced elected county-level councils (1888 in England and Wales, 1889 in Scotland, 1898 in Ireland) and then a Liberal Government an elected lower tier in 1894 (1898 in Ireland). The Liberals favoured the free market and in principle intervened only to improve economic efficiency – but used this argument to modernize the civil service (1854), provide public utilities in industrial cities (from the 1850s), and introduce social health and welfare insurance (1911).

Though the newly formed Labour Party (1906) wanted collective services, when it entered government in the 1920s it lacked solid parliamentary majorities and the behind-the-scenes bureaucratic help for coordinating and driving change across the various departments. During the 1939–45 war the Cabinet Office expanded, bringing in 'outsiders' to prepare for the post-war reconstruction and developing its coordinating role. A landslide victory for the Labour Party in 1945 enabled the new government to introduce the welfare state, nationalize the major industries and manage the economy using Keynesian economic theories. These substantial reforms were made possible by the same features that 40 years later enabled the Conservatives to implement New Public Management (NPM) reforms (Pollitt and Bouckaert 2004: 40): namely a centralized and coordinated state, a majoritarian political executive, a non-politicized bureaucracy that acts on behalf of ministers (not its own sense of 'the public interest'), and an input of ideas from outside the bureaucracy (see Chapter 2).

Most post-war Conservative Governments accepted the changes to public management, though Labour governments tended to initiate the reforms to institutional structures, such as economic planning regions in 1964 or the restructuring of local government in 1966 to match urban growth, whereas Conservative Governments tended to water them down. However, Britain's economic problems in the 1970s brought a different approach from the Conservative government led by Margaret Thatcher, 1979–90. Combining nineteenth-century economic liberalism with an even earlier Conservative emphasis on responsibility and authority (Heywood 1998), Thatcher's efforts to 'roll back the state' produced an impact on public sector management that will be evident throughout this book. In the area of territorial management, the Greater London Council and six other metropolitan county councils were abolished, ostensibly to 'streamline' the administration of conurbations, though there were also political reasons. The Blair Government restored Greater London government in 2000 with a directly elected mayor and assembly, and created English regional chambers that could have become directly elected assemblies where regions wanted them. The original chambers were appointed but in the first referendum on an elected assembly for North East England, 78 per cent of voters rejected the idea. No chamber ever became an elected assembly and the Labour Government abolished the regional chambers before it left office in 2010. The Coalition Government seems unlikely to revive them, though it legislated to transpose the concept of powerful elected mayors to other major English cities.

Wales and Scotland

Although Wales was incorporated into the English administrative system by the sixteenth century, the government's reliance on the local gentry to carry out public duties gave Wales some local responsiveness. From the nineteenth century, special boards were created for Wales whenever its concerns were different from those of England (agriculture, health and education) or when Wales demanded the same treatment as Ireland or Scotland, such as on National Insurance in 1910 (Mitchell 2009: 40–4). However, projects to combine these 'quangos' (quasi-autonomous non-governmental bodies) into a single executive body for Wales failed because of long-standing divisions within Wales. As ministerial departments developed in London in the early twentieth century they created specific 'Wales' divisions. The post-1945 Labour Government set up a Welsh advisory council and asked the Home Secretary to coordinate the 'Wales' divisions but without specific executive powers (O'Neill 2004: 18–20). In Wales itself there was no clear mandate for further action until 1964, when the Labour Government was forced by growing pressure from Plaid Cymru ('Party of Wales') to set up a Welsh Office with 'a Minister for Wales'.

Unlike Wales, Scotland had long been an independent state, and has always possessed some independent functions. When Scotland joined England and Wales in 1707, the Treaty of Union protected Scots law, royal burghs, and the Church of Scotland with its education system. As the British government increased its activity, it did so in Scotland by creating quasi-autonomous boards under the distant supervision of the British Home Secretary. Worries about the boards, like those about quangos today (lack of coordination, poor accountability of unelected appointees), and also about a loss of Scottish distinctiveness in other policy areas, led in 1885 to the creation of the Scottish Office (Mitchell 2009: 19), and the appointment of a Scottish Secretary to present Scotland's interests in Cabinet, Parliament and Whitehall. Further functions tended to be devolved whenever Scots law or the context was distinctive. The Scottish Office was relocated to Edinburgh in 1939 (Rhodes *et al.* 2003: 72–4), acted as a mini-Whitehall for Scotland's affairs and over the decades negotiated a favourable financial treatment for Scotland. Yet the Office could vary how the funding was spent only within the UK's overall financial, administrative and policy framework. Scotland had a strong form of administrative devolution before 1999, but not political power, because the wishes expressed by Scots could always be over-ruled by legislation passed in Westminster by an English majority, even in the relatively protected area of education.

The growth of nationalist parties in both Wales and Scotland led to the Labour Government setting up a Royal Commission (Kilbrandon 1973), which recommended devolution. In 1974, Labour was elected with only a slim parliamentary majority of nine overall, and increasingly needed the support of the eleven Scottish Nationalist Party (SNP) and three Plaid Cymru Members of Parliament (MPs) as its majority declined through deaths and by-elections. The government had to offer referendums on devolution in 1979. Welsh voters rejected devolution (20.3 per cent for devolution) and the vote in Scotland (51.6 per cent in favour) did not reach the required 40 per cent of the total electorate.

The radical policies of the Thatcher Government created a coalition in Scotland of those who wanted devolution with those who opposed the Conservatives (Mitchell 2003: 36). The impact on Labour Party opinion was greater in Scotland than in Wales because it was losing more votes to the 'home rule' party. From 1989, an unofficial Scottish Constitutional Convention of the main parties and civil society made plans for a devolved parliament. The referendums held soon after the Blair Government took office in 1997 produced a large Scottish majority in favour of a parliament (74.3 per cent) but only a bare majority in Wales for the less powerful assembly (50.3 per cent).

The 'constitutional rules', notably the policy areas reserved to the UK parliament, were set out in the Scotland Act 1998 and Government of Wales Act 1998. 'Concordats' set out the ground rules for the interactions between Whitehall ministries and the devolved governments, and guidelines on civil service personnel management. These guidelines, like the legislation, assumed that devolution would have little impact on the civil service, which remained unified, though the roles of civil servants in the different territories are diverging (Burnham and Pyper 2008: 94–102). Elections to the Scottish Parliament and Welsh Assembly were first held in 1999, but the process of devolution continues, with both Labour and Coalition Governments in London acceding to Scottish and Welsh demands for further powers.

Northern Ireland

Northern Ireland, too, started to govern itself again in 1999, after nearly four decades of Direct Rule by the UK government. Ireland was ruled by force and colonization from Great Britain until the Act of Union 1801 when the 'United Kingdom of Great Britain and Ireland' was formed. Three attempts by Liberal Governments from the late nineteenth century to introduce 'home rule' failed to become law because of parliamentary objections. Irish Nationalists were themselves divided between those who wanted independence and those who wanted decentralization, while 'Unionists' wanted to remain under British government. The Anglo-Irish civil war in 1919 was resolved in 1920 by a separation between northern Ireland ('Ulster') and southern Ireland, each having control over its internal affairs. This decentralization was insufficient for the majority in southern Ireland, which became entirely independent in 1949.

The Northern Ireland parliament ('Stormont') had law-making powers except in international affairs, defence, social welfare and taxation. The Northern Ireland Civil Service (NICS) was created from the Irish Civil Service as a separate body from the British civil service, and remains separate today. Ulster Unionist leaders used their powers over jobs, housing, education and the police to increase support among Protestants (O'Neill 2004: 41): discrimination against Catholics was identified by Lord Cameron (1969) as a cause of the 'troubles'. After the civil rights demonstrations in 1968, there was an escalation of political conflict into civil war. In 1972 the UK Parliament suspended and then abolished Stormont, and transferred most local authority functions to the Northern Ireland Departments staffed by the NICS or to area boards. Northern Ireland was governed directly by the UK's Northern Ireland Secretary, assisted by a new Northern Ireland Office and the British army was sent to maintain law and order.

Attempts to re-introduce devolved structures failed in the mid-1970s and again in the mid-1980s, but a long collaboration between the UK and Irish governments resulted in 1995 in a plan for a Northern Ireland Assembly that would operate under Irish-British supervision. It would have a power-sharing Executive elected from the different communities represented in the Assembly. Elections took place in 1998 and powers were devolved under the Northern Ireland Act but disputes between the parties often led to the Assembly being suspended. Progress continued, however, towards 'normal politics' and additional policy domains, including policing, were transferred by the Labour Government. The Coalition Government has offered to transfer further powers, such as the levying of corporation tax on businesses and air passenger duty. In all three cases, therefore, the relationships between the devolved governments and the UK government are continuing to evolve.

Evolving approaches to public services

The Conservative Party's election manifesto in 2010 deplored 'big government' and proposed to replace it with the 'Big Society':

> a society with much higher levels of personal, professional, civic and corporate responsibility; a society where people come together to solve problems and improve life for themselves and their communities; a society where the leading force for progress is social responsibility, not state control. (Conservative Party 2010a: 37)

David Cameron (2010a) described the concept in more formal terms as 'the post-bureaucratic age', which, as academics explained to parliament (Hood and Lodge 2011: 56), could mean, depending on the particular public activity concerned:

- it would be delivered as locally as possible, and preferably by independent individuals or private or voluntary groups, unless the tasks were beyond their capacity;
- it would be organized and delivered with the least possible formal intervention by the state;
- it would involve as much public participation as possible;
- it would simply be abandoned by the public authorities without alternative arrangements being made.

As we have seen, the historical and cultural tendency in the UK, especially in England, was to resist the systemic provision of collective services; governments only reluctantly accepted these were public responsibilities. Yet the state intervened in the end because of the failure of local, voluntary and private providers to solve the problems arising from industrialization and its consequences: population movement and mass urbanization. Social welfare concerns joined with the economic need for healthy, educated, mobile workers to bring about state intervention and a coordinating public management that had advantages (efficiency, equity, probity, comprehensiveness) as well as disadvantages (standardization, 'bureaucracy', weak responsiveness to citizens or adaptability to social change). Yet 'the Big Society' may still find a need for 'bureaucracy'. These points can be illustrated with a brief survey of three different types of services: education, social welfare and public utilities.

Education

Except in Scotland, education in Britain was a rather random affair until the end of the nineteenth century: it was left up to the voluntary sector (churches and charitable donors), private schools and various borough corporations. Schools had originally been provided by the monasteries to train priests but, during the English Reformation of the sixteenth century, most monastery schools were destroyed. Grammar schools were then founded by some boroughs and merchants but educated mainly the well-off. In contrast, the Scottish Reformation stressed bible-reading literacy, and a system of parish schools was established in the seventeenth century, alongside the burgh grammar schools. It was public provision in the sense it was paid mainly from property rates (local taxes) and was universal but it was overseen by the Church of Scotland. In England and Wales, disputes between different churches and concerns in parliament about the social and political impact –

the 'threat of mass education' – held back the provision of schooling (Chitty 2009: 3–6). In 1802, parliament rejected a bill to introduce a system of parish schools like those in Scotland; however another bill of the same year required factory owners to provide tuition to child workers. The churches then became more active, especially once the government provided grants. Yet the historical pattern of church parishes did not match the urbanization of the industrial revolution, leaving many areas without adequate school provision. Even in Scotland, schooling was very variable in quality, unable to cope with demand and increasingly reliant on central government grants (Smout 1986: 209–30).

In 1870, with nearly half the children in England and Wales having no education (the rest in voluntary and grant-aided schools), the Liberal Government made a compromise with the churches (Jenkins 1997: 322–5). The Education Act 1870 enabled school boards to be set up to organize state schools in areas where no church schools existed. The boards were locally elected, could charge a local property rate and levy small fees. Churches could apply for state funding, church schools would not be absorbed into the state system, and religion would be taught in state schools. In Scotland the equivalent Act of 1872 set up a comprehensive system of elected local boards, enabling responsibility to pass from the church to a new Scottish Education Department. In England and Wales, arrangements remained rather ad hoc and confused until 1902, when the recently created local authorities were made responsible for planning primary education for all children in their areas. These 'local education authorities' (LEAs) were to include the church schools (except Catholic schools) in their planning, including their secular curriculum. Grammar schools too were later brought into the system, enabling councils to provide a coherent service that could be linked to other local government services. At national level, the Board of Education was created in 1900 to provide a unifying impetus on standards and qualifications, essential in an era of increasing mobility, but central authority was intentionally weak in what was designed as a locally decided service, even after the 1944 Education Act made education 'a national system, locally administered' (Chitty 2009: 21).

Concern grew across the parties in the 1970s about the power of chief education officers and teachers and the general quality of the education being provided and its usefulness for business needs. The response of the Conservative Government of the 1980s was to reduce the LEA's scope, emphasize the strategic role of the Department for Education, and decentralize: to parents, business, governing bodies and school sponsors. Market competition was introduced by making it easier for parents to choose a particular school, guided by 'league tables' of performance. Some could choose between schools managed by different providers: either public (LEA or individually grant-maintained), voluntary (state-aided church schools), partly in private hands (sponsored schools), or even one of the continuing 'public' private schools. The positive features of the earlier 'bureaucratic' system were now exposed. For example, LEAs, though still responsible for providing an efficient system in which every child had a place, were unable to plan provision to match demographic trends because schools, good or bad, that feared closure would 'opt out' and seek more generous treatment directly from central government.

On taking power in 1997, the Labour Government retained the different types of school, but it brought them back within the LEA administrative system. Now the Coalition has made autonomous 'academy' status available to a much larger number of schools, and added 'free schools' – state-funded schools with a freer choice of curriculum set up in a variety of premises by virtually any group, subject to central authorization, but outside the local authority system. Both Blair's former Head of Delivery Unit, Michael Barber, and the Coalition-appointed head of the schools inspectorate, Michael Wilshaw, have drawn attention to their fears if large numbers of 'standalone' schools are left without the 'middle tier' support and supervision provided by LEAs (*Financial Times,* 26 December 2011). The contemporary range of school provision has much in common with the 'public schools', 'private venture schools', 'church schools' and 'board schools' that failed to answer nineteenth-century needs. Even though a 'Big Society' approach to education has certain attractions, local or central bureaucracies are still needed to plan provision, allocate public funding and monitor standards, and advise schools when problems arise, to ensure that every child receives an education of an acceptable and equivalent quality.

Social welfare

The evolution of social welfare provision in the UK shows a similar pattern to that of education. An ad hoc approach by governments and parliaments reluctant for the state to intervene, and relying on local voluntary provision, produced a confusing and inadequate service; its failings only started to be addressed once a comprehensive public service was organized. Following the abolition of the monasteries, the English parliament in the sixteenth century decided that parish churchwardens and JPs should help the impoverished but it took several Poor Law Acts before their resources moved from voluntary to compulsory local donations, and then local taxes with the Poor Law Act of 1601. By the early 1800s many parishes were unable to cope with the distress arising from poverty and disease, though some more prosperous boroughs were able to promote individual Acts of Parliament to build workhouses that helped the needy more efficiently (and discouraged the needy from seeking help).

Arguments about efficiency persuaded parliament to pass the 1834 Poor Law Amendment Act that set up locally elected boards that straddled several parishes and were big enough to build workhouses, which were expected to be economical and reduce the 'poor rate' bills they levied. The board concept was adopted for an increasing number of public health and welfare functions: not only the poor law and school boards but also highways boards (1835) and public health or sanitary boards for water, sewers and street cleaning (1848). It produced a chaotic overlapping of special-purpose authorities, each with their own boards of local gentry, their own officials, levying their own rates, operating within their own boundaries. As in education, there was a parallel development in the voluntary and private sectors – charitable 'almshouses' for the homeless elderly, and 'friendly societies', trade unions and insurance companies that assisted workers in periods of unemployment or sickness but which chiefly covered skilled workers in long-term employment who could afford to pay contributions. The complex structure offers an image of what David Cameron's 'Big Society' might look like if 'people come together to solve problems for … their communities' (Conservative Party 2010a: 37) without a supporting bureaucracy to integrate provision and fill in the gaps where no community groups come forward.

Some rationalization took place in 1875 when a complete system of public health authorities was introduced throughout England and Wales and combined with the poor law boards in rural areas. The new public health obligation on urban boroughs to clear slums led to them being permitted to build replacement council housing, financed from the rates. After the 1914–18 war, councils were enabled to develop a housing programme with government subsidies. Urban poor law boards remained separate, and continued to fund services from the 'poor rate'. Yet without the modern national system of cross-subsidies (taxpayer-funded local government grants or welfare benefits) this arrangement meant that householders in areas in greatest need faced the highest poor rate bills, though they themselves were likely to be poorer. A question for the 'Big Society' strategy, therefore, will be how far issues can be managed by community groups without a commensurate 'back office' bureaucracy at national level for equalizing or sharing resources.

The Liberal Government of 1911 answered this question with the National Insurance scheme to which employees, employers and the state all contributed. It was delivered until after the 1939–45 war by the voluntary societies under the supervision of National Commissions in England, Scotland and Wales. Yet the scheme did not cover the self-employed and some other groups, for whom local councils and poor law boards retained responsibility. The welfare state legislation of 1946–48 (the National Health Service Act; the National Insurance Act and the National Assistance Act), at last provided universal rights to basic 'cradle to grave' health and welfare.

In the 1950s, local government was asked to plan and provide mass social housing. Housing in the UK has however long been a mixture of private ownership, private renting and charitable, voluntary or public sector renting. The public rented sector became larger than the private rented sector only in the 1960s, and has since been sharply cut back by successive governments, who directed subsidies towards voluntary and private-sector provision (see

Chapter 3). Yet it is still a public bureaucracy – local government social services and then the housing department – that has continued to bear the ancient 'poor law' responsibility of housing vulnerable citizens, even if the practical arrangements are now mostly made through other providers.

The health and welfare function was a large factor in the growth of the UK's national bureaucracy, even though healthcare and social services are delivered by other agencies. In the mid-1970s, when the number of British civil servants was at its peak (see Figure 1.1, p. 18), the departments responsible for these services employed 134,000 officials. Despite very substantial cuts in the overall size of the civil service under the Conservative Governments (a 30 per cent cut 1979–97), the departments for employment and for health and social security continued to grow, to 138,000 by 1997 (*Civil Service Statistics*). Adding to this negative impression of a public welfare bureaucracy resistant to control is the judgement that the welfare state encouraged the creation of an extensive professional bureaucracy that treated service users as passive, dependent clients not as individual citizens (Needham 2007: 49–50). Such attitudes can be ameliorated and public sector reforms such as the Citizen's Charter (see Chapter 6) have tackled them directly. Specifically in the welfare area, the Blair Government implemented an imaginative reform to the welfare system by integrating the employment and social security departments into a network of Jobcentre Plus offices. The organization has been restructured to deliver services efficiently with the aid of communications technologies that respond to the modern demand for instant access but allows most attention to be given to those most needing it. This project enabled staff to offer a better 'front office' service individually tailored to people seeking work and claiming benefits (PAC 2008a: 9–11). Yet staff making allocation decisions will always have, at some level, to be acting in a 'bureaucratic' way – equitable, accountable, and therefore regulation and rule-regarding – because they are transferring a significant proportion of the public budget to private individuals.

The public utilities

Despite the very different character of infrastructure-based services from personal services, the historic approach of UK governments to their provision treated them in much the same way. National governments did not much intervene in public utilities until the 1914–18 war showed the advantages of planning and coordinating the production of supplies and transport. Until then, governments regulated to ensure safety but were against restricting competition. Infrastructure-heavy services (highways, water, sewers, railways, gas, electricity, telephones) were supplied by private entrepreneurs. Private companies, borough corporations and quango-like 'Turnpike Trustees' and 'Improvements Commissioners' sought permission from parliament to build infrastructure in a specified area and charge for their services.

The new urban MPs elected in 1832 passed thc 1833 Scottish Burgh Reform Act and the 1835 Municipal Corporations Act for England and Wales that permitted all councils to provide lighting, water and sewers without special legislation. By the end of the nineteenth century, many larger boroughs had created companies to supply these services. However, services elsewhere were sparse and offered mainly by the private sector.

During the 1914–18 war the government controlled the rail companies and its experiences led it to amalgamate them into four monopoly operators before handing them back to the private sector in 1921. It was unable to persuade local electricity companies similarly to join forces to provide a nation-wide network to uniform standards. It therefore created the Central Electricity Board in 1926, as one of the first public corporations, to construct a national grid and supply it with electricity, leaving local public and private electricity companies in place. The 1939–45 war, followed by the election of a Labour Government in 1945, stimulated a more intense round of government intervention. Not only did the Labour Party's founding constitution at the end of the 1914–18 war commit it to 'the public ownership of the means of production', but also there was a more widespread urge for infrastructure that would facilitate reconstruction and economic development, which the private sector had failed to provide. During the war, a public hydro-electricity board had taken over the private electricity companies in northern Scotland to increase production, and the rest of the electricity industry was nationalized in 1947; the gas industry was nationalized in 1948. The rail companies were not returned to their owners but nationalized in 1947, along with many other transport companies, to be managed by the British Transport Commission as 'a properly integrated system'. The 1945 Water Act allowed larger councils to retain their water companies but others were required to form joint water boards. Even these authorities were not large enough to provide for increasing demand, and responsibility for water was transferred in 1973 to public regional water authorities – with a difference in Scotland, where local authorities retained this function until 1995 and continue to help define this public service.

Public ownership of the utilities was not much questioned until the 1980s. The traditional economic argument in favour of state-owned utilities, supporting Labour's position, is that an operator of an existing network is a natural monopoly (no new operator can hope to construct from scratch a similar service at a lower price). Utilities should therefore be in public hands to stop consumer exploitation. From the 1980s, the Conservative leadership followed economic theories that assumed public bureaucracies promoted their own interest, and that privatization and competition would force them to offer better value for money (see Chapter 2). This argument applied to the public corporations even more forcefully because ministers had legally only a general objective-setting and accountability role, and because the corporations were delivering a technical service which few ministers or civil servants could question – it was only during electricity privatization, for example, that ministers learned the 'financial and economic truths' about nuclear power, according to the then Chancellor of the Exchequer (Lawson 1993: 236–7).

Conservative Governments privatized nearly all the network utilities between 1984 and 1996, in each case appointing a regulatory office to control the behaviour of the monopolistic companies it had created, and to promote competition (see Chapter 7). The Labour Government did not seek to re-nationalize the privatized utilities, and its rescue of some rail and electricity organizations and banks was seen as temporary measures. It part-privatized National Air Traffic Services (NATS) and made preparations to part-sell Royal Mail that the Coalition Government has continued but has been unable to bring to fruition in the current financial climate. While there can be an expanding role for communities in those utilities that can be run locally (such as rural community buses), the major public utilities have shown that even if they are privately owned and managed they will be publicly regulated, and often part-publicly funded, for the foreseeable future.

The Cameron thesis expressly contrasts 'post-bureaucracy' with 'bureaucracy', much as all recent governments have contrasted 'front office' with 'back office', as if one were always good and the other bad, though there is little that organizations can achieve without back office, and indeed 'bureaucratic', support.

The international context

In the present economic climate, the greatest international constraints on UK public management would seem to be the global financial markets and budgetary weaknesses in the UK's trading partners in the European Union (EU), which adversely affect the UK's public finances, reducing the resources available, while placing greater demand on public services. However, the intensity of these problems should not obscure the constant but less dramatic ways in which national public managers are affected by the international environment.

The UK has for a century and more cooperated in intergovernmental organizations such as the International Telecommunications Union (ITU, since 1871), or the Organisation for Economic Cooperation and Development (OECD, since 1948). Membership hampers its own freedom to act but the restrictions are believed to be balanced by wider benefits. Most such organizations affect policy, not management, strictly speaking. However, some intergovernmental organizations, such as the Council of Europe (1949), which promotes democracy and human rights, are directly concerned with public administration. The Council's Charter of Local Self Government was signed by the Labour Government in 1998 and supported the campaign by UK local authorities for a 'general power of competence' (common in Europe) which the Coalition Government agreed to enact. The Council's

European Court of Human Rights (ECHR) implements the European Convention on Human Rights, ratified by the UK in 1950, but its judgements are recommendations that governments are not compelled to follow, though they generally do. The ECHR principles were incorporated directly into UK law as the Human Rights Act by the Blair Government in 1998, and must now be taken into consideration by civil servants and other public officials. The ECHR developed the principles on data protection which, following legislation by the EU, now govern how data processing is used in UK public services. The OECD's membership comprises the more highly developed economies and its main objective is to pursue that development; thus its public management programme over the last twenty years or so has been very much in the spirit of the efficiency reforms pursued by the UK since the 1980s, although the UK has followed (and inspired) the OECD's preferred strategies in some areas more than others (more on human resources reforms and deregulation, less on financial and budgetary planning, see OECD 2009a: Annex C).

As the examples above suggest, decisions and agreements of intergovernmental organizations constrain but do not absolutely bind member states. In contrast, the EU is a supranational organization. Once agreements are made jointly by member states in those policy domains in which the EU has supreme competence, members must abide by them or face action in the European Court of Justice (ECJ). Although 'public administration', like education, is not an EU competence, other areas of competence, especially private-sector employment law and public purchasing are within the EU domain and have an indirect but substantial effect on UK public administration (just like mutual recognition of university degrees and professional qualifications has an indirect effect on education and training).

There are three core areas in which EU law makes an everyday impact on UK public management (and which are explored further in Chapter 4): human resources issues, especially equal remuneration for work of equal value, and the protection of employees' accrued rights if transferred to another employer; procurement decisions by public authorities: bidders must be treated equally and the lowest cost or best value for money offer accepted (to ensure that governments do not discriminate against traders from other EU countries or subsidize national suppliers 'unfairly'); and regulations on the network utilities, to ensure that they too trade 'fairly' and are open to competition. Governments do not need to privatize public enterprises but they must structure them in such a way (by separating the rail network operator's accounts from the train operator's accounts, for example), that operators from other member states can compete to supply services. All these provisions derive from the EU's objective of achieving a 'common' or 'single' market. This objective has always been shared by UK governments and was driven hard from the 1980s by the Thatcher Government and the then EU Trade Commissioner, Leon Brittan, previously Trade Secretary under Margaret Thatcher. The EU has, on the whole, moved in the direction that the UK and other free-trading nations preferred but some of the subsidiary provisions to complete the single market have placed unexpected and often unwelcome constraints on public organizations.

Some academics and public management consultants see the UK's membership of international and supranational organizations as one dimension ('upwards') in the transfer of power away from once largely self-sufficient Whitehall bureaucracies – the other dimensions being the transfer of functions 'downwards' to departmental agencies and devolved assemblies, and the transfer of implementation 'outwards' to the private and voluntary sectors; together these processes have created a 'hollowed-out state' (Foster and Plowden 1996; Weller *et al.* 1997). The Big Society or de-bureaucratization approach would continue this movement, even perhaps along the international dimension too, led by the oldest intergovernmental organization, the ITU, which brings together not only the governments' official representatives but also their partners in business.

Charting the evolution of the public sector

The numbers in public sector employment can serve as a summary of the evolution in public intervention that has been outlined above. Figure 1.1 illustrates the growth of the civil service as the 'night watchman' state turned into the beginnings of a welfare state under the Liberal Governments of 1905–15. Expansion during the two World Wars was followed each time by some 'retrenchment'. But the 1945 Labour Government's reforms needed civil servants to plan, manage and deliver new services, and the 'non-industrial' civil service continued to grow to its peak of 571,000 in 1977, making a total of 745,000 when the 174,000 industrial civil servants who worked in the dockyards and government departments are added. In 1976 the economic crisis forced cutbacks on the Labour Government. On arriving in office in 1979 the Conservatives continued to put pressure on the civil service to reduce its numbers. The number of non-industrial staff had been reduced to 429,000 by 1999 but the number of industrial staff fell even more sharply as manual work was contracted out and the dockyards were closed or sold. Yet the level of non-industrial staffing in 1999 was the same as in the mid-1960s, one sign that 'the hollowed-out state' still had considerable capacity. From 1999 the civil service even expanded again, partly as a result of policies which required more officials (in prisons and immigration, tax and employment offices), partly because Labour had a greater 'willingness to spend money and employ people' (Flynn 2007: 11). From 2009 numbers started to decline again as first Labour and then the Coalition confronted another economic crisis.

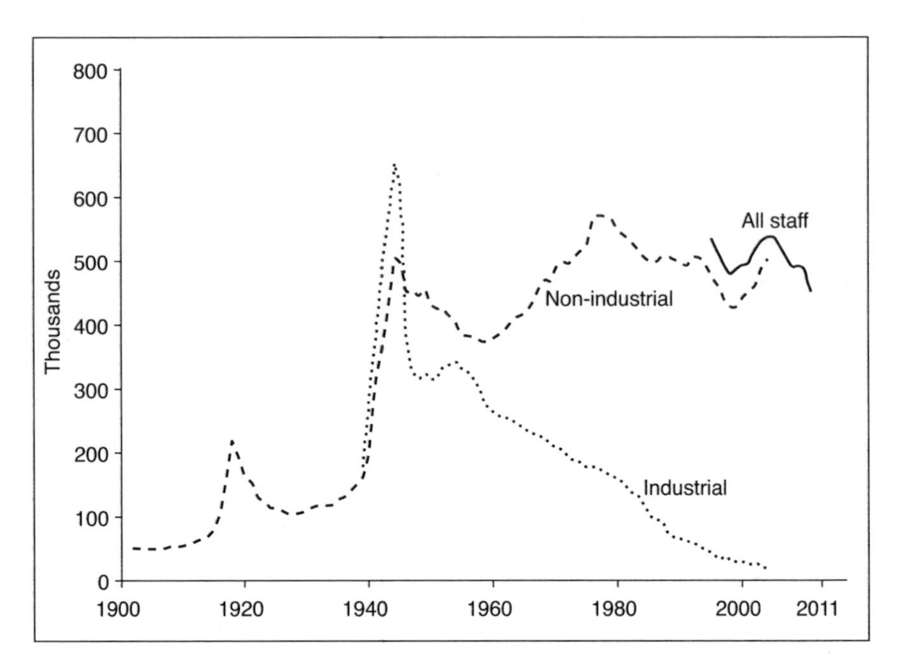

Figure 1.1 ***Historical trends in the size of the civil service***

Note: 'All staff' includes industrial and non-industrial civil servants and casual staff, but post office workers are excluded throughout. Headcount figures.
Sources: Adapted from data from the Office for National Statistics (ONS) in HM Treasury, Civil Service Statistics 1993, Cabinet Office, Civil Service Statistics 2004. Available from www.civilservice.gov.uk/management/statistics/reports/2004/history/index.asp, accessed 29 March 2007.

Figure 1.2 shows how the size of the public sector as a whole has changed since the 1960s. (Figures for recent years are provided in Chapter 3.) The biggest change overall occurred among the 'nationalized industries', otherwise known as 'public corporations'. Most were privatized between 1982 and 1995; Royal Mail and London Underground are now the only large entities in this sector – though the temporarily nationalized banks also come into this category and caused the 'blip' after 2008. The 'local government' here includes not only local councils but also schools and police forces. Though local government was cut back from the late 1980s, there were increases in resources and staff in social work, education and the police; these were reversed from 2008, and especially from 2010 following the Coalition's sharp budgetary cutbacks. Central government is usually taken as including the NHS and the armed forces. The chart separates out the NHS, to show first its gradual expansion, then a substantial step change in the Labour Government's second term, 2001–5. The size of the defence forces continues to decline. Finally, 'central government' in the graph consists of the administrative arm of the state, meaning not only the civil service (in the devolved administrations too), but also officials in 'non-departmental public bodies' controlled by ministers – the quangos.

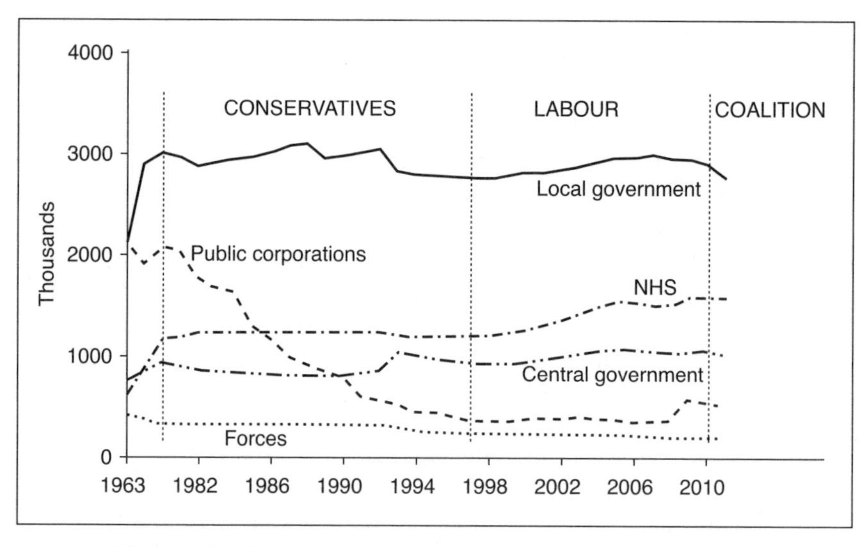

Figure 1.2 ***Trends in the main components of the public sector***

Note: The years to the left of the 1979 vertical line are compressed.
Sources: Adapted from data from the Office for National Statistics in Black, O., Herbert, R. and Richardson, I. (2004) 'Jobs in the Public Sector mid-2003', Labour Market Trends, July, 271–81: 272–3; and on-line Time Series C9KA, C9KC, C9KD, C9KE, C9LB, C9LG, available from www.ons.gov.uk.

The rest of the book

Some reference has already been made to the ideas underpinning government action on public services but Chapter 2 examines more broadly the theories of how the public sector should be managed. Ideological views about how bureaucracies should be organized guided British politicians and officials during most of the twentieth century. 'Leave it to the market' was already a familiar theory, provided notably by the eighteenth-century Scottish philosopher Adam Smith. However, as the chapter explains, this principle may work better in 'consumer' public services that can be equated to 'consumer' private services than in 'collective' public services, such as defence, justice and transport, as Adam Smith and his followers acknowledged. While the Conservative Governments 1979–97 preferred delivery by the market and if not, then market-like mechanisms for managing the public services, after 1997 the rhetoric and often the practice was more about collaboration and partnerships and participation, even co-production by communities.

Chapter 3 focuses on the organizations responsible for providing public services or ensuring that they are provided, and the recent changes to those services. It takes an institutional approach, structuring the information around the categories of public authority illustrated in Figure 1.2. It tracks the reform processes in central and local government, the NHS and the public corporations, identifying their problems and the responses from government across policy areas and institutional sectors.

Chapter 4 considers these reforms in terms of generic processes. Devolution, decentralization, deconcentration, delayering and delegation have all been present in the rhetoric of public management. A second set of processes has altered the relationship between the public, private and voluntary sectors: privatization, marketization, contracting-out and local partnerships, followed, it appears, by the Big Society and post-bureaucracy. We look at the consequences, whether for democratic control and accountability or fragmentation of delivery. Other broader trends – the expansion of IT solutions and Europeanization – are not special to public management but have particular impacts on it, affecting the day-to-day processes of public administration and public sector employment.

These changes have created a turbulent environment for public organizations, and strategic management and leadership are now widely seen as essential. Ministers and council leaders demand strategic plans and strategic leadership from their senior officials; managers themselves are conscious that strategic choices are necessary in the face of conflicting expectations, and that leadership is required if organizational change is to occur. Chapter 5 shows that strategic management has a longer history in UK government than is often recognized but that there remains much scepticism about the application of this private-sector principle to the public sector. The chapter defines and explains the concepts and assembles the arguments for and against, and concludes that, despite the significant differences between public administration and private business, strategic management has 'caught on' throughout the British public sector.

Moving on from the strategic themes of the previous chapter to the techniques used to achieve more from the organizations being managed, Chapter 6 traces the introduction of performance and quality management into the public sector. Here again, the question of the appropriateness of importing private-sector management techniques into the public sector arises. The chapter notes the criticisms and the complexities, and the caution with which New Labour adopted, and adapted, an approach introduced under the Conservatives, but which is now widely seen by public organizations as helpful for ensuring that resources are used effectively and that the public services respond to the public's needs and expectations. The main procedures used are presented and the issues surrounding their practice debated.

Still on the practicalities, Chapter 7 examines financial management and economic regulation. It uses the budget-making process to explain how public organizations are funded and their resources allocated, and to analyse the Coalition's cutbacks and the recent reforms to the systems of financial planning, accounting and control. The newer forms of engaging the private sector in public investment, project management and operating services, from the Private Finance Initiative (PFI) to the economic regulation of the privatized public utilities, are explained.

One of the principal claims of all public services is that 'people are our major asset and our most important resource'. There have been significant changes in the way people are managed over the last 30 years, coinciding with the introduction of NPM but also with changes in the role of the public sector and in its relationship with the private and voluntary sectors. As traditional public administration and government have given way to NPM and governance, so traditional personnel management (TPM) has given way to new forms of people management collectively referred to as human resources management (HRM). Chapter 8 examines the reasons for that change, its effect on the ways public officials are currently managed in the public services, and the major issues confronting HRM in the public sector today.

Chapter 9 considers the roles of the thousands of other auditing and inspection bodies that make up what some critics refer to as 'the regulatory state'. While Chapter 7 deals with regulation of bodies outside government, Chapter 9 deals with the control of organizations delivering publicly funded or subsidized services which are inside government. Paradoxically, as the Conservative government moved towards a 'steering' and 'arm's length' approach, the list of regulatory bodies lengthened. Though Labour in opposition had criticized these bodies, in government they used them and invented new ones, especially in the education, health and social care sectors – some to be abolished in their turn by the Coalition Government. The chapter identifies the positive features, such as in their role as change agents, but also explores the perverse effects and the costs, financial and otherwise, of regulation.

In the concluding chapter we present a comprehensive and contemporary picture of public management in the UK. Reconsidering and putting together the evidence as a whole, we identify the roles of history, culture and place in the development of a UK style of public management, with its distinctive national variations. The theories explained in the early chapters of the book are judged against the practical outcomes of the reforms they stimulated. Their application to four crucial aspects of public management: strategic management, performance management, financial management and human resources management, is summed up in terms of the continuities and changes each represents, their impact and the issues they raise. This brief survey of public management in the UK today considers the 'audit explosion' of recent years and its uncertain costs and benefits, a stark contrast to the new Conservative leadership's aim of a post-bureaucratic state. What, finally, can we say about the evolution of public management in the UK? Against the background of national heritage and international volatility, we pull together the evidence from each of the chapters for the signs that help make the prognoses for the future.

Chapter 2

The Politics and Theories of Public Management in Britain

If 'the Big Society' promoted by David Cameron turns out to be more than a campaign slogan, it will be the third reform agenda for the public sector in Britain in thirty years. The Big Society gives the major responsibility for public services to social groups, not the state. By labelling the era in which this system would prevail as 'the post-bureaucratic age', Cameron (2010a, 2010b), as we saw in Chapter 1, made a contrast with a 'bureaucratic age' which had its heyday in Britain after the Second World War. Public bodies were characterized as working to an organizational model that was hierarchical, impersonal and operated according to standardized procedures that ensure accountability but give rise to the form-filling routines with which the word 'bureaucracy' is popularly associated.

This 'traditional' model of administration was rejected by the 'New Right' Government of Margaret Thatcher, which analysed the world in terms of the interests of individuals not of society: 'There is no such thing as society…. There are individual men and women and families. People look to themselves first.' (Thatcher 1987). The Conservatives' reform agenda was to 'roll back the state' by privatizing or contracting-out functions wherever feasible. The public sector was to be managed in the way private companies are managed to produce outcomes that satisfy customers in a competitive marketplace. These practices were soon labelled by academics as 'the New Public Management' (NPM).

The 'New Labour' politicians who came to power in 1997 had a different agenda. Blair's Third Way (1998a) combined state intervention in the cause of social justice with retaining some advantages of the market. The Blair Government would work through public, private and 'third sector' organizations, arguing that 'what matters is what works', not ideology (Cabinet Office 1999a: 40). Its choice of solutions could therefore seem rather ad hoc, but the concept of 'public value', capturing the wider impact on society of policy decisions, provided a principle to guide decision makers. Community-based solutions were favoured, as were collaboration and partnerships, but they never replaced competition as a drive to performance, especially in England. Furthermore, enough 'top-down', 'centralizing' bureaucracy remained to substantiate Cameron's arguments for yet another change.

As these last examples indicate, although the political leaders had distinctive ideas about public management, certain elements overlapped in principle or in practice. Reforms cannot be applied uniformly even if they are not opposed, and reformers are frequently distracted by other events. Analysts are unrealistic in trying to identify coherent management models from the variety of patterns observed. Nevertheless, such analysis is valuable for understanding the evolution of public management in the UK. This chapter therefore presents an outline of the basic models of public sector management that co-exist in the UK today, their characteristics, rationales and relevance to current practice and problems.

The traditional model of public administration

There is general agreement on the main items that make up the traditional model of public administration even though it is rarely applied fully in practice. From the UK's Northcote-Trevelyan Report (1854) comes the idea that officials should be recruited to lifetime careers on merit, not political preference, and form a unified civil service. The separation of administration from political decision making, analysed in a classic paper by Woodrow Wilson (1887); and the concept of a hierarchical bureaucracy, set out by the German sociologist Max Weber in the early twentieth century, formed the other two main planks of 'traditional public administration' (see Table 2.1).

Non-partisan recruitment to a lifetime service

The Northcote-Trevelyan Report examined the problem of recruitment of civil servants at a time when they were appointed as personal favours. It recommended (1854: 22–3) that, to improve efficiency, a reformed civil service be based on certain principles:

- recruitment of young officials through competitive examinations;
- opportunities for promotion to the highest grades, based on quality of work;
- reduction of fragmentation between departments by common first appointments, and subsequent promotions to different departments; and
- transfers of officials from over-staffed departments to those with increased workload.

These principles at first met opposition, not only from those who would lose their power of appointment but also on principle. Walter Bagehot, editor of the free-market review *The Economist*, argued in a book that is now regarded as part of Britain's constitution (Bagehot [1867] 1963: 197) that, although it might look 'scientific' to recruit top civil servants at 20, and train them in civil service ways for 30 years, this system would restrict the renewal of people and ideas. Successful businesses, Bagehot said, were run by people

Table 2.1 *Models of public management*

	Traditional Public Administration	**New Public Management**	**Collaborative Community Governance**
Underlying organizational principle	Bureaucracy	Markets	Networks
Organizational relationships	Hierarchical and function-based	Competitive/ contractual	Collaborative, trusting partnerships
Relationships between politicians and public servants	Separation of roles between non-partisan officials and political leadership	Separation of policy-making and arm's length delivery by managers	Interaction between public managers and political leaders on policy and delivery
Ways of working and allocation of tasks	Scientific management – one best way – procedural manuals	Many possible ways: – flexible responses – market preference	Menu of partnership alternatives selected pragmatically
Policy advice and delivery	Monopoly of provision by public organizations – elimination of overlap	Competition in supply between public and private suppliers – customer orientation	Policy produced through interaction with social and interest groups
Motivation of public officials	Public interest	Interest maximization	Public value
Employment terms	Permanent, standardized, linked to hierarchical grade	Flexibility in hiring and rewards; individual contracts	Variety of terms, including voluntary co-production
Task/function	Administrative, following instructions; no personal responsibility	Taking personal or team responsibility for achieving results	Steering stakeholders to find and deliver effective solutions to community problems
Accountability mechanisms	Hierarchical chain of reporting and accounting	[Quasi] contracts, performance measures	Challenge through elections, referendums, forums

Main sources: Hughes (2012), Kelly *at al.* (2002), Kickert (1997), Stoker (2011).

mostly *not* trained or bred to that business. These ideas would be heard again a century later in the Fulton Report on the reform of the civil service (1968a, and see Chapters 5 and 8). Other critics feared an over-powerful bureaucracy like that of Prussia/Germany (Albrow 1970: 24–6). Competitive recruitment and promotion nevertheless became the norm in the UK. While British ministers have always made some partisan appointments, more than in the Danish and Dutch civil services for example (Christensen 2004: 17–28; van der Meer 2004: 219), there are far fewer such appointments in the UK than in the USA, France or Germany. In British local government, a non-partisan career administration also became the norm, although no unified 'local government service' emerged comparable to that in France.

Separation of politics and administration

Woodrow Wilson, later US President, wanted to reform the disorganized and corrupt management of many US cities and federal bureaux. In an academic paper he praised the orderliness of French and German bureaucracies, though rejected their authoritarian regimes. Wilson (1887: 192–222) recommended a disciplined, professional bureaucracy that would be protected from corruption by separating administration from politics. Officials would apply the law: political leaders would connect the system to public demands. Wilson accepted as self-evident that politics is concerned with great and universal matters, and administration is about small and individual matters – though he recognized the difficulty of establishing the dividing line.

In practice, British civil servants, as indeed officials everywhere, participate to some degree in the political and policy-making process. Pyper (1995a: 19–20) observes that, while Wilson had good reason for promoting his ideas in the context of corrupt nineteenth century American politics, 'his thesis represented neither an accurate description of the real world of government, nor a sensible proposal for reform'. Page (1997: 2) goes further, pointing out that 'civil servants everywhere not only have the opportunity as permanent officials with expertise in decision-making to shape the decisions they are also responsible for implementing – they are expected to shape them.'

Senior officials advise ministers and help them answer to parliament and citizens. Local government officials have an equivalent role. The policy process does not split neatly into stages: officials need to understand the political implications of policy options and they also modify these options, unconsciously or not, when they turn to expert groups for advice (Pollitt and Bouckaert, 2009: 3). Nevertheless, Wilson's theory remains a basic, if unrealistic, assumption of public administration in the UK. If the eventual political decision goes against their best technical advice, British officials still work 'loyally', even 'enthusiastically', to implement it (Lodge 2010: 100). Unlike some bureaucracies in Continental Europe, which once had to substitute for failed governments, and where 'the State' has a personality, which officialdom is assumed to incarnate (Lynn 2006: 62), British public servants do not expect (nor are they allowed in law) to decide what is 'in the public interest' (see also the discussion on public value below).

A hierarchical bureaucracy

Max Weber's theory of bureaucracy is the most important underpinning of the 'traditional model of administration' outlined in Table 2.1, although it was published after modern bureaucratic institutions were already established. Weber (1921/1947: 324–9) analysed the relationships between rulers, their administrative staff and the social culture, and classified the exercise of legitimate authority into three types: charismatic authority (staff act for heroic leaders from devotion); traditional authority (staff accept the status given to their chief by historic custom); and legal authority (staff obey a person's requests because they believe he or she has the right to issue them within a framework of law). In Weber's view, the purest form of legal authority is one with a bureaucratic administrative staff. Offices are organized in a hierarchy and their functions specified. Officials are selected for their professional knowledge; and they have a contract and a salary related to their position. There is a career structure, which includes promotion by seniority or merit as judged by superiors. The supreme chief can be appointed by election or nomination – but that person can give orders only within a defined sphere of competence (*ibid.*: 329–34). Weber regarded this form of administrative organization as the most 'rational' or efficient. Officials do not act arbitrarily or corruptly, but have the knowledge and the discipline to apply the rules, and thus political leaders are virtually certain that the organization will produce the output they specify (*ibid.*: 339).

Large public organizations in Britain tended to conform to the Weber model but less than in countries of mainland Europe where it made a better fit with the concept of a State founded on law and with a special public or administrative law. Some important principles in British government, such as political responsibility and the confidential relationships between top politicians and officials, look more like Weber's 'traditional' or 'customary' type. However, Weber himself raised the problem of who would control an expert bureaucratic machinery (Chapter 9 asks this very question). A 'trained permanent official is more likely to get his way in the long run than his normal superior, the Cabinet minister, who is not a specialist' (Weber ([1921] 1947: 338). His question found echoes in Britain, especially during the 1960s and 1970s when the public sector expanded fast (see Figure 1.2, p. 19), and 'entrenched professional groupings' held considerable power on the ground, and were able to ignore demands for reform (Greener 2009: 54).

Scientific management and 'one best way'

Associated with the traditional model of administration was a particular idea of management that assumed that each organization could be structured in the best way for efficiency. Frederick Taylor's (1911) work in the USA on scientific management, including time-and-motion studies, is particularly associated with this view. Formulae were devised for the optimum administrative mechanism, such as Gulick's (1937) POSDCORB set of functions for the chief executive (Planning, Organizing, Staffing, Directing, COordinating, Reporting, Budgeting), or the 'Purpose served, Process used, Persons or Things dealt with, and Place of service' principles for allocating functions and workers to departments.

UK governments paid only intermittent attention to such questions. The recommendation of the Haldane Committee (Ministry of Reconstruction 1918) for a regular overhaul of the whole machinery of government was generally ignored, and nor was there much attention by departments to improving work procedures (Campbell 1955: 69). During the 1939–45 war the Treasury introduced 'Organisation and Methods' (O&M) studies, and after the war also advised local authorities. The Association of Metropolitan Boroughs set up an O&M section in the 1950s, but at that time the use of the word 'management' (rather than 'administration') was unorthodox (Lynn 2006: 8). Efficiency was a major motive for the creation of larger local authorities in the 1960s and 1970s and in the enthusiasm for corporate management in the 1970s, following similar trends in the private sector (see Chapter 5). Though central government occasionally reorganized functions for strategic management reasons (Heath's Government 1970–74 notably created a number of 'super-departments'), departmental restructuring mostly responded to political imperatives (splitting functions to give additional Cabinet posts, or combining them to give a senior politician a more important-sounding title). The traditional model of administration still holds up well in the UK at the level of formal 'principle': ministers claim to make the decisions and take responsibility for errors, and prime ministers claim to allocate functions between departments on grounds of administrative efficiency – but the practices often differ.

New Public Management

In contrast to the well-established traditional model, the NPM model is a looser grouping of concepts (summarized in Table 2.1), which were synthesized by academics from empirical observations and promoted by management consultants and think tanks. It is partly grounded in an economic theory of bureaucracy that gave NPM a political rationale, especially in the UK.

The doctrines of NPM

Hood's 'A Public Management for All Seasons?' (1991) provides the most widely cited definition of 'new public management' in 'a hugely important' paper on the transition to NPM (Greener 2009: 68). While accepting that 'NPM, like most administrative labels, is a loose term', Hood (1991: 3–4) considered that it was nevertheless a convenient 'shorthand term for the set of broadly similar administrative doctrines which dominated the bureaucratic reform agenda in many of the OECD group of countries from the late 1970s'.

From observations of reforms that had taken place during the 1980s in the UK, Australia, New Zealand, Sweden and other OECD member countries, Hood defined NPM by synthesizing its 'doctrines' into seven components (see Box 2.1). In this new administrative model, managerial control and responsibility for performance is delegated from political leaders to senior officials. Policy objectives are set out in advance and performance measured. Output is emphasized by allocating resources and rewards in relation to performance, which implies the breaking up of centralized personnel management. Bureaucracies are disaggregated into budgetary units, each managed appropriately for its function. There is more use of competition, with public bureaucracies being challenged by private contractors to produce higher standards at lower cost. Private-sector practices, such as performance management, flexibility in human resource management, attention to public relations and responding to customer and consumer needs and wants, replace traditional precepts like uniform and standardized services, emphasis on due process and 'the public service ethic'. Finally, the stress is on making economies, whether by cutting government's own costs, or by reducing the compliance cost to business of government regulations

Almost simultaneously with Hood's academic research, Osborne and Gaebler's *Reinventing Government* (1992) popularized among American and British politicians and officials many of the principles of NPM. US Vice-President Al Gore's National Performance Review of 1993 was 'strongly indebted' to Osborne and Gaebler (Van Dooren *et al.* 2010: 8) and their book

BOX 2.1 Doctrines of New Public Management, 1991

- Hands-on professional management by senior officials.
- Explicit standards and measures of performance.
- More emphasis on output controls.
- Disaggregation of public organizations into single-purpose units.
- More competition in the public sector.
- Private sector management practices (flexibilities, public relations).
- Reducing expenditure (within public sector, and in businesses' compliance costs).

Source: Summarized from Hood (1991: 3–5).

BOX 2.2 Principles of 'entrepreneurial government', 1992

1 Competition between providers.
2 Empowerment of citizens and community.
3 Measurement of performance by outcomes.
4 Goal or mission driven.
5 Customers to be offered choice.
6 Prevention of problems before they emerge.
7 Earn money, not just spend it.
8 Decentralize authority, including participatory management.
9 Market mechanisms not bureaucratic mechanisms.
10 Instead of providing public services enable others, from all sectors, to provide them.

Source: Summarized from Osborne and Gaebler (1992: 19–20).

was used by the Major Government in the UK as justification for its reforms (Burnham and Pyper 2008: 134–5). Osborne and Gaebler's 'ten principles' (see Box 2.2) added the 'doctrine' of decentralization, which was more prominent in Scandinavia, France and Italy than the UK. Whereas Hood (1991) interprets the increased use of competitive tendering as being a means to improve performance and/or cut costs, Osborne and Gaebler emphasized its function of 'steering not rowing', that is, separating policy makers' goal-setting from front-line execution. The 'Hood' model treated the split in economic or purchasing terms, as a 'principal–agent' or 'customer–client' relationship: the 'Osborne and Gaebler' model treated it in more political terms, as decentralizing the choice of delivery mechanism. The 'market' included as potential suppliers the local community – treated not as dependent clients but as co-producers of the service with the public service professionals (Osborne and Gaebler 1992: 52) In the Thatcher Government of the 1980s, 'contracting-out' was the chief means of 'enabling not providing', in the words of her New Right local government minister (Ridley 1988), and the most efficient way to conduct local government. Yet, at local government level, many practitioners – politicians and officials – already saw that 'the enabling council' could 'catalyse all sectors', facilitating the provision of services in a wider variety of ways (Clarke and Stewart 1988; Brooke 1991). This view would then develop into the 'Third Way' model, considered below.

The theories underlying NPM

In traditional public administration, the theoretical model of the organization is a bureaucracy: in public management it is a market (Ostrom 1973). Scholars who analyse public organizations in terms of a market tend to use the methods and assumptions of economics instead of discussing law or institutions. This section discusses, first, the economic theories that inspired the market-oriented NPM reforms, before considering the political factors that enabled the UK government to introduce such radical change.

Adam Smith, self-interest and the free market

Political economists adapt the classical free-market theories of the Scottish philosopher Adam Smith, set out in *The Wealth of Nations* (1776) which includes many ideas directly relevant to NPM strategies. Smith asserted that traders such as brewers and bakers acting from their own interest were likely to work more efficiently than if they were thinking of the public good. When trading is subject to market competition, they have an incentive to keep prices low, and to innovate. Thus, without any deliberate intention on their part, their actions are to the benefit of society. In contrast, if traders had a monopoly or grouped together as a combined monopoly, they would charge the highest price people would pay. 'People of the same trade seldom meet together, even for merriment and diversion, but the conversation ends in a conspiracy against the public, or in some contrivance to raise prices' (Smith 1776: Book I.10.82).

Although Smith called for a *laissez-faire* attitude to the economy, he argued that there was sometimes a place for state intervention, whether in sovereign responsibilities such as defence and justice, or in ensuring the supply of collective services that increase national wealth but which individuals would not find it in their own self-interest to provide. 'The ... duty of the sovereign ... is that of erecting and maintaining those ... public works, which, though they may be in the highest degree advantageous to a great society, are, however, of such a nature that the profit could never repay the expense to any individual or small number of individuals' (Book V.1.69).

Although in these cases the market fails to provide an answer, and the state must intervene, the whole burden need not fall on taxation: for instance, road users could help pay for their cost in proportion to their use. 'A highway, a bridge ... may in most cases be both made and maintained by a small toll upon the carriages which make use of them' (Book V.1.73). Furthermore, charges for public services would be an incentive to the supplier: teachers could be remunerated in proportion to their hard work, partly by fees from satisfied students, partly by enhanced professional status. 'In some universities the salary makes but a part... of the emoluments of the teacher, of which the greater part arises from the ... fees of his pupils. The necessity of application... is not in this case entirely taken away' (Book V.1.135).

Niskanen's budget-maximizing model

'Public choice' theory applies classical economics to choices made in the public sphere. In 'public choice' analysis it is assumed that bureaucrats, like other individuals, are rational actors who choose strategies that maximize their own self-interest. Among the most important modern writers using this approach have been Hayek (1944) and Friedman and Friedman (1980), who provided the intellectual theories for the New Right politicians in the USA and UK in the 1970s, and Niskanen, who served on Reagan's Council of Economic Advisers, and whose work on bureaucracy was read by Thatcher, who pressed her colleagues to read it (Campbell and Wilson 1995: 304). Hayek argued that government intervention eroded the freedom of the individual (*The Road to Serfdom*), and Friedman and Friedman claimed that individual choice (*Free to Choose*) was not only better than bureaucratic command but was more efficient, because the market provided incentives. Niskanen (1971, 1973, 1994) asserted that public agencies tend to grow in size because officials benefit personally if they can maximize their budgets, increase their staff complement and thereby advance to more senior, more highly paid grades. He suggested a number of personal goals that bureaucrats might maximize which would involve increasing the bureau's budget.

According to Niskanen, public organizations make a case for a larger budget by 'over-supplying' their service. They do not need to consider the excess cost because, as a monopoly, the service cannot easily be compared and challenged by the political authorities. If a technological advance means that the cost of the service falls, budget-maximizing bureaucrats are likely to find ways to keep it high, becoming less efficient or providing more surplus product. At the end of a military conflict, a general might propose extending intervention in another sphere of operations rather than risk the government reducing the size of the army, as a British diplomat suggested happened in 2007 (Foreign Affairs Committee 2011: memorandum 17). In contrast, in the private sector, competition and consumer pressure are permanent incentives to reduce costs. Niskanen (1973: 33) demonstrated theoretically that a public bureau's budget and output might be twice that of a private firm operating under the same economic conditions. Changes to a bureau's incentive structure, such as performance management techniques, could resolve some problems, but Niskanen suggested that the simplest strategy was to transfer work to the private competitive sector wherever this was feasible (1973: 54).

The New Right reform agenda in the UK

The Conservative 1979 manifesto adopted an ideological tone on the public sector. It promised not only to cut back waste and 'bureaucracy' but also to reduce the role of the state and 'over-government' (Drewry and Butcher 1991: 198). A further signal of Thatcher's preference for the market was the appointment of Derek Rayner (director of Marks & Spencer) as her 'adviser on efficiency and effectiveness in government', and John Hoskyns (former company director) as the head of her policy unit. Hoskyns came from the Centre for Policy Studies, a private think-tank founded by Thatcher and her

New Right colleague, Keith Joseph. Together with the Adam Smith Institute and the Institute of Economic Affairs (which published Niskanen's 1973 paper), this organization promotes pro-market policy ideas. Joseph urged civil servants to read Adam Smith, Hayek and Friedman (Richards and Smith 2002: 94–5, 216). John Redwood MP, a subsequent head of Thatcher's policy unit, who advised her on privatization and became a minister in the Major Government, personifies this New Right approach in the twenty-first century.

Norton (2004: 347) explains the New Right's approach to the state sector as being 'motivated by the economic philosophy of the free market'. State intervention distorts the free play of the market and takes away the consumer's freedom to choose between competing alternatives. 'The state should therefore withdraw from economic activity. This viewpoint entails a contraction of the public sector, with state-owned industries being returned to the private sector'. However, the Thatcher and Major Governments combined these 'New Right' ideas with centralized control and an authoritarianism in social matters. The mixed message was driven by the need to retain majority parliamentary support despite ideological divisions within the Cabinet and between the government and its backbenchers, making Conservative reforms piecemeal and evolutionary (Richards and Smith 2002: 101). Yet, on the whole, the New Right was well-represented among those forming Conservative policy and this was especially true of Thatcher's policy advisers, such as Redwood and her economics adviser, Alan Walters, and Major's ministers in charge of public sector reform, such as William Waldegrave and Stephen Dorrell.

Critiques of NPM

The NPM model of public management assumes a greater use of the market, and the introduction into the public sector of private sector techniques such as contracting, delegation of authority and greater managerial freedom. Critiques of this approach are grouped below under three headings: economic theories; management questions, and political or democratic issues.

Economic arguments

In the traditional bureaucratic model, hierarchy and the trust built up within a permanent career service are seen as the basis of effective collaboration. In the NPM model, assumptions that officials pursue their own interest leads to preference being given to contractual '*principal–agent*' relationships, in which the public client (the principal) aims to specify exact requirements from a public or private supplier (the agent), measure the output, and replace an inadequate supplier. However, principal–agent theory suggests that it is not possible to be sure that agents will act in their principals' interest. Accountability is difficult because only the agents have complete information about the activities actually carried out. The private sector can use controls such as shareholder pressure, non-executive boards and contractual obligations, and incentives such as performance bonuses, but in the public sector the interests of the public stakeholder are diffuse and difficult to identify; and the political principal is poorly informed (Hughes 2012: 13–14). Performance incentives are often particularly resented because the traditional relationship has been one of trusting professionals to act in the public interest. Therefore the public sector is even less likely than the private sector to gain the maximum benefit from contractual relationships.

Transaction cost theory was developed, notably by Williamson (1975), to help companies decide whether to buy in goods and services or to produce them with their own staff; these arguments need to be applied equally to public sector contracting (see Flynn 2007: 223–44). The difficulties include the 'agency problem' described above: neither side has all the information needed to draw up the perfect agreement, but the purchaser is likely to be at a bigger disadvantage than the provider. The more the contract tries to cover all eventualities the more expensive and less efficient the process becomes. For some products, there may be few competent suppliers and therefore no real competition. Even if there is competition for the first transaction, the winner gains information that puts the others at a disadvantage in future tenders, making them reluctant to compete again. New Labour's solution was to seek a more participatory and yet still competitive collaboration (Erridge 2009: 97; and see below).

A particular economic debate is about the provision of *collective services – 'public goods'* in economists' term – that require substantial investment before there is any reward, and then the service may be open to use by the public without full payment (the 'free rider' concept). The classic example is street lighting which benefits not only local residents (who could be charged) but the public, both individually and as a collective (from increased safety). The lessons from Marks & Spencer do not apply to large capital projects as they do to consumer goods, as Adam Smith had observed. The state may have to provide the collective goods that benefit the community but do not interest private companies. The *laissez-faire* government of 1855 was eventually persuaded to set up the Metropolitan Board of Works to build a sewage system for London because cholera epidemics hit all social classes. State intervention is therefore required for some services. However, this argument can easily be used to defend public provision where the need no longer applies. Alfred Kahn (1970) used marginal cost theory to argue for the deregulation of services such as airlines and telecommunications. Kahn's implementation under President Carter of airfare deregulation in the USA led not only to low-cost travel but also to the deregulation of other industries (telecommunications, electricity, gas) under Thatcher and Reagan (*The Economist* 22 January 2011). Market competition, however imperfect, can be preferable to state regulation, and it is for governments to make the political, as well as economic, judgement about which services will be treated as public goods.

Management arguments: how far is it generic across sectors?

As NPM established itself, its lack of fit with public services was a point often made by those arguing against 'government by the market' (Self 1993: 169–70; Kickert 1997: 731–4). Some other authors (Allison [1979] 1982; Farnham and Horton 1999; Boyne 2002; Rainey and Chun 2005) made systematic comparisons of public and private management. Writing at the beginning of the NPM movement, Allison ([1979] 1982: 16–18) identified many generic functions – but also substantial differences in what these functions meant in practice and in their operating environments. After synthesizing a considerable body of research, Rainey and Chun (2005: 92–4) concluded that private management theory and techniques could apply to public management – but only with important modifications. The governmental environment puts greater constraints on managers: they are more closely directed; have more complex accounting procedures; and lack the clear goals and incentives found in business. Public managers have to negotiate parliamentary and political processes and relationships with interest groups, and work within more complicated rules on financial and human resources. Public managers have greater problems linking pay and discipline to performance, although they themselves are no less motivated than their private-sector counterparts – rather their motivations are different: more altruistic and work-related (*ibid.*: 85). Performance outcomes were on the whole better under private-sector management, but in many cases and in some sectors outcomes were mixed (*ibid.*: 89). These findings suggest that governments need to be selective in transferring activities to private management, and to consider the contextual constraints too when reforming public management.

Political arguments: ethos, accountability and politicization

Comparing management in public and private settings brought out some of the particular expectations that society has of public officials. Horton (2006) provides a historical institutional analysis of the effects of NPM on the *public sector ethos*. Chapman (1997) and O'Toole (1993, 2006) examined the traditional public service values and feared that, with private contracting and short-term appointments, the ideals of probity, working for the public good, and political impartiality would be lost. Brereton and Temple (1999: 471) argue that 'Civil servants are no longer the disinterested servants of democratically accountable ministers, which has been the cornerstone of the British system of democracy and parliamentary government'. Peters (2000: 127) links this question to accountability because ethical standards in traditional public administration were inculcated through a career service backed up by hierarchical internal controls and both these mechanisms are undermined by NPM. O'Toole (1993: 2) speculated that open competition would bring in managers who would feel frustrated by the 'inefficiency' of democratic accountability. However, Mellon's survey of 'Next Steps' agency chief executives (mostly recruited by open competition) found they were similar to senior civil servants in having strong principles, though different from civil service managers in favouring new ways of working (2000: 204–5). Agency chief executives, with less experience of Whitehall practices, were in fact less willing than senior civil servants to bend the rules to achieve results. Others have shown that ethical standards are linked more closely to specific societies or generations than to sectors (Doig 1997: 95–6, 105–6).

NPM in the UK removed or reduced the traditional *accountability* to elected political representatives of former public utilities and some local services (schools, social housing), but offered some new accounting mechanisms. For example, performance indicators are now available to clients, the general public and the media; and regulated utilities provide more information about price and quality of services to customers than under the former public monopolies. Traditional arrangements for government accountability were, in practice, weak. Public inquiries, such as Scott (1996, on 'arms-to-Iraq'), Hutton (2004, on the death of Dr David Kelly) and Butler (2004, on Iraq intelligence), confirmed that ministers and civil servants can fail to account truthfully to parliament or to behave in a principled way or to keep the records required for accountability. Local government is sometimes corrupt (Westminster and Doncaster are notable recent cases) and poor election turnout undermines the claims for democratically accountable local services. Indeed, one reason that the NPM reforms occurred was because the public bureaucracy was not seen by the public as accountable (Peters 2000: 137).

In contrast, the NHS Trusts introduced by the Conservatives had to issue annual reports and accounts, business plans, and hold annual open meetings. New Labour from 1998 required national quangos to hold management board meetings in public. Local bodies can be less transparent, yet the local government chief executive is, it seems, 'accountable to everyone' in the 'post-modern' public management era: to elected political representatives, to staff, to clients, and to the wider public of taxpayers and citizens (Quirk 1997: 585; 2011: 46). In general the Conservatives' reforms to public services could be interpreted as improving their citizen orientation in response to widespread dissatisfaction with the existing bureaucratic state (John 2009: 19).

NPM opens up closed career systems and creates more semi-autonomous public bodies, increasing possibilities for *political patronage*. Specialists distinguish between politicization of posts (politicians intervene in appointments), and partisan politicization (appointments influenced by party affiliation), though both can undercut professionalism, efficiency, merit-based career systems and, in the end, an apolitical public service (Pierre 2004: 49). It is not possible to relate politicization directly and clearly to NPM. 'Party-card' appointments have increased less in Sweden, the UK and the Netherlands, which adopted NPM relatively early and widely, than in France and Germany, even though these two countries were already more politicized

(Peters and Pierre 2004). In the UK, political interference in appointments appeared to grow before NPM reforms had been adopted (Peters and Pierre 2004: 9). Although Thatcher and her leading ministers believed that officials were social democrats who would withhold the 'last ounce of commitment' (Lawson 1993: 267), the 'party card' was much less important to them than a 'can do' approach. However, Blair and Brown relied more on personal advisers chosen for their political affiliation as well as their expertise.

The strong presence on UK quangos, such as NHS Trust boards, of people thought to be Conservatives, and then later to be Labour, also raised questions of politicization, which were examined by the Office of the Commissioner for Public Appointments (OCPA) created by Prime Minister Major. The Commissioner issued a code of practice for appointments, and the proportion of political activists on national quangos declined from 19 per cent in 2000/01 to 8 per cent in 2009/10 (OCPA 2010: 40). In local government, Boyne *et al.* (2010) demonstrated that most senior managers are vulnerable to changes in party control, independent of organizational performance, but that the chief executive is likely to survive a political change if the council's performance is strong. In short, politicization is not directly related to NPM, but NPM provides opportunities for politicization, which then brings into disrepute some useful management tools, such as executive agencies and open competitive recruitment.

Factors governing adoption of the NPM model

The UK was in the vanguard of NPM reforms, with New Right ministers adopting early many components of the model, although decentralization was a notable exception until New Labour's devolution programme. The basic concept of a smaller state was adopted by many governments, including Left and Coalition governments (Hughes 2012: 36–7). In Australia, Sweden and Denmark the rise of Conservative parties or 'anti-welfare tax' movements were triggering factors. In New Zealand, the reforms were led by a Treasury 'run by public choice disciples' (Self 1993: 68; New Zealand Treasury 1987). The international financial crisis of the late 1970s and budget deficits forced most Western governments to reduce their public sectors (Bovaird and Löffler 2009a: 15), but the responses adopted varied greatly.

Pollitt and Bouckaert (2004: 39–44) suggest that the impact of the new ideas depended on the country's political and administrative regime and its social context. First, in the vanguard NPM states, the general social culture is individualist and favourable to business, rather than statist or hostile to private profit. Pollitt and Bouckaert (2004: 54–7) draw on Hofstede's (2001) work on the impact of culture on institutions to contrast the highly individualist USA, UK and Australia with the more collectivist Finland and Germany. Another cultural feature is the attitude to risk (and therefore to accepting new flexibility in personnel policies and to reorganization); people surveyed in

Sweden and the UK felt less threatened by such uncertainties than those in France and Belgium.

Second, administrative culture in liberal democracies tends to fall into one of two camps: either primacy is given to the public interest as defined by parliament and ministers (parliamentary sovereignty) or parliament and ministers are seen as subordinate to the established constitution and body of law (the *Rechtsstaat* or State of law principle). In the UK, Australia and New Zealand, public servants are socialized into implementing ministers' wishes, even if it means their own reorganization. In contrast, in many Continental European countries the *Rechtsstaat* principle, coupled with a Weberian bureaucratic model, produces a highly professional, almost autonomous body of public officials applying administrative law, less susceptible to politicians' managerial ideas (Kickert 2007). In between these two attitudes come Dutch, Swedish and Finnish administrators, who facilitate ('steer') the political accommodation of the diverse societal interests (Pollitt and Bouckaert 2004: 42; Kickert 2003: 139).

A third factor is the diversity of advice available to ministers (Pollitt and Bouckaert 2004: 57–8). Thatcher appointed personal advisers from business and think-tanks who brought in new managerial ideas, and distrusted the advice of officials (Foster 2001: 728). The more radical Australian governments too were able to call on advisers from outside the civil service. In the Netherlands and New Zealand, information came mainly from the civil service but in New Zealand the Treasury was itself a purveyor of market ideas, as noted above, while in the Netherlands advice on reform came from a variety of sources, not just business and free-market think-tanks. In France, on the other hand, advice to ministers comes from top civil servants from the same administrative training school networks and with little to gain from change.

Fourth, the 'Westminster' or 'majoritarian' parliamentary system in the UK, Australia, New Zealand and Canada gives a prime minister with a single-party parliamentary majority great political power at national level. Leaders of multi-party governments and US presidents (who often confront two powerful assemblies) are less able to implement radical ideas. Constitutional systems that concentrate most powers at central level, as in New Zealand and the UK (before 1999), enable governments to carry out widespread reform including to local government. In contrast, the constitutions of the US, Canada, Australia and several European countries give regions substantial autonomy. Some countries have specific legal obstacles to administrative change: for example, French trade unions have a veto over changes to the public service statute whereas the UK did not have a civil service statute until 2010, and its provisions remain limited. The UK government was able to create a hundred 'Next Steps' executive agencies without new legislation, unthinkable in Germany, Sweden or France (Pollitt 2007a: 17).

Contingent factors make their contribution – notably the unusual longevity of the UK's Conservative government (1979–97): in contrast, French governments of Left and Right alternated in quick succession 1981–97, each insisting their reforms were different from their predecessors (Rouban 1998: 98). In general terms, the UK was among the more radical adopters of NPM because its society was more comfortable with the market and change, its political leaders had stronger political and constitutional powers to introduce sweeping reforms, and its officials accepted that they had to be implemented.

Governance, community and the Big Society

The variation between countries in their take-up of the NPM model depended not only on the capacity of governments but also on whether its principles were acceptable to their societies. The new managerial model, promoted by pro-market organizations such as the OECD, World Bank and European Commission (Lynn 2006: 1), was seen by some Continental critics as an 'Anglo-American' private-sector approach not applicable to their public services (Kickert 1997; Pollitt 2007a). Premfors (1998) demonstrated that the Nordic countries were not NPM 'laggards' but following a different trajectory, one that put more stress on political and administrative decentralization.

Kickert (1997) proposed an alternative model, that of 'public governance'. He argued that public sector management is not merely an internal organizational matter but also an externally oriented activity, because government actors engage with each other and with other public, private and voluntary groups. Whereas 'government' in the traditional model implied that politicians and officials decided and implemented policy in a way that excluded others, 'governance' encompasses networks of governmental and non-governmental bodies in a more inclusive environment. The model of public management should therefore be broadened into one of 'public governance', which takes account of the interaction with the socio-political environment, the complexity of administrative relations and the specific character of 'governance' within networks (Kickert 1997: 732; and see Table 2.1 for other elements of this model). Many European critiques of the 1990s developed this concept further, seeing 'partnership between administrative agents and users in the production of social services' as a third model, separate and different from the Weberian and managerial models (Rouban 1999: 3). New Labour too moved in this direction, as outlined below.

Collaborative community governance

In the UK, the concept of governance through networks is closely associated with the work of Rhodes (Rhodes 1997, 2000) and, for local governance, with that of Stoker (2004, 2011). They built on earlier work by Richardson and Jordan (1979; and Jordan and Richardson 1987) which showed that UK government policy making involved not only ministers and officials as in the conventional 'government' model but also the social and economic groups that helped develop and implement policy. In some Continental countries, as Kickert suggests, facilitating policy networks has long been a recognized role of officials – to link across the historical cultural 'pillars' in the Netherlands or to promote 'cooperative federalism' in Germany, for example. However, the vitality of unofficial networks in the UK was at variance with both the traditional model of administration and that of NPM. In the NPM model, officials are certainly expected to deal extensively with other actors, but the relationships are assumed to be contractual, competitive or at least at arm's length whereas 'governance' implies that officials engage in collaborative bargaining with other participants in a policy network or policy community.

Rhodes drew attention to the importance of the informal networks that had grown as a result of the fragmentation of service providers under NPM. He argued that effective service delivery therefore depended on linking organizations (Rhodes 1997: 100). More debatably, Rhodes claimed that policy networks in an era of governance are self-organizing, acting autonomously of central government departments, developing their own policies – and thereby 'hollowing-out' the power of the state, weakening its capacity to steer (Rhodes 1997: 51–5; for more details see Bevir and Richards 2009).

Viewed from a different angle, the concept of self-governing policy networks, autonomous of the state, would support the Conservatives' model of a Big Society; a 'society where people come together to solve problems and improve life for themselves and their communities; a society where the leading force for progress is social responsibility, not state control' (Conservative Party 2010a: 37). Under the Coalition Agreement (Cabinet Office 2010: 29), neighbourhoods, social enterprises and groups of public sector workers are being invited to organize their own community plans, schools and other public activities. However, empirical research and theoretical analysis have failed to sustain the idea that self-organizing policy networks exist to any extent in the UK (Davies 2002: 316–19; Richards and Smith 2002: 23). More typically, local community networks in the UK have been stimulated by a centrally funded project led by local or regional officials (Davies 2002; and see examples of Action Zones and Partnerships in Chapter 4). Only a small minority of citizens seems willing to engage in 'neighbourhood governance', which requires considerable commitment. In a MORI survey of one local authority, 82 per cent favoured the idea but only 2 per cent became involved (Durose and Richardson 2009: 43).

Stoker and colleagues (Stoker 1999, 2000) researched network governance primarily to understand the management and politics of local government. However, their identification of a more networked, partnership-based, participatory solution to delivering public services entered the realm of practical management with the Blair Government; their findings influencing Blair's *The Third Way* and *Leading the Way: New Visions for Local Government* (Blair 1998a; 1998b), and the Lyons Report (2007) on *Place-Shaping* (Stoker

2011: 16). The Third Way claimed to leave behind the statist Old Labour Left of the 1960s and 1970s – but retain its values of social justice and inclusion. It similarly rejected the New Right ideology – but nevertheless acknowledged that the UK needed to be a competitive market economy in a globalized world (Giddens 1998). The role of the state should change from that of direct provider to that of an enabler of services, but an enabler with a more active social purpose than that conceived by the New Right (Ridley 1988). In particular there would be a larger role for local bodies and citizen participation in the delivery of public services (Prabhakar 2006: 2–3). On the one hand the government would move away from the 'one size fits all' approach that was associated with public bureaucracies and which no longer met voters' aspirations; on the other, the government would cease the 'denigration' of public service that had been implied by the New Right's turn to the market (Cabinet Office 1999a: 5) while still using markets as tools to increase fairness, productivity and efficiency (Giddens 2007).

Networks, in institutional forms such as 'joined-up government', 'partnerships' and 'community leadership', became the proclaimed approach of New Labour to public provision (though many hierarchical controls and market mechanisms remained in place). 'Joined-up government' was short-lived as a slogan, but it could be seen in several initiatives: the Social Exclusion Unit in Whitehall; the bringing together of Benefits Agencies and Job Centres as welfare to work 'one-stop shops'; the English regional development agencies and Government Offices for the Regions; the elaboration of cross-departmental Performance Service Agreements (see Chapter 5); and the DirectGov and council websites as cross-sector public portals. Partnerships proliferated, whether public–private investment contracts or partnerships led by local authorities and/or the regional offices, covering high-level local concerns as in Local Strategic Partnerships, or specific themes as in Community Legal Service Partnerships.

In contrast to Thatcher's 'there is no such thing as society', 'community' is 'often seen as a key motif in New Labour's governing agenda' (Needham 2007: 92). Blair used the term 'community' in a higher proportion of speeches related to public services than any other keyword of the New Labour years (*ibid.*: table 6.3). Community figured frequently in the Blair Government's policies (New Deal for Communities 1998, Community Strategies 2000), institutions (Department for Communities and Local Government 2006, Homes and Communities Agency 2008), and White Papers: *Strong and Prosperous Communities* and *Communities in Control* (DCLG 2006, 2008a). The 'community governance' model of multi-agency service planning and delivery replaced the earlier concept of local councils providing services under their own management with their own employees.

However, a sceptical tone is evident in Flynn's (2007: 187–90) 'spectrum of collaboration' that starts with 'meetings, no action' and ends with 'merger/acquisition'. Collaboration between public, private and voluntary sector organizations is often a condition of government funding, such as for the local partnerships discussed in Chapter 4. Actors seeking funding may well meet to agree a bid prepared by the main public partner or, perhaps, work together to prepare a joint bid, but without subsequently working cooperatively within the project. Cooperation implies each organization providing its own specialized input with its own staff to the joint project. Greater collaboration would come from sharing management and seconding staff to the shared project, but a shared budget can be one step too far, often for legal reasons. Finally, Flynn notes, the end of the spectrum of collaboration is a merger, which could be relatively spontaneous (as in the sharing of top officials between neighbouring London boroughs from 2011 to reduce budgets) but could have the nature of a take-over, as in the Education Act 2002's provision for maintained schools to federate under a single governing body – mostly to save a 'failing' school by enabling one to 'turn round' the other. Official surveys of Local Strategic Partnerships (LSPs, see Chapter 5) showed that LSPs were satisfied with the input of some actors (generally local authorities, police and health bodies) and felt able to secure some change in the priorities of these bodies towards the agreed partnership priorities. However, input from other groups (especially education, voluntary and community bodies) was poor, and from business and transport interests very poor. Links upwards to regional agencies and downwards to neighbourhood structures were very limited (Geddes *et al.*: 2007: 6–7). Partnership and collaboration do not sit easily with the spirit of competition in England that has been encouraged by league tables and the like for some decades now (see Chapter 4 for more evidence and discussion).

Public value

In the community governance model, the preferred system for service delivery is developed by the network of stakeholders from a 'menu of alternatives selected pragmatically' (Stoker 2011: 18). The Blair Government announced its intention to choose service suppliers on the basis of 'what matters is what works' (Cabinet Office 1999a: 40), an approach that could be seen as ad hoc and discretionary. Quirk (2011: 51) advised public managers, especially those who adopted an entrepreneurial or leadership role, not to pretend their actions were purely pragmatic and value-neutral but to make explicit the values they were advancing.

Blair's Strategy Unit responded to this problem by promoting the concept of public value as a guide to governmental decisions (Kelly *et al.* 2002). The public value approach had been set out by Moore (1995) but received less attention than the Osborne and Gaebler (1992) book which was used to back up NPM strategies. Like that book, Moore's *Creating Public Value* broke away from the traditional model of public administration by conceiving public management as an entrepreneurial and community-enhancing activity.

It differed by proposing the notion of 'public value' as a strategic aim for public managers in the way that adding shareholder value is a strategic driver for private managers. Table 2.2 sets out a summary of the conceptual framework outlined by Moore, to assist public managers to think strategically and take entrepreneurial action to resolve community problems (Benington and Moore 2010: 1). The public value framework does not neglect the traditional roles of the public administrator but adds new roles, to help governments meet challenging environments and deliver more responsive services.

The Cabinet Office Strategy Unit revived the concept of public value as an assessment tool governments could use when deciding public service reforms. It suggested a framework for evaluating publicly funded or regulated activities, using 'a broader measure than is conventionally used within the new public management literature, covering outcomes, the means used to deliver them as well as trust and legitimacy'. Outcomes, services, and trust seemed to be the three criteria most valued by citizens (Kelly *et al.* 2002: 2–4; and see Mulgan 2010).

The assessment of UK government projects, programmes and regulations already encompassed a wide variety of considerations, including environ-

Table 2.2 ***Public value***

	Traditional administration	**Added public value**
Governments (local or national)	Rule-setter; service-provider; guarantor of social welfare net	+ Creator of public values; shaper of the public sphere: politically, economically, socially, culturally
Public managers	Bureaucratic clerks; servants to political leaders	+ Stewards of public assets, using imagination to help governments discover what can be done with public assets; and ensuring responsive services to users and citizens
Public management techniques	Procedures to ensure consistency; reliable routines in public organizations	+ Orchestration of policy processes in partnership with stakeholders to ensure choices are made in public interest and improve outcomes for public; and help governments adapt to changing environments and aspirations

Source: Adapted from Benington and Moore (2010: 3–4), citing Moore (1995).

mental impact, access to jobs and services, and health benefits, even where these cannot be quantified (see Glaister *et al.* 2006: 232–6). Yet these appraisals were usually conceived in terms that mirrored the private sector – they evaluated benefits deriving from personal consumption of public services as they would benefits from goods produced by the private sector. However, the proponents of public value argue that measuring the total benefits of a government action should reflect criteria specific to the public sphere – public preferences – such as the value people place on fair distribution of public goods, trustworthiness (for example in the health and police services), due process, or user involvement in defining or co-producing services (Kelly *et al.* 2002: 6). A public value framework would be unlikely to come up with a single answer but would be a tool for debating the value of different options.

Not everyone accepts the public value argument. Rhodes and Wanna (2008: 367) questioned whether Moore's proposals, developed in the context of US government, were translatable to the Westminster-style arrangements of Australia or the UK. The US gives a large role to partisan or locally elected public officials (such as school administrators or police commissioners) who have the legitimacy to act in an entrepreneurial way: Westminster-style public managers are required to be neutral, and elected political leaders are in principle and practice the 'pre-eminent actors' in the policy network (see also Rhodes and Wanna 2007). It may therefore be inappropriate to urge officials to be the arbiter of the public interest, and build coalitions to pursue their own initiatives on public value; that role belongs to party politicians within the political arena. Nevertheless, public value frameworks have been tested and applied in the UK: Benington and Moore (2010: 2) provide a substantial list, though it is notable that all are governmental or quasi-autonomous bodies with the decision-making legitimacy sought by Rhodes.

However, under the Coalition Programme (Cabinet Office 2010), the entrepreneurial public official steering the local community to maximize public value is destined to become more frequent with the creation of locally elected police and crime commissioners; more elected mayors of large cities with delegated powers from central government; and a new generation of community organizers to support the creation of community groups.

Bureaucracy, markets, community, Big Society

This chapter has presented three models of public management – traditional public administration, NPM, community governance – and the beginnings of a possible fourth, 'the Big Society'. These models are idealized versions, in two senses. First, they are ideal-types – the pared-down essentials of alternative ways in which public management can be or is being organized, that are used to compare and contrast options for government. Second, they are normative ideals, that is, they are models which some would like to see copied in a particular country or specific public sector. The arguments reformers use in promoting a model are often based on strong principles, whether political or philosophical.

As the chapter has shown, none of the models is, or ever was, integrally present in the public management of the UK. Even the historical bureaucracy model, which is the most embedded in democratic states, matches public organizations in only an approximate way. In the UK, there has always been greater involvement by officials in policy making and weaker interest in rational scientific management than the model suggests; and there has always been some departure from the model with respect to politicization and on who takes responsibility (ministers or officials), though these departures are modest compared with many countries of similar economic standing.

Although the NPM model emerged during the Reagan and Thatcher administrations of the 1980s and key definitions were published in the 1990s, opinions on its content still vary. Combinations of plausible elements of the model are present in many countries, though more often in countries that are anglophone and/or were engaged in budgetary restructuring. In many countries, NPM reforms were underpinned by a theoretical view that officials were self-interested individuals whose behaviour was more effectively controlled by market-like incentives than by motives of altruism. NPM reform was strongly driven in the UK – partly because the British (English) political culture had always favoured the market over the state, and partly because the UK political system gives substantial power to a majority government intent on reform. The features of NPM in Britain, in the sense of changes away from the traditional model, are therefore relatively clear.

Yet, even in Britain, many elements of the traditional model remain. Some researchers are therefore sceptical about NPM as a widespread phenomenon, arguing that any convergence on a central model is in terms of rhetoric not reform content (Pollitt 2001: 945). Some observe a 'layered' effect in the UK, as parts of the public service come to a new arrangement with political leaders and are reformed, and then co-exist with other parts of the traditional system that have proved more resistant (Lodge 2010: 100–5). Others consider that the NPM agenda was so loosely defined that a variety of reforms (such as decentralization) could be rolled into it to make it seem more universal than it was, and that it was then unduly promoted by academics, civil servants and management consultants; failures to adopt it were explained as political setbacks rather than more profound problems with the NPM model itself (Goldfinch and Wallis 2010: 1099–113).

In the 1990s, networked 'governance' appeared in academic texts as a description of how policy making and implementation 'really' worked in hierarchical bureaucracies. It seemed especially relevant in NPM-model administrations because of the fragmentation of delivery partners. Governance was also presented as a public management model appropriate to administrative cultures that placed more stress on negotiating with, and accommodating, different interests. The rise of the community network governance model in the UK was associated with the advent of a New Labour Government and its Third Way approach that incorporated both the state and the market. The government opened up the range of possible service providers and required local authorities to lead them in network partnerships and a mixed economy of welfare. The concept of 'public value', and notably the need for public participation in its assessment, was presented as a useful criterion for deciding on public action, in the absence of any strong ideological rationale.

In practice, though New Labour spoke about governance through networks and decentralization to communities, its desire for greater political and bureaucratic accountability brought a continuity of the Conservatives' top-down performance management and target-setting. Though the Labour Government ensured that local community representatives sat on NHS Trusts, it soon reversed its abolition of the Conservative Government's internal market in the NHS (Needham 2007: 69–71; Durose, Greasley and Richardson 2009: 5). Governance seemed, in part, to be a development of NPM, even if the public funding was greater and the intentions different.

These continuities between models cause some observers to query their pertinence. Lynn (2006: 10–12) notes that NPM was sufficiently ambiguous that some people used governance to cover both traditional and new public management. Governance was generally used to indicate that administrative practice was shifting from a bureaucratic state and direct government to government by third parties, with a looser boundary between state and society. Yet public management already incorporated the idea of indirect relationships with dispersed entities, therefore governance was little different from the broader definitions of public administration and public management. Hood (2005: 12) considered that the changes in terminology from public administration to public management and then to governance were nevertheless more than just changes in words: they referred to both ideological and analytical shifts. Stoker (2011: 28) is more pessimistic about the real world of UK governance at local level. Community governance is favoured by academics as a model but it has not entered popular understanding. With local government in the UK now having so little functional capacity for welfare provision or economic development, its ability to play a community governance role has an air of 'desperate rhetoric'.

The 'public value' invitation to local government managers to take on an entrepreneurial role as community leaders runs contrary to the concept of the neutral public servant, which is a basic tenet of traditional public administration that is not disputed by the NPM model. Senior civil servants and local government chief officers have always worked in a grey area between promoting the decisions of political leaders and promoting their own solution to a policy problem. Ambiguity grows when a local government chief executive steers a series of community partnerships. In the Big Society model, it is this type of active entrepreneurial behaviour which seems to be expected of public servants (loosely defined). Many of the new forms of management role being carved out by the Coalition give individuals or self-selected groups direct responsibility for public services for which they will be accountable to the local community, sometimes through direct election. It has yet to be seen whether these innovations will become operational, and whether, at a time of severe reductions in public spending, the invitation to public sector agencies to relaunch themselves as social enterprises is merely a short-term cost-saving measure, not the foundation of a new model that will capture the imagination of communities. These questions are raised again in the chapters that follow.

Chapter 3

The Institutional Framework of Public Service Provision

The organization of public service provision in Britain was complex even before the Coalition Government invited neighbourhoods, social enterprises and groups of public sector workers to become involved and offer alternative services (Cabinet Office 2010: 29). The NHS is being restructured again, another type of school has been introduced, and new regimes are being installed for police authorities and large cities. The relatively simple structures of the 1970s – central departments, local authorities, the NHS, the nationalized industries and other public corporations – were sub-divided in the 1980s into self-managing units, or contracted-out or privatized, in the pursuit of economy, efficiency and effectiveness. The Labour Government then argued for more joined-up, responsive services. It said people had become used to products being available when they wanted them; that level of service should be available in the public sector too, and without users having to know which branch of government to deal with (Cabinet Office 1999a: 23). Labour linked some organizations in a variety of partnerships while separating others differently or reconstituting them under different names. Networks and relationships between bureaucratic organizations became as important as the organizations themselves.

A 'post-bureaucratic' age will be advantageous for people as consumers if, as suggested, it gives them direct access to, and control of, the particular service provider of their choice, perhaps one they themselves are producing as part of Cameron's Big Society (Cameron 2010a; Conservative Party 2010b; and see Chapter 1). However, for people as citizens, as political leaders or as public managers, a general understanding of the governmental system would seem to be a fundamental requirement, and one more than ever necessary at a time of financial stringency when choices have to be made and services will not be available to all on demand. This chapter provides an overview of the now complicated institutional structure and its continuing changes, arranged for clarity around the four traditional types of public body that dominate the UK public sector: central government, local authorities, the NHS and public corporations. Although many public services are provided by voluntary and private sector entities, or by cross-sectoral partnerships, it is the formal public bodies, with specific powers and responsibilities assigned by parliament, which, in the end, set the parameters of public service provision, make the strategic decisions, supply the public funds, and are held accountable by citizens' political representatives.

The four categories of public organization

Box 3.1 sets out the features that define each of the four distinct categories of public body in the UK. These arrangements sometimes differ in detail from the patterns of administration in other countries. In the UK there is a separate civil service which works only for government departments, whereas in other countries there may be a combined local and central public service (as in Slovenia), or indeed no career service (as in Sweden). The British civil service also works for the devolved governments in Scotland and Wales but not for the Northern Ireland Executive, because Northern Ireland has its own civil service, as we saw in Chapter 1. However, the British civil service is present throughout the UK in departmental offices (for example in tax offices or Jobcentres). Local government officials are recruited by individual councils, whereas in other countries they may form one unified career service (as in France). Councils combine together to share expertise and present their case to parliaments and ministers (for example in the Local Government Association (LGA) of English and Welsh councils, and in the Convention of Scottish Local Authorities (COSLA). Through COSLA and the Local Government Employers section of the LGA, they deal jointly with questions on conditions of service, for example, on salary levels or implementing judicial decisions on equal remuneration. Yet councils remain free to make their own arrangements: some, especially in south-east England, opt out of national terms and conditions (LGE 2006: 10; and see Chapter 8 for human resources issues). Because education in Britain is a local authority service (in Northern Ireland it is run by a special-purpose public authority), teachers are not civil servants as they are in some other countries, but neither are they considered to be local government officials.

The NHS organization is idiosyncratic: it is not a government department – though organized by one – whereas in other countries the hospital service may be modelled more closely on the central government service (France) or not be in the public sector at all (as in the Netherlands). The NHS shares some of the characteristics of the public corporations – in its semi-autonomy as a public body carrying out technical functions 'at arm's length' from politics. The public corporation is a category of organization that developed strongly with the creation of nationalized industries: it gives governments the power to set the overall objectives and level of public funding for functions to which civil servants in central departments are not suited, which do not need daily attention from ministers, and which need to be managed more flexibly to suit the particular market. In some cases, as with the BBC, it is important the public corporation is seen to be independent of political manipulation.

The public corporation formula, as set out in Box 3.1, has been used by government for a disparate set of bodies. Often called 'quangos' (quasi-autonomous non-governmental organizations), those responsible to central government are more accurately termed 'non-departmental public bodies'

BOX 3.1 Features of the four main types of public body

Central Departments (Ministries)

- A political authority, normally headed by a Cabinet minister (the Secretary of State), or under the umbrella of a minister
- The prime minister decides the functions of the department and appoints its ministers
- The minister is accountable to parliament for the work of the department
- The department focuses on particular functions, people, or places
- Officials belong to one UK civil service
- Senior officials are 'generalists', whose career across departments helps coordination.

This model applies to the UK, Scottish and Welsh governments, but Northern Ireland has its own civil service for devolved functions

Local Authorities (Councils)

- A political authority, whose decisions are made by elected councillors or in a few cases by a directly elected mayor
- Parliament decides a council's functions*
- LAs are responsible for multiple services
- LAs are funded by central government grants but have some local taxing power
- Officials are employed by the individual authority but there are national agreements on basic conditions of service
- Senior officials specialize, and advance by moving between authorities

The Scottish Government has devolved powers on local government. Local authorities in Northern Ireland have few powers

National Health Service (England)

- Accountable to the Department of Health but its staff are not civil servants
- The Secretary of State for Health is accountable to parliament for its work
- The NHS Chief Executive is responsible to the minister for its performance
- The NHS is publicly funded from taxation
- Hospital doctors and nurses are nearly all employed by the NHS
- 'Family doctors' (GPs), dentists, opticians are self-employed, contracted to the NHS
- From 2012 in England, GPs are set to play the major health commissioning role

The NHS is a devolved function in Scotland, Wales and Northern Ireland

Public Corporations and other Non-Departmental Public Bodies (NDPBs)

- A public body operating at arm's length from government
- It has a separate legal identity
- Sponsored by a government department
- The minister makes the top appointments and sets out the body's overall aims
- The minister accounts to parliament for its independence, efficiency and performance
- It has substantial operational autonomy
- It employs its own staff
- It can own and dispose of assets
- Many are trading companies

Examples of NDPBs are the Royal Mail Group, the BBC, the Environment Agency and the Equality and Human Rights Commission

* *Notes*: Parliament has in the Localism Act 2011 given local authorities 'a general power of competence' but its scope has yet to be tested and is not embedded in a written Constitution: under the British 'constitution' another Act could restrict the power.

(NDPBs); they arc introduced and sponsored by departmental ministers but not part of the department. They are often created because government wants their advice or decisions to be seen to be independent of politics (for example, the Commission for Equality and Human Rights), or because they have quasi-judicial functions (such as the Environment Agency or the Pensions Ombudsman). In the last two decades a similar 'quango' arrangement has frequently been used at local level too to deliver public services through smaller, individualized units (such as housing associations or self-managed state schools, operating at arm's length from local councils). All these structures are typical of the set of reforms called New Public Management (NPM), which focused responsibilities, dividing functions between policy and delivery, agent and principal and/or contractor and client (see Chapter 2).

Table 3.1 ***UK public sector employment 1979–2011 (selected years)***

Year	Civil service (departments)	Local government	NHS	Public corporations	Total public sector (including armed forces)
1979	739,000	2,997,000	1,152,000	2,065,000	7,449,000
1984	630,000	2,942,000	1,223,000	1,599,000	6,900,000
1994	578,000	2,786,000	1,189,000	445,000	5,681,000
1997	516,000	2,762,000	1,190,000	370,000	5,426,000
1999	504,000	2,762,000	1,212,000	347,000	5,446,000
2001	522,000	2,799,000	1,285,000	376,000	5,618,000
2005	571,000	2,950,000	1,528,000	380,000	6,108,000
2008	523,000	2,948,000	1,506,000	356,000	5,996,000
2009	527,000	2,936,000	1,572,000	558,000	6,288,000
2010	522,000	2,912,000	1,596,000	537,000	6,270,000
2011	489,000	2,766,000	1,565,000	509,000	6,030,000

Note: Mid-year headcount figures, including casual staff from 1995. Local government here includes police authorities and teachers. Total public sector includes staff within central government who are not civil servants, chiefly in the armed forces and non-departmental public bodies.

Sources: Office for National Statistics (ONS): Black, O., Herbert, R. and Richardson, I. (2004) 'Jobs in the Public Sector mid-2003', *Labour Market Trends*, July, 271–81, pp. 272–3; and online Time Series C9KE, C9KA, C9LG, C9KD, available from www.ons.gov.uk.

Figure 1.2 in Chapter 1 gave an overall view of the relative size of the main categories of public bodies since the 1960s. Table 3.1 gives more detailed figures on the changes in recent years. The public sector was cut back overall during the Conservative years 1979–97, then grew under Labour until the financial crisis. Numbers rose in 2009 because of the transfer of failed private banks into the public corporation sector, and the NHS also continued to grow, reflecting the priority given by Labour to this policy area. The Coalition Government responded to the budgetary deficit with cutbacks to all sectors. Local government remains the largest provider of public services, even taking account of the fact that the official statistics include police and some other authorities that are not directly controlled by local councils (Chapter 8 provides an extensive analysis of human resources management across the public sector).

Reshaping central government departments

Reshaping the central administration is easier in the UK than in most liberal democracies, as the prime minister has powers to move functions between ministries and to manage the civil service without being obliged to consult parliament or civil service representatives. Labour's Constitutional Reform and Governance Act 2010 put these traditional powers into law, transferring the Royal Prerogative powers over the civil service (already exercised by the government) directly to the prime minister. As we see below, the government has in the past few decades used this power: to transfer the tasks performed by civil servants to other organizations to improve efficiency; to restructure departments to increase managerial control; and to realign departments to provide a more 'joined-up' approach.

Reallocating and reducing civil service functions

The Thatcher Government made slimming the state a policy goal. It had been elected on a promise to reduce 'waste' and 'bureaucracy'; and embraced the public choice theories discussed in Chapter 2, pushing departments to identify efficiency savings. Some tasks were transferred to other public organizations (housing benefit to local authorities). Some processes were simplified (the income tax regime) or abandoned (collection of some statistics). The largest reductions came from privatizing work. Munitions factories and dockyards were sold. Buildings maintenance and computer services were contracted-out.

Labour, whilst in opposition, had opposed cutting back and privatization, but the new Blair Government in 1997 wanted to demonstrate it could manage the public finances efficiently. The first paragraph of *Modern Public Services for Britain* said it would 'root out waste and inefficiency' (HM

Treasury 1998). The Blair Government privatized half a dozen departmental agencies (see below), notably the Defence Evaluation and Research Agency, DERA, its 8,000 civil servants moving into the private sector. Overall, however, the number of civil servants increased between 1998 and 2005, as we saw in Chapter 1. More staff were needed for new policies which were labour intensive, such as the working family tax credit, and for the expanding prison services.

In Blair's second term, two official reports examined the location and efficiency of the civil service. The Lyons review (2004) identified 20,000 civil service posts that could be relocated outside London by 2010, saving £2 billion. The Gershon Review identified changes to organizational structures, processes and purchasing that could produce £21.5 billion of 'efficiency gains' by 2008. Some gains would come from producing similar output with fewer staff, freeing others for 'front line public service delivery' (Gershon 2004: 5). Others would take the form of higher quality output from similar levels of resources. It was estimated that over £23 billion had been saved by 2008 (about £21.5 billion in 2004 prices), although there were substantial problems measuring these savings (Treasury Committee 2007). There were also adverse impacts on users, such as in Jobcentres (Work and Pensions Committee 2006). The House of Commons suggested that the Treasury's loss of 20 per cent of posts had crucially weakened the UK Government's capacity to respond to the financial crisis (Treasury Committee 2009: 9). Some departments had continued to grow despite Gershon, and by the time of the 2010 election there were 6,000 more civil servants than the number Labour inherited in 1997. The Coalition's answer was more cutting back on staffing, with very substantial reductions (33,000) in its first year in office, driven by departmental business plans for reform (see Chapter 5) and, even more, by huge budget reductions for nearly all departments (see Chapter 7).

Restructuring to improve managerial control

Other Thatcher projects added up to improving departmental management. An Efficiency Unit project helped ministers direct budgets towards their priorities and monitor progress by identifying 'units of accountability', their staffing, costs, objectives and performance. Promoted by Thatcher throughout Whitehall as the Financial Management Initiative (FMI), it introduced financial management systems with budgets allocated to managers, who had to account for their expenditure and report monthly. However, parliament's Public Accounts Committee (PAC 1987: paras 20–43) found that 'progress was very slow': few ministers or civil servants were interested in management.

Another important report from the Efficiency Unit (1988), *Improving Management in Government: The Next Steps*, argued that ministries should be divided internally by 'business' so that each unit could be managed appropriately and effectively for that function. First, 'political' areas of daily concern to ministers (policy development, budgetary negotiations, parliamentary liaison), should be separated from implementation. Second, implementation divisions should be divided by function into 'executive agencies', whose 'chief executives' would have substantial freedom to adapt human resources strategies to the needs of the work. Administrative tasks could be managed more appropriately and ministers could focus on major decisions, including drawing up the framework of objectives and performance levels for each agency. This reform raised concerns, especially about ministerial accountability and civil service anonymity (Pyper 1995b), and about varying conditions of service across the traditionally unified civil service. Since the reform was strongly backed by Margaret Thatcher it proceeded quickly; almost three-quarters of civil servants were in over 130 executive agencies by the 1997 election (Horton and Jones 1996). Box 3.2 shows how the concept has been applied in the Department for Work and Pensions (DWP).

Civil servants assigned to executive agencies remain civil servants, full members of their 'home' department, though senior officials have considerable day-to-day managerial freedom (see Chapter 4 for an assessment). These 'Next Steps' agencies differ from NDPBs, which, as their title implies (and see Box 3.2), are outside the departmental framework and have a separate legal identity. NDPBs are loosely tied to a minister (for top appointments, overall objectives and accountability), and their staff are public officials but rarely civil servants. Confusingly, many NDPBs have 'executive' or 'agency' in their title (for example, the Health and Safety Executive or the Environment Agency), while many departmental executive agencies have kept their pre-Next Steps title (the Planning Inspectorate, for example).

This new management system was not a political issue until the Major Government started to privatize executive agencies. By 1997 a dozen agencies had been transferred to the private or non-profit making sectors, while others had been merged or dissolved (Horton and Jones 1996). The Labour Government created several new agencies, as did the Labour–Liberal Democrat Scottish Executive to deal with powers devolved in 1999 and 2005. The Northern Ireland Civil Service adopted a similar strategy during the period of Direct Rule from London (see Carmichael 2002). In contrast, the SNP-led Scottish Government elected in 2007 re-integrated several Next Steps agencies, including those dealing with housing, fishing, and agriculture, back into their parent departments. In the UK as a whole, agencies have undergone a continuous process of review and restructuring. A few have been privatized (such as DERA). Some have merged with others and/or transferred as agencies to other departments. For example, the Rent Service was transferred in 2004 from the local government department to DWP but then merged in 2009 into the similar Valuation Office Agency of HM Revenue & Customs (HMRC), to make efficiency savings. Some have lost their agency status and become conventional divisions of their parent departments, as did several small agencies of the Ministry of Defence in 2004 and 2005.

BOX 3.2 The Department for Work and Pensions in 2012

<table>
<tr>
<td colspan="3">Core Department
Providing policy advice and personal advice to ministers; managing finance and relations with the Treasury; human resources; IT and legal advice; parliamentary and media communications; linking the core department to its executive agencies and quangos</td>
<td rowspan="2">DWP's 'quangos'
(with examples)

6 executive bodies
• Child Maintenance and Enforcement Commission
• Health and Safety Executive

5 advisory bodies
• Industrial Injuries Advisory Council
• Equality 2025

2 tribunals
• Pensions Ombudsman
• Pension Protection Fund Ombudsman

2 public corporations
• Remploy
• National Employment Savings Trust</td>
</tr>
<tr>
<td>Jobcentre Plus Executive Agency

• helps people find a job or training
• helps employers find recruits
• assesses claims and pays unemployment benefits</td>
<td>The Pension Service Executive Agency

• assesses claims and pays state pensions and pension credits
• makes pensions forecasts</td>
<td>Disability and Carers Service Executive Agency

• assesses and pays disability living allowance, attendance allowance, carer's allowance and vaccine damage payments</td>
</tr>
</table>

Note: DWP plans to merge the two tribunals and to bring the work of the Child Maintenance and Enforcement Commission into the department as an executive agency.
Source: Information from Department for Work and Pensions, www.dwp.gov.uk.

During the early years of the Next Steps programme, the main problem with agencies seemed to be that of separating policy and management. Who was responsible when prisoners escaped from Parkhurst prison on the Isle of Wight – the chief executive of the Prison Service Agency or the Home Secretary? There was a highly public disagreement about whether it was a policy or a managerial issue, which ended with the removal of Derek Lewis, the Prison Service chief executive (Talbot 1996). A similar conflict occurred over the Child Support Agency (CSA), which seeks child maintenance payments from non-resident parents; its performance was poor but there was also considerable opposition from clients and members of parliament to the policy itself. Again it was the agency chief executive who left. In both cases, ministers refused to accept responsibility for what were policy rather than management matters. The political difficulties were resolved by creating an NDPB, the Child Maintenance and Enforcement Commission, using the CSA as its delivery arm; this arrangement put ministers at a greater political distance from controversy. In 2010 the Commission was reviewed as part of the Coalition Government's 'cull of quangos'. Ministers decided that this organization should be brought within the DWP as an executive agency (like the former CSA) to make it 'democratically accountable through a Minister' (Cabinet Office 2011a: 4). Other departments have chosen to keep political aspects within the core ministry: for example, in the Department for Transport (DfT) the Highways Agency is responsible for constructing motorways but not for the often controversial decisions on where they will be built.

Some ministers intervene greatly in delivery, to the extent that the Benefits Agency, for example, turned to address ministers' current political priorities rather than the performance targets it had been set (James 2005). In other departments, including the Ministry of Defence, ministers have almost ignored agencies (Hogwood, Judge and McVicar 2000: 213). Following a review of executive agencies by Blair's Office of Public Services Reform (OPSR 2002), attention turned towards ensuring that agencies did not become too separate from the core department, because gaps were developing between policy and implementation. The OPSR report (2002: 6–11) recommended that the departmental leadership should include people with delivery experience as well as policy skills (see Chapter 9), that agencies should have at least one annual discussion with their minister, and that the targets set for departments and their agencies must be aligned, and supported by spending decisions.

Reshaping for coordinated policy and delivery

The fragmentation of public services was a powerful critique of the Conservatives' market reforms. Such considerations lay behind the 'joined-up government' promoted by the early Blair Government as part of the *Modernising Government* programme (Cabinet Office 1999a: 15). It was implemented most effectively in the early years by the small Social Exclusion Unit set up in the Cabinet Office. Yet Labour's continual reshaping of ministerial functions to improve coordination produced its own management problems.

In Blair's first term the Department for the Environment, Transport and the Regions (DETR) integrated departments dealing with these issues as well as local government and social concerns. DETR proved too difficult for its minister, John Prescott, to manage, and lasted only one parliamentary term. The break-up of DETR enabled environmental issues to be combined with agriculture in the Department for Environment, Food and Rural Affairs (DEFRA), but mainly aimed to change the culture of an agriculture ministry accustomed to promoting one small sector, yet unable to handle its crises (see the Anderson Report 2002 on the foot and mouth epidemic).

In Blair's second term, combining the Employment Service and the Department of Social Security into the DWP facilitated the merger of their respective executive agencies (Job Centres and Benefits Agency offices) to form Jobcentre Plus, a major delivery plank of Labour's 'welfare to work' reforms. The huge Inland Revenue (77,000 employees) and HM Customs & Excise (22,000), both highly autonomous organizations for a century or more, were combined in 2005 as HMRC. Ministers said this ambitious restructuring would provide a 'joined-up' department for businesses, save 3,000 posts and bring the institutions under closer ministerial control (Seely 2004: 3–4, 13–17). However, the merger was hampered by the simultaneous introduction of working family tax credits and the Gershon programme for cutting 24,000 posts (PAC 2008b). The Jobcentre Plus change project was eventually judged by parliamentarians to have been highly successful (PAC 2008a: 3), but also handicapped by having to deal concurrently with 'Gershon' and telephony and new process programmes: Jobcentre Plus provided 'truly appalling service levels' in summer 2005 (Work and Pensions Committee 2006: 3).

Prime ministers change departmental responsibilities in order to secure improved performance, to fit a minister's interests or limited managerial skills, or to pursue more principled goals. All these elements could be seen in recent restructurings, such as the transfer in 2007 of some former Home Office functions (courts, prisons and the constitution) to a new Ministry of Justice (the former Lord Chancellor's Office), allowing the Home Office to concentrate on immigration and policing. Gordon Brown renamed the Department of 'Trade and Industry' as 'Business, Enterprise and Regulatory Reform' (BERR) in 2007 to denote the shift in Labour's economic policy. A year later he transferred BERR's energy role to a new Energy and Climate Change Department, to reconcile the aims of the Climate Change Act 2008 with the constraints of a privatized energy industry. A former head of the civil service, Robin Butler, told parliament's Public Administration Select Committee (PASC 2007: Q16) that 'the frictional cost of making changes very often does exceed the benefits'. The National Audit Office (NAO 2010) put just the direct financial cost of the 90 changes made to departments and their agencies between 2005 and 2009 at £780 million, with no evidence that they were value for money.

The Coalition Government has not so far made major structural changes to departments (a few suffered further name changes) or departmental executive agencies. Furthermore, ministers from both parties were mostly appointed in 2010 to departments whose policies they were shadowing in opposition, ensuring an unusual continuity of expertise. Perhaps for that reason they have, in contrast, been active in reshaping the delivery agents of their departments: the NDPBs, the NHS, schools and local government, as can be seen below.

Changing territorial responsibilities for public services

Local authorities in the UK are less autonomous than those in most liberal democracies. They have no constitutional protection (other European countries guarantee the status and general competence of local councils in their written Constitutions). The Westminster parliament is free to change local government structures and add or subtract responsibilities to fit current political needs or management theories. The extreme case is Northern Ireland where, as we saw in Chapter 1, most local services were removed from district councils, whose impartiality was in doubt, and transferred to appointed local boards.

From monopolistic provider to enabling authority

The outlook for local government under Thatcher was signalled at the beginning of her premiership. On the hypothesis that bureaucracies supplied goods at higher prices than markets (see Chapter 2), councils were obliged from 1980 to allow companies to tender for construction and maintenance work in competition with council staff. This 'compulsory competitive tendering' (CCT) was extended in 1988 and 1992 to other functions. Council departments had to be restructured into internal companies for the purpose of introducing a client–contractor or purchaser–provider split, even where work remained 'in-house'. However councils still specify and 'enable' the service to be provided.

Similar reasoning led the Conservatives to favour solutions that allowed users to manage services for themselves. Councils had to let tenants buy their homes at a discount and were prohibited from using the receipts to replace their stock. Central funding for housing was directed to the Housing Corporation, an NDPB that subsidized housing associations, seen as better managers than council housing departments. Property companies were encouraged to take over council estates, if tenants agreed. Some councils transformed their housing estates into housing companies or associations in order to access grants. By 1997, only 18 per cent of UK homes were managed by councils, as against 29 per cent in 1981; by 2009 this figure had fallen to 9 per cent (DCLG 2007a, 2010a). Yet it is the council that has the legal duty to re-house vulnerable citizens, even in 'the Big Society'.

Another tendency of the Conservative Government was to transfer responsibility from councils to quangos. Urban Development Corporations were set up to renovate areas free of local government controls. The London Docklands Development Corporation and the Welsh Development Agency were the most controversial, because of their huge government funding and lack of accountability to local people. The Conservatives used the quango model extensively in education. The polytechnics left the local authority sector in 1988 to become self-governing and funded through NDPBs, followed in 1993 by sixth-form colleges and further education colleges: these became Higher and Further Education Corporations. New categories of schools were introduced: City Technology Colleges were governed and part-funded by boards led by private entrepreneurs; Grant Maintained schools had funding allocated by a central NDPB and managed by school governors not local authorities. Councils still had to ensure that every child had a school place, and plan for that provision, but through a mix of state schools and other maintained schools.

Equivalent reforms occurred in other functions. From 1994 each police authority (43 in England and Wales, 12 in Scotland) combined a slim majority of councillors from one or more councils with magistrates and Home Office appointees and a chair nominated by the Home Secretary. Because the boundaries of local authorities and police authorities have both been much altered, a quarter of English police forces and all in Scotland and Wales have lost the historic link to a single council. Local councils have to collect a precept (charge) for policing along with the council tax but have less influence than ministers over local policing objectives. The Coalition Government's introduction of directly elected 'police and crime commissioners' (see below) will restore some local responsiveness but in a different form.

By the end of the Conservatives' 18-year tenure, councils were providing some services directly and other services through private or voluntary sector bodies. Despite the political conflict between ministers and councillors, local government chief executives generally made it their business to engage in productive relationships with the new providers (Travers *et al.* 1997; and see Chapters 4 and 5 on partnerships). As principal adviser to councillors and the senior professional officer, the chief executive in particular had to manage the change from a 'providing' to 'an enabling authority' (Wilson and Game 2011: 24–5).

From enabling authority to community governance

The Blair Government's most revolutionary action on local government was to devolve full competence on structures, taxation and policies to Scotland and Northern Ireland, and allow the Welsh Assembly Government full discretion on implementation (see section below). In England, Labour was more positive about local government than the Conservatives had been, speaking of 'community' and 'new localism', yet just as prescriptive in its approach, in a bid to improve service standards (for the processes, see Chapters 4 and 5). The Blair Government did not restore local public service monopolies and warned councils of 'the need for change' (DETR 1998a: Chapter 1). *Best Value* in the Local Government Act 1999 was a modification not a replacement of CCT. Local authorities had regularly to review each service, and decide whether it should be provided in-house or not, based on the comparative performance of other suppliers. The procedure did not give preference to outsourcing, and it allowed councils to take into account user opinion and equity of provision. On the other hand, it required councils to use competition 'wherever practicable', and performance outcomes would be measured and inspected (see Chapters 6 and 9). The Coalition Government lightened the burden of performance reporting but expected that its financial cutbacks to local government would, of themselves, force councils to look for efficiency savings.

The housing service provides an example of the limited *institutional* changes to local services in England since the Conservatives left office in 1997 (although housing *policies*, such as on the levels of benefits, have changed). Labour gave councils more freedom to spend housing sales receipts on new homes but central capital funding still went primarily to Partner Programmes with housing associations. The duty of local authorities to house vulnerable people was extended to additional groups in 2002, along with the need to network with voluntary and private-sector partners to reduce homelessness. In 2008, the Housing Corporation in England was combined with English Partnerships (an NDPB set up by the Blair Government to replace Thatcher's Development Corporations) to create a new Homes and Communities Agency to fund and plan housing provision. It could take over a council's planning role if necessary to achieve the number of homes the government wants. The Coalition Government abolished some NDPBs but kept this one, consolidating it with the Tenant Services Authority (another NDPB, which regulated social housing), except in London, where both functions were devolved to the Mayor.

In English education, the most distinctly 'New Labour' or 'Third Way' initiative (see Chapter 2) was the short-lived Education Action Zone programme which offered additional funding and curriculum freedoms to schools in educational priority areas which formed partnerships with the wider education sector and local businesses. However, these projects did not prove as effective as a more conventional schools programme run by local authorities (Excellence in Cities) and were abandoned in Labour's second term (OFSTED 2003: 69). Labour's 'Fresh Start' programme relied on Conservative legislation that allowed ministers to close down 'failing' primary schools and re-open them under new and possibly private management. Although the Blair Government brought Grant Maintained schools back within the local education authority system as Foundation Schools, they retained their autonomy on managing assets and on teacher and pupil recruitment. The 203 sponsored City Academies promoted by Blair's policy unit were modelled on the Conservatives' City Technology Colleges, but with the significant difference that their public funding (allocated centrally) was concentrated on inner-city areas.

The Coalition Government had transferred Academy status to over 1000 schools in England by 2011, and intended that all schools rated at least 'good' by the schools inspectorate, OFSTED, should become academies, to introduce further competition into the system. Additional categories of schools were introduced. 'Free Schools', which are centrally funded, non-profit making schools with a freer choice of curriculum, can be set up in a variety of premises by virtually any community group, subject to central authorization, and best typify the Big Society approach to education. Two dozen had been created by 2011 at the initiative of parents, faith groups or existing Academy trusts. Partly because decisions on status and funding were now being made centrally for a large number of schools, a new executive agency, the Education Funding Agency, was created within the Department for Education to carry out this task from 2012, integrating some functions of existing NDPBs and, indeed, of local education authorities.

There were few areas of local services where Labour abstained from organizational change. One partial exception was in policing but only because Home Office proposals to combine forces to save money faded away in the face of opposition from police authorities and some forces. Nevertheless the Policing and Crime Act 2009 required police authorities in England and Wales to promote collaboration between forces, and enabled the minister to order collaboration. The restoration of Greater London government gave the opportunity to create a Metropolitan Police Authority and make the police answer to Londoners, as demonstrated by Mayor Boris Johnson's informal but effective removal of the Metropolitan Police's chief officer in 2008. The Coalition presented its proposals for elected police and crime commissioners as adding accountability by making forces subject to 'oversight by a directly elected individual', and whose judgement on the appointment of a chief constable and overall policing plans would be 'subject to strict checks and balances by locally elected representatives' (Cabinet Office 2010: 13). Although local police and crime panels will (except in Wales) consist of committees of councillors from each authority covered by the force, the Home Office specifically reminds them they are not there to represent the local community – which is the task of the commissioner – but to 'support and challenge' the commissioner. The panels will have the legal right to veto the chief constable appointment and local precept (charge), but are asked to treat these powers as a last resort (Home Office 2011). The Welsh Assembly had to accept the introduction of police commissioners (because policing is not devolved to Wales), but refused to assent to local authority panels (over which they have competence). The Home Secretary responded by creating bodies to which she or he will nominate members, with invitations going to selected local councillors.

Overall, there has been substantial continuity between Conservative, Labour and Coalition Governments on local services in England in the way that they saw local councils as only one possible provider among many. Despite much talk of 'localism' they often preferred to give a task to a specialized quango. However, Labour did not emphasize the private sector and sometimes gave local government a special leadership role to play in multi-agency working, and that did constitute a different approach from the Conservatives, while the Coalition shared Labour's concern with 'localism' but interpreted the 'entrepreneurial leadership' role as one for a locally elected individual.

Restructuring territorial government: local, regional, national

The Blair Government's devolution reform of 1999 somewhat eclipsed the Conservatives' abolition of local councils between 1985 and 1994, but this earlier restructuring of councils had aroused passions in Scotland and Wales that helped drive the more radical constitutional change (Jones 2002: 49–50). The Coalition Agreement ruled out further structural change to local councils.

Local government in Britain had already been restructured in 1974 into a two-tier system, with county authorities for some services and district or borough authorities for the rest. The Thatcher Government abolished the Greater London Council (GLC) and metropolitan county councils in 1986. It argued that the two-tier configuration was administratively inefficient and led to conflict where competences overlapped, although the decision was also influenced by the fact that the metropolitan councils were at that time dominated by the Labour Party and were vocal opponents of Conservative policies. Some GLC and metropolitan county functions were devolved to boroughs or transferred to central government ministries, but many continued under joint committees of the districts or new local quangos. The resulting fragmentation of services was acknowledged by the Major Government when it created a coordinating Regional Office for London in 1992, followed by Government Offices for the Regions in eight other metropolitan cities (see Chapter 4). They were abolished by the Coalition Government in 2010 to cut expenditure, though most departments will continue to need regional offices.

As Conservative minister for local government in 1992, Michael Heseltine (instigator of managerial reforms in central government a decade earlier), inspired a manifesto commitment to move to a unitary (single-tier) system of local government. A consultative review started in England but there were so many objections (including by Conservatives) that it was halted early, leaving most counties and districts untouched and a small number recast as unitary authorities. The UK Secretaries for Scotland and for Wales replaced all councils with unitary authorities with legislation approved by a parliamentary majority of English Conservatives, fuelling the demand for devolution.

The Labour Government started the devolution process immediately it was elected. Devolution had already been well prepared in Scotland, as Chapter 1 explained. Because the majority of Welsh voters had historically shown themselves content with the status quo, the enabling referendum proposed a lower level of devolution than that for Scotland. The Welsh Assembly gained support after its establishment in 1999, and further powers were added, as also happened in Scotland. Labour's 1997 manifesto commitments on

Northern Ireland were cautious because of uncertainty about the peace process, but the concept of a devolved parliament had already been agreed between Ireland and the UK, and was put in place after the Good Friday Agreement of 1998. The powers devolved at that time included most domestic policy areas but not justice and policing, which were devolved in 2010 after further negotiations.

The continuing process of devolution is outlined in Chapter 4 but it is already clear that divergence is emerging between the four governments on preferred organizational structures. The Labour Party in Wales had vigorously opposed Conservative-created and appointed NDPBs, such as Housing for Wales, the Wales Tourist Board, the Welsh National Education and Training Council and the Welsh Development Agency. Within a few years of devolution, all had been brought into departments where they could be made accountable to the Assembly. It was noted earlier that the Scottish Government brought some politically sensitive executive agencies back into core departments. The Northern Ireland Executive in contrast has retained the concept of delivering education through special-purpose bodies, combining the former education boards with services from the Department of Education and other bodies to form a new NDPB, the Education and Skills Authority (see Chapter 5). The Scottish and Welsh Governments have, like the UK Coalition Government, embarked on programmes for reducing the number of public bodies to help meet the new financial circumstances: Scotland proposed to cut the number by a quarter (Scott 2009: 83), and Wales decided to merge three environmental bodies to save £160 million over ten years (Government of Wales 2011).

The different organizational approaches of the four governments can be seen in the delivery of social housing. As noted above, the UK Government created for England (and for Wales) an NDPB (Homes and Communities Agency, Housing for Wales) for the planning and regulatory aspects. Housing for Wales was abolished with the Welsh devolution legislation and its functions transferred to the Welsh Assembly Government's housing department. In Scotland the same functions were performed until 2007 by civil servants in an executive agency, Communities Scotland, part of the Scottish Government's Housing and Regeneration Directorate. The SNP-led Scottish Government then followed Wales by bringing Communities Scotland fully within the core housing directorate. In all parts of the UK, housing associations are important voluntary sector providers but in Northern Ireland the housing role, equivalent to that of local councils in Great Britain, is in the hands of a regional board, the Northern Ireland Housing Executive, these powers having been taken away from Northern Ireland's local authorities in 1971 because there were suspicions of discrimination.

The only English region to have been organized comprehensively is Greater London. In 2000, the Greater London Authority (GLA) and its directly elected mayor were given fewer but stronger and clearer functions than those of the former GLC. The GLA's budget can be (and has been) cut back by the Greater London Assembly members elected by the boroughs. Yet it is more powerful strategically, with a duty to plan integrated land-use, transport, environment and economic development strategies, and to direct the boroughs' plans. Much depends on the mayor's personal capacity to direct GLA executive bodies, such as Transport for London (TfL), and on the people he or she appoints to lead and manage them. Good coordination with the boroughs is still required for effective delivery.

In other parts of England there is little popular demand for regional government, as the failure of a referendum in the North East in 2004 indicated. Labour's 1997 manifesto had promised elected regional assemblies but only where 'there was demonstrable demand', and Regional Development Agencies (RDAs). However, there was tension within the Blair Government between John Prescott, Deputy Prime Minister, in charge of regions and a strong supporter of them, and other ministers who saw that, now Labour was in government, 'a degree of centralized coordination' would drive national manifesto commitments more effectively than devolved regional assemblies (Rhodes *et al.* 2003: 138).

The RDAs were created in 1999 as appointed bodies, to develop economic strategies in consultation with regional assemblies. Assemblies were set up with members appointed mainly from local councils, with some representation of regional social groups. The 2004 Planning Act gave the assemblies the task of elaborating spatial and transport strategies, but some assemblies found it hard to develop a 'regional' outlook in such a short time (see West Midlands Regional Assembly 2008 for a discussion of the issues). Labour dissolved the assemblies in 2010, transferring their planning functions to the business-led RDAs. The RDAs were in turn abolished by the Coalition Government, which invited community leaders to set up their own cross-sectoral Local Enterprise Partnerships (LEPs) within the boundaries they thought relevant to their needs.

The concept of unitary councils was taken up again in 2006 by the Blair Government after a campaign by several city councils. Three dozen proposals were assessed on criteria that included leadership, neighbourhood empowerment, value for money, equity and local support as well as affordability (DCLG 2006). Seven applications were approved by the Brown Government in 2008. Five counties (Cornwall, County Durham, Wiltshire, Northumberland and Shropshire) absorbed the staff and functions of 28 district councils, which would save £75 million, according to the local government minister (DCLG 2007b). In Bedfordshire and Cheshire, proposals from the districts succeeded: the county councils were abolished and each replaced by two unitary councils: Bedford Borough Council and Central Bedfordshire, and Cheshire West & Chester and Chester East respectively, all first elected in April 2009. The Coalition Agreement announced that plans initiated under the previous government for restructuring other councils (in

Norfolk, Suffolk and Devon) would be abandoned as would the plans to restructure fire brigades (Cabinet Office 2010: 12).

Reorganizing the NHS for management and the market

The Department of Health, responsible for the NHS, public health and social care, was among the leaders of NPM in the UK (Day and Klein 2000: 238). It pioneered performance measurement of outputs rather than inputs; developed professional, private-sector style management; introduced the concept of market competition and the purchaser–provider split; and was among the first to bring in outsiders to senior posts traditionally staffed by career civil servants. On the other hand, the constant structural reforms – to the department itself, to the local health authorities, and to the providers of the service – gave Pollitt (2007b) the material for 'a cautionary tale' about the high costs of organizational change.

Management reforms and the purchaser–provider split

The Conservative Government's first NHS reorganization in 1982 concerned the territorial restructuring of hospital services, and sought greater business-like efficiency (Ham 2009: 30–4). The new larger District Health Authorities (DHAs) in England and Wales (Health Boards in Scotland) were more efficient for hospital management but broke the link with county-level social care services and with the GPs who determined hospital inflows (see Table 3.2). Next, the top-level internal management structure was reformed, following recommendations by the managing director of the supermarket chain Sainsbury's, Roy Griffiths (1983). An NHS Management Board of officials became accountable for hospital performance to a ministerial Supervisory Board, which took the strategic decisions. This arrangement was designed to split policy from delivery, but had the disadvantage that departmental officials advising ministers on policy lacked contact with hospital implementation issues, while the more expert Management Board represented a producer interest; furthermore, the GPs remained outside the NHS management structure.

A third reorganization in 1991, following a working party chaired by Thatcher, resulted in a clearer chain of command linking DHA to Regional Health Authority (RHA) to the Chief Executive of the NHS Management Executive and thence to the Secretary of State. A more radical option, similar to that now being implemented by the Coalition Government, was put forward and would have made the NHS an independent agency or corporation, insulated from the short-term political pressures weighing on ministers. This solution was preferred by Griffiths and by Major, as the then Treasury minister, but was rejected because it put technical efficiency before local

Table 3.2 ***NHS purchasers in England***

<table>
<tr><th>1982</th><th>1991</th><th>1996</th><th>1999</th><th>2002</th><th>2006</th><th>2013?</th></tr>
<tr><td colspan="2">14 Regional Health Authorities</td><td colspan="2">8 Regional Offices of NHS Executive</td><td>28 Strategic Health Authorities</td><td>10 Strategic Health Authorities</td><td>NHS Commissioning Board</td></tr>
<tr><td colspan="2">201 District Health Authorities</td><td colspan="2" rowspan="2">100 Health Authorities</td><td rowspan="3">303 Primary Care Trusts</td><td rowspan="2">152 Primary Care Trusts</td><td rowspan="3">about 300 GP commissioning groups</td></tr>
<tr><td rowspan="2">Family Practitioner Committees</td><td>Family Health Service Authorities</td></tr>
<tr><td colspan="2">– GP fund holders
– 175 Locality (GP) commissioning groups</td><td>481 Primary Care Groups</td><td>GP Practice based commissioning</td></tr>
</table>

Source: Adapted from Audit Commission (2008a) *Is the Treatment Working?*, London: Audit Commission, p. 16.

responsiveness and parliamentary accountability for a huge budget service (Day and Klein 2000: 241–9).

At the same time, an 'internal market' was introduced by creating 'purchasers' and 'providers'. The market was seen as the answer to the problem of poor services that survived only because most users had no choice (see Chapter 2). The purchasers of secondary (hospital) care were the DHAs, GP fund holders (large practices with delegated budgets), and private insurance companies. The providers of secondary care were DHA-managed hospitals and hospitals which had 'opted out' to become self-managed NHS Trusts (quangos). GPs were 'providers' of primary care, earning additional payments if they attracted more patients or reduced prescription costs. Local councillors were removed from the DHA boards, leaving mainly business people and the Family Practitioner Committees were replaced with more business-like Family Health Service Authorities, FHSAs. Outside the official scheme for GP fund holders, many groups of GP practices formed collaborative 'locality commissioning groups' to work with DHAs and NHS Trusts to meet specific needs, such as primary mental health care, or planning local provision; this voluntary community action would later be resuscitated by Labour.

Within a few years, the wider NHS structure in England and Wales was further 'streamlined' (Ham 2009: 45). The RHAs were replaced by regional offices of the NHS Executive, required to focus on strategy and control of outcomes. DHAs and FHSAs were merged into 100 Health Authorities covering both primary and secondary care. The government abandoned the policy–delivery split: the NHS Executive became responsible for policy deliberations on NHS matters.

New Labour reorganization; return to local purchasing

Labour's first reorganization (DH 1997) retained the purchaser–provider split but replaced GP fundholding and commissioning groups with Primary Care Groups (PCGs). They 'commissioned' (purchased) services from NHS Trusts and local authorities, trying to match NHS budgets to users' needs. GPs were persuaded to join the PCGs by being offered majority control of PGC boards, but their professional views dominated the definition of local needs as opposed to users' demands (Sheaff, Pickard and Smith 2002: 444–51), a finding that suggests problems ahead for the Coalition Government's scheme, which gives GPs the prime purchasing role. Parallel White Papers were produced for Wales, Scotland and Northern Ireland, with that for Wales (DH 1998) notably making PCGs match local council areas and adding other measures to improve cooperation between health care and social services.

Further reorganization for England (DH 2000, 2002) was announced by the Blair Government and encouraged by vociferous criticism of the NHS during the 2001 election. The reforms challenged NHS traditions by emphasizing competition with the private sector, and a more devolved health service to provide user choice (Audit Commission 2008a: 9). Primary Care Trusts (PCTs) integrated both Health Authority and PCG roles: they were given health budgets to commission hospital services (from any sector), become direct providers of community services and run non-Trust hospitals. Each PCT was to be managed by a board, part-appointed and part-representative of GPs and other health professionals. Strategic Health Authorities (SHAs) were created to ensure the PCTs and NHS Hospital Trusts worked to DH medical and budgetary priorities; two years later, another reform introduced a 'Foundation Trust' status that allowed better-performing hospitals to become 'not-for-profit businesses' outside the control of SHA and DH officials, but licensed to practice and overseen by a new regulator, Monitor.

The Wanless Report on the long-term funding of healthcare (2002), and the Gershon Review on efficiency (2004) stimulated more streamlining. In 2006, PCTs merged and SHAs were reformed, to cut office costs and obtain value for money in procurement. Another advantage was that the boundaries of most reformed PCTs matched those of local authorities providing social care (some PCTs were even located in council offices), and the SHAs matched the Government Offices for the Regions (though the latter were abolished in 2010 by the Coalition). At the same time, to increase local choice, GP fundholding was reintroduced under the title of GP practice-based commissioners, a system at the heart of the 2010–11 reform.

Responsibility for the NHS in Scotland and Wales was devolved in 1999. The Welsh Government replaced Health Authorities with Local Health Boards in 2003. Welsh NHS Trusts cover all hospitals and community care within an area that matches a group of local councils. In Scotland, major reform in 2004 brought all Health Boards and hospitals under the management of one body, NHS Boards. NHS Hospital Trusts were abolished in Scotland, and local authority councillors were appointed to Health Boards to improve coordination of health and social care. The SNP Government of 2007 rejected Labour's partnerships between the NHS and the private sector; and proposed Boards be elected. Legislation on elections for a proportion of Board members was approved by all parties in 2009, and pilot schemes introduced in 2010.

By 2010, the territorial structure of the NHS in the UK had largely gone back to the position before 1982, helping link clinical treatment to community care, and there was more effort to coordinate primary and secondary care. In Wales and Scotland, the reforms aimed at providing an overall integration, but in England, hospitals, and especially Foundation Trust hospitals, had substantial autonomy. The structural changes also had a price. In its report on the government's implementation of NHS reforms in England, the Audit Commission identified 'structural reorganization' as a significant barrier to progress. The Commission recommended 'a prolonged moratorium' on any further reorganization of those who commission health services (2008a: 74).

The Coalition's reform of NHS organization in England

The Coalition Programme of 2010 made NHS reform a 'flagship' example of the benefits of cross-party collaboration: 'GPs with authority over commissioning; patients with much more control; elections for your local NHS health board' (Cabinet Office 2010: 8). It promised to 'stop the top-down reorganizations' while 'enabling' (not requiring) consortia of GPs to commission treatment for their patients. PCTs would contribute to 'the new localism'. Some of their board members would be elected to provide 'a stronger voice for patients locally' (Cabinet Office 2010: 24). Local authorities would appoint the remaining members and ministers would control the appointments of top PCT officials. The proposal that seemed most likely to provoke opposition was that of establishing 'an independent and accountable NHS Commissioning Board' which would allocate resources and issue commissioning guidelines.

The White Paper *Equity and Excellence: Liberating the NHS* (DH 2010) confirmed the concept of the Commissioning Board, including the intention to protect Board decisions from 'political micromanagement'. About four-fifths of the NHS budget would be spent directly by groups of GPs, who would choose between public and other providers, which would be paid according to performance, not output. All NHS Hospital Trusts would become self-standing Foundation Trusts (forcing them to become financially viable). The primary role of the Trust regulator, Monitor, would become that of promoting competition. The new proposals gave a place to local authorities by adding 'health and wellbeing boards' that would promote public health and coordinate social care. Having given the PCT's commissioning function to GPs (mainly a Conservative aim), and its other functions to local health and wellbeing boards (mainly a Liberal Democrat aim), the White Paper proposed abolishing the PCTs by 2012, and therefore also the SHAs, to reduce duplication and layers of management. There was an immediate 'change management' problem of relying on PCTs to transfer the commissioning and contracting process to GPs while they themselves were being abolished.

Among the many points of contention over the reform were:

- the reduced role of the Secretary of State – from safeguarding and accounting for the NHS to 'enabling' health services to be supplied, and not necessarily by the NHS;
- the enormous power given to GPs – who were a strong producer interest, in the private sector, not accountable to parliament, and not trained and perhaps not prepared to manage large budgets; and
- the potential privatization of the NHS, which all these 'market' provisions seemed to encourage, in the name of choice, improving standards and cutting costs.

Implementation of the reforms (announced for 2013) seemed to run ahead of the legislation. PCTs were losing so many staff that they had to be grouped into 'clusters', while many GPs were 'piloting' a yet-to-be-created role. The dispute threatened to split the Coalition and parliament to the extent that legislative progress was halted for a 'pause' while options were reconsidered by an 'NHS Future Forum' of experts before amendments were presented to parliament (Purvis 2011).

The government ultimately conceded that the Secretary of State would have explicit legal and constitutional responsibility for providing a comprehensive health service in England and for accounting directly to parliament for the health budget. The role of the local health and wellbeing boards was also strengthened; they would play a larger part in developing local commissioning plans, and in joining up the commissioning of hospital treatment with health and social care provision.

The rules for GP commissioning groups were modified following the advice of the Forum. The boards of groups would have to include other professions (a nurse, a hospital specialist), and they would have to consult other specified bodies when developing commissioning plans. To improve accountability each group would have an additional governing body, including non-health professionals, which would meet in public. GP group practices would generally be required to work within one local authority area to facilitate coordination. To reassure those GPs (and their patients) not ready to take on the new responsibilities, the deadline for becoming operational would be relaxed, and the NHS Commissioning Board would support these groups.

The primary role of Monitor was changed: it would instead protect and promote patients' interests – which could be by ensuring fair competition but also by integration, by setting NHS prices (to rule out price competition), and by ensuring that services would continue to be supplied if a private provider or Foundation Trust failed. Trusts have been given a few extra years to reach Foundation Trust status, with advice from the NHS Trust Development Agency and Monitor. Hospitals that are still not financially viable could choose to merge with another Trust, or call in a private operator to try to achieve a turnaround (King's Fund 2011). Monitor is, in effect, the regulator of 'the health economy' with a task equivalent to the regulators of the privatized utilities discussed below. It has an additional function of 'provider of last resort', with the power to levy charges on providers and commissioners to cover the risk of having to organize an alternative supply of health services. The similarity of its role to that of utility regulation further added to the impression that the NHS was being privatized.

The legislation required further amendments before it was completed in 2012, because of the opposition from doctors, nurses, midwives and paramedical professional groups, and from the House of Lords, the Labour Party and some government backbenchers, and is likely to require more change when early implementation reveals problems.

Privatizing and regulating public enterprise

The Thatcher Government led the world on the privatization of public corporations. Nevertheless, there were still more than 500,000 jobs in the public corporations sector in 2011, including 200,000 in the banks rescued by the Labour Government in 2008 (Office for National Statistics). Initial intentions on nationalized enterprises were based on the belief that competition would benefit the consumer, but later privatizations had elements of 'selling the family silver', as former Conservative Prime Minister Macmillan described it. In this chapter, we are less concerned with the principles underlying the various strategies, which are discussed in Chapters 2 and 7. Here we set out the changes governments made to the organization of the public sector.

Privatization, liberalization and competition

The first privatizations by the Thatcher Government concerned sectors in which a market already existed. British Aerospace and British Shipbuilders had recently been in the private sector; the oil firms had been part-privatized by previous governments; and others operated in competitive markets. For the second set of privatizations the government had first to encourage a more competitive environment by removing the regulatory controls that kept out rival providers. British Airways (BA) was not sold until 1987, after opening up some routes to other airlines had taken effect. Bus routes were deregulated in 1985 (except in London) and the government privatized the National Bus Company, splitting it into smaller companies first, to avoid reproducing a monopoly.

Creating competition was more difficult where the service depended on huge investment in a network infrastructure. In telecoms, the government encouraged Mercury to become an alternative supplier to BT by guaranteeing that there would be no other entrant until 1989, and by creating the Office of Telecommunications (Oftel, now Ofcom), to supervise access to BT's network (Whitehead 1988: 18). Subsequent privatizations of infrastructure-based companies (gas, electricity, water, railways and airports), were accompanied by the creation of a regulatory agency. As problems arose (such as non-payment of bills by poor households, or the national need for modernized infrastructure) the regulators' work became more complex, trying to judge companies' rates of return and efficiency and specifying consumer rights (see Chapter 7). The privatized utilities remain real 'public services' in that their activities are the daily concern of public regulators. The state continues to play a large role in these services.

Strengthening government controls

For those nationalized industries still in the public sector, the Conservative Government found new ways to monitor and control performance. The 1980

Competition Act empowered the Monopolies and Mergers Commission (now the Competition Commission) to examine the efficiency, costs and service quality of public corporations. The Conservatives also turned increasingly to management consultants to carry out efficiency reviews.

Another tactic was to restructure a corporation to expose its weak sectors. The Post Office was restructured in 1986 into three businesses: Parcelforce, Royal Mail and Post Office Counters, which highlighted their different contributions to the Post Office's performance. In 1989 the government started to offer the centrally run (Crown) post offices as franchised agencies (UK sub-post offices have always been run as a business by shopkeepers), but the Major Government's proposal to sell 51 per cent of Parcelforce and of Royal Mail had to be dropped because of parliamentary opposition (Hillyard 1999: 10). The Scottish Transport Group was split between the bus companies, which were sold, and the heavily subsidized Caledonian MacBrayne ferry business, which remained in the hands of the UK Scottish Secretary.

The Civil Aviation Authority's National Air Traffic Services (NATS, air traffic control) was separated from the Authority's regulatory operations. Substantial investment was needed to modernize the traffic control system but the government was reluctant to increase public sector borrowing. Privatization was proposed instead and NATS was constituted as a public company. Its sale was strongly contested and abandoned. The privatization process was coming to an end, partly because few nationalized industries remained, but also because the government was politically weak at this time. Some half-resolved problems, such as NATS, were left for the next government to tackle.

New Labour: semi-privatization; semi-nationalization

By 1997, the Post Office and NATS were the only substantial national industries, but other significant public corporations remained, such as the Bank of England, the BBC and regional utilities such as London Underground, the Scottish water companies and local authority airports (Manchester for example). Furthermore, Labour in opposition had pledged to bring some services back into public ownership, rail in particular.

The Labour Government proved reluctant to buy back the railways but improved coordination between the train operators and the network operator, Railtrack, by creating a Strategic Rail Authority (SRA). The SRA negotiated franchises and considered infrastructure planning, freight development and consumer protection. Following a fatal accident at Hatfield in 2000 and construction cost overruns, Railtrack had severe financial problems. Ministers seized the opportunity to 'bankrupt' the company. The government replaced Railtrack with Network Rail, a not-for-dividend company with a large appointed board, whose debts are guaranteed by the state. The network has in effect been re-nationalized. The SRA was abolished in 2005 and its functions are now carried out by the DfT. In essence, private companies run the trains but the rest of the railway is as much under government control as it was under the nationalized British Rail (see Glaister *et al.* 2006: 60–2, 200–12). The Labour Government also rescued London & Continental Railway (owner-constructor of the Channel Tunnel Rail Link) by guaranteeing its debts. The Brown Government offered to 'sell' the company on a 30-year lease and the Coalition Government completed the sale in 2010.

Labour resolved the problem of NATS with a public–private partnership (PPP), agreed in 2001 between ministers and the Airline Group (of major UK airlines), which bought 46 per cent of NATS; 5 per cent went to NATS staff to give them a stake in the modernization. These arrangements allow NATS and its debt to be categorized as private sector, but the government remains the largest shareholder, though the Coalition has plans to sell this now-profitable business. The Blair Government promised the Post Office greater commercial freedom. The Postal Services Act 2000 changed the Post Office to a public limited company, to operate within a five-year strategic plan approved by the government. This legislation also created a postal services regulator, which would promote competition by offering licences to other companies, such as DHL and Business Post. The Conservatives' plans to privatize Royal Mail having failed, the Coalition Programme proposed an alternative strategy based on Labour's solution for NATS, of enabling private capital and employee ownership to be introduced into Royal Mail. The government's goal was for the whole organization to become a mutual company, owned by employees, sub-post offices and local communities. However, the general economic situation, coupled with Royal Mail's declining mail business, made it difficult to attract the proposed private investment.

A PFI/PPP arrangement was used for London Underground, with the difference that the operation of the trains would remain in public hands while the modernization of the infrastructure would be undertaken by two private consortia. The PPP was a compromise between those ministers who wanted to keep the Tube public, and those who were not impressed by London Underground's management of previous projects. Responsibility for London Underground's operations was not devolved to the Mayor of London (Ken Livingstone) and TfL until the two PFI contracts were settled in December 2002, because they had argued strongly against this method of financing. After one consortium went into administration in 2007, the Mayor negotiated the transfer of its project (and debts) to London Underground. Under the new Mayor, Boris Johnson, TfL bought the second consortium in June 2010, leading to the public corporation, London Underground, becoming responsible for both operating and renovating the Tube.

The BBC had a historic reputation for authoritative factual broadcasting, but the Blair Government's news management made for fraught relationships, which culminated in the resignation of the Chair of the BBC Board of Governors and the BBC Director General in 2004. The government then used the regular review of the BBC Charter and licence fee to reshape the BBC constitution. In 2007 the Board of Governors was abolished and replaced by the BBC Trust, which is appointed by the prime minister; it includes four members to represent audiences in the four nations as did the former Board. The Trust appoints the Director General. The 'public service' duties of the BBC were redefined to include, notably, 'sustaining citizenship and civil society', and 'representing the UK, its nations, regions and communities'. The BBC is funded by household licence fees, which are collected by a private company. It remains highly dependent on the goodwill of the government.

The Scottish Caledonian MacBrayne's virtual monopoly of scheduled ferry crossings on the west coast became an issue for the Scottish Government shortly after devolution. EU rules require subsidized ferry services to be open to competition. In 2006, the enterprise was split into two state-owned companies: one, CMAL, owning the harbours and ships; the other, CalMac Ferries, leasing the ships from CMAL. CalMac Ferries then bid for the tender to operate Clyde and Western Isles services, which it won by default when early private-sector competitors withdrew. Under a different name, Caledonian MacBrayne also operates subsidized ferry routes to Orkney and Shetland, which means that a large part of Scotland's 'lifeline' ferry traffic is in the hands of one state company.

The first Scottish Government (a Labour–Liberal Democrat coalition) kept the water service in the public sector, but brought its organizational arrangements closer to those in England and Wales. The service had been run by local authorities until their restructuring in 1994–5, when it was transferred to three public water companies. The devolved government reorganized these companies as a public corporation, Scottish Water, regulated by a Water Industry Commission. The subsequent SNP Government agreed to opposition demands in 2008 to study a possible conversion of the corporation into a mutual organization but there seemed little prospect of change. In Wales, a not-for-profit company Glas Cymru Welsh Water, with the support of the Welsh Assembly and the regulator Ofwat, stepped in to take control when the private water company in Wales failed. Like Scottish Water, it works mainly through private contractors. In Northern Ireland, water is still a public service, and was supplied by the Department for Regional Development's Water Service Agency until 2007. The Water Service Agency was reconstituted as a state-owned contracted business, Northern Ireland Water; the Northern Ireland Authority for Utility Regulation, already regulating gas and electricity, became the regulator for water services too. Scotland and Wales are establishing distinctive identities from England where public services are concerned (keeping some in the public or not-for-profit sector rather than privatizing them), while Northern Ireland remains both different from England (in not privatizing its public operator), and yet taking on some of the same organizational characteristics (introducing a regulator at arm's length from government).

Many corporations privatized by the Thatcher and Major Governments had been nationalized by the Labour Government in the 1940s in pursuit of 'Clause 4' of Labour's founding constitution (1918), committing the party to 'the public ownership of the means of production'. Subsequent nationalization projects – by Conservative and Labour – concerned the rescue of loss-making industries (aerospace, the vehicle industry). By 1995, Blair had been able to persuade his party to revise Clause 4, ending the goal of state socialism, and his government did not anticipate reversing the privatization process. However, the crisis in the financial sector in 2008 led to the Brown Government taking over two regional building societies (Northern Rock and Bradford & Bingley), and buying substantial proportions of two much larger banks (60 per cent and eventually 80 percent of Royal Bank of Scotland, 40 per cent of HBOS-Lloyds TSB). However, neither the Labour Government nor the Coalition suggested that these 'nationalizations' were anything other than temporary measures; and the commercial banking activities of the two smaller banks have since been re-privatized.

Permanent reorganization but strong continuity

In terms, therefore, of the classic four-part structure, how can the evolution of public institutions in recent years be summed up? In central government, the executive agency model associated with delegated management and more generally with the NPM reforms of the 1980s has not been called into question by UK governments, and the agency landscape for the most part evolved along the lines established under the Conservatives, including the privatization of agencies. More significantly, the fusion of the Benefits Agency with the Employment Service Agency's Job Centres was a bold and effective response to the fragmentation that Labour had deplored during opposition years, as was the creation of the Social Exclusion Unit in the Cabinet Office in an attempt to coordinate at the policy level. The conclusion of former top officials and parliament's NAO was, however, that there had been rather too much organizational change to central departments and their agencies under Labour. 'The costs are not just financial … Governments stand to lose expertise, institutional memory and strategic focus' (PASC 2007: 10). The Coalition Government did not immediately change the configuration of departments but its review of a long list of NDPBs, and the merger or abolition of some of them (see Chapter 4) had repercussions on the organizations that would absorb their functions and staff.

The inventory of changes to local government shows strong continuity since the 1980s on principles. The appeal to the market, competition and citizen choice are still strong themes, although both Labour and Coalition Governments have emphasized communities and neighbourhood, at least in their rhetoric. The local authority is now seen as an enabler, not a provider, yet it is the 'provider of last resort' for the disadvantaged and vulnerable whose needs are not addressed by the private and not-for-profit sectors. The cutbacks in funding during the period of Coalition Government as a consequence of UK budgetary difficulties will make it difficult for local councils to interpret their role in a more entrepreneurial way. There was also continuity of organizational forms, both specifically (Coalition academies extending Labour's programme of City Academies that copied the Conservatives' City Technology Colleges, for instance), and generally, with the tendency to turn to quangos as a way of combining some local responsiveness or flexible management with central control over appointments. Despite the Coalition abolishing some NDPBs, this form of institution is very likely to re-emerge in England, in contrast to Wales and Scotland, whose hostility is explained by the history of NDPBs run by Conservative appointees of Westminster.

Labour was as prescriptive as the Conservatives in its relationships with local councils – on how their leadership structures should be organized, for example, and the Coalition Government, while being more 'hands-off' in relationship to performance monitoring (see Chapter 6), is deciding for itself where elected mayors could be introduced. Yet Labour governments were distinctive in their more even-handed approach to the public, private and voluntary sectors, and their insistence that organizations should work in partnership to provide a more community-wide and joined-up service. They differed most from the Conservatives in their readiness to devolve powers to Scotland, Wales and Greater London – and only in part because these governments were likely to be run initially by Labour.

Governments have searched obsessively for the perfect NHS configuration for forty years. The 2006 reforms in England came closer to the structures already adopted in Wales and Scotland, and aligned most health care authorities along the boundaries of local authorities, following the 'joined-up' principle and encouraging the development of Labour's distinctive multi-agency and area partnership model. The Coalition Government's approach to health will continue along the path of reorganization, including within the Department of Health itself, in a market-based approach to reducing costs and matching provision to new patterns of demand.

The difference between Conservative and Labour governments was greatest over nationalized industries. Labour was cautious on what remained, using PPPs where the Thatcher Government might have privatized outright. It took the rail network back into quasi-public ownership, and lent sufficient funds to British Energy and London & Continental Railway that they were categorized by the Office for National Statistics as 'public'. Its financial support for banks was seen as temporary – New Labour was no more committed than Conservatives to national ownership and its decisions were pragmatic not principled. The diversity of regional approaches to utility privatization, along with differences on NDPBs and the NHS, constitute clear signs of the 'differentiated polity' within the four parts of the UK identified by Rhodes *et al.* (2003).

The organizational architecture is now very different from that in 1979, but the most radical changes were made by the Thatcher Governments of 1979–90, not Labour nor the Coalition. The Conservative Governments brought about the use of multiple providers instead of the directly managed State services of the post-war period. Later modifications have often been a response to the consequences of the Conservative restructuring: fragmentation and problems of coordination. Labour therefore emphasized partnerships and collaboration rather than outsourcing and competition. The Coalition promised 'de-bureaucratization' and the shrinking of the formal organizations of government, though implementation so far concerns mainly cutbacks in staffing in response to difficult times and, in the end, it is the 'bureaucrats' in government institutions who will always be responsible for housing the vulnerable, and ensuring schools and social care and hospital treatment are provided when the market sector fails.

Chapter 4

Delivering Public Services: Processes and Problems

Decentralization, devolution, deconcentration, delegation and delayering represent one set of processes central to the rhetoric of public management since the 1980s. They are seen as ways to improve public services, taking them closer to the people they are meant to serve and moving decision making closer to front-line delivery. A second set of processes have been transferring the supply of services from public bureaucracies to other agents. While the New Right preferred delivery through the private sector, New Labour supported the voluntary sector and David Cameron talks about the 'Big Society' and the 'post-bureaucratic state' described in Chapter 1. Other contemporary processes affect society in general but have a special impact on public services: the use of information and communication technologies with their potential for better but more intrusive governance; and internationalization, especially Europeanization, most explicitly in the liberalization of public utilities, but also in imposing new rules on terms of employment and public procurement.

Chapter 2 introduced the theories and political arguments that underpinned many of these processes; and Chapter 3 gave examples of how they have been applied to public sector institutions. This chapter now considers the processes generically, referring readers to relevant chapters for more detailed information.

Redistributing public governance

'Decentralization' and related terms are used to describe processes that transfer responsibility away from the centre and can refer to both political and bureaucratic decentralization (Rhodes *et al.* 2003: 4). Here we consider 'decentralization' to mean more specifically the transfer of political or policy-making power. 'Devolution' was used by the UK Government to denote the asymmetrical process in which some responsibilities were transferred to Scotland, Wales and Northern Ireland but remained centralized in England.

Deconcentration, delegation and delayering refer to ways in which executive responsibilities are redistributed to lower hierarchical levels, or outwards to other public bodies. The OECD groups these three as 'distributed public governance' (OECD 2002). On this type of strategy the UK was among the leaders internationally, and we make frequent reference in other chapters to its impact on the delivery of public services.

Centralization, decentralization and devolution

The UK is one of the more centralized liberal democracies (OECD 2009b: 63). Local government has only the powers specifically granted by parliament (which can always be removed by the next parliament) and these are circumscribed by central government financial controls. Although new functions are sometimes decentralized to local government (responsibilities for residential care and child protection in 1990, and the Connexions youth service in 2008), these are counterbalanced by the distancing from local councils of other functions, such as higher and further education (1990, 1993), policing (1995) and the probation service (2001 in England and Wales). Under Labour, the central–local relationship improved only by comparison with the low baseline of the 1980s. Yet there has been decentralization: government and parliament have transferred power and influence to users and citizens, whether as groups or individuals, and to three of the 'home nations'.

Decentralization to users

First, UK governments have been transferring power directly to the users of public services – Thatcher, Major, Blair and the Coalition have all had greater faith in public choice than in public bureaucracies. This strategy was adopted for many services – education, housing, the NHS and the public utilities, as we saw in Chapter 3. Yet decentralization was often accompanied by centralizing measures, as Box 4.1 shows for education, to make public bureaucracies provide choice, and to ensure users could make comparisons.

Decentralization to neighbourhoods

A second trend is for public services to give influence to neighbourhoods. By 1997 about 20 per cent of English authorities had some form of user management, and 60 per cent had neighbourhood forums (Lowndes *et al.* 2001: 45). Scottish authorities had powers to create community councils and authorize them to act as their agents, as Glasgow City Council chose to do, giving them a number of explicit roles (see Box 4.2). English metropolitan authorities, such as Birmingham, introduced neighbourhood offices but found their functions were legally restricted; they campaigned for town councils. Legislation by the Major Government enabled parish or town councils to be created and provide a larger range of services as an agent of the 'principal' councils (county, district, unitary), or in partnership with other public bodies. By subsidizing a post office or part-funding a neighbourhood police officer, these services too were encouraged to adapt to local demand.

BOX 4.1 School reforms in England: decentralization and centralization

Conservative Governments 1979–97

1986 Education Act

- More parental choice on admissions
- Governing boards to include more parents and business people and more responsibility for curriculum, staffing, discipline

1988 Education Reform Act:

- Open access widens parental choice
- National Curriculum and attainment targets
- Local Management of Schools
- Grant Maintained Status (GMS): central funding, governors manage school, employ staff
- City Technology Colleges (CTC): firms share costs, control curriculum; management

1992 Education (Schools) Act

- Performance league tables published
- Her Majesty's Inspectorate of Schools recast as Office for Standards in Education (OFSTED)

Labour Government 1997–2001

1998 School Standards and Framework Act

- Fresh Start: ministers can take over 'failing' schools, appoint new management
- Performance tables to show rate of progress
- Fair Funding: financial delegation from LEA to schools using pupil-based formula
- Foundation Schools: GMS schools brought back under LEA; board controls admissions, assets

2000 Learning and Skills Act

- City Academies: 'CTCs' for inner cities

Labour Governments 2001–10

2002 Education Act

- Academies: businesses or voluntary groups share costs, manage school, control budget
- Inspectors to report on management and leadership of school as well as on teaching

2006 Education and Inspections Act

- Trust Schools: own buildings, employ staff, set (mixed) admissions policy, opt out of curriculum
- Dedicated Schools Grant: indicative education funding to LEAs replaced by 'ear-marked' grant

Coalition Government 2010–

2010 Coalition Programme

- Pupil Premium; additional school funding for disadvantaged pupils; implemented 2011

2010 Academies Act

- Any state school can apply for academy status; have freedom on curriculum, pay, management
- Non-profit state-funded 'free schools' to be run by a community group
- University-sponsored Technical Colleges: post 16 vocational schools, some work-based training

2010 White Paper: Importance of Teaching

- National formula funding per pupil, related to educational needs; to replace local formula

2011 Education Act

- Ministers given more powers to intervene
- Schools inspection to focus on achievement, teaching, leadership, behaviour and safety

Labour's 'new localism' strategy looked to neighbourhood councils to reverse the decline in civic participation and deliver more responsive services (ODPM 2004: 13). Neighbourhood councils approved by the minister (Quality Parish Councils) could pursue activities that 'promoted well-being', provided they did not conflict with the principal councils. However – to put this reform into context – parishes are mostly of a size that would constitute a fully fledged local authority in the rest of Europe.

BOX 4.2 The role of community councils in Glasgow

- Positively support local government and establish close, constructive relationships with their local authority.
- Form close relationships with local ward councillors.
- Provide local views to public agencies, private-sector suppliers of water, gas, electricity, and other organizations providing local amenities.
- Consult a full cross-section of residents to ensure the views expressed are representative.
- Advise the authorities on planning applications, liquor licensing and community plans.

Source: Glasgow City Council, 'Key Roles of Community Councils', 20 December 2007 (www.glasgow.gov.uk, accessed 16 March 2011).

Decentralization to citizens

The third decentralization process is the transfer of power to citizens. *Modern Local Government: In Touch with the People* (DETR 1998b) treated people as citizens as well as consumers: people's opinions mattered, whether or not they were personally affected by the activity in question. At national level the government organized a 5,000-strong 'People's Panel'. It required local authorities to consult residents and businesses on Best Value reviews, and involve them in setting performance targets and drawing up service improvement plans (see Chapters 5 and 6); and it produced evidence-based guidance on useful techniques (Table 4.1).

In Labour's third parliamentary term *Strong and Prosperous Communities* (DCLG 2006) announced the government's aim to give people greater influence. A new 'duty to involve' was imposed on English local authorities, and later extended to bodies in 'partnerships' with councils, such as probation boards. Those involved must accurately reflect the community, which obliges councils to seek out under-represented groups (DCLG 2008b: 20). *Communities in Control* (DCLG 2008a) asserted that community empowerment could drive improvements to councils, the NHS, and police and justice systems. Labour introduced a new 'duty to promote democracy' in 2009, but because of the financial climate postponed its implementation (Parry 2010: 5). The Coalition's Localism Act 2011 replaced this duty with 'a community right to challenge' the way a local authority delivers its services, forcing it to go out to tender. It strengthens existing rights for a local referendum but without making the outcome binding on the council, unless the referendum is about the council tax.

Pratchett *et al.* (2009) found the tools proposed in *Communities in Control* could certainly empower active participants but not the community as a whole. Being a board member of a decision-making body offers substantial control but requires significant long-term commitment. Petitions require little

Table 4.1 *Tools for consulting on local authority tax levels*

Consultation tool	Potential advantages and disadvantages
Quantitative surveys	
Opinion surveys	• The more representative the more costly • The questions must be right
Survey of 'permanent' Citizens' Panel members	• More knowledgeable, informed responses • Usually a good cross-section but not representative
Qualitative surveys	
Focus groups	• Can home in on groups often not heard • Gains deeper understanding of citizens' views but their interpretation is complex • Never representative
Informed discussions	
Community workshops	• Produces better-informed opinions that take account of policy implications and impact • May be dominated by small groups with own agenda
Public meetings	• Provides information and options in a variety of ways • Participants are not representative • Hard to reach groups unlikely to attend
Shared interest forums	• Existing special interest forums (youth parliaments, ethnic minority forums) can be used for tax issues • Forum can consult the wider interest group too
User forums	• Existing user groups can form part of general consultation • Need to balance user demands with views of taxpayers
Neighbourhood forums	• Can explore impact in practical terms at area level • May lead to bidding wars between neighbourhoods
Other methods	
Interactive web site	• Information can be at the level wanted by each participant • Likely users are those already in contact with the council
Stakeholder mail shot	• Suitable for detailed discussion of established partners • May generate alternative, better options • Depends on quality of local authority networks

Source: Summarized from Office of the Deputy Prime Minister (2002) *Council Tax Consultation: Guidelines for Local Authorities: Summary* (ODPM), pp. 7–8.

effort but have less chance of making a widespread impact. Empowerment tends to vary with the effort expended – a problem for Cameron's Big Society strategy.

The Coalition's localism agenda

There is much continuity between Labour's approach and the Coalition programme 'giving power back to people and communities' (DCLG 2010b: 3), and a similar scepticism about whether this shared aim will come second to the centre's responsibility for ensuring that service providers are neither failing citizens nor undermining national economic strategies. The provision for local referendums on 'excessive tax levels' suggests centralism on important topics is likely to remain. Fear of an expensive referendum will force councils to keep close to central government's calculation of what is not 'excessive' rather than make their own evaluation and be guided by voters (Sear and Parry 2011: 45). The Coalition sent a mixed message about councils' political management structures. It inherited a system from Labour that had required all but the smallest councils to replace their traditional committee-based structure with a small executive comprising a directly elected mayor or a leader elected from among councillors. The Coalition's Localism Act is decentralist in permitting councils to return to the committee system but is also centralist in enabling the Secretary of State to propose directly elected executive mayors for 12 large English cities, subject to local referendum. Labour's provision in 2000 for a mayoral system had resulted in only 13 elected mayors (Parry 2011: 1). Central government's view that communities are looking to replace traditional councils is therefore probably misplaced. However, it has been argued that organizing a valid petition is difficult without party organization, that some councils have put administrative barriers in the way, and that the three main local parties are often united in their campaign against the mayoral option (Copus 2006). The type of mayoral governance being offered by the Coalition is similar to that of Greater London, where the mayoralty has proved to be a focus for promoting the city, even if some council tax payers remain sceptical of the benefits.

Similar claims for popular control and identifiable leadership are made by the Coalition for their policing reform. Directly elected police and crime commissioners replace the local police authorities from 2012. Commissioners are expected to work with community safety and justice partners, including county and borough councillors, to set priorities for the police, to control the police budget, and to appoint chief constables. They will be held to account ultimately through the ballot box. The government insisted everyone would have a role in cutting crime, such as in neighbourhood watch schemes, through volunteering as community safety officers and as vigilant citizens. However, police forces will retain their traditional control of operations, and continue to work within national priorities and resources decided by the Home Office.

In what may become a more long-lasting change, the Coalition's Localism Act 2011 gave local authorities in England and Wales 'a general power of competence'. The intention is that it 'will result in greater innovation and a new, more confident and entrepreneurial approach which should, in turn, lead to greater efficiencies, improved partnership working and the ability to help their communities in ways previously outside their remit' (DCLG 2011a: 1). If the 'general power of competence' proves to be the same as local government's long-awaited 'power of general competence' (and opinions differ) it will be a reform of constitutional significance to compare with Labour's 1999 devolution (both could always be repealed by a later government though it seems unlikely). Yet simultaneously, elected local councils are being bypassed as a consequence of the education, police, financial and local governance reforms described here and in other chapters.

Devolution

The beginnings of devolution to Scotland, Wales and Northern Ireland were described in Chapter 1, and examples of organizational variations given in Chapter 3. Here we observe that devolution is a process, as illustrated ironically by New Labour's faltering attempts to establish English regions. Government proposals for regional assemblies were not attractive locally, and probably unworkable, but were all that ministers and departments were prepared to offer at that time (Sandford 2002: 28).

Devolution has deepened in Northern Ireland, following the path anticipated should the peace process continue. Police and justice responsibilities were transferred in 2010 from Westminster to the Northern Ireland Assembly and Executive. The Executive has now revised public management structures (the local government system, education and skills, and the health service) to meet its own aims in the new context.

Welsh Assembly powers were limited in 1999 to the Secretary of State's former powers to make regulations. There was considerable local support for the recommendation of the Richard Commission (2004) that the Assembly should have legislative power, but the Blair Government did not want further devolution (Jeffery 2006: 143). Nevertheless, two major concessions were made. First, the Government of Wales Act 2006 provided a type of legislative competence: 'Assembly Measures'. Measures are primary legislation in a narrow field (such as education for children with special needs), which Westminster agrees to devolve to Wales. Second, the 2006 Act offered the Assembly primary law-making powers providing the change was first approved by a two-thirds Assembly vote and a referendum. The choice was between gaining competences incrementally with Assembly Measures, or all at once in a risky referendum (All-Wales Convention 2009: 3–5). That referendum was held in 2011 and approved by a majority of voters, and notably in all counties bar one (Monmouth), indicating a widespread acceptance of the devolution process.

In Scotland too arrangements have continued to evolve. The Calman Commission (2009) recommended adjusting the division of competences – in both directions. It wanted Scotland to have more financial power but also more financial responsibility (see Chapter 7). The Brown Government welcomed most of the Calman recommendations but refused to devolve powers on welfare benefits since they transfer resources that reduce inequalities between regions. The Coalition Government's Scotland Act 2011 omitted welfare benefits and the government argued that the proposed Universal Credits would underpin 'the social union' (Scotland Office 2010: 64–5). The financial changes make Scotland responsible for raising a third of its own budget. The minority SNP Government wanted the Scottish Parliament's new powers 'to allow for independence'; it proposed to hold a referendum on that issue but did not do so (Scottish Government 2009). The SNP Government elected in 2011 demanded the devolution of additional tax-raising powers, and proposed a referendum on further devolution or independence by 2014.

Overall, the devolution process has stimulated further and deeper changes. The extent of subsequent divergences can be judged by each country's arrangements for strategic management (Chapter 5), public finance (Chapter 7), and performance auditing (Chapter 9).

Deconcentration, delegation and delayering

Deconcentration, delegation and delayering mean the redistribution of administrative responsibilities away from central authorities, downwards within the organization or outwards to another public body. There is a clear contrast between decentralizing housing management to a tenant association and deconcentrating housing management by relocating officials to estate offices. Deconcentration is one way of reallocating administrative functions; others include the delegation of a ministerial responsibility to arm's length bodies, and the delayering of bureaucratic organizations: all these processes are important in UK public management strategies.

Deconcentration

The weakest form of deconcentration is a relocation of staff: by itself it has no impact on services, and its usual aim is to stimulate local economies or reduce office costs (see Chapter 8). More relevant is the deconcentration of local services to 'areas', 'patches' or 'neighbourhoods'. Starting with neighbourhood units providing a single service the trend has been towards offering a multi-service presence, sometimes with management authority delegated nearer the front line (Leach and Percy-Smith 2001: 169). When Conservative ministers placed the emphasis on single-purpose housing providers, such as housing associations and the business-led Housing Action Trusts, the integration of area services was undermined, both in practice and politically. In any case, there were problems associated with deconcentration (some now resolved by technology): balancing the 'right' size in terms of population, geography and efficient delivery with people's sense of a 'neighbourhood'; communication difficulties between the centre and local offices; and the capacity of performance review systems to replace direct line management (Lowndes 1992: 56–7). Once in power nationally, Labour pushed the idea of 'one-stop shops' as a way to join up government (Cabinet Office 1999a: 7). 'Customer focus' became a criterion in the Comprehensive Performance Assessment (see Chapter 5), and councils were 'named and shamed' if access to services was sparse outside the council's main office (Audit Commission 2005a, 2005b).

In central government too, there was a move to deconcentrate functions to 'joined up' offices. The Major Government was persuaded that integrated regional offices were needed for the coordination of departments' regeneration programmes and EU regional fund submissions. In 1994, the Government Offices for the Regions were set up with civil servants from five departments; more departments joined in 2001. Their position as local-centre interface was enhanced by Labour's creation in 1999 of Regional Development Agencies and regional chambers, but they were typical deconcentration devices, coordinating on behalf of their parent departments, and co-opting local bodies into the implementation of national public policy (Rhodes *et al.* 2003: 135). The Communities Secretary, Eric Pickles, agreed, asserting that the Government Offices were not 'voices of the region in Whitehall'; they had 'become agents of Whitehall to intervene and interfere in localities', and 'a fundamental part of the "command and control" apparatus of England's over-centralised state' (Pickles 2010). Yet it seems likely that regional 'mini-Whitehalls' will be reconstituted some day in some form.

Delegation

The term 'delegation' is commonly used to denote authorization to exercise another's powers. Delegation of pay and grading decisions for junior officials to heads of executive agencies enables them to adjust recruitment to agency tasks. Most OECD members have delegated personnel matters from central bodies to departments and agencies, with the UK among those that have implemented 'a fairly high' degree of delegation, though not as high as in Australia, New Zealand, Finland, Iceland and Sweden (OECD 2005a: 170).

A different type of delegation is the transfer of governmental functions to arm's length public bodies. Governments use it to add efficiency or give greater legitimacy to decisions by demonstrating their independence of politicians (OECD 2005a: 110). The first argument is relevant for executive agencies, whereas the second applies to economic regulators (see Chapter 7) and to advisory bodies and inspectorates (Chapter 9). Either or both arguments have been used to justify the 'quangos' described in Chapter 3.

The term 'quango' can be defined in different ways. It was first used to describe bodies such as the General Medical Council that were legally private but carrying out statutory functions for the government in a quasi-autonomous way – quasi-autonomous non-governmental bodies (Wilson 2003: 371). The word was extended to cover public-sector bodies whose executives were appointed by, funded by, and directly accountable to, departmental ministers but operating autonomously of the department – the non-departmental public bodies (NDPBs) of which many examples, such as the Homes and Communities Agency, the Commission for Equality and Human Rights and the Environment Agency, were given in Chapter 3. An even broader definition of quangos was then used by critics of quangos, such as Stuart Weir at Democratic Audit (Weir and Hall 1994), who charted the transfer of many local government and health service functions to semi-autonomous bodies (grant-maintained schools, career service companies, NHS trusts and so on), and worried about the impact on democratic accountability. The Commons Public Administration Select Committee put emphasis on the accountability question when it defined quangos 'in a wider sense' as:

> all bodies responsible for developing, managing or delivering public services or policies, or for performing public functions, under governing bodies with a plural membership of wholly or largely appointed or self-appointing persons. (PASC 2001: paragraph 4)

Although the number of the more traditional quangos (the NDPBs) almost halved during the Conservative years, many more of the new types were created by both Conservative and Labour Governments. The mapping exercise carried out by Weir for the Committee, using its definition quoted above, identified over 5,000 local quangos (see Table 4.2). While party-political factors were involved, quangos were mainly seen as agents for change, either (for the Conservatives) because board members could import innovative practices from the private sector (Flinders 1999: 34), or (for Labour) because they were a more energetic, diverse set of people than the councillors dominating local government (Wilson 2003: 381). Governments come to power promising to 'cull quangos', citing their disadvantages (not directly accountable to citizens, potential for party patronage) but once in office they recognize their advantages over line departments (flexible design, ring-fenced budgets, performance targets, independent image).

On taking office, the Coalition announced a speedy 'quango' review of all NDPBs and some independent statutory bodies and non-ministerial departments, such as the Export Credit Guarantee Department. The objectives expressed were to improve accountability of ministers to parliament by bringing functions more directly under their command in departments and to make financial savings, though the motives became mixed (PASC 2010a: 27–8). Departments are now told to assume that, if a function still needs to be carried

Table 4.2 ***Quangos in the UK***

Type of quango	Number
Further education institutions	511
Foundation schools	877
City technology colleges	15
Training and enterprise councils/ Learning and skills councils (England)	72
Local enterprise councils/ Career service companies (Scotland)	39
Registered social landlords and housing associations	2,461
Housing action trusts	4
Police authorities	49
Health authorities or boards (England, Wales, Scotland)	121
NHS and primary care trusts (England, Wales, Scotland)	441
Primary care groups (England)	434
Health and social services councils/boards (Northern Ireland)	27
TOTAL	**5,051**

Source of data: Public Administration Select Committee (PASC) (2001) *Mapping the Quango State*, HC 367 (TSO): table 6, data for April 2000.

out by the state, it should not be given to an arm's length body unless it either performs a technical function, its activities require political impartiality, or it needs to act independently to establish facts (Maude 2011). However, little guidance on these points was initially given to departments in what parliament judged was a too hasty and poorly managed project, whose principles had not been 'properly thought through'; 'impartiality' should have been the relevant test. Ministers had made little effort to clarify the 'chaotic landscape' of public bodies or determine the functions that each category of organization should perform (PASC 2010a).

A number of organizations, such as the Food Standards Agency, were told in early 2010 they would be abolished and then had the decision rescinded, before an announcement in October 2010 that just over half the public bodies examined (481 out of 901) could usefully be reformed to some degree. The advantages of quangos in some contexts re-emerged as ministers decided to 'retain and reform' a third (171) of the reform candidates. Where the precise reform is known, it mostly refers to cost savings rather than accountability, as in the case of the Financial Reporting Council, for which the 'substantial reform' promised would be to 'remove reliance on Government funding' (Cabinet Office 2011b: 3; and see PASC 2010a: 29). In others it might be a change of ministerial location, such as the transfer of the Big Lottery Fund from the Department for Culture to the Cabinet Office. Most of the 171 were simply 'retained'. However, 192 public bodies would be abolished. Another 118 would be merged into others with related functions, such as the Tenants Service Authority becoming part of the Homes and Communities Agency, or the integration of DWP's two Pensions Ombudsmen (see Chapter 3). These changes would lead to an overall reduction (after some revised decisions) of about 250 quangos, just over a quarter of the 901 public bodies examined, if the programme is completed (Cabinet Office 2011c).

By October 2011, 53 non-statutory bodies and 3 statutory bodies had been removed from the list of quangos (Cabinet Office 2011d); prior legislation was needed for some in the form of the Public Bodies Act 2011 or other Acts. The government claimed that it expected to see 'cumulative reductions in administrative spending of £2.6 billion' by 2015 (Maude 2011), but most of what was spent by quangos is still being spent. The functions of most NDPBs that were abolished would still be carried out, usually within departments, raising the question of whether the improved accountability of the new arrangements and any cash savings were worth the upheaval. The proposed abolition of the Audit Commission, which has financial oversight of local and health authorities, was a particular case in point, since it was debatable whether overall accountability for public governance would be improved (Chapter 9 provides the detail).

The most frequent reason given by ministers for retaining a quango was that it was performing a technical function which required independence of government (Cabinet Office 2011b), the classic reason for creating an arm's length body. Much of the increase in delegation, whether in the UK or internationally, has arisen from the tendency since the 1980s to privatize and then regulate economic activities, and from the expansion of regulatory action in social and environmental domains, all of which require demonstration of impartiality.

Delayering

Delayering takes a variety of forms. Usually it means removing hierarchical layers that add least value to the organization, often because their functions are redundant following advances in communications systems or because financial savings must be made. In local government, the need for middle managers declined, partly as a result of contracting out or the transfer of management functions to schools and housing associations, and partly as councils devolved responsibilities to first-line managers, because they were closer to the consumer and more likely to be flexible and innovate. Severe budgetary cutbacks from 2010, coupled with the need to preserve front-line services, led to further reductions in middle management posts. For central government, delayering can mean removing whole organizations, as with the Coalition's decision to abolish the Strategic Health Authorities (SHAs) and Primary Care Trusts (PCTs): 'Over the past decade, layers of national and regional organizations have accumulated, resulting in excessive bureaucracy, inefficiency and duplication' (DH 2010: 43; and see Chapter 3).

In the civil service, delayering has meant both shortening the chains of communication and removing a tier of officials. The creation of executive agencies brought ministers into contact with operational managers and (should have) diminished the role of senior staff in central departments. Official reports suggested that cutting headquarters staff by a quarter would force departments to stop double-checking agency decisions. Senior Civil Service (SCS) officials should be classified by job titles (director general, director, deputy director) to displace the hierarchical grade structure and ways of working (Efficiency Unit 1991, Trosa Report 1994, Cabinet Office 1994). The Treasury's Fundamental Expenditure Review estimated that a 're-organized and delayered Treasury' would save a quarter of senior management posts (HM Treasury 1994: summary). The number of Treasury staff dropped significantly during the 1990s. However, there was much less decline in overall SCS numbers – a small reduction from 1994 to 1999 was followed by growth (*Civil Service Statistics*). Critics warned that delayering had two adverse consequences: a reduction in the quantity of expert advice; and a reduction in the quality of advice because officials sent advice direct to ministers without prior challenge by colleagues (Lipsey 2000: 83–4; Foster 2001: 733). As noted in Chapter 3, parliament in 2008 questioned whether the Treasury had the capacity to respond to the financial crisis; by 2011 it was back at 1994 levels and with a much higher complement of senior officials.

Problems of distributed public governance

The OECD (2005a: 118) saw three 'challenges' facing arm's length bodies internationally: complexity, poor coordination and problems of accountability.

Complexity and ambiguity

The number and variety of structures created have produced a complex landscape that is more difficult for politicians and officials to control and steer, and more complicated for citizens to understand, weakening accountability and trust in government (OECD 2005a: 118). The UK has historically taken an ad hoc approach to defining types of public bodies. This attitude adds flexibility and speed and enables bodies to have specially tailored management structures, but departments have constantly to adapt their steering mechanisms to the variety of relationships. The Cabinet Secretary concluded that the current pattern of public bodies 'owes far more to history than it does to operational effectiveness' (PASC 2010a: 42), while Talbot pointed out that 'randomness and historic accident' have shaped the allocation of functions between central and local government and between departments and quangos (PASC 2010a: 66–7). This confusion hampers public debate about the relative merits of the different ways of allocating responsibilities.

Problems of coordination

The OECD (2005a: 118) found that delegation made coordination more difficult. Policy coherence suffered as arm's length bodies worked to their own objectives and priorities. Outcomes of national policies diverge more dramatically when powers are decentralized or devolved to more local units – but that is also usually their purpose. The principal concern of the Labour Government coming into power after decades of NPM reforms was to 'join up government': improve coordination between individual service providers, and reduce the gaps between policy makers and delivery agents, as Chapter 3 explained. Yet 'joined up government' runs so contrary to the in-grained silo organization and accountabilities that characterize UK Cabinet government that some academics regard the Blair Government's efforts as producing even greater complexity (Bogdanor 2005). Furthermore, poor coordination can manifest itself as overlap and duplication, as discovered by reports on Next Steps and the Coalition's quango review.

Risks for democratic control and accountability

The third risk identified by the OECD was that of loss of democratic control and accountability. Arm's length bodies may follow their own interests and not that of their principals (see the discussion of the principal–agent problem in Chapter 2). This fear has led to ever-more stringent procedures to monitor the expenditure and performance of these bodies. The risk that non-performance goes undiagnosed, or that corruption occurs, is relatively low in the UK, but the possibility was a factor in the opposition to the Coalition's proposal that NHS commissioning be put in the sole hands of GPs. Even decentralization to local communities can raise issues for conventional forms of accountability and democracy. Should a 'minority' neighbourhood or tenants' association be allowed to decide different priorities from those of the elected council majority, especially when, as in the more radical schemes, such as in Tower Hamlets in London's East End, the advantages of locality for service delivery are then unable to be balanced with the need for strategic management of wider issues (Stoker 1991)?

De-bureaucratizing the state?

Alongside the process of redistributing responsibilities within and between public organizations has come an expansion in the traditional ways that bureaucracies shared public service delivery with other actors in a variety of relationships.

The private sector and competition

A characteristic of today's public management is the increased use of the private sector. In the UK, the aim to cut public debt was underpinned by the theory that bureaucracy was inherently inefficient and that competition drove efficiency (Chapter 2). Services that could not be privatized were likely to be contracted-out or subject to some other competitive purchaser–provider relationship.

Privatization

Britain led the way on privatizing the public sector (Hughes 2012: 157). State industries were sold and, if rivals were lacking, the government gave regulators the role of promoting competition (see Chapter 7). There was less for Labour to privatize but it sold several executive agencies and took the first steps to privatize Royal Mail. The Coalition returned to the theme of privatization; and not only postal services, but an expansion in private sector delivery of NHS services and the potential for public servants to set themselves up as 'coops' (see 'the Big Society' below).

Contracting and the PFI/PP

The Thatcher Government expanded the outsourcing of manual activities and extended it to administrative tasks in central departments and local government (see Chapter 3). *Competing for Quality* (HM Treasury 1991) led to the cost of 'in-house' supply being compared with private provision – 'market testing' – possibly followed by contracting out (Chapter 6). Similar procedures were introduced in the NHS. Market testing in both central and local government saved about 20 per cent of costs, whether or not the work was contracted out (Minogue 1998: 27; Wilson and Game 2011: 369). Competition seemed to encourage officials to examine procedures and find cheaper methods. However, when departmental work was outsourced despite it costing more, or without officials being allowed to bid (Theakston 1995: 150–1), the aim was more clearly to shrink the public bureaucracy.

Public–private partnerships (PPPs) have been adopted across the OECD but the UK was again the originator, and remains the largest user internationally (OECD 2005a: 141). Companies compete for public projects, which they design, finance, build and operate or maintain over a long period, during which the public authority pays to use the facility. This strategy enables governments to substitute private finance for public borrowing, and to gain the advantages claimed for the principal–agent split. The company has an incentive to consider project risks and build efficiently and well, so that its running costs will be reduced (HM Treasury 1993). The dangers are that 'buy now, pay later' tempts politicians to announce projects that will burden future generations (see Chapter 7).

Quasi-markets and choice

In many public services, a market operates based on performance rather than price. Funding schools on the basis of pupil numbers, publishing their test results, and allowing parents to choose, gave schools the motive to do better. In healthcare, the NHS and Community Care Act 1990 introduced an 'internal market'. However, choice between alternative providers was limited; purchasers rather than users made the choice; and hospitals were reluctant to see complex statistics published (Chapter 6 explores the issues on performance measures). After some hesitation, New Labour continued that strategy. Since 2006, patients have had some choice between hospitals, and hospitals have been paid by volume of activity. In the civil service, the 'cost centres' of the Financial Management Initiative (FMI) created a purchaser–provider split. The need to allocate costs, and charge other departments for services supplied, helped departments identify the comparative value of, for example, providing training within the department or paying for training offered by the Civil Service College/National School of Government (Chapter 8). Local authorities are not in an open market, but from the mid-1980s, until the arrival of the Coalition Government, their comparative performance was published in a benchmark system that pressurized them to emulate higher performers. Moreover, the restructuring of council areas pitted candidates for unitary status against each other, bringing the principles of competition and choice even into the design of public authorities.

The voluntary sector and partnership

Blair's 'Third Way' rejected both the Conservatives' marketization and the bureaucratic state that had been favoured by Labour after 1945. 'The choice of delivery mechanism will be determined by what works best' (HM Treasury 1998: para. 4.2, and see Chapter 2). Labour wanted the different sectors to collaborate in partnerships, as *Modernising Government* explained: 'Distinctions between services delivered by the public and the private sector are breaking down in many areas, opening the way to new ideas, partnerships and opportunities for devising and delivering what the public wants' (Cabinet Office 1999a: 9).

Collaboration in Action Zones

The Labour Government hoped that innovative working across organizations and sectors would overcome persistent inequalities. In Education Action Zones (EAZs), schools bid for grants in partnership with businesses, universities and others. They were freed from the National Curriculum to find new activities that improved attendance, attainment and social inclusion. In Health Action Zones (HAZs), health and social care organizations tackled health inequalities and problems such as drug abuse, especially through modifying local funding policies. However, few zones lasted longer than seven years. An official report found the Excellence in Cities school programme (run through Whitehall and local authorities), was more effective than EAZ (OFSTED 2003: 69). EAZ partnerships were more difficult to manage; planning, evaluation and dissemination were all weaker. They were subsequently incorporated into the 'Excellence' programme. HAZs made little impact because their influence was affected by national policies: NHS reforms, the creation of Local Strategic Partnerships (LSPs), changes to HAZ priorities and their own uncertain future (Health Development Agency 2004: 2), and they were absorbed into PCTs. Out of the fifteen Employment Action Zones, in which contractors worked with employers and local organizations to help clients find work, four remain – as Jobcentre Plus programmes.

Partnerships and partnerships of partnerships

Partnerships can tackle problems that single organizations cannot resolve; they allow expertise, resources, risk-taking and project findings to be shared; they fill in gaps in services; and they encourage learning from other organizational cultures and experiences (Bovaird and Tizard 2009: 234). Most local partnership schemes originated centrally, in London, Edinburgh or Cardiff. In 2000, there were over 2,200 partnerships covering eleven different policy areas (PASC 2001: table 7). The three programmes outlined below illustrate some of the issues – their aims and the members in one example of each of these partnerships (which are not necessarily typical) – are summarized in Tables 4.3, 4.4 and 4.5.

Community Legal Service Partnerships (CLSPs) in England and Wales were initiated by the Legal Services Commission to help it steer legal aid towards gaps in provision, especially for disadvantaged groups. Half were established by 2000 and virtually all by 2002, but only a third had published their first strategic plan at that time (some were still mapping provision in 2004). The main problem was the weak input from local authorities, which had other priorities (NAO 2002: 4, 27). For providers and politicians, progress in reshaping services was too slow, and in 2006 the Commission stopped facilitating CLSPs.

Connexions Partnerships (CPs) were introduced in England to extend the careers service into multi-agency youth support. Services were 'rolled out' between 2001 and 2004. After a poor start, relationships with employers and the voluntary sector improved and CP advisers provided innovative, effective help. Schools were satisfied with CPs' work with problem students, on whom resources were targeted – but not with its 'universal' careers advice (OFSTED 2002: 4; NAO 2004a: 3–8). The need to pay VAT on contracts (often a problem with partnerships) made CPs restructure in 2004: some changed to direct delivery; others contracted through a local authority to avoid the VAT problem (PAC 2004: 12). The government addressed these points in 2005, trans-

Table 4.3 ***Community Legal Service Partnerships (CLSPs)***

National aims	Partners in one of the Partnerships	Comments
• Improve access to legal aid and advice, especially for disadvantaged people • Funders and providers to work together to map local provision, identify local needs, and plan how to fill gaps • Encourage better referral arrangements between providers • National partner: the Legal Services Commission (LSC)	County Council, Age Concern, Citizens Advice, Library Service, Primary Care Trust, Solicitors, Neighbourhood Advice Centre, Association of Disabled People, Healthy Living Project, Social Services, Law Centre, Association of Voluntary Services, Borough Council, Housing Advice Service, Trading Standards, Community Relations Forum Crime Prevention Panel [Woking CLSP]	• Promoted from 1998 to limit legal aid costs but ensure access to quality advice • By 2002 nearly all CLSPs in place; but slow progress with planning and shaping provision • Not all councils committed to this project: had other local and national priorities • In 2006 LSC stops supporting CLSPs

Sources: Official reports and partnership websites.

Table 4.4 ***Connexions Partnerships (CPs)***

National aims	Partners in one of the Partnerships	Comments
• Encourage 13–19 year olds to learn and move smoothly into adult life • Information for all; personal support for those most in need • Target: to reduce numbers not in education, training or employment • National partner: Department for Education and Skills	Youth Service, Schools, Substance Misuse Service, Probation Service, Health Service, Education Welfare Local Authorities, Chamber of Commerce, Children's Services, Youth Offending Service, Jobcentre Plus, Learning Providers, Fire & Rescue Service, Colleges, Legal Services, Police, Unions, Voluntary Sector [Connexions Northumberland]	• Initial partnership problems especially with business • 'Rolled out' from 2000 to 2004 • Good individual service for difficult cases • Other pupils given less personal attention • VAT problems when contracting-out • 2005: decision to transfer to local authorities by 2008

Sources: Official reports and partnership websites.

Table 4.5 ***New Deal for Communities Partnerships (NDCPs)***

National aims	Partners in one of the Partnerships	Comments
• Reduce differences in housing, crime, educational attainment, health, and job prospects between deprived and other areas • National partner: Department for Communities and Local Government	Councils, housing association, Primary Care Trust, Development Agency, transport organization, tourism, charity and arts quangos, charities, healthy living project, Office of the Third Sector, Social Enterprise Coalition, London Community Resource Network, galleries, theatres, arts centres, private companies, orchestra, college, university, bank, architects [Hackney-Shoreditch NDCP]	• Ten-year projects • Well-resourced and extensive evaluation • Community satisfied overall • More successful on crime and dereliction and education than on jobs or health • Some planned to continue under other formats, after funding ceased

Sources: Official reports and partnership websites.

ferring CP funding to local authorities, and general careers advice to schools (DfES 2005: 8–10). Local authorities happy with their CP continued to contract from CP providers; others established their own in-house service. Authorities then received a service that better matched their demands, but the needs of the most vulnerable were no longer being met (OFSTED 2010a: 6–9).

New Deal for Communities Partnerships (NDCPs) were initiated in 1998. Government did not give local authorities the lead role but previously difficult relationships with the neighbourhood improved during the programme. Partnership with the police, who could operate within the same patch, was more successful than with PCTs, which were undergoing reorganization, or schools, which prioritized national targets (Batty *et al.* 2010: 30–1). People's satisfaction increased more in NDCP areas than in the authority area or similarly deprived neighbourhoods without NDCPs. However, while there was positive change on crime and dereliction and educational attainment, there was little change to job prospects, and health indicators were worse. Despite great efforts by NDCPs to engage with communities, they had little impact on social capital, such as people believing they can influence decisions (*ibid.*: 7, 22). Although many, such as Centre West in Newcastle, planned to continue beyond the funded programme, the financial and economic climate is likely to test their optimism (*ibid.*: 32–4).

Partnerships were administratively costly because of 'separate management structures with separate reporting requirements, with separate inspection arrangements' (PAC 2004: Ev 2). In 2005, the government proposed that the LSP become 'a partnership of partnerships', encompassing all these local projects, to clarify responsibilities and reduce duplication (Flynn 2007: 193). Only one existing partnership seemed likely to continue under the Coalition – the Sure Start programme to improve the prospects for disadvantaged pre-school children, and that had become more of a child-minding exercise to enable mothers to work, according to the official who led this Treasury initiative, Norman Glass (2005).

The Big Society and post-bureaucracy

The Coalition Government did not abandon partnerships entirely; indeed, an early decision was to replace the government-appointed Regional Development Agencies with Local Enterprise Partnerships (LEPs). Yet the tone was already different since it was left to LEPs to decide their own boundaries. Chapter 1 outlined the Conservative Party's (continuing) move towards replacing 'big government' and 'state control' with 'a Big Society' in which people assumed personal, professional and community responsibilities (Conservative Party 2010a: 37). Cameron described these proposals in a more formal way as the 'post-bureaucracy age' – Box 4.3 offers an academic definition. The Network for the Post-Bureaucratic Age argues that technological advances have eroded government's monopoly on information and empowered people. Before modern communications it was more practical to let bureaucracies develop policy and hold them to account afterwards: now public organizations and citizens can interact continuously (PASC 2011a: Ev w11).

BOX 4.3 The post-bureaucracy age

Depending on the policy domain, the post-bureaucracy age may mean:

- Delivering public services and welfare services at the most local level possible and, wherever feasible, by private and independent organizations.
- Pulling public organizations out of delivering some kinds of services that they might once have delivered, without making alternative arrangements.
- Conducting public services, whether by public organizations or by other kinds of organizations, with as much public participation as possible.
- Organizing and delivering public services with as little use as possible of the legal powers of the state to permit, compel, prohibit or punish.

The skills, competencies (and perhaps rewards) required for public servants will depend on what type of meaning of post-bureaucracy is dominant in the specific policy domain.

Source: Summarized from oral evidence of Christopher Hood and Martin Lodge to Public Administration Select Committee (2011) *Change in Government: The Agenda for Leadership*, HC 714 (TSO), pp. Ev 2–3.

According to Cameron (2010a), the significance of modern technology is not the new tools themselves but the changes they have brought about in society. In the bureaucratic world, 'regulation, laws and diktats' could be used to control other people's lives: in the 'on-line' era, people control their own lives. The information gap between public service experts and citizens is narrower than ever before (Quirk 2011: 47). Governments that want change are more likely to achieve it through influencing people, by providing incentives and removing obstacles. 'The post-bureaucratic age is just as much about behavioural economics as data transparency' (Cameron 2010a). Behavioural economics is about 'nudging' people to behave in a civic-minded way rather than assuming they make thoughtful rational choices between sticks and carrots (John *et al.* 2009). The Conservative manifesto proposed that 'neighbourhood groups, charities, social enterprises and other non-governmental bodies' would play a 'leading role' in public services. 'Parents' would be able to start new schools, 'communities' would run parks and libraries, 'neighbourhoods' would control the planning system and local police. Public servants would be encouraged to 'own' their services, setting themselves up as coops and bidding to take over services (Conservative Party 2010a: 27, 37–8; 2010b).

All these processes are taking place to some extent. Power is passing from bureaucrats to the on-line public through an increase in the data being made available: all items of government expenditure over £25,000, and of council expenditure over £500; new government contracts published in full; hospital death rates revealed, with, of course, the risks of misinterpreting data published out of context. Two dozen 'free schools' opened in 2011, in church halls, listed buildings, former office blocks and libraries and in temporary classrooms; some were organized by parents or faith groups, others (on a non-profit basis) by education providers already operating academies. The government countered some criticism by funding poorer pupils more generously (in addition to the 'pupil premium'), and by requiring a mixed ability intake; half the schools are located in relatively deprived areas (DfE 2011). Sutton Borough Council (selected by the government to be a 'Big Society Pioneer' council), is piloting an on-line book exchange scheme which was welcomed – though not initiated – by some residents, while Dorset County Council is among a number of councils willing to transfer library management to local groups. However, other members of these communities regarded the schemes as 'elitist' or too demanding of volunteers' time and funds (*Financial Times*, 29 March 2011). NHS staff already had, under Labour, the right to set up social enterprises to contract their services, and about 30 'spin out' companies (such as Central Surrey Health with 650 nurses and therapists), were in operation in 2010 (*Financial Times* 18 November 2010). Yet there are issues still to be resolved, such as whether the right to a public service pension will continue, the ownership of assets, and the difficulty of building up a financial reserve to cushion possible gaps between contracts.

An example of a more 'grass-roots' approach is the campaign by Dover's Chamber of Commerce, MP, district council (and 97 per cent of voters in a referendum) for the mutualization of the Port of Dover (a not-for-profit trust port) instead of its proposed part-privatization to fund expansion. The Coalition Government has, in response, changed the conditions for selling a trust port to include the need for significant community participation and DfT officials facilitated discussions between the Dover People's Port Trust, Dover Harbour Board and other interested parties on the options for the port (*Dover Life*, autumn 2011; *Financial Times* 3 August 2011; DfT 2011). Such schemes are more typical of the successful mutuals of the past (coops and building societies, for example) than are the top-down 'spin offs' being promoted by ministers.

Cameron's distinction between a bureaucratic world of diktats and a post-bureaucratic world of communities over-simplifies. It has long been known that bureaucrats share decision making and implementation with politicians and interest groups (Finer 1958; Richardson and Jordan 1979; Jordan and Richardson 1987; Pyper 1995a: 89–97); and that most people in most communities are reluctant to become engaged, as the NDCPs showed (Batty *et al.* 2010: 7). Public institutions and public bureaucracies are still needed to facilitate community action. The important question is whether bureaucrats are managed and equipped to perform the consulting and empowering role that will be required of them in a 'post-bureaucratic' world (Pratchett *et al.*: 2009).

Problems of de-bureaucratization

De-bureaucratizing public services, whether by transferring delivery to other suppliers, asking public servants to work with other actors, or enabling co-production by community groups, not only shares the problems of 'redistributing public governance' but has its own specific issues.

Complexity

Privatization, competition and choice have made services more complex to organize and use than when dealing with a single supplier. For officials and their political chiefs, as they tackle the bidding process and manage the contractors, contracting adds complexity but has a trade-off in helping to clarify the essential service requirements, and can resolve (or transfer to others) difficult labour relations. Partnerships and the Big Society are inevitably complex for governments to steer, as was acknowledged by the Labour Government in introducing the LSP; indeed the bureaucracies of multi-purpose local government and the NHS replaced the fragmented provision of the early twentieth century for this very reason.

For users, making choice drive performance adds complexity that may be worthwhile if it incites the most convenient school or doctor's surgery to provide a better service. Setting up a new school can be advantageous for a group only in special circumstances, which may be poor local provision but is usually the aim of an alternative, probably faith-based, curriculum. The Swedish Free School, the model for the Conservatives (Conservative Party 2010a: 50), survives mainly as commercial ventures. Bureaucratic complexity cannot be avoided if public funding and the credibility of public authorization is required. The Department for Education (DfE 2011) stressed that 'groups that were successful in applying to open a Free School went through a robust process to make sure they were suitable and capable to run a school'. Details had to be provided of likely demand, the curriculum, the type of teachers, the admissions system, financial plans, an appropriate site that provided value for 'taxpayers' money', and Criminal Record Bureau checks. Due diligence vetting, OFSTED inspections and league tables would apply. Quirk (2011: 58) warns of the complexities of the tasks awaiting not only community groups but also councils when transferring under-used public buildings or land. Even if legally justified in selling below market price – and the Coalition Government did not seem inclined to alter the law – the financial loss is to the detriment of the wider community or other particular social groups. Taylor (2011: 240–6) refers to this type of challenge as reconciling community cohesion and diversity.

Fragmentation as well as coordination

Privatization and contracting can fragment a service between multiple providers. Partnerships were intended to overcome fragmentation whether from contracting or the silo tendencies of bureaucracies. Yet partnerships set up to focus on particular social problems are likely to be working with different agencies, funding arrangements, time scales and regulation regimes, and on different geographical bases, even if co-located within one local authority. Partnerships can lead to a fragmentation of structures and processes, which in turn engenders blurred responsibilities and accountabilities (Bovaird and Tizard 2009: 235). Blair's policy adviser, Geoff Mulgan (2005) observes that the efforts to join up government brought awareness that bureaucratic silos and joined-up initiatives were complementary: both are needed.

Risks for democratic control and accountability

Using private companies to deliver public services can raise questions about the safety of confidential data, the potential for lower ethical standards, and conflicts of interest between political donations and tendering for contracts. Parliament's Public Accounts Committee (PAC 1994) found cases of irregularities and improper spending by outsiders in Whitehall, and the National Audit Office (NAO) complained that it could not track the expenditure of public money by private companies to check for their probity and efficiency

(Theakston 1995: 152–3). Ministers often treated questions on contracts as 'commercial-in-confidence'.

At local level, most statutory partnerships have council members on their boards, giving them democratic legitimacy. Nevertheless, it was a cause for concern to parliament that about 75,000 people were serving on local partnerships with little official attention being paid to the appointments process (PASC 2003a: 5, 9). Action Zones in particular were 'very small, newly formed charitable bodies with little corporate experience of handling public money or the proper conduct of public business'. Some did not ensure that purchasing did not favour business partners, or specify how grants should be spent and accounted for properly (NAO 2001: 1–3). The DfE claims that free schools 'are run by teachers – not local councils or Westminster politicians – and have freedom over things like the length of the school day, the curriculum, and how they spend their money' (DfE 2011). Yet it is unlikely that the probity of their expenditure of public funds and their value for money (VfM) will not come under official scrutiny.

Inefficiencies

Outsourcing incurs higher transaction costs because much is taken on trust when public-sector norms are secure; and because bidding for contracts and grants demands resources which have to be recouped in higher prices. The Labour Government tried to reduce these inefficiencies by moving from competitive contracts to partnership working (Erridge 2009: 97); the NHS 'spin out' companies it introduced combined the performance advantages of contracting with a shared culture. Making choice available logically requires inefficiency in the form of spare capacity (such as school places or hospital beds), and can create inefficiencies from loss of scale (such as when overlapping training schemes are offered to civil servants) though policy makers may, of course, decide that these inefficiencies are outweighed by the performance incentives (PASC 2005: 35–6).

Market problems

Markets are more efficient when multiple bidders compete, but many sectors (utilities, data management, back office functions, accountancy and now welfare provision) are dominated by a few large companies. The small companies and voluntary providers that all governments want to encourage are unable to respond to large projects or to carry the administrative costs and long lead times associated with contracting. The Coalition Government put a further obstacle in the way of social enterprises by adding payment by results – for example, for finding Work Programme placements that last – which further delays reimbursement. Although the third sector enterprises have the multiple skills that are needed for difficult cases, and are used for this reason as sub-contractors by large companies (AfE, Serco, G4S, Reed in Partnership, PwC), few win tenders themselves. Once public bureaucracies outsource an activity they risk losing the competence either to write effective contracts or to take the service back in-house. The OECD (2005a: 137) points to the special problems faced by governments that outsource in conjunction with downsizing (as Britain did in the 1980s and early 1990s and is now doing), and in the process lose skilled staff to the private contractor.

Finally, de-bureaucratized delivery is likely to be – and is intended to be – more attentive to local demand and conditions than to the regularity and equity that are the hallmarks of the public sector (OECD 2005a: 138). The Big Society therefore poses the problem of 'post-code lottery' as the counterpart to the criticisms of 'bog-standard' and 'one size fits all' services which were made by the Blair Government.

Information and communications technologies

Blair's *Modernising Government* expected 'electronic information-age services' to produce public services that were both better for all and tailored to individual citizen's demands (Cabinet Office 1999a: 5). At the time, only six local authorities in England had a web site offering a good level of interaction; 72 per cent had no interactive content at all (Lowndes *et al.* 2001: 208). The 24-hour telephone help lines such as NHS Direct in 2000 were among the earliest signs of the new strategy. By 2004, the Jobcentre Plus change programme relied on complex information and communications technology (ICT) that included: replacing paper-based payments with payments to bank accounts; introducing telephone call centres underpinned by a computerized Customer Management System; and updating benefit processing by replacing multiple legacy computer systems with an integrated, more flexible system (Work and Pensions Committee 2006: 8–9).

Bellamy (2009: 136–43) identifies four processes of transition in the relationship between ICT and management. First, using technology to support a business strategy evolved into using it to shape the strategy or even the organization. Whereas the ICT department's mainframe computer made the traditional hierarchical bureaucracy work more efficiently, the personal computer and computer networks allowed organizational deconcentration without losing managerial control. Software development subsequently enabled posts that once needed long experience to be filled by more junior staff (Hughes 2012: 277–8, 286). Second, there was a move away from the function-based ICT systems that replicated traditional bureaucratic silos (employment records, welfare benefits records, housing tenancy records) towards a vision of 'joining-up' systems, both horizontally across departments and vertically from the first enquiry to the delivery of the service. However, making this vision real is hampered by practical problems (such as the Jobcentre Plus legacy systems), and by ethical issues on sharing data (see below).

Third, New Labour had a deliberate policy of making advances in e-government, whether meaning public organizations using ICT to improve their own handling of business, or citizens and companies being able to use ICT systems to seek information and documents, obtain a public service or fulfil a public duty (filing tax returns or paying the London congestion charge). This process depends on the electronic networking of related back-office systems. In the case of the congestion charge it means bringing together the operator's records of camera and vehicle number plate readings and of people who had paid the charge, the DVLA database of registered vehicle owners, and borough databases of residents entitled to a discount. The technical problem of mass data-handling has been eased by identifying client groups, such as the 'working age', 'pensioners' and 'disabled people' around which the DWP structured its business (Bellamy 2009: 138). Organizing information around 'client groups' or 'life events' is used too for electronic 'one stop shop' access to public services on the internet, whether the Business Link portal or Direct Gov for individuals. *Transformational Government enabled by technology* (Cabinet Office 2005a) was commissioned by Blair from chief information officers in the public sector, and set out the Blair Government's 'vision' of seeing the public sector use ICT in the same way as the private sector: to respond to customer demand, to give citizens' choice and to increase efficiency (see Box 4.4).

Local councils, however, have yet to fulfil Blair's expectations, let alone Cameron's assumptions of an on-line era. Whitehall's National Strategy for Local Government in 2002 expected them to develop contact centres and call centres; use smart card technology (to pay benefits, for example); use digital TV to communicate with citizens; use mobile and wireless technologies (for example in traffic control), improve back-office functions through document imaging and other electronic processes; develop customer relationship databases; and enhance routine procedures for procurement and payments using

BOX 4.4 The vision for twenty-first-century government

The specific opportunities lie in improving *transactional* services (e.g. tax and benefits), in helping front line *public servants* to be more effective (e.g. doctors, nurses, police and teachers), in supporting effective *policy outcomes* (e.g. in joined-up, multi-agency approaches to offender management and domestic violence), in reforming the *corporate services* and *infrastructure* which government uses behind the scenes, and in taking swifter advantage of the *latest technologies* developed for the wider market.

Source: Cabinet Office (2005a), *Transformational Government: Enabled by Technology*, Cm 6683 (TSO), p. 3.

ICT (Pratchett 2004: 26). In 2009 the majority of council websites were yet to provide acceptable transactional capabilities, according to a survey by the Society of Information Technology Management (Wilson and Game 2011: 13).

Bellamy's fourth evolutionary process is that of moving from collecting data to manipulating data to produce additional knowledge. Comparing data sets shows gaps in the take-up of benefits, or fraudulent claims, or local variations in the impact of interventions. While many applications of this idea seem unproblematic, there are ethical issues about the use of personal data for purposes beyond that for which it was supplied. While some CPs shared information on young people within the rules of the Data Protection Act, many partner organizations were reluctant to transmit their clients' history to twenty or so public or private partners (PAC 2004: Ev 17). The NAO advised that young people be given a 'unique identification number, making it easier to track their progress' for evaluation purposes (NAO 2004a: 11), but there is a tension between obtaining information to improve services and 'the surveillance society'; namely, the growing collection, storage and use of personal data. Similar dilemmas confronted the Labour Government's ambitions for the National Identity register and card; ContactPoint, with details of every school child in England; and the National DNA database, which stored samples of people arrested even if they were not subsequently charged.

Opposition to the expanding deployment of ICT grew during Labour's third term. The Information Commissioner published a report by the Surveillance Studies Network (2006). The Home Affairs Committee (2008: 5–6) asked the Home Office to exercise restraint in collecting personal information and the government to 'adopt a principle of data minimization'. Three practical aspects of ICT management increased the doubts: the costs in resources and public trust compared to the value of such unfocused information; the financial and security risks of relying on the few large private-sector ICT suppliers (though it was the public-sector HM Revenue & Customs that lost child benefit records in October 2007); and the 'government sector's poor record with ICT projects and change management more generally' (Kawalek 2007: 170).

The Conservative and Liberal Democrat manifestos, under headings of 'civil liberties' and 'freedom', said they would 'scrap' identity cards and ContactPoint, and scale back the DNA database to the Scottish model (Conservative Party 2010a: 80; Liberal Democrats 2010: 94); this consensus was carried forward into the Coalition Agreement (Cabinet Office 2010: 11), and implemented in August 2010 (ContactPoint), February 2011 (National Identity register), and with the Protection of Freedoms Act (National DNA database).

Hood and Margetts (2007) synthesize Bellamy's fourth stage in the ICT evolution into a general distinction between governments moving from using digital tools as 'detectors' – taking in information – to using them as 'effectors'

– making an impact on the world outside. Their summary of the evidence (*ibid.*: 184–203) leads them to judge that digital technologies have so far augmented governmental capacity for 'detecting' more successfully than they have for 'effecting', and that even 'detecting' has a rather variable quality (sometimes decreasing costs, sometimes increasing them, for example). They remind us, however, that the digital era is at a relatively early stage, because only with the mass penetration of the internet at the end of the 1990s could ICT really make a difference: its full effect is yet to be seen (*ibid.*: 202).

Internationalization and Europeanization

The spread of ICT throughout public management is an international process in which the UK sometimes runs ahead. In 2007 Britain was second in the EU for its national e-portal, and third for its e-government services (OECD 2009a); while its DNA database (5 per cent of the population and over five million records) was the largest anywhere (Home Affairs Committee 2008: 77). More generally, in adopting the changes to public management described in this book, the UK has been part of an international movement (see Chapter 2). Yet international does not mean global. Even among the advanced economies of the OECD, more than a quarter of OECD governments have no non-financial performance data in their budget documentation, nearly half do not reward if targets are met; and less than a fifth link pay to performance (OECD 2005a: 64–6). Spreading 'best practice' has worked better amongst Nordic countries and countries linked historically to Britain; countries with other systems are less interested, and transfers to non-OECD countries have sometimes been harmful (OECD 2005a: 197). Even countries that broadly adopted the new approach pick and choose: Sweden has agencies, education vouchers and free schools but also the highest proportion of public expenditure to GDP and second highest proportion of public sector employees in the OECD (OECD 2009a: 1, 4).

The concept of 'Europeanization' has more validity, because 27 states have approved the same EU laws, and 47 European states have agreed to respect the judgements of the European Court of Human Rights (ECHR). Despite a Europeanization of policies, there have, however, been no dramatic changes to the structures and processes of national governments (Bulmer and Burch 2000: 46). In the UK, there is little Europeanization in central government: for most civil servants who negotiate in Europe it is only one part of their work; those in Europe-facing posts are rarely given specialized training or subsequent posts that confirm the Europe connection; and Treasury budgeting rules make departments resistant to EU funding programmes (Bulmer and Burch 2000, 2005; Burnham and Pyper 2008). Academic experts on the EU dismiss the idea that sharing decision making with Europe means a 'hollowing out' of central government control (Holliday 2000).

Nevertheless, both the ECHR and the EU have Europeanized certain aspects of public management. As Bellamy (2009: 144) notes, data processing in the UK is regulated by principles developed by the ECHR and set out in the EU's 1995 Data Protection Directive (law). The ECHR's ruling in 2008 that the UK, by retaining a suspect's DNA profile after acquittal, had violated the European Convention on Human Rights, did much to discredit the National DNA database.

EU policies to develop the Single Market have had significant implications for public services. In particular, the EU's 1977 Acquired Rights Directive, implemented in UK law as the Transfer of Undertakings (Protection of Employment) Regulations (TUPE) of 1981 and 2006, was a major constraint on privatization. (It safeguards the terms of employment of staff transferred to another employer and came into force just as the Thatcher Government was restructuring the civil service and imposing CCT on local government.) The Labour Government treated TUPE as a way to implement PPPs without harming labour relations and asked all public organizations to apply TUPE when transferring staff, even where not legally required (Cabinet Office 2007a). More directly in the area of employment, the EU member states agreed to gender equality on pay in 1971 and on occupational pensions in 1990, and outlawed other aspects of discrimination in 2000. These conditions already existed in the civil service but have proved financially burdensome for local councils that were slow to give equal pay for jobs of equal value (Local Government Employers 2006, 2008). While some EU employment laws, such as the 2003 Working Time Directive, have been a challenge (the NHS had to reduce the hours worked by doctors in training from 58 to 48), on others, such as opening most posts in the public services to other EU nationals and recognizing their professional qualifications, the EU has become more like the UK.

All government bodies are affected by EU public procurement rules, which require that even low-value contracts must not discriminate against other EU countries. From 1977, various directives regulated higher-value contracts for supplying goods and services, or for constructing buildings and other public works. The purchaser must treat all bidders equally, the specification must not be discriminatory, the call for tender and eventual award must be transparent (published in the EU's on-line Official Journal), and the 'lowest cost' or 'most economically advantageous' (VfM) bid wins. The 2004 Public Sector Directive enabled environmental and social criteria to be included, and it also permitted a 'competitive dialogue' procedure much used in the UK, where bidders help define the terms of the eventual contract.

The 1990 Utilities Directive made the public utilities (water, energy, transport, postal services, telecommunications), even if privatized, subject to equivalent procurement rules. Early EU intervention focused on these enterprises because they and their industrial purchasing decisions often subsidized state companies. The EU regulates state aids, which are permitted only for short-term restructuring support (such as when Labour was slimming the sub-post office network), and for socially necessary subsidies (such as the Scottish ferry services mentioned in Chapter 3). From the 1980s, the EU liberalized the utilities in order to open up state enterprises to 'foreign' competition. This free market agenda was very much the UK's approach (see Chapters 3 and 7) but opposed by many other EU states. The 'regulated competition' used in Sweden (and for contracting London's bus services) is now the European Commission's compromise solution. However, most public utilities have already been 'Europeanized' in practice by the strong presence across the EU of a handful of operators in each sector, such as UK-owned bus and coach services.

Processes of change in public service delivery

The processes described in this chapter can almost all be summed up by Flynn's (2007: 66) observation that one of the themes in delivering services over the last three decades has been a 'move from equality of treatment to the promotion of responses tailored to individual need'. However, the tailoring can run from the relatively superficial modulation of a script-based call centre response, which leaves little room for discretionary decision-making, to a service organized with the participation of citizens, or even wholly organized by them.

Decentralization, devolution, deconcentration and delegation, whatever their other distinctions, all have this element of moving from standardized, centrally managed and controlled arrangements in favour of a diversification that meets local conditions. Nonetheless, typical public service values and rules such as equity and conformity will still apply wherever public officials or funds are involved. Equality does not need to mean identical if the recipient or context of the service differs; indeed a general characteristic of public policy is that it differentiates and discriminates, because the aim is to solve differentiated problems (those that affect some people or communities more than others). Yet where levels of service are easily compared across administrative areas, citizens and their representatives will readily complain of post-code lottery, or bureaucratic incompetence, even if there are genuinely different community priorities in different areas – a familiar problem in the NHS. The reaction of some schools and local authorities to CPs that gave special attention to pupils in difficulty shows the political limits to non-universal services. As Rhodes *et al.* (2003: 5) point out, the advantages of centralization then emerge: it promotes territorial justice and equality. Strong central authorities can uphold service standards, supervise the uniform application of national policies, and allocate resources in a rational way. Delayering is different in being a management process internal to the organization but it still contains the idea of a more flexible, less centrally controlled process that should allow a wider range of options to emerge from officials nearer the front line; indeed it might almost have been discussed under the heading of de-bureaucratizing.

De-bureaucratizing the state is more likely to involve moving away, sometimes expressly, from the equity and conformity with regulations that are the trademarks of a public bureaucracy, to prioritize other goals, such as market efficiency or innovative answers to intractable problems, or other values, such as citizenship and community. Outcomes are more uncertain, whether they concern privatization or partnerships or, especially, the Big Society. Privatization, whether as outright transfer or in the form of contracts and PPPs, poses the biggest question in this regard, particularly where former national industries are regulated lightly or not at all (regulation ensures at least a minimum universal service). Some privatized industries have gone on to provide services that better match the needs of more individuals than under the previous state-run regime (telecommunications, airlines, buses, leisure train services), though others (the energy industries) have not. Local partnerships seemed to offer a 'third way' that combined the active engagement of users, providers from different sectors, and the local community with the structured funding and administrative support of the public sector. However, one of the best evaluated and longest partnership initiatives (NDCPs) demonstrated the difficulty in gaining the commitment of local people, on the one hand, and of public service organizations driven by their own priorities, on the other. The silo effect is still evident even at neighbourhood level.

Developments in ICT have provided the support for many of these reforms in service delivery, but have also shaped those reforms and, according to some proponents of the 'post-bureaucratic age', are driving social changes to which public management is being forced to respond. The next five chapters examine the key functions today of public sector management.

Chapter 5

Strategic Management and Leadership

Systems of government in the UK and throughout most OECD countries have been transformed in recent years. The reasons for this have been discussed in Chapter 1 and the influence of private sector management ideas and practices on these transformations have been examined in Chapter 2. The relevance of these practices and ideas to the public sector, however, has been and still is hotly debated (Greener 2009). But strategic management, initially seen as a vehicle for transforming the traditional public administration culture to a new managerialist one, is now at the core of that new culture and is accepted as an essential approach to dealing with the turbulent and dynamic environments in which public organizations now operate.

Governments require public organizations to act strategically, and demand strategic plans from public organizations and agencies to demonstrate how they intend to achieve the strategic objectives set down by central government – or the politicians at other levels of government – and to demonstrate how they intend to manage the increasing number of strategic partnerships. Furthermore, all public organizations today, faced with declining resources and government cut backs, recognize the need to make strategic choices and to find ways of meeting their responsibilities – legal and political – as efficiently and effectively as possible. There is an imperative to act strategically especially in times of recession, when there are even greater demands to use limited resources to meet rising expectations from an increasingly demanding and educated public. Paradoxically it is both more difficult to act strategically in the increasingly complex systems of governance, which occupy both political and administrative space, but more possible with the advanced technology with which to collect, access, analyse and disseminate information. Strategic management is now a major concern of both domestic and international public organizations (Flynn and Strehl 1996; Proeller and Siegel 2009). 'To be without a strategy [today] is to appear to be directionless and incompetent' (Bovaird 2009: 61). However, to have one is no guarantee of avoiding crises and reactive politics.

Strategic management involves change and change requires leadership. Strategic leadership is now seen as the key to successful strategic management and organizational change (Morse *et al.* 2007; Raffel *et al.* 2009; Joyce 2012). Local authority chief executives, directors of agencies and permanent secretaries of departments are chosen on the basis of their 'leadership', 'strategic' and 'change management' skills and competencies. Although there are similarities in the approaches to strategic management and strategic leadership amongst public and private organizations, there are also some significant differences which will be the focus of this chapter.

The chapter will first examine the core concepts associated with strategic management and strategic planning. Second, it traces the introduction of strategic management in the public sector before focusing on the current practices and problems at the centre of government and devolved and local governments. Finally, it examines the current emphasis on strategic leadership and its links to transformational change.

Definitions of core concepts

What is strategy?

Strategy is a disputed concept and there is no single definition that everybody agrees on. It is usually associated with setting goals and objectives and planning how to achieve them but Hax (1990: 28–31) identifies six different definitions:

- strategy is a coherent, unifying and integrated pattern of decisions;
- strategy is a means of establishing an organization's purposes in terms of its long-term objectives;
- strategy is a definition of a firm's competitive advantage;
- strategy is a response to external opportunities and threats and internal strengths and weaknesses as a means of achieving competitive advantage;
- strategy is a logical system for differentiating managerial tasks at corporate, business and functional levels;
- strategy is a definition of the economic and non-economic contribution the firm intends to make to its stakeholders.

(If organization is substituted for firm, the definition applies to the public sector.)

By incorporating all these perceptions Hax arrives at his own definition:

> Strategy [is] a fundamental framework through which an organization assesses its vital continuity, while at the same time purposefully managing the adaptation to the changing environment to gain competitive advantage. Strategy includes the formal recognition that the recipients of the results of a firm's actions are the wide constituency of stakeholders. Therefore the ultimate objective of strategy is to address the stakeholders' benefits to provide a base for establishing the host of transactions and social contracts that link a firm to its stakeholders.

Another management guru, Henry Mintzberg (1996), offers a further list of descriptors of strategy as a plan, a ploy (to outwit competitors), a pattern in which strategies emerge as a result of decisions and behaviours, a position of an organization within its environment, and a perspective or shared way of seeing the world within an organization. Mintzberg argues that all these views of strategy hold some truth as to what it is.

Strategic decisions

Determining a strategy involves taking decisions. The essence of strategic decisions is that they are *fundamental* not low level decisions, and that they are *important* decisions. Important decisions are ones that have an impact on an organization. They are likely to be concerned with the scope and the boundaries of the organization and linking the activities of the organization to its external environment. Strategic decisions are also about matching the organization's activities to its resources. All public organizations have limited resources, and decisions about how to combine and use those resources are strategic. Strategic decisions may relate to the organization's culture. Decisions to change the values and the behaviours within the organization amount to a change of the culture: this is often signified by a new mission statement or a statement of core values. Strategic decisions also generally have long-term effects on the direction of the organization and they are complex. But they do not always achieve the effects that were intended as we will see later.

Strategic planning

There are different types of planning, such as, operational planning and long-range planning, but strategic planning involves taking decisions aimed at removing uncertainty and identifying a future you wish to achieve and how you intend to get there. Bushnell and Halus (1992: 357) define strategic planning as 'a process that an organization can use to visualize its future and develop the necessary strategies and operations to achieve that vision'. Strategic plans usually cover three to five years and decisions are normally made after a great deal of information gathering, analysis and forecasting. They also involve political judgement (even in private companies) about what would be acceptable, supported and doable. Strategic planning, once popular in the 1970s, but derided by anti-planning Conservative ministers Margaret Thatcher, Nicholas Ridley and Keith Joseph, was reincarnated as strategic management in the 1990s.

Strategic management

Strategic management is concerned with the process of formulating, implementing, monitoring and controlling organizational strategies (Thompson

1997). Strategic management is also the way that an organization is structured, allocates resources and establishes systems for taking and implementing strategic decisions. It is how managers and management systems identify issues which require a strategic response and how the organization manages the interface with its environment. Some organizations will have special strategy units, whose job it is to undertake environmental scanning and alert the senior management to situations that present risks or opportunities; they may also be expected to make plans for dealing with these issues. Other organizations may have a regular sequence of meetings of the senior management team to raise issues on the agenda and to discuss what action, if any, needs to be taken. Most, but not all, public organizations today draw up strategic plans and annually review those plans and related policies to ensure they are still relevant and appropriate (Darlow *et al.* 2008).

Strategic management is also about who is involved in the making and taking of strategic decisions and what are called the soft issues in the organization such as 'the formal and informal power relationships between people, their attitudes to change, their values and beliefs, the culture of the organization, the status relationship and the morale of the staff' (Bowman 1990: 6). There is no standard structure or process in strategic management but, today, all public organizations are aware of its importance and the need to formulate, implement, monitor and control organizational strategies within the systems of performance management imposed by central government under both Conservative and Labour governments and adapted under the Coalition (see Chapter 6).

The ingredients of strategy

The core concepts used in strategies include vision, mission statements or core values, strategic goals, objectives, targets and levels of strategy.

Vision is best thought of as an image of the future – a desired future state, which is the aim or the intention of the organization. It is where or what the organization wants to be and it underpins the purpose and the strategy of an organization. The new Head of the Civil Service in 2006 – Sir Gus O'Donnell – presented his vision of the future 'civil service for the 21st century' encapsulated in the '4Ps': pace, passion, pride and professionalism (see Box 5.1).

A *mission statement* tells the public and the people working in an organization what the purpose of the organization is and the broad direction that it seeks to follow. It may derive from a leader's vision and values and those of its major stakeholders or out of government policy. A mission statement may be seen as the starting point of a strategic analysis and should be written in a way that will help the process of strategy formulation by making clear what the organization exists for – what it does – who the beneficiaries are and the scope and boundaries of the organization as well as the shared values and beliefs. See Box 5.2 for an example of the key ingredients of a mission statement.

BOX 5.1 Gus's vision of a twenty-first century civil service: the 4 Ps

- Pride – civil servants should take pride in the value they add, working with others to inspire and create.
- Passion – civil servants should care about their work and the people they serve. A culture that values passion will also keep attracting the most talented people to join the organization.
- Pace – the civil service needs to ensure it gets on with the job as quickly as possible and provides value for money.
- Professionalism – this can be achieved by constantly lifting standards and promoting a culture that values lifelong learning.

Source: Summarized from '*Gus' vision*', archived from the Cabinet Office website, 5 July 2006. Available from http://tna.europarchive.org/20060715185433/http://www.civil service.gov.uk/reform/

Core values – not all organizations have a mission statement but they may have a statement of core values, for example:

- to be the best;
- to be customer focused;
- to value and empower staff.

Strategic objectives state more precisely than a mission statement what the organization wants to achieve and when it hopes to achieve them.

Targets are the more specific objectives and are expected to be SMART – specific, measurable, achievable, realistic and time-bound.

Levels of strategy

Generally three levels of strategy are identified within an organization:

- *Corporate level* – these decisions are about the purpose of the organization, what 'markets' it is responding to and who are its stakeholders; how the organization should be structured, the allocation of resources between the functions and businesses of the organization; how the organization intends to establish a competitive advantage and what are the aims and objectives.
- *Business level* – Here strategies are developed to achieve the corporate plan and may involve plans to indicate how the organization will meet the more specific issues facing it. These strategies should be consistent not only with the corporate strategy but also with strategies in other parts of the organization, including other departments or divisions, production, HR and marketing.

BOX 5.2 Mission statement of a NHS Hospital Trust

A motto summarizing the organization's desired outcomes:
'Effective Care, Well Delivered'.

A prose statement setting out objectives and strategies for achieving them:
We believe that the patients' needs and experiences are the first consideration and that the best outcomes come from active participation by patients, their carers and relatives and staff. We believe that all relationships between staff and patients, their families and each other should be courteous, professional, open and respectful.

Explicit performance objectives:
A confident, high performing organization, in the top 10 per cent of NHS Trusts.

Values supporting the goals that should be shared across the organization:

- patients' individual needs and experience are our first consideration;
- we should behave with compassion, courtesy, professionalism, integrity, openness and respect in our relationships with patients, their families and each other;
- we are most effective when we are highly skilled, motivated, patient focused and work together as a team.

Source: Modelled on the mission statement of a NHS Hospital Trust.

- *Functional level* – At this level decisions are about how the business level strategies can be operationalized and delivered; for example, HR strategy, marketing strategy.

Strategic leadership

Strategic leadership provides the vision and direction for the growth and success of an organization. It requires the vision to create and carry through plans and to take decisions in today's volatile, complex and ambiguous strategic environments. Strategic leaders are able to anticipate, envision, maintain flexibility and empower others to create strategic change.

The origins of strategic management in the public sector

According to Hughes (2012: 213) 'Strategic planning in the public sector is a phenomenon of the early 1980s – significantly later than its development in the private sector'. There is evidence, however, of strategic planning taking place much earlier than the 1980s, even if it was not as systematic or as wide ranging as it is today. Not only was planning necessary during the Second World War (1939–45) to design military action but also to plan ahead for the period of reconstruction after the war and to prepare for peace. It became still more important to plan after 1945 when the Labour Government introduced the welfare state and assumed responsibility for management of the economy. The government proceeded to nationalize the major industries of gas, electricity, coal, railways and the airlines; introduce a national health service (NHS), transform the educational system; and introduce a system of town and country planning. The government was in effect replacing the market in major areas of the economy and dividing the new state responsibilities between a range of organizational structures including public corporations, central government departments and local authorities (See Chapters 1 and 3). These were clearly highly important decisions and needed to be strategically managed.

All the new functions of government required forward looks or forecasting, whether it was estimating how many children would be entering the education system, at ages five and eleven, to ensure there were enough school places and teachers, or planning for the numbers of people needing pensions, or to ensure that there were sufficient council or private houses built to meet social needs or demands. The under-investment inherited in the newly nationalized industries required huge long-term investment and planning, while 'forward looks' were taking place in areas of defence as well as longer-term programmes or ten-year plans for hospital building, major roads and, later, motorways. In other areas of government, planning or forward looks were not always very comprehensive, long-term, coordinated or effective and there were significant gaps. The projections were sometimes wrong, which brought planning into disrepute. There was also an ideological resistance to economic and social planning, particularly within the Conservative Party, because of its association with the Soviet Union and totalitarianism. Nevertheless, both Conservative and Labour governments did have strategies but they tended to emerge and were more incremental than clearly planned.

Two landmarks in the evolution towards strategic management in the public sector were the Plowden Report (1961) and the Fulton Report (1968a). Plowden revealed that, in spite of the planning referred to above, there was no real planning of public expenditure. It recommended radical changes in the process for determining and allocating government funds and a new system was introduced in 1961, which provided information on the financial implications of continuing existing programmes, costing new policies and projecting forward the financial implications over the next five years. Each year adjustments were made and another year added to the unrolling programme. These changes in public expenditure planning and control were important and, by international standards, a pioneering step in the strategic planning of government expenditure as a whole' (Garrett 1973: 110). However, they were not supported by any analysis of alternative programmes nor by any evaluation of the results of the public expenditure (Pollitt 1977) and they were input rather than output oriented. The Fulton Report (1968a) came to the conclusion that what was needed were planning units in every department staffed by young civil servants and people recruited from outside the service to prepare future scenarios and identify likely policy needs and the associated demands for resources (Fulton 1968b). During the 1970s, Policy Units were introduced in every department and a Central Policy Review Staff (CPRS) was set up in the Cabinet Office to work for ministers collectively under the supervision of the Prime Minister. It advised the government and assisted it in relating departmental policies to the government's strategy as a whole. It also undertook issue analysis particularly of a cross-departmental type (the precursor of Tony Blair's Strategy Unit).

In the 1960s, new ideas about strategy and corporate planning were being taken up by governments in the USA under the title of Planned Programme Budgeting System (PPBS). The essential characteristic of PPBS was that it presented budgets in terms of specific programmes and set out the aims and objectives of each programme (Garrett 1973: 115–41). Some policy transfer took place when the Conservative government, under Edward Heath, experimented with PPBS in the early 1970s, under the title of Programme, Analysis and Review (PAR). (See Garrett 1980: 100–9 on the role of PARs.)

These developments were not confined to central government, as local authorities also flirted with corporate planning in the 1970s. The *Maud Report* (1967) followed by the *Bains Report* (1972) led to many local authorities adopting a more strategic approach to corporate management after 1974, when local government was reorganized into bigger units. Many appointed chief executives, created planning units within the Chief Executive's Office and had Chief Officer teams designed to ensure coordination and systematic planning across the authority. At the political level, Policy and Resources Committees anticipated the Cabinet systems of today. By the late 1970s, however, the verdict was that most of these attempts at forms of corporate management and strategic planning had failed (Caulfield and Schultz 1989).

Although strategic management and corporate planning were widespread in the private sector in the 1970s, there was a view that such practices were inappropriate in the public sector (see Box 5.3).

Twenty years later, however, in a very different context from the 1970s, Isaac-Henry (1999) provided a strong case *for* strategic management in the public sector, arguing that governments need to think more strategically because of the fast changing, unpredictable and dynamic environments in which they operate. The introduction of New Public Management (NPM), the re-engineering of public organizations and the fragmentation of large bureaucratic departments into executive agencies, plus the reform of local government and other government organizations during the 1980s, had resulted in far more autonomy and therefore the ability of public organizations to decide

BOX 5.3 Reasons that strategic management is inappropriate for the public sector

- Public sector management is too complex to lend itself to the simplistic models of private-sector management.
- Strategies are handed down by politicians leaving little room for managers to manoeuvre and they are essentially left with the problems of implementation or operational matters.
- Clear goals and objectives are rarely found in the public sector as there are reasons for politicians to be vague and ambiguous.
- Goals are sometimes stated to placate and mislead rather than to be achieved.
- Political leaders are often temporary and tend to be short-term oriented.
- There are far more stakeholders in the public sector.
- A rationalistic strategic planning approach downgrades the political process and seeks to managerialize or technologize it.
- It gives political judgement a spurious scientific character and seeks to remove it from discourse, negotiation and compromise.

their own strategies. Public organizations were now operating in market contexts and in competition, not only with each other but also with private and voluntary organizations. Defining goals and objectives, developing action plans and designing effective ways of implementing plans were as important in the public sector as in the private sector. While there are still differences between strategic management in the public and private sectors because of the political contexts within which public organizations exist (a point emphasized by Bovaird 2009: 75), strategic management is essential.

In the 1980s and 1990s under the guise of NPM, public organizations were managerialized and performance management systems were introduced throughout the public sector. All public organizations were urged to produce mission statements and strategic plans, setting out their goals and objectives and measurements for evaluation. The environmental scanning techniques were increasingly used to generate information on which these plans could be formulated and decisions could be made, although the comprehensiveness of these reviews varied. PESTLE analysis involves examining the political, economic, social, technological, legal and environmental contexts to identify current and potential changes which could impact on the organization. SWOT analysis focuses on the threats but also the opportunities confronting management. FORCE FIELD ANALYSIS is similar to SWOT but identifies all those forces which are supportive and enabling and those which, on the other hand, are constraining. Some organizations also used stakeholder analysis and resource inventories and a range of other techniques imported from the private sector (Joyce 1999, 2012). In particular, those organizations operating in the commercial sector used Porter's model (Porter 1980) which identifies five forces within a competitive market – the threat of new competition, substitutes for the product or service, the intensity of the existing competition, and the bargaining power of both the organization's buyers (customers) and suppliers.

Although scepticism about using these private sector techniques remained, and some saw as sinister the cultural changes that were transforming the traditional public administration way of thinking into a new managerialist thought-mode, open to the ideas and mind-set of the Conservative government of the day: the private was clearly penetrating the public.

First, the Financial Management Initiative (FMI) in 1982 laid the foundations for the introduction of performance management, while the Next Steps Report (Efficiency Unit 1988) led to the beginnings of strategic management in central government. All Next Steps Agencies were issued with framework documents, which set out the purpose and aims and missions of the agency, and the agency chief executive then agreed, with the parent department, objectives and targets for which he or she was held personally accountable. Performance management was the main driver of the strategic management approach. Performance management was not confined to central government departments and agencies but also imposed by central government on the NHS, education (schools, further education and universities), the police and eventually the armed forces. Because of the significant differences between the various parts of the public sector and because context is important, forms of strategic management at first varied. The Next Steps Agencies model was one in which framework documents set out the strategies for the agency while their business plans, developed by the agency itself, set out their implementation strategies. Local authorities used strategic analysis to identify their purpose, what business they were in and how they could meet the needs and expectations of their stakeholders. As Leach *et al.* (1994: 51) pointed out 'it was necessary to adopt the latest management "totems" to strengthen your legitimacy whether or not they are effective or have any real impact'. The newly privatized 'national industries' were already practising many of the commercial sector's business techniques but were free to develop new strategies and, soon immersed in a competitive environment, were encouraged to do so.

Public sector strategic management under Labour

The election of the New Labour Government in 1997 brought new ideas and a new vision into the public sector and important developments in strategy and strategic management followed. The strategic priorities of the government were based on the major concerns of the public and an attempt was made to create a consensus in the centre of government on the top strategic priorities. There was a concerted effort to create a capability at the core of government to formulate strategies, monitor progress on the strategic priorities and to support the delivery of government's priorities as well as being transparent about government achievements. Major changes occurred in the centre of government in Whitehall, the new devolved governments in Scotland, Wales and Northern Ireland and in local government.

Strategic management by the centre

When in opposition, the Labour Party recognized weaknesses at the centre of government and was determined to strengthen it as well as to provide strong leadership as 'the means of formulating and driving forward strategy for the government as a whole (Mandelson and Liddle 1996: 240). The centre here is taken to mean the Prime Minister's Office (No. 10), the Cabinet Office and the Treasury. This triad collectively provided some leadership and strategic direction but there was a lack of an institutional coordinating body and, in reality, departmentalism was rife. Although performance management systems were in place throughout the civil service they were often compromised by the continuous intervention of the Treasury over annual budgets and spending and there was, in fact, too little coordination at the centre of either policy or implementation. Government was not joined up, and different parts of the system pursued their own strategies, which were often in conflict with each other, impeding the delivery of government policies. In addition, the capability of the different parts of the system varied in terms of strategic leadership, competencies and structural coherence.

During the first New Labour administration significant developments took place. First, came the introduction of Comprehensive Spending Reviews (CSRs) and Public Service Agreements (PSAs); second, the government's Modernizing Agenda; third, the strengthening of the institutional support for the Prime Minister and the Cabinet, and fourth, the Capability Reviews, although these commenced during Blair's second term of office.

Comprehensive Spending Reviews

In 1998, the government published its first CSR. This was a review of departmental aims and objectives alongside a zero-based analysis of each spending programme to determine the best way of delivering the Government's objectives (see Chapter 7 for further discussion of budgetary planning). The CSR also introduced PSAs. Spending reviews set firm and fixed three-year Departmental Expenditure Limits and the PSAs were national targets agreed by the Treasury and the departments to make sure that measurable outcomes were delivered in return for the resources agreed. In other words, they defined the key improvements that the public could expect from the resources allocated by parliament. Successive spending reviews after 1998 targeted significant increases in resources for the government's priorities and set ambitious

PSA targets for improvements in key public services including education, health, transport and criminal justice.

The initial 1998 CSR set spending plans and PSAs for 1999–2002. In 2006, there was a second CSR which undertook a long-term, fundamental review of government expenditure. It provided departmental allocations from 2008 through to 2011. To lay the groundwork for this CSR, the government undertook an examination of the key long-term trends and challenges that it considered would shape the next decade. These included demographic and socio-economic change, globalization, climate and environmental change, global uncertainty and technological change. A series of zero-based reviews of departments' baseline expenditure was undertaken, as in 1998, to assess their effectiveness in delivering the government's long-term objectives. Further, a more strategic approach to asset management and investment decisions was intended, to ensure that the UK would be equipped with the infrastructure needed to support both public service delivery and the productivity and flexibility of the wider economy (HM Treasury 2006: 135–6). Of course there was always potential for disagreement between the Prime Minister/Cabinet ministers who shaped the five-year strategies for government priorities (education, health and law and order) and the Treasury/Chancellor who presided over the CSR and PSAs, as these were carried out separately and over different periods.

Public Service Agreements

From their introduction in the 1998 CSR, every government department, including the Cabinet Office, had to produce a PSA detailing the department's aims and objectives for the forthcoming three years. These set out the key priority outcomes the Government wanted to achieve. Each agreement described how these targets would be achieved and how performance against the targets would be measured. Each PSA was underpinned by a single Delivery Agreement (DA) shared across all contributing departments and developed in consultation with delivery partners and frontline workers. The DA described the national outcome-focused performance indicators used to measure progress towards each PSA. The set of PSAs for 2008–11, shown in Table 5.1, illustrates the attempt to integrate the work of separate departments and ensure they were focusing on the major goals of the government seen in the far left column.

Modernising Government

The government's new strategy for reforming central government was set out in the White Paper *Modernising Government* (Cabinet Office 1999a) which listed a programme of reforms focused around three aims and five key commitments. The three aims were:

Table 5.1 ***Public Service Agreements 2008–11***

Overarching goal	Public Service Agreement priority outcome
Sustainable growth and prosperity	• Raise productivity • Improve skills • Ensure controlled, fair migration • Promote science and innovation • Deliver reliable, efficient transport • Provide conditions for business success
Fairness and opportunity for all	• Maximize job opportunities • Halve the number of children in poverty by 2010–11 • Raise educational achievement • Improve children's safety, health and well-being • Help young people improve their lives • Tackle inequalities • Help socially excluded adults find homes, jobs and training • Enable older people to remain independent
A better quality of life	• Improve the health and well-being of all • Better care for all • Increase housing supply • Deliver a successful Olympic Games and Paralympic Games
Stronger communities communities	• Build more cohesive, empowered and active • Make communities safer • Provide a more effective criminal justice system • Reduce the harm caused by alcohol and drugs • Reduce the risk from international terrorism
A fair, safer and sustainable world	• Lead the effort to avoid climate change • Conserve the natural environment • Reduce poverty in poorer countries • Reduce the impact of international conflict

Source: Summarized from HM Treasury (2007a) *Pre-Budget Report and Comprehensive Spending Review: Meeting the aspirations of the British people*, Cm 7227 (TSO): pp. 187–96.

- to deliver joined-up and strategic policy making;
- to ensure the focus was on service users and not providers;
- to deliver high quality and efficient public services.

And the five key commitments were:

- better policy making;
- responsive public services;

- high quality public services;
- information age government;
- valuing public service.

Blair directed the new Head of the Civil Service, Richard Wilson, to undertake a review of the civil service at the centre of government, a form of SWOT analysis. Wilson's report identified a list of major weaknesses including poor linkage between policy formulation and implementation, a lack of coordination of policy and service delivery across departments, an underdeveloped strategic management process with too little strategic analysis, failure to generate strategic choices and failure to evaluate policy outcomes. His report set out an agenda for change of the civil service which was systematically pursued over the next decade (Cabinet Office 1999b).

Strengthening the centre

It was clear that, at both the political and the administrative levels, strategic policy making and strategic management were weak. There was too little policy analysis, the options presented to ministers were limited and not evidence based and policy implementation was poor, so that policies were often not delivered. There was too little coordination of policies or implementation and very little evaluation to assess their effectiveness. Structural changes were needed at the centre and Blair made changes to both the Prime Minister's Office and the Cabinet Office in an attempt to centralize policy making and strategic control on taking office (Richards and Smith 2002). A large number of full time special advisers, 25 by 1999, were appointed to No. 10 to shadow specific policy areas. A Chief of Staff (Jonathan Powell) and a Director of Communications (Alistair Campbell) coordinated the work of No. 10 and the Cabinet Office and sought to ensure government spoke with one 'voice'.

The Cabinet Office was also restructured to strengthen its strategic role. A variety of new units, project teams, task forces, working parties, and ministerial and official networks were created (Taylor 2000). A Performance and Innovation Unit and a Prime Minister's Forward Strategy Unit were introduced to begin formulating new strategy and to move to 'joined-up-government' (see Richards and Smith 2002: 243). In Blair's second administration (2001–5), a whole new raft of units was set up including a Prime Minister's Strategy Unit (PMSU), a Delivery Unit (PMDU) and the Office of Public Services Reform (OPSR). The Strategy Unit conducted strategic reviews, and gave policy advice on domestic policy, helped departments develop effective strategies and policies and identified emerging issues and challenges. According to Fawcett and Rhodes (2007: 84), the Cabinet Office 'worked in project teams organized around five clusters: public service reform, home affairs, economic and infrastructure, welfare reform and social justice, and communities'.

At the official level, reform of the civil service was proceeding in parallel with political reforms. A Civil Service Management Command was created consisting of the Permanent Secretaries Group and the Civil Service Management Board. A special Modernising Government Project Team was established with special responsibility for overseeing the implementation of the reform programme. This team was further divided into a number of groups assisted by interdepartmental networks. A labyrinth of project teams and networks was formed although quite how effective these were is not clear.

After the 2001 election, the Prime Minister announced a second phase of reform building on the *Modernising Government* programme but acknowledging disappointment in the slow progress that had been made. In spite of a massive majority and the full backing of the party in parliament and the strengthening of the centre it was still not possible to make change happen. As Tony Blair admitted:

> You try getting change in the public sector and the public services. I bear the scars on my back after two years in government.... People in the public sector [are] more rooted in the concept of 'if it has always been done this way, it must always be done this way' than any group I have ever come across. (Quoted in Barber 2007: 46)

So the failure was seen as one of implementation or the failure to deliver. Although many of the objectives remained the same during the second Labour Government, the key priority now became delivery. There was a clear strategy emerging based upon active government, backed by increased public expenditure on health, education, transport and law and order. In 2003–4 the government produced five-year strategies for each department, which were largely shaped or set by the Prime Minister and 10 Downing Street, but informed by the concerns of the Chancellor (Barber 2007). Each strategy included performance targets from PSAs and was funded by budgets decided by the CSR – both of which were developed by the Treasury. The Strategy Unit helped to develop a strategic policy-making capacity in the departments but the challenge was how to get policies delivered and that was the task of the Delivery Unit (Barber 2007). Figure 5.1 shows the government's model of how public service reform was being implemented and the various strategies involved.

The Capability Reviews

The Capability Review programme, started in 2006, was part of the wider reform of the civil service. The objectives were to bring about a step change in the capability of departments to meet current delivery needs and to be ready for future challenges. A capability model consisting of ten elements,

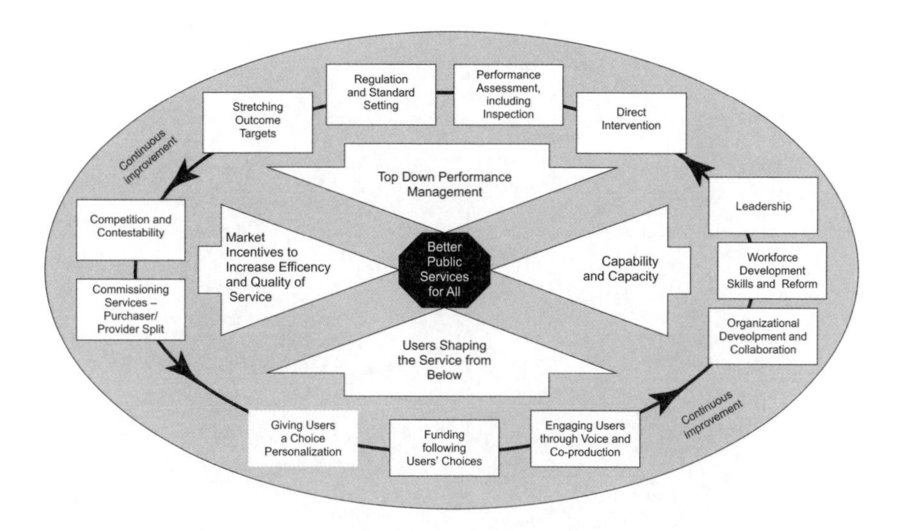

Figure 5.1 ***UK Government model of public service reform***

Source: Cabinet Office (2006) *Capability Reviews: The Findings of the First Four Reviews* (Cabinet Office), p. 9.

grouped around the three areas of leadership, strategy and delivery, was used in all 17 government departments to assess their capability. Where it was found lacking, action plans were drawn up. The major areas of weakness were found to be in leadership and the skills of staff at every level. All departments responded to critical reports by taking remedial action and the Capability Reviews were institutionalized on a bi-annual basis. A new Capability Framework was introduced (see Figure 5.2) based on *Capability Reviews: Refreshing the model of capability* (Cabinet Office 2009a). A new Strategic Leadership model was also developed and the National School of Government provided training in developing the competencies of the Strategic Leadership group within the civil service (see below).

Strategic management in devolved governments

The Labour Government did not have strategic management in mind when it devolved powers to Scotland and Wales in 1998 but devolution has made overall strategic management of the UK much harder. It has had implications for the strategic management of the civil service, the NHS and UK-wide public organizations.

Scotland

From the outset, the newly elected Scottish Government took a very strategic approach by setting out its aims and objectives. The aim was: to focus the

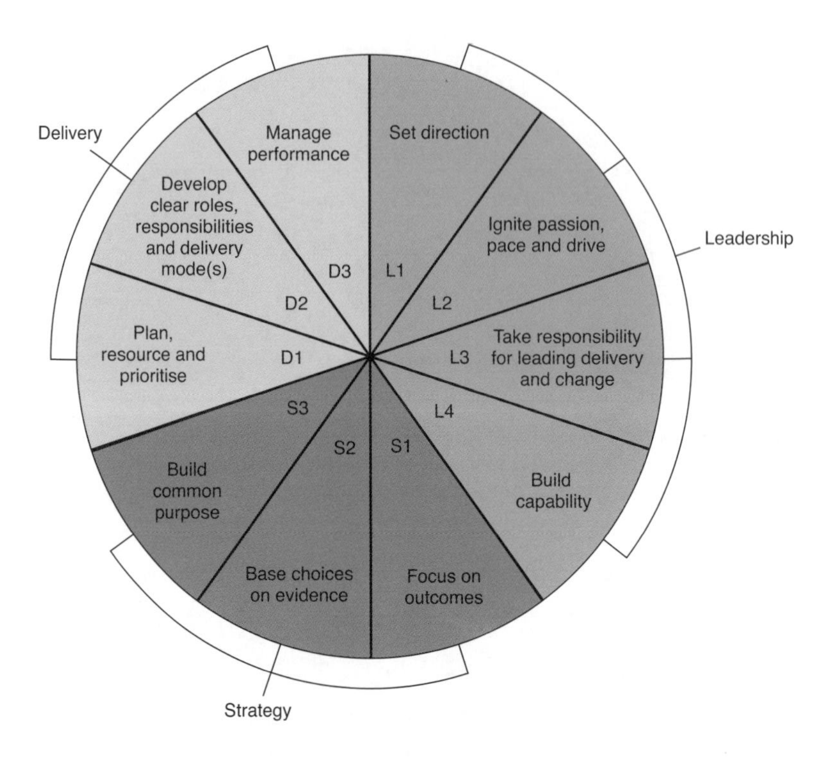

Figure 5.2 ***Capability framework***

Source: 'Model of capability', http://www.civilservice.gov.uk/about/improving/capability/model. Accessed 4 February 2011. Originally published as Cabinet Office (2009a) *Capability Reviews: Refreshing the Model of Capability*, p. 7.

Government and public services on creating a more successful country, with opportunities for all of Scotland to flourish, through increasing sustainable economic growth. The five main objectives were to make Scotland: wealthier and fairer; healthier; safer and stronger; smarter; and greener. These goals were to be achieved by:

- generating greater and more widely shared employment;
- creating more highly skilled and better paid jobs;
- providing better quality goods and services and additional choices and opportunities for Scotland's people;
- stimulating higher government revenues and supporting better quality public services;
- fostering a self-sustaining and ambitious climate of entrepreneurial advance;
- encouraging economic activity and investment across Scotland, thereby sharing the benefits of growth;

- bringing a culture of confidence and personal empowerment to Scotland; and
- securing a high quality environment today and a sustainable legacy for future generations. (Scottish Executive 2005)

This strategy was distinctive in that it focused Scottish central government and the wider public sector on one 'Purpose': namely increasing sustainable economic growth. It was also an over-arching strategy that set the direction for the whole of Scotland's public sector – the Scottish Government, local government, the enterprise networks and other key agencies – to work collaboratively with the private, academic and third sectors, in pursuit of increasing sustainable economic growth.

In 2007, because of the change from a Labour–Liberal Democrat government to one run by the Scottish National Party (SNP), a new strategy and target framework was introduced based on advice from a new Council of Economic Advisers. The latter was a group of leading international economists and business people established to advise the Scottish Government directly on how to increase sustainable economic growth. The government also looked at studies of successful small independent economies including Norway, Finland, Iceland, Ireland and Denmark, which are similar to Scotland in scale and geographically close. Figure 5.3 illustrates how all the elements within the strategy interacted with each other and fitted together. It can be seen that it built very much on the framework developed by the former Labour–Liberal Democrat coalition.

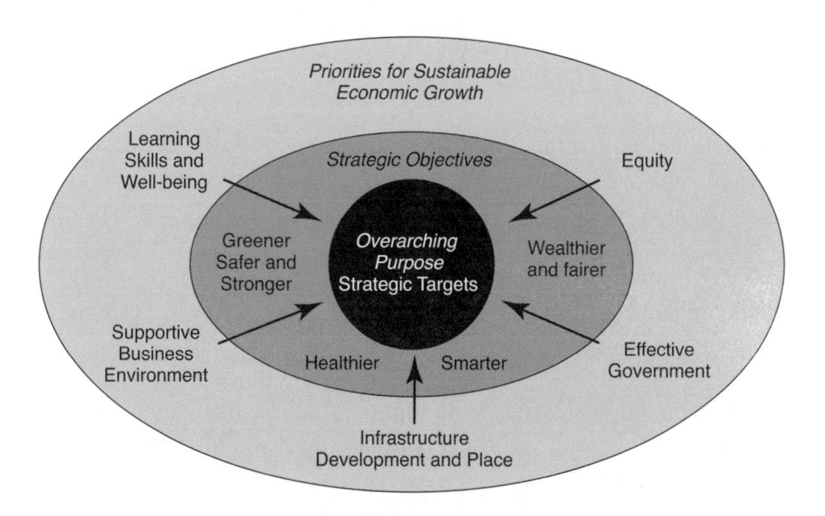

Figure 5.3 ***The strategic approach***

Source: Scottish Government (2007) *The Government Economic Strategy*, Edinburgh: Scottish Government, p. 2.

The starting point was still the 'Purpose': to increase sustainable economic growth. Financial and other resources were sharply focused on the delivery of the five strategic objectives which are designed to make Scotland wealthier and fairer, smarter, healthier, safer and stronger, and greener. The central purpose was still the unifying factor across all levels and institutions of Scottish Government. In deciding which course of action to take, a range of options – financial incentives, regulation, direct provision, better information and doing nothing – were appraised on the basis of sound analysis and evidence. According to the government, the strategy was designed to balance economic growth and social, regional and inter-generational equity objectives. Its strategic objectives play a key role in focusing all the activity of the government on increasing sustainable economic growth.

In order to integrate all levels of government, to pursue its reform agenda and to improve the performance of all government organizations, the first Scottish Government chose to use a Best Value strategic framework, analogous to that adopted by the UK Labour Government in 1998 for local government in England and Wales (see below). Best Value was intended to balance both quality and cost, ensure regard for the '3 Es' plus equal opportunities and also secure continuous improvement. Best Value also placed the emphasis on the customer. The performance management principles of Best Value cover:

- Commitment and Leadership
- Sound Governance at a Strategic and Operational Level
- Accountability
- Sound Management of Resources
- Responsiveness and Consultation
- Use of Review and Options Appraisal.

Scottish national government and local government work in partnership to develop the Best Value framework to ensure that management and business practices in local authorities improve and provide more responsive public services. The Local Government in Scotland Act 2003 placed a statutory duty of Best Value upon all 32 local authorities, and audits of Best Value and Community Planning were intended to assess local authority responses and provide an overview of a council's performance across services and its joint working with community planning partners. Audit Scotland published a report, based on the Best Value Audit reports of all 32 local authorities, which was very positive about the workings of both the Best Value and Community Planning frameworks:

> The introduction in 2003 of the statutory duty to demonstrate Best Value has had a significant impact on local government. The concept of Best Value had been around for several years by then, but the statutory duty on

> councils, and the introduction of the BV audit, focused the minds of elected members and senior officers and provided a catalyst for change and improvement. It encouraged councils to take a more systematic approach to improving performance and emphasised the importance of medium to long-term planning. (Audit Scotland 2009: paragraph 9)

The report focused on the corporate assessment elements of the Best Value reports, concentrating on strategic leadership and how well local authorities were organized to develop Best Value. It highlighted the fact that making audit reports public was increasing transparency and attracting a lot of media coverage but two critical reports (for Aberdeen and West Dunbartonshire) exposed weak leadership and a lack of transparency. After public enquiries, progress reports were demanded of these two authorities and these produced significant improvements in both areas.

In 2007, following the introduction of proportional representation and multi-member constituencies in local government, and the formation of the SNP minority Government, a Concordat between the national government and local authorities was negotiated along with Single Outcome Agreements (SOAs). These developments required local authorities to find new ways of working both politically and managerially. This was helped by the recruitment of a cohort of new chief executives, but SOAs meant that local authority leaderships had to learn to work in effective partnerships across the public sector.

Parallel developments in Scotland and Whitehall included debates on reform of the civil service. Several reports (*Changing to Deliver* 2003; *Efficient Government* 2004; *Taking Stock* 2006) culminated in the *Shaping Up* report (Scottish Government 2010a). There were 21 recommendations in *Shaping Up* involving the need for more strategic direction from senior staff, more coordination and effective communication and improvements in leadership. Similar recommendations were made in the capability reports, which stressed the need for stronger leadership and strengthening the delivery chain. Following the 2007 election, a small strategic board of senior civil servants was created in the Scottish Executive; heads of department were replaced by Director Generals (DG) and each DG was given responsibility for one of the government's five strategic objectives similar to the champions in Whitehall's Senior Civil Service (SCS).

Wales

The Welsh Assembly adopted *The Wales Spatial Plan: People, Places, and Futures* in November 2004. This was modified in 2008, following the election that brought Plaid Cymru into a coalition with Labour, bringing the Plan into line with their policy statement on *One Wales* (www.assemblywales.org). It was a broad 20-year agenda, which set out a vision for Wales:

- to ensure decisions are taken with regard to their impact beyond the immediate sectoral or administrative boundaries and that the core values of sustainable development govern everything;
- to set the context for local and community planning;
- to influence where money is spent by the Welsh Assembly Government;
- to provide a clear evidence base for the public, private and third sectors to develop policy and action.

As with the overall plan in Scotland, the major principle and aim of the Wales Spatial Plan was sustainable development and to improve the well-being and quality of life of the Welsh people by integrating social, economic and environmental objectives in the context of more efficient use of natural resources. The Plan aimed to deliver sustainable development through six area or sub-regional strategies, each with its own area spatial plan. But the Welsh Assembly set out cross-cutting national spatial priorities, which provided the context for the application of national and regional policies for specific sectors, such as health, education, housing and the economy, reflecting the distinctive characteristics of the different sub-regions of Wales and their cross-border relationships. Although there are six Welsh sub-regions they do not have hard boundaries, reflecting the different linkages involved in daily activities. In each area, local authorities, the private and third sectors, and the Welsh Assembly Government and its agencies work together in Spatial Plan Area Groups to achieve the strategic vision for that area – the Welsh version of joined-up government. Each regional plan sets the context and identifies the actions required to achieve the objectives, both for service delivery and land use. They inform, and in turn are informed by, community strategies, local development plans and the work of the Local Service Boards.

Northern Ireland

Northern Ireland elected a new assembly to Stormont in 2007 and a power-sharing Executive was appointed. Its first programme for government set out its strategic priorities and key plans for 2008–11. This followed a very participatory process between the parties representing the opposing communities and involved numerous drafts before the final document *Building a Better Future* was agreed. It set down a set of principles on which it intended to base its decisions and actions including:

- providing good leadership and working energetically in the interests of everyone;
- working in partnership as an Executive, and across the public, private and voluntary sectors;

- raising standards across government, both in terms of the openness and accountability of the Executive, and in driving improvements in essential public services;
- delivering fair outcomes and social improvements in terms of the implementation of policies and programmes.

The strategic priorities were to:

- build a peaceful, fair and prosperous society in Northern Ireland, with respect for the rule of law and where everyone can enjoy a better quality of life now and in years to come;
- pursue an innovative and productive economy and a fair society that promotes social inclusion, sustainable communities and personal health and well-being;
- protect and enhance the physical and natural environment;
- use resources as efficiently and sustainably as possible;
- eliminate all forms of inequality.

The strategic and inter-dependent priorities identified were:

- growing the economy;
- building a peaceful, prosperous, fair and healthy society;
- providing good public services and infrastructure.

In 2002, a Review of Public Administration was launched. This was the first major examination in thirty years although, during the period of direct rule from London, the Northern Ireland Civil Service had adopted some of the strategic management techniques introduced during the 1980s in the British civil service, notably FMI and restructuring into executive agencies. Major structural changes to the rest of the public sector followed the 2002 review with local government councils to be reduced from 26 to 11 by 2011 and Health Trusts from 18 to 5, a new Education and Skills Authority and a Library Board replacing five previous Education and Library Boards. These changes in structure should make it easier to coordinate, monitor and control the work of these organizations. Major changes in departmental structures were introduced in 2010 to reflect the changes in the wider machinery of government. This strategic management process appeared to be mirroring that found in other parts of the UK. For example, the Northern Ireland system had spending reviews, PSAs and performance indicators and the hub is focused in the Department of the First Minister and Deputy First Minister, which is responsible for developing the overall strategy for the government. There are targets and performance indicators enabling an assessment of their achievement and the success of the strategies. These may be abolished if policy follows that of the current British Coalition Government or of the other devolved governments.

Local government

As we have seen, strategic or corporate planning is not new to local government and during the 1980s and 1990s systems of performance management were introduced followed by the Best Value initiative in 1998. As in the Best Value approach outlined for Scotland, a duty was placed on all local authorities in England and Wales to achieve effective services by balancing quality and cost. All authorities were required to undertake fundamental performance reviews of all local services, over a five-year period, starting with the worst performing and using the '4Cs' approach: challenging the purpose of the service; comparing its performance against other authorities; consulting the community; and competing with other organizations for the delivery of the service (Rouse 1999).

Most local authorities have always been constrained in their ability to formulate and implement strategic plans largely because of their financial dependence on central government and the statutory frameworks within which they have to exercise their powers. The extent of central control, however, increased significantly after 1997. Starting with *Local Government in Touch with the People: Agenda for Change* (1997), central government set about changing local government's political and official management structures by offering four models from which all local authorities had to choose. Most opted for the Cabinet model and introduced features supporting a corporate managerial approach. Chief executives are generally supported by senior management teams made up of heads of directorates including corporate services. These report to Cabinets of elected councillors in most authorities, although there are a small number of elected mayors who are political executives (there were 14 elected mayors in England and Wales in 2011). The Labour Government promoted mayors, and their numbers will increase as they are supported by the Coalition Government, which made provision for them in the 2011 Localism Act. A majority vote in a referendum is still required to introduce a mayoral system so it is therefore a local decision (see Chapter 4). However, the Coalition wants mayors to provide strategic leadership and expected the 12 biggest cities to elect them, with potential powers similar to those of the Mayor of London, but 9 of those cities rejected mayors in referenda in May 2012.

From 1997, local authorities were expected to have mission statements or core values, corporate and business plans and were required to produce annual performance plans. As the Labour Government moved to the use of PSAs in 1998, these were imposed on local authorities where they were responsible for implementing national policies. Some of the larger authorities had strategy units which undertook environmental scanning and identified issues which required a local response. Until 2010 unitary authorities, county councils and most districts operated within a national framework of strategic plans, PSAs, local area agreements (LAAs) and Strategic Partnership

Agreements (SPAs). Best Value was imposed in 1998 and the earlier performance framework was added to with PSAs in 1998 (see above), followed by Comprehensive Performance Assessments (CPAs) in 2002, as the government strengthened its monitoring and assessing of local authorities' performance. CPAs looked at how well LAs delivered their core services, used resources, and how the LA managed itself as an organization, to arrive at an overall assessment. That assessment came in the form of a star rating – from zero to four stars – and a 'direction of travel' judgement about the rate of improvement in services and the outcomes for local residents. From 2009, the CPAs were replaced by Comprehensive Area Assessments (CAAs) which became the major driver for improvement.

There were fewer central targets and reporting systems, as LAAs replaced the multiple national performance frameworks and, by the end of the Labour Government, each LAA contained up to 35 priorities for specific performance improvements (chosen from a National Indicator Set containing 188 outcome indicators across Whitehall spending departments), plus 16 statutory education outcomes. The aim was to strengthen the ability of LAs (together with their partners, including local people and Local Strategic Partnerships) to determine the actions required to address locally determined and agreed priorities. They set out improvement priorities for the local area, along with targets that needed to be hit to deliver improved outcomes for local people set out in a Sustainable Community Strategy. There was also a single annual performance review to examine the findings of the CAA and to assess responses to changing priorities in the area.

In line with Labour's commitment to 'joined-up government', in 2002, local authorities were encouraged to establish Local Strategic Partnerships (LSPs). These non-statutory bodies, consisting of representatives of statutory and voluntary organizations, business and other stakeholders within the community, developed community strategies to deal with the issues and problems in the local area. LAAs were supposed to help design what sort of place people wanted to live in and were intended to set strategic direction and focus on the priorities to make a town, city or community a better place. The government called it 'place-shaping'. LAAs were three-year agreements between the members of the strategic partnership, including health trusts and police authorities, other local partners and the government. LAs were required to ensure systems were in place for participation of the public in the formulation of LAAs.

Strategic management under the Coalition

The Coalition Government published an agreement on its programme of reform (Cabinet Office 2010) within a week of taking office. Its strategy became clearer as the details emerged but priority was given, initially, to reducing the public sector deficit through cuts in public expenditure, while the three key aims of the government were to *support growth, reform public services and build a fairer society*. The 2010 Spending Review (HM Treasury 2010a) set out the ways in which the government planned to reduce the overspend by first promising a £6 billion saving on administrative budgets in departments and their quangos (HM Treasury 2010a: 9). The original figure of a head count reduction of 490,000 staff by 2014/15 was later revised by the Office of Budget Responsibility to 330,000 (OBR 2010: 6) The latter would be achieved by natural wastage, not filling vacant posts, some redundancies and shedding contract staff where possible (for example, in the NHS) but the strategy would be decided by individual organizations. Departmental budgets, except for health and overseas aid, were to be cut by an average of 19 per cent over the next four years (see Chapter 7 for more details), and every government department had to produce a business plan setting out the details of its reform plans and how it would ensure the reductions required (see Box 5.4).

The Chancellor also promised to reshape public services and to institute a dramatic shift in the balance of power from the centre to the local level, from bureaucrats to professionals in the health service and education and from politicians to the public. He described the policy under Labour as one of rising burdens, regulations, targets, assessment and guidance which had undermined local democracy and stifled innovation and promised to completely reverse that with a dramatic shift in power.

There was structural reorganization at the centre of government with six ministers appointed to the Cabinet Office including the Deputy PM (Nick Clegg), Minister for the Cabinet Office (Francis Maude), Minister for Government Policy (Oliver Letwin), Minister for Civil Society (Nick Hurd), Minister for Political and Constitutional Reform (Mark Harper) and Minister without Portfolio (Baroness Warsi). The Prime Minister's Office was re-

BOX 5.4 Departmental Business Plans for reform

The Coalition Government's requirements for a departmental business plan included:

- vision and priorities 2011/12 to 2014/15;
- structural reform plan, to include action and deadlines for implementing reforms over the next two years;
- key indicators that show the cost and impact of public services and departmental activities;
- draft indicators to be published for consultation and Government approval by April 2011.

Source: Summarized from HM Treasury (2010a) *Spending Review 2010*, Cm 7492 (TSO), p. 9).

staffed with his political appointments but there were also 178 civil servants linked to major areas of policy. A strategy group was established, but it was not clear to begin with whether Prime Minister Cameron would try to keep control from No. 10 or resort to a more collective style of leadership appropriate to a Coalition Government.

One of the first acts of the new government was to create an Office for Budget Responsibility (OBR) to make an independent assessment of the public finances and the economy and to advise the government on how it could reduce the deficit within the lifetime of the Parliament. It obtained a statutory basis when the Budget Responsibility and National Audit Act was passed in March 2011. The changes in the Cabinet Office and its greater political weight reflected the priorities of the Coalition Government and were intended to enable the Office to act as a strong centre for reform. Various units were transferred from the Treasury, the Justice Department and the Department of Work and Pensions into a large Efficiency and Reform Group (ERG), which was assigned both strategic and operational responsibility for a wide range of activities including procurement; information and communication technology; civil service capability, reform and human resources; communication policy covering marketing, advertising and the transparency of government; governance reform; the office for civil society; and responsibility for cross-cutting work. The strategic direction of the group is overseen by an Efficiency and Reform Board chaired by the Minister for the Cabinet Office (Francis Maude) and the Head of the Civil Service. This massive group was designed to ensure that improvements in efficiency and cost cutting dominated government activities. Also supporting the Cabinet and the Prime Minister are a European and Global Affairs Secretariat, an Economic and Domestic Affairs Secretariat and the Strategy Unit. The latter, with a staff of 27 in 2011, advises the central executive on the whole spectrum of policy areas including decentralization, political reform and society, public services, home affairs, development and climate change, economy and welfare and strategic reviews. It bears a close resemblance to the former Labour Government Strategy Unit. Developments in the hub of the executive, which is constantly changing, can be followed on the Cabinet Office website (www.cabinetoffice.gov.uk).

One of the major commitments of the Coalition Government was to decentralization and, within a year of taking office, it had abolished CAAs, PSAs and most performance indicators relating to local government and only the value for money reviews by the Audit Commission remained (see Chapter 9). There is now much more emphasis on area-based service delivery but the Labour Government was moving towards giving local governments more freedom in spending decisions and reducing the number of specific grants. The Coalition Government's commitment to localism reinforces the idea of freedom of local authorities to decide on local services and their own spending priorities. However, the reduction in central government funding and the constraints imposed by the Coalition Government on increases in council tax suggests that freedom, at least in the short to medium term, will amount to how to make cuts! (See Chapter 7).

What is quite clear is that under the Coalition Government both central and local government are continuing to practise strategic planning although the effectiveness of the various processes involved in producing strategies, which deliver the intended results, is open to debate (Seddon 2008). Business plans have replaced PSAs and business plans are not negotiated with the Treasury or the Cabinet Office, as were the PSAs. According to Oliver Letwin, Cabinet Minister for Government Policy, in oral evidence to the House of Commons (12 January 2011), the only rule for a departmental business plan is that it has to enable the department to fulfil the task it had been allocated by the Government's programme. He thought that micro-management had not produced results on the ground and that 'a power shift' to the people, to be achieved by more transparency on departmental business, could be a more effective strategy (PASC 2011a: Ev 1–3).

The Coalition Agreement remains the over-arching framework within which the government was operating but in the first two years the government has found it difficult to get its legislation through parliament. Over twenty bills were announced in the first 'Queen's Speech' and the government extended the parliamentary session until May 2012 to enable them to complete this programme. Much of the legislation was very contentious and many revisions, including to the Localism Bill, had to be made before receiving the Royal assent. Some one thousand amendments were put to the Health and Social Care Bill, which eventually received the Royal assent in March 2012, after significant changes had been introduced. There was particularly strong opposition in the House of Lords and from the medical profession. It was also a policy that strained the coalition parties. Both these reforms had major implications for strategic management as they envisaged significant changes in the delivery of public services and the potential providers and, in the case of the NHS reform, involved the abolition of the Strategic Health Authorities and Primary Care Trusts. Similarly, the abolition of the Regional Development Agencies and Government Regional Offices, replaced in part by Local Enterprise Partnerships, will leave gaps that may in time have to be filled.

Managing strategic partnerships and coordinating the work of diverse public and private organizations is a challenge, which requires strong leadership as well as a range of incentives and penalties to keep stakeholders on course. The frameworks under Labour saw a move away from the silo mentality and rigid departmentalism, which had plagued earlier attempts at corporate management in the 1980s and 1990s, and were certainly achieving a degree of joined-up government, although that should not be exaggerated. Perhaps more significantly, they were enabling far more public participation in strategic management at all levels. The Coalition Government is going further by reducing the control of central government and encouraging more participation and involvement in its vision of the Big Society. However, in its determination to cut public expenditure, it has not so far removed the key controls over spending, although the Localism Act will give the public more direct control over local spending through greater transparency, while the use of referenda to authorize or reject a local authority's budget if the minister decides it is 'excessive' will represent a radical change. So far this power has not been used, and there are strong arguments suggesting it may not be used (see Chapter 7).

The Coalition is committed to an ill-defined post-bureaucratic age which again involves moving away from top-down decision making towards decision making by individuals, communities and local authorities and increasing personal and local responsibility away from state responsibility. The Deputy Prime Minister refers to this strategy as horizontal shifting and long-term orientation. It is questionable whether its emphasis on strategic planning is adequate as a strategic management approach in the highly turbulent environment facing the UK in the second decade of the twenty-first century. Uncertainty about the future of the euro, the unstable situation in the Middle East, especially among oil-producing countries, and the threatened double-dip recession with its implications for demand, unemployment and taxation are likely to leave some, if not all, of the Coalition's financial targets unmet and further changes to its public expenditure plans and reforms are likely. Strategic management may become even more important and yet far more difficult.

Strategic leadership

While the call in the 1980s and 1990s was for improved management, in the last decade it has been for improved leadership. *Modernising Government* (Cabinet Office 1999a) and *Civil Service Reform* (Cabinet Office 1999b) both identified the need for stronger leadership. The report on *Strengthening Leadership* (Cabinet Office/PIU 2001) referred to the scarcity of top-level or strategic leaders and to the fact that demands on them were increasing all the time. One of the three foci of the Capability Reviews in central government was leadership and although examples of good leadership were found throughout the departments there was clearly a general need for more effective leadership in the future.

This story was repeated throughout the public sector with persistent calls for stronger leadership in local government, the NHS, education and the police. The government promoted the establishment of academies for training head teachers (The National College for School Leadership which confers the National Professional Qualification for Head Teachers); the Gateway to Leadership in the NHS; the strategic leadership programme at Bramshill for the police; and not least the Strategic Leadership programme for all members of the SCS. The latest competency framework, Professional Skills for Government, places leadership as a core competency required at all levels of the service (see Chapter 8).

Although there are volumes of literature on leadership in the private business sector there is far less on public sector leadership. In the last decade, however, academics, consultants and international organizations have produced a burst of scholarship on public sector leadership, both national and international (OECD 2001; Koch and Dixon 2007; Raffel *et al.* 2009). Leadership is now seen as the key to successful implementation of change (Joyce 2000, 2012; Hughes 2012) and a key factor in organizational performance (Andrews *et al.* 2006). However, exactly what it is and how to define it is still disputed. Some see it as an individual capacity, others as a social relationship within groups. Some see leadership as concentrated at the top of organizations while others write about distributed leadership and servant leadership (Yukl 2002; Horton and Farnham 2007).

Although leadership training programmes have existed in the civil service and other public services since the 1980s, significant changes have taken place in the last ten years in the type of leaders required and this is reflected in both the literature on leadership and the approach to training. Classical theories traditionally saw leaders as individuals with certain traits and exceptional abilities who 'emerged 'and took control. Management theorists saw leadership as a function of management which managers either performed well or badly. Different types of leader were recognized and it was argued that different situations called for different styles of leadership. The contingent factors were identified as the type and size of organization, the industrial setting, the nature of the staff, and the economic situation. These theories were focusing on leadership rather than leaders – seeing leadership as a relational concept between leaders and led. The more recent theories examine that relationship more closely and identify transactional and transformational relationships, distributed leadership and subject leadership. Today the emphasis is on strategic leadership and there is a mixture of approaches found in the literature ranging from writings on the individual strategic manager (Joyce and Woods 1996; Davies and Davies 2009) to the role of strategic leadership in creating a learning organization and empowering staff to lead (Bolden 2004). Box 5.5 describes the differences between these types of leadership.

A continuing debate is about the difference between management and leadership. The words 'management' and 'leadership' have different origins and, by looking at those origins, we can perhaps get an insight into their true meanings. 'Management' comes from the Latin 'manus' or 'hand' and 'management', therefore, is basically about being 'hands-on', in planning, organizing, staffing, directing, coordinating, reporting and budgeting – the famous acronym of POSDCORB (Gulick and Urwick 1937). 'Leadership' on the other hand has an Anglo-Saxon root and comes from words meaning

BOX 5.5 Concepts of leadership

Autocratic or Authoritarian Leaders: all decision-making powers are centralized in the leader. They do not entertain any suggestions or initiatives from subordinates. The autocratic style permits quick decision making and may be appropriate in crisis situations where speed is essential.

*Participatory or Democratic Leader*s favour decision making by the group. The decisions of the democratic leader are not unilateral as with the autocrat because they arise from consultation with the group members or participation in joint decision making. The most democratic style is one in which the leader delegates to the group to take the decision.

*The Transactional Leade*r is given power to perform certain tasks and reward or punish the group's performance. The group agrees to follow his/her lead to accomplish a predetermined goal in exchange for something else: it may be money, promotion, training or retention of the job.

The Transformational Leader is highly visible and focuses on the big picture, needing to be surrounded by people who take care of the details. The leader is always looking for ideas that move the organization to reach the vision which he/she has presented. Communication is the basis for goal achievement focusing the group on the final desired outcome or goal attainment.

Distributed Leadership is about leadership practice rather than leaders. Leadership practice is a product of the interactions of leaders and followers and not a product of a leader's knowledge and skill. These interactions, rather than any particular action, are critical to leadership practice which involves multiple leaders, some with and some without formal leadership positions. Leadership practice is not something done to followers, rather followers are one of the three constituent elements and their interactions are critical.

Servant Leadership is a philosophy of leadership) which is demonstrated through specific characteristics and practices including listening, empathy, healing, awareness, persuasion, conceptualization, foresight, stewardship, commitment to the growth of others, and building community. It is based on a desire to serve others and a commitment to lead. Servant leaders continually strive to be trustworthy, self-aware, humble, caring, visionary, empowering, relational, competent, good stewards, and community builders. Servant leaders are individuals of character, put people first, are skilled communicators, are compassionate collaborators, use foresight, are systems thinkers, and exercise moral authority.

'forward', 'path', 'route' and 'journey'. Leadership, therefore, is about 'movement', 'progress' and 'change'. Managers tend to get things done by controlling people whereas leaders tend to get things done by inspiring people and motivating them. Motivation from managers is often transactional and rational using 'reward or punishment' to get people to do what they want them to do. Motivation from a leader is often emotional and appealing to people's values. 'Do this and you'll feel good'. 'Do this and we can make a difference'. Leaders inspire, raise morale and energize. In summary, managers appeal to people's rational thinking, whereas leaders appeal to people's emotions; managers appeal to people's logic and leaders to their feelings, which engage different parts of the brain (CIPD 2010).

It is recognized today that successful leadership is underpinned by sound management and the performance of most people in managerial positions, at whatever level, is monitored and judged on managerial criteria. However, combining management skills with leadership skills leads to better results. The Professional Skills for Government framework indicates the managerial skills in which civil servants are expected to demonstrate competence, and likewise in other parts of the public sector, skills councils are providing frameworks for the development of similar management skills. However, strategic management and strategic leadership are singled out as needing special training as they involve distinctive skills.

All members of the SCS, who are deemed to be operating at the strategic level, and equivalent senior staff throughout the public sector, have to undertake leadership training and the number of training and development programmes in leadership is rapidly increasing. The dominant view is that strong strategic leadership is necessary to develop and implement new strategies and that it requires special competencies including vision, persuasion, judgement, team building as well as the management skills necessary for achieving results. In the new world of governance, partnerships and joined-up government, it is the ability to lead coalitions and multi-agency federations and confederations that is the new core competency that is being demanded. It requires negotiating and diplomatic skills and highly developed interpersonal and social skills as well as those identified in Box 5.1 – the ability to set direction, to ignite passion, pace and drive; taking responsibility for leading, delivering and changing; and building capacity (see Chapter 8 for a discussion of leadership training).

Review

Strategic management is about shaping an organization's development. It is about a way of thinking within an organization, and among its actors, in analysing the organization's development. Although it may involve strategic planning it is more accurately described as 'planned evolution'. Strategic management is a collective learning process and embraces all issues considered important to an organization's development. The key questions with which it is concerned are: what is the purpose of the organization and how does the organization want to develop in response to the changing environment in which it operates? The transformation that strategic management strives to achieve is something that can be influenced, but not necessarily directly planned or managed. Influence can be gained, however, by shaping four fundamental dimensions – content, actors, processes and instruments – as well as coordinating and integrating them into the organization as a whole. This chapter has sought to demonstrate how that has been attempted in all parts of the UK administrative system and how it is continuing to evolve.

It has shown that the strategic framework for the public services has changed in the last decades. Although the Labour Government inherited a commitment to improving public services and ensuring they were responsive to the users, it strengthened that commitment by continually emphasizing the need to deliver better public services through increased public expenditure especially on education, health and law and order but also by improving efficiency and performance. It also strengthened participation and joined-up government to overcome the fragmentation and lack of coordination which was, in part, a consequence of many of the Conservative reforms. Labour first used instruments such as PSAs to set targets, and strengthened performance management frameworks to improve internal management controls. Performance measurement and benchmarking (see Chapter 6) drove standards up but also had unanticipated consequences which undermined their credibility.

Five-year strategic plans, three-year funding settlements, the publication of targets and results changed the rules of the policy game. Although performance management predated the Labour Government elected in 1997, both Blair and Brown went further in laying down targets and requiring all public bodies to publish their results. Governments in the devolved administrations have all used similar processes and techniques as well as extending the participation and hence the actors involved within the strategic process. Local government was driven by PSAs as well as their own LAAs. The development of strategic management driven by politicians at the centre was predicted as the epitaph of New Labour (Joyce 2008).

The Labour strategies were not disruptive junctures – as all had originated or had seeds planted in the past. There was therefore much continuity along with the change. Greater use of performance indicators and targets, competition for league table positions and incentives and penalties in the form of increased autonomy or loss of funding amongst local authorities and health trusts were new. The centre of government was strengthened and the great effort made to direct and coordinate both policy and the work of government from the Prime Minister's and the Cabinet Offices was also new. There was strategic direction, but it did not always succeed in getting the results hoped for because of the implementation gap which, in spite of all the efforts, was not always filled.

The Coalition Government, whilst continuing to pursue a strategic approach, has made some significant changes. It has implemented policies designed to decentralize and reduce the degree of central direction and control by abandoning PSAs, LAAs and the raft of performance indictors used by the former Labour Government to control local, health and police authorities. These have been replaced by business plans (at national level) and financial targets, leaving public bodies at both central and local level to determine how they will achieve the cuts in public expenditure required by the government and the 2010 Spending Review. New forms of accountability are being introduced with the powers now given to the public under the Localism Act and the proposals to introduce elected police commissioners and more elected mayors. The question remains, however, in the vacuum left by the bonfire of controls and the decentralization of powers, how will the government ensure that its strategies are able to steer the machinery of governance or will it be left ultimately to the market?

The UK is not alone in adopting a more strategic approach to public management. The study of twelve countries by Proeller and Siegel (2009) showed it is now widely practised. Although each country is adopting a unique approach, and strategic management is context specific, there are some similarities. These include a focus on objectives, results and outcomes, the production of mission statements, strategic plans and planning documents and the use of performance management systems. There are, of course, many differences reflecting those countries' different political and administrative systems and the stage of development of performance management they have reached. They all appear, however, to be moving in a similar direction.

Chapter 6

Performance and Quality Management

The strategies of recent UK governments with respect to public services have been focused on how to improve their performance – how to get more for less, how to ensure that resources are being used in the most efficient and effective way, how to be more responsive to the public's needs and expectations, and how to ensure that quality is central to the workings of all public organizations. This reflects governments' preoccupations with outputs and the need to demonstrate how they are using public money. In fact, performance measurement has become a core element of public management reform not only in the UK but world wide (Pollitt and Bouckaert 2000; Bouckaert and Halligan 2007; OECD 2009c).

The ideas of performance and quality management have been imported from the private sector, again on the assumption that private organizations do things better: and their practices can be applied within public organizations because good management is generic across organizations. A fundamental assumption, too, is that performance and quality can be measured and therefore standards can be set and assessed over time. This enables governments to demonstrate their achievements and for all government organizations to be accountable – internally to central government and externally to the public – for the way they spend public money and for the results.

This chapter examines the concepts of performance and quality management, traces their introduction into the public sector and debates the issues surrounding their practice.

The context

A concern with performance is not a recent preoccupation as Heinrich shows in her brief chronology of systems of performance measurement (Heinrich 2003) and Bouckaert and Halligan (2007) demonstrate in their comprehensive examination of performance measurement. According to Hood (1991), by the 1990s, a broadly similar set of administrative doctrines, including 'explicit standards and measures of performance', could be found in many OECD countries and a study of seven European countries by Flynn and Strehl (1996) also confirmed a preoccupation with performance in their public services. The factors influencing this trend were the same factors influencing the introduction of New Public Management (NPM) – namely changing market conditions, increased international competition, globalization and the search by private sector organizations in the advanced economies for competitive advantage through an emphasis on productivity, performance and quality. This provided a model, which some governments sought to emulate in their public sectors although not in a standardized way. In the UK, for example, governments demanded reduced costs and improvements in productivity which forced public managers to focus on performance. Further, market conditions were created in some public services to inject competition and this too led to a much sharper focus on performance management to achieve competitive advantage.

Other factors at work were management ideas and changes in thinking about management, reflected in the writings of gurus such as, Peters and Waterman (1982) and the quality gurus Deming (1982), Crosby (1984), Juran (1992), and Oakland (1993). Technology was also acting as both a stimulus and a tool. Many of the systems used in controlling and monitoring performance were only possible because of developments in ICT. But the main driver in the UK was government policy. The top-down approach to NPM forced public organizations to move toward performance management, starting with the creation of cost centres and accountable management introduced by the Financial Management Initiative (FMI) in 1982, which is seen by many commentators as the real beginning of performance management in central government in the UK. This was followed by the Next Steps policy of creating agencies from 1988, quality charters and Total Quality Management (TQM) (1990s), market testing (1991), benchmarking (1997) and later, under New Labour, Public Service Agreements (PSAs), clinical governance in the NHS, Best Value and then Local Area Agreements (LAAs) in local government, and finally quality management in the first decade of this century.

But why the emphasis on measuring as well as managing performance? Flynn points out it is because it is a means of increasing accountability and enables politicians to obtain information about what is happening. 'They need evidence of what policies and services produce the desired results and a system of measurement and monitoring to make sure that people are doing what they are told and achieving what the government wants them to' (Flynn 2007: 126). Performance management and measurement also helps managers exercise more control over their staff and curb the power of the professionals (doctors, teachers, social workers, police), who, in the past, have been the standard setters and the allocators of resources. Finally, it is a means of holding governments and public organizations to account to the public whom they are there to serve. Information is now more transparent and parents can see how well their children's schools perform; patients can see the records of their hospitals; and local residents can see how well their local authorities are doing compared to other councils.

Concepts and definitions

Performance management

Performance management can be described as a rational approach to management in which:

- organizations identify their goals and objectives;
- the role of management is to achieve those goals and objectives in the most efficient and effective way;
- targets and performance indicators are set and used as a basis for measuring the efficiency and effectiveness of the organization; and
- individual goals, objectives and performance are also set and appraised as a means of linking individual performance with the performance of the organization overall.

Williams (1998) conceptualizes performance management in three ways, as:

- a system for managing organizational performance;
- a system for managing employee performance; and
- a system for integrating the management of organizational and individual performance.

The first system is often based on a mission statement which sets out the purpose and the values of the organization; corporate plans which state the goals and aims of the organization; business plans which set out specific action plans, budgets and targets and standards of performance; and the monitoring and review process.

The second, a system for managing individual/employee performance, involves planning and setting down individual performance targets, behaviours and criteria for measurement of their performance; monitoring and appraising that performance; rewarding or sanctioning the performance and determining future development and/or re-planning.

The third system is based on the assumption that there is a compatibility and complementarity between organizational objectives and individual objectives and that they are planned accordingly. Ideally, when they are integrated, the maximum performance can be achieved because Human Resource Management (HRM) will be both vertically and horizontally integrated with the business plan and overall strategy of the organization.

Williams' first system focuses on vertical integration and translating the goals and objectives of strategic management into business targets and, in turn, into individual performance, cascading down through the organization. It is aimed at achieving optimum results through the most effective arrangement of work and is a system for directing, controlling, and monitoring human resources. His second system describes an approach to raising

Table 6.1 ***Performance management system***

Planning	Managing	Appraising
Establishing performance objectives and targets	Monitoring performance and results	Reviewing and recording results
Identifying job behaviours	Adjusting goals and objectives as necessary	Formally appraising staff
Providing direction	Reinforcing behaviours and objectives through rewards	Focusing on the future and employee development
	Re-directing inappropriate behaviour	
	Providing control	

performance standards and managing people, which aims also at horizontal integration. These two approaches to performance management might be said to reflect what are called 'hard' and 'soft' HRM respectively (see Chapter 8). Nevertheless, both are based upon the idea of a system of interrelated and inter-connected parts, which are shown in Table 6.1, and which, when integrated, offer a sophisticated approach to performance management and match Williams' third system.

Armstrong offers a nice summary:

> Performance Management is about getting better results from the organization, teams and individuals by understanding and managing performance within an agreed framework of planned goals, standards and competence requirements. It is a process for establishing shared understanding about what is to be achieved and an approach to managing and developing people in a way which increases the probability that it will be achieved in the short and long term. (1994: 429)

Performance measurement

Performance measurement is also multifaceted. Basically it is a tool with which to measure how successful an individual or organization has been in achieving its objectives or its intended performance. There are several concepts which are central to performance measurement. *Performance indicators* are variables that enable us to see how near we are to achieving our objectives; *performance standards* provide a benchmark against which an organization and individuals can be measured and a *benchmark* is a standard or point of comparison.

Benchmarking is the process of comparing one organization's performance against others in an attempt to discover 'best practice', which can be imported to improve operations (Keehley and Abercrombie 2008) and it is a way of seeking excellence through a systematic comparison of performance measures with reference standards (Cunha Marques and De Witte 2010)

There are several types of performance indicators, some of which are shown in Box 6.1.

Since the 1980s, all governments have placed great emphasis on the traditional 3Es of performance: economy, efficiency and effectiveness, but these are not the only Es which are considered important in assessing the performance of an organization (Box 6.2).

Performance indicators (PIs), therefore, are any financial or non-financial metrics used to help organizations define and measure progress towards organizational goals. Although some PIs were used in the 1970s and 1980s in the NHS, they began to be used more widely after the FMI in 1982, and the introduction of performance management (Carter and Klein 1992). Performance standards, which facilitate the measurement of performance and the identification of performance gaps, also appeared in the 1980s. A minimum standard is the performance that must be met but standards may be aspirational, normative or comparative. Where the comparative method is used, as in benchmarking, 'it requires a high degree of comparability between the organizations to be compared – otherwise the comparisons are likely to be regarded as unfair (especially by those who appear in a bad light)' (Bouckaert and Van Dooren 2009: 156).

In summary therefore:

> The central idea behind performance measurement is a simple one – a public organization formulates its envisaged performance and indicates how its performance may be measured by defining performance indicators. After the organization has performed its efforts it may be shown whether the envisaged performance was achieved and what the cost of it was. (De Bruijn 2002: 7)

BOX 6.1 A typology of performance indicators

Input indicators: number of pupils, number of job seekers, number of hospital beds, miles of track;
Output indictors: passes at GCSE, number of jobs filled, numbers of patients treated, rail passenger mileage;
Intermediate outcome indicators: numbers continuing in education, changes in unemployment rate, number of recovered patients, change in use of rail travel;
End outcome indicators: numbers obtaining new skills, increase in GNP, increase in health, change in greenhouse gas emissions;
Societal/environmental indicators: higher percentage of population with higher education, rising standard of living, changes in life expectancy; cleaner, more sustainable society.

BOX 6.2 Definitions of the Es

Economy is concerned with inputs and ensuring they are obtained at the lowest cost and that outputs are also produced at the lowest cost.

Efficiency is the ratio between inputs and outputs. To increase efficiency means reducing the ratio between inputs and outputs. An average cost may be identified for example for processing an application for disability allowance. Offices where the average cost is above that level will be deemed inefficient and those where it is below that average will be classed as efficient (*ceteris paribus* – other things being equal).

Effectiveness is concerned with impact and it is possible for an organization to be both inefficient and uneconomical but yet be effective. For example, a hospital may have an above average unit cost for undertaking an operation and a below average bed occupancy rate but its patients do not return to hospital and are released in a good state of health,

Ethics is concerned with the standards of behaviour of public officials and the values that guide their performance,

Equity is concerned with fairness and ensuring that the circumstances of an individual are taken into account when decisions are taken. Treating people equally does not necessarily produce a fair outcome,

Ecology: economic costs do not necessarily consider the impact on the environment and the long-term effect on society. Environmental impact should be incorporated into assessment of efficiency and effectiveness.

Empathy incorporates an understanding of the impact that decisions have on individuals and groups both psychologically and emotionally.

League tables enable individual organizational performance to be compared with that of other similar organizations. They inform individual organizations how they are doing compared to their competitors, while the government and the public can also see how well a particular school, health care trust, university or local authority is performing or not. *Time trends* are another form of performance indicator as it enables this year's performance to be compared with previous years to see whether there has been an improvement or deterioration in performance.

Since the 1990s, governments have used targets to drive up the performance of public organizations and to provide a tool by which they can control, monitor and compare performance against standards. Target setting means that organizations have to be explicit about their aims and objectives and what they want to achieve over a specific period of time. For example, targets might be a reduction in the waiting time for an operation over the next year; an increase in the number of visits made by a district nurse each week; the number of children obtaining five GCSEs at grade C or above year on year. Targets can also be cost and economy targets, efficiency targets or quality targets; for example, to make a 5 per cent efficiency saving or to increase the number of very satisfied patients by 20 per cent.

Advantages of performance measurement and PIs

Performance measurement and PIs have a wide variety of objectives including encouraging efficient use of scarce resources, informing managers of areas of weakness, influencing resource allocation and in many organizations, including the NHS and the civil service, serving as a basis for performance related pay (PRP). Hood (2007) points out that PIs can be used for 'targets', 'ranking' or 'intelligence'. There are also a number of wider functions that PIs can perform including making organizations more transparent and strengthening their accountability (see Box 6.3).

Problems with performance indicators

There are as many critics of performance measurement as there are advocates (De Bruijn 2002; Johnsen 2005; Heath and Radcliffe 2007). First, it is argued, performance measurement is predicated on the assumption that a public organization has a 'product' that can be measured. In reality, public organizations may have multiple products, multiple stakeholders and also multiple values, sometimes in conflict with each other. Therefore, it is possible that

BOX 6.3 Functions of performance measurement and performance indicators

- *Transparency*: enabling members of the public to see how organizations are performing and facilitating more informed choices, for example, choice of school, university, hospital.
- *Control*: more information enables managers and politicians to improve the quality of their policies and their decision making.
- *Managers* can use measurement to judge and improve their own performance as well as the performance of their staff.
- *Accountability*: pinpoints responsibility and provides information about public expenditure, what is being spent on what and how efficiently that money is being spent.
- *Enables learning* to take place – organizations can learn what they are doing well and where improvements are needed.
- *It facilitates improvements in staff appraisal* where performance targets are set down.
- *Enables inspectorates* to concentrate on those organizations appearing to be under-performing.
- *Performance measurement* is an incentive to innovation because the comparison with other organizations encourages the search for improvement and comparative advantage.

improved performance in one aspect may be at the cost of reduced performance in others. Public agencies are also often responsible for difficult, insoluble problems and have no control over how they respond because it may be legally prescribed. They cannot choose to whom they deliver a service nor can they respond to demand with variable supply because of lack of control over resources. There is, therefore, a tendency to go for things that can be easily quantified and to ignore things that cannot, even though they may be important to the performance of an organization. As Flynn points out: 'If managers have little discretion in the choice and arrangements of inputs, any judgement on their performance is in practice a judgement only of how well they manage a given set of people and equipment' (2007: 137). However, where the managers are determining their own performance criteria, they are likely to go for the easily achievable targets and not the challenging ones.

Second, many public organizations are highly process oriented especially those involved in policy making and negotiation. Outcomes here are very difficult to predict and also there may be disappointing outcomes although the process may be good. Third, in all comparisons, such as league tables, organizations do not start from the same base. For example, school intake is a major factor in explaining deviations in performance of children at SATs and GCSE. This issue was eventually acknowledged by the government when it introduced the idea of value added but not until many schools had been 'named and shamed'. League tables also tend to focus only on the targets to be achieved to the detriment of other aspects of performance. Fourth, once a measurement becomes an instrument of policy then it actually ceases to tell you what you want to know because people act to ensure the target is reached. This is referred to as 'gaming'. There are many examples of this happening – such as shortening waiting lists by not referring patients to hospital; schools not accepting applicants with low SATs grades to maintain high pass rates at GCSEs.

Fifth, another problem is that targets come to dominate activity and adversely affect other aspects of the service. Here, accountability becomes reduced to meeting pre-stated PIs and this skews the priorities of staff and the organization; for example, targets for recruiting students may lead to a lowering of entry requirements while targets for retention may lead to lowering of acceptable standards of performance often referred to as 'debasing the coinage' or 'grade inflation'. Also with targets there is a tendency to short-termism, especially where managers are on short-term contracts and PRP. The PIs become more important than what they are measuring.

Finally, the quality of public performance is very difficult to assess and to measure and therefore it is down-graded and pushed out by the emphasis on quantity. Perhaps the most fundamental criticism is that as PIs become more sophisticated it becomes an 'expert system' and an industry emerges and an 'insider' group of experts displaces the politicians and the public, who become outsiders with less influence or control. Research embarked on by

Pollitt and colleagues in 2004 on performance indicators in the NHS found that they did result in improved performance in the first instance, but they then began to dominate activities and priorities and their relevance and reliability are now continually challenged. The creation of more and better PIs did not increase transparency or greater public trust in the services provided and, if anything, it has led to loss of confidence in the NHS. It has also produced an insider group, familiar with increasingly sophisticated PIs, and an outsider group, with politicians often in the latter. PIs now constitute an expert system (Pollitt *et al.* 2010).

These criticisms of PIs have led to a great deal of thought, research and refinements of performance indicators and performance measurement systems, which are examined below.

Quality management

Quality is another concept which has no universal definition. There are a number of general definitions such as 'worth' or 'goodness' of something and there are also specific definitions which originate from the writings of the quality gurus. Quality is 'fitness for purpose or use' (Juran 1951), 'conformance to requirements' (Crosby 1979), 'a predictable degree of uniformity and dependability at low cost and suited to the market' (Deming 1982).

The person credited with starting the quality movement is Dr W. Edward Deming, an American statistician, who recognized that greater efficiency in industry could be achieved by eliminating faults and poor quality. His ideas were not popular in America in the 1950s and so he took them to Japan. Some 20 years later the success of Japanese industry attracted the interests of Western businessmen who saw a commitment to continually raising the quality of what was produced in Japanese organizations as the key to their success.

The idea of TQM took hold first in the private sector, where it was recognized that unless you meet customer expectations and produce goods that do what you say they will do and are reliable, you will not be competitive. So the original focus was on ensuring that manufactured goods were fit for purpose, conformed to requirements, were reliable and represented value for money. Deming had pointed out that poor quality was very costly and Crosby (1979) identified these costs in terms of wasted materials, replacements, dealing with complaints and dissatisfied customers and argued that the performance standard in any activity should be 'zero defects' or 'right first time'. But Peters and Waterman (1982) argued you need to continually improve the product and 'delight' your customers not just satisfy them in order to keep them.

It is obvious that defects can arise at any point in the production process so it must be TQM. TOTAL because it involves everybody, every activity and every process within an organization; QUALITY because it meets customers' needs and is fit for purpose and MANAGEMENT, which designs and controls the quality processes and systems to ensure the desired results and outcomes. TQM is actually a management philosophy and approach and not a narrow concept of product or service quality. TQM is:

> a cost effective system for integrating the continuous quality improvement efforts of people at all levels in an organization to deliver products and services which ensure customer satisfaction. (Collard 1989)

> a strategy for improving business performance through the commitment and involvement of all employees to fully satisfy agreed customer requirements at the optimum overall cost, through the continuous improvement of the products and services, business processes and people involved. (Institute of Management Services 1992)

There was initial scepticism about the relevance of TQM to the public sector because it provides services which are very different from goods. Services are intangible performances and cannot be stored, counted or measured. They are also heterogeneous and provided to individuals with different needs and priorities. Finally, it is impossible to separate production and consumption as they occur simultaneously. Services, therefore, are happenings, deeds or efforts and consumers are an inherent element of the service. Whilst you can test the quality of a product at the end of the production cycle before distribution you cannot do that with a service. It was also argued that TQM was not appropriate if there was no market and people could not choose or control quality by their purchasing actions (Morgan and Murgatroyd 1994 Bovaird and Löffler 2009b).

There was also the problem of deciding how the quality of a service could be determined. If the customer is the judge of quality then what do they look for in the service and what preferences make up the components of quality in a service? Customers may have different priorities in terms of their idea of quality, which makes it difficult to set a standard. Criteria that customers may apply in judging quality include reliability; responsiveness; easy access; the competence of staff; good communication and courtesy; understanding and knowing the client, the overall appearance of the staff and the general environment of the organization.

Work in the USA by Donabedian (1980), acknowledged as an international guru of quality in health care, identified three components in evaluating a quality health service, which are interpersonal, technical and professional, and environmental and amenities components. The first refers to the relationships between the patient and the medical and nursing staff; the second to the perceived skill and competence of those staff; and the third to the amenities and general environment. These three components are all important aspects of quality – the technical care links directly to the ability to achieve cure or care of the patient; interpersonal relations are a key to the patient/medical practitioner component, but could also include other relationships with clerical, administrative or support staff. Finally, the quality of amenities is very important and includes convenience, comfort and the environment, such as single room or a clean and bright ward and good food. Donabedian went on to produce a model of quality care based on three further inter-connected variables – structure, process and outcomes – generally referred to as the Donabedian triad (Donabedian 1988) and his work continues to inspire international research into quality systems (Kunkel *et al.* 2007).

Government policy and practice in performance and quality management

Conservative governments 1979–97

During the 1980s, government was preoccupied with increasing efficiency, eliminating waste, improving performance and managerializing public services. During the 1990s, it turned its attention more to standards of performance, the quality of public services and engendering a customer orientation. A paradox of decentralization and centralization was a major feature of the 1980s. In response to the financial crisis, in part created and in part inherited by Conservative Governments, performance management was seen as a tool to make all organizations review what they were doing and why, and whether they could do things more efficiently. The FMI resulted in all departments reviewing their activities and their programmes and linking budgets to each programme with managers responsible and accountable for performance. There was a move from input to output budgeting. Starting in core government departments, it spread to the new agencies created after 1988 with their policy frameworks and negotiated targets. It also spread to education after the 1988 Education Reform Act and to colleges and polytechnics after 1992. By the 1990s, all public bodies were required to adopt a rational approach to management and the wider availability of information technology meant that more complex information systems could be constructed upon which performance management systems depend.

Paradoxically, the more decentralized the system became the more governments found a need for centralization to ensure that government policies were being implemented. The use of centrally determined PIs directed the priorities of public services and the requirement to make information on results available enabled central government to see what was being achieved. The use of an army of regulators and inspectorates enabled government again to monitor performance and enforce its policies. And to ensure that hospitals and schools and local authorities responded, central government used carrots and sticks, or incentives and penalties, to encourage conformity. The creation of the Audit Commission in 1983 was the first of a family of regulatory bodies to enhance the control of the centre (see Chapter 9), and during the 1980s it produced a multitude of comparative statistics on performance on housing and local authorities.

The Citizen's Charter and Market Testing

In 1991, Prime Minister John Major published the Citizen's Charter (Cabinet Office 1991a), and quality entered the government's agenda in a more explicit and personalized way through imposing performance standards. The main theme of the Charter was a commitment to responsive and high quality services, and privatization and competition were seen as one means of achieving this. But where that was not possible, Charter standards were set down for each part of the public sector and publicized so that external bodies and individual consumers, patients or users of the services could judge performance against these expectations. Charters applied to all services including the NHS, local government, nationalized industries, the police and the courts and they were implemented in the hospitals, schools, police stations and tax offices. The Charter also signalled a new emphasis on consumers and users of public services who were expected to be involved.

The Citizens Charter identified six principles of public service:

- explicit performance standards should be set down;
- information on the purpose, costs and performance of the service should be made explicit;
- there should be provision of choice wherever possible;
- consultation with users;
- courtesy at all time;
- effective remedies if things should go wrong.

All public services were also required to demonstrate VfM (Cabinet Office 1991b). In 1997 more standards were added, requiring targets to be set for:

- answering letters;
- operating a help-line;
- consulting users on a regular basis;
- operating a redress system;
- catering for the needs of all people including those with special needs.

In 1996 a review of the charter policy (Cabinet Office 1996) claimed it was intended to raise standards of quality and to act in lieu of markets and that it had done so. It claimed that there was a new culture in which citizens, users and consumers of services came first, which was bringing about constantly rising quality standards. There was some evidence of change but the rhetoric far exceeded the reality. By 1997, there were over 40 charters for ministries and over 10,000 charters issued by local authorities and other public bodies (Bovaird and Löffler 2009b: 170). There was also extensive use of customer or user surveys to assess levels of satisfaction; the spread of PIs related to quality issues; and greater use of league tables. There was far less evidence, however, to support the claim that citizens now came first or that the quality of public services was generally better.

Accompanying the Citizen's Charter in 1991 was the White Paper *Competing for Quality* (HM Treasury 1991). This was complementary to the Charter with its commitment to increasing choice and standards through privatization and contracting. The introduction of compulsory competitive tendering (CCT) in 1980, followed by the market-testing programme in 1991 and the use of internal markets within public organizations, had all rendered the old arguments against TQM in the public sector redundant.

CCT was first enforced upon local authorities in 1980 but only in their Direct Labour Departments. It was encouraged in such services as catering, cleaning and security in the civil service and the NHS but was not compulsory. The *Competing for Quality* White Paper, however, set out proposals for central government, the NHS and local authorities to extend their market testing. The emphasis moved from searching for efficiency savings to competing for quality. Government departments were told to introduce more competition and choice into the provision of services, especially their non-core ones, and were mandated to improve the quality and standards of service provision to citizens. Health Authorities and NHS Trusts were required to report annually on their plans and progress in market testing and new guidelines for local authorities were laid down.

Government departments had been required to examine their activities using a process called Prior Options since 1988. This was initially to determine whether to set up executive agencies. It involved identifying in sequence whether the activity was still needed, and if so did the government need to do it? (If not, privatize.) If government needed to do it did public officials need to do it? (If not, contract out.) If public officials needed to do it did ministers need to be involved on a day-to-day basis – if not agencify – and if yes, keep in the core department. Market testing was not the same as contracting out but it could lead to it. Market testing, or perhaps more accurately, testing the market, was at first a rigorous comparison between the cost of doing something 'in house' and what it would cost a private company to do it. The government set down clear guidelines on market testing and the criteria to be applied in evaluating the bids (see Bendell *et al.* 1994: 170–82). The government also later set down financial targets for market testing although they were rarely met and were soon abandoned. The Civil Service White Paper *Continuity and Change* (Cabinet Office 1994) delegated decisions about whether to market test or not to departments without drawing attention to the change. However, by the late 1990s a culture of market testing had been embedded.

The last innovation of the Conservative Government in 1996, in this field, was the introduction of a benchmarking exercise. Anxious to keep up the pressure on departments and their executive agencies to seek continual improvements in service delivery, the government required agencies to identify and adopt best practice whether from the public or private sector. A pilot study was undertaken involving 30 agencies, using the European Business Excellence model (BEM). BEM was developed by the European Foundation for Quality Management (EFQM) and used extensively in the private sector. It was a system whereby an organization examined all its internal processes to assess its performance against other organizations using the same model. A further project began in 1997 involving 45 departmental executive agencies and non-departmental public bodies (NDPBs, see Chapter 3). A Cabinet Office report (Samuels 1998) summarized the benefits of using BEM and demonstrated the relatively high performance of the public agencies. By the end of the 1990s, BEM was widely used in central and local government, the NHS and other public bodies. The results of the self assessments were collated by the Civil Service College and a data base known as BENchmark was established. The UK became an international leader in using the BEM model in the public sector, although there were critics of its suitability (Talbot 1999) and alternative models have since been developed. These include the Common Assessment Framework (CAF) favoured by the European Commission and the Public Service Excellence Model developed by Colin Talbot (1999). Neither of these models has been used as widely in the UK as BEM (later renamed the EFQM Excellence model), although CAF is extensively used at all levels of government in other EU member states. By the end of the 1990s, quality was a mainstream issue in the UK public sector and the philosophy of TQM had been widely accepted. New ideas and models were being developed, however, and many public organizations were becoming interested in the Balanced Scorecard (see below).

New Labour 1997–2010

After 18 years of Conservative Governments and a landslide victory for New Labour in the 1997 election, there were high expectations of radical changes. However, apart from some significant constitutional changes in the first couple of years, there was a great deal of continuity especially in the management of the public sector. Labour emphasized its commitment to promoting quality, efficiency and responsiveness in all public services but with a greater emphasis on increasing citizen participation and accountability to service users. The Citizen's Charter was re-launched as *Service First – The New Charter Programme* (Cabinet Office 1998a), which included extensive guidance to public services on how to draw up national and local charters, how to conduct participation exercises and how to deal with complaints. The government also created a national focus group of some 5,000 people – The People's Panel – which was to be used by government departments, agencies and other public organizations to find out people's views on a whole range of service delivery issues. Many government departments and local authorities created customer care departments and ran their own customer services initiatives and a number of consortia was established and led by the Cabinet Office.

The Labour government was elected on a platform of modernization, which, as Newman (2001) points out, was little more than a metaphor for change. The changes were set out first in the White Paper *Modern Public Services for Britain: Investing in Reform* (HM Treasury 1998) and then in the White Paper *Modernising Government* (Cabinet Office 1999a). In fact the changes were largely more of the same, as the government did not abandon the idea of the mixed economy of welfare, although they gave more importance to the third sector. They did abandon CCT but replaced it with Best Value. Far from increasing decentralization, which was in their manifesto, they introduced more regulation and central control, albeit to raise standards. The ideas of better government as securing more efficiency, best value, better quality and greater responsiveness to the public were not new, however, as they were the aims of the previous Conservative Government. The publication of *Better Quality Services* (Cabinet Office 1998b) simply provided new guidelines for departments and agencies on reviewing services and creating partnerships but the government resolved to increase performance through setting down clear objectives and targets for public organizations, including local authorities, schools, police forces as well as departments and agencies, to achieve. This was a particular type of partnership akin to a principal–agent relationship. By setting clear performance objectives and targets, the government aimed to mobilize the public services to focus on performance and outputs. They used benchmarking as a means of identifying relative performance and examples of good practice and it was anticipated that performance and standards would rise. By centralizing control and reforming the centre of government (see Chapter 5), the fragmentation of services from the customers' perspective would be overcome through central coordination and, later, partnership working at the local level. This, however, took time as it needed structural reform, not only in the centre but of local government management and the NHS before new forms of strategic partnerships could emerge. These were to come after the second Labour election victory in 2001.

After 2001, Labour concentrated on finding ways to bridge the implementation gap between policy and practice (see Chapter 5), increasing the transparency and accountability of public services and their responsiveness to rising public expectations. During its first administration, Labour had been quite cautious. For example, it chose to experiment with its Best Value strategy by introducing it into local government as a pilot in 1997. It only became a statutory duty in 2000 (DETR 1998a). Best Value was a means of changing the culture of local authorities to one committed to continuous improvement and development in performance and efficiency; and also receptive to more radical changes in future (see Box 6.4).

BOX 6.4 Best Value framework in local government

All local authority services had to be fundamentally reviewed at least once every five years. Clear performance targets were to be set down in Local Performance Plans which would be the basis for regular audits by the Audit Commission and a new Best Value Inspectorate.

Every review had to apply the so called 4Cs methodology:

- Challenge the need for the service and how it was delivered.
- Consult with all relevant stakeholders.
- Compare the performance of the service against other providers.
- Compete – test the competitiveness of the service.

Every local authority had to compare its services with other local authorities against the 'best value performance indicators' of which there were over 100 in every local authority, and more in some types of council. They ranged from input indicators through to output and outcome indicators and from efficiency to quality. There was a mixture of national and locally determined indicators all designed to raise standards and over a five-year period. Local authorities receiving excellent status in particular services would be rewarded with Beacon status while those with unsatisfactory status would be sanctioned and in extreme cases the service could be removed from LA control.

There was some contradiction in the policies and strategies being pursued by the Labour Government. The rhetoric was that of decentralization, participation and local responsiveness but in the major services of education, health and policing the modernization was centrally driven and top down. The call for joined-up government and partnership working was frustrated by the vertical directive style of central government departments. This was part of the explanation of the government's failure to deliver (Barber 2007) and the use of more sophisticated models of Best Value (in local government) and the Excellence model meant that agencies were being continually assessed. There was clearly more accountability as current overall performance and the reasons for the level achieved were being identified and areas for improvement were targeted. There was also the development of good practices, which were copied (Massey 1999). However, there was increasing evidence of some of the traps of performance management and measurement identified above (Bovaird and Löffler 2009b: 159).

Throughout 13 years in office, Labour governments led from the front and adopted a very top-down approach to raising quality standards in public services. As we have seen in Chapter 5, from 1998 they used PSAs to lay down standards and targets not only for government departments and agencies but also for local government, the police, the NHS and most other public bodies. In addition they required all public organizations to seek 'Investors in People' status (see Chapter 8) and encouraged the use of the Business Excellence

Quality Framework to assess and benchmark performance. Many organizations, however, started using the Balanced Scorecard framework (Kaplan and Norton 1996) which acknowledges that performance reporting is multi-faceted and that there are multiple stakeholders whose perspectives of performance and quality are likely to vary.

The Balanced Scorecard is a performance measurement framework that adds strategic non-financial performance measures to traditional financial metrics to give a more 'balanced' view of organizational performance. It involves four perspectives: 'Learning and Growth', which includes employee capabilities and competencies, training, corporate self-improvement and learning; and the 'Internal Business Process' perspective, which focuses on the values that drive the business, the support processes that deliver those values and the processes which seek to maintain good relationships with all stakeholders. Metrics based on this perspective allow managers to know how well the business is doing, and whether its products and services conform to customer requirements. The third perspective is the 'Customer Perspective' which relates to customer satisfaction; and the fourth is the 'Financial Perspective – accurate financial data remains a priority, but the traditional emphasis on finance leads to an 'unbalanced' assessment with regard to other perspectives.

The Kaplan and Norton framework can be used to show a logical, step-by-step connection between strategic objectives and value added in the form of a cause-and-effect chain. Improving performance in the objectives found in the Learning and Growth perspective enables the organization to improve its Internal Business Process objectives which, in turn, enables the organization to create desirable results in the Customer and Financial perspectives. The Balanced Scorecard is being adapted and increasingly used throughout the public sector.

Individual performance management

Individual performance is a critical element in the performance management system but individual appraisal is one of the most controversial management activities. Some form of staff appraisal has existed since organizations emerged and has been the basis of selection of staff for appointment, promotion, reward or dismissal. It was very ad hoc, however, and managers undertook appraisal on the basis of observation and subjective judgement without any participation by staff. Today appraisal is widespread for managerial, administrative, technical and professional staffs although less frequently used for manual workers.

Types of staff appraisal

There are many types of staff appraisal and they can be classified in terms of purpose and procedure. In terms of purpose, the three classic types are development, performance and reward appraisals. Randall (1974) argued that these different types of appraisal should remain separate and should be conducted at different times and, in some cases, by different people. Development appraisals he suggested should be conducted by personnel or human resources (HR) specialists while performance and reward appraisals should be carried out by line managers but at different times. This is still the practice in some public organizations but not where there is performance related pay.

In terms of procedures Fletcher (2001; 2002) points out that traditionally, in the public sector, line managers appraised staff and produced narrative reports that remained confidential. Staffs were rarely involved or interviewed and the outcome was a totally subjective management assessment used mainly for decisions on promotion. Gradually appraisals developed as an informal part of the 'natural process of management' (Fowler 1990) with meetings taking place between managers and staff to discuss their work. During the 1960s, joint appraisals with agreed procedures and reports, countersigned by both parties, became common. In the last 30 years, however, more advanced forms of appraisal have been used including: results oriented appraisals; appraisal centres; trait and competency rating forms; electronic self and manager administered assessment; peer assessment and 360-degree appraisals. All these types of appraisal can be found throughout the public sector and also internationally with 360-degree appraisals and electronically recorded appraisals increasing in popularity (see Box 6.5).

There are two main approaches to appraisals: those oriented towards results (outputs) and those oriented towards competencies (inputs) (Rees and Lowman 2009). Results oriented appraisals are based upon quantifiable objectives most often in a participatory process involving a line manager and a subordinate and are geared towards achieving organizational objectives. Competency appraisals, in contrast, are geared towards assessment of individuals' demonstrated skills and behaviours thought to be associated with high performance. In the UK, there has been a trend towards combining both results and competencies in an attempt to achieve results but also to support the development of staffs and ensure they have the capabilities to meet the needs of ever changing public organizations. Another trend, however, is to decouple the link between performance and rewards and increase the emphasis on development, skills and competencies.

Appraisals are an essential element of performance management and also of quality management and they can benefit individuals, managers and the organization by virtue of the information they generate. Depending on the type of appraisal, individuals can gain from the opportunity to discuss their jobs and the demands made upon them, their training and development needs and ways of meeting them, and career development as well as their performance. They will have a better understanding of what is expected of them by the organization and their managers and there will be recognition of their

BOX 6.5 Types of staff appraisal

Top-down

The line manager conducts the appraisal and produces a written report that is entered into the employee's file. The appraisee does not see the report and has little opportunity to influence its content.

Joint appraisal

Here the appraiser and the appraisee are both involved in setting the agenda for the appraisal meeting and agreeing the outcome. In the event that there is disagreement over the final report the matter will be referred to the 'grandfather' – the line manager's line manager for resolution.

Self appraisal

This is sometimes incorporated informally into the top-down schemes as a mechanism for encouraging openness and employee self-reflection. It enables the employee to participate in the appraisal process by influencing the agenda to be discussed and is a normal part of the joint appraisal.

Peer appraisal

This version involves peers and colleagues in the assessment of performance. It can be done by interviewing all relevant people, which is time consuming. It is more often done by use of questionnaires or open discussion forums. The latter is most appropriate where organizations are structured in teams

Upward appraisal

This approach involves inviting the views of those who report to a manager or are affected by a person's performance, such as pupils and teachers and students and lecturers. The questionnaire usually relates to managerial style and effectiveness and in the case of student feedback to the goals and objectives set for the course. Views and comments are often not individually identified. The results of the appraisal can provide a forum for discussion within the group or the department and may encourage a problem-solving approach to management or staff development. Upward appraisal is often perceived as threatening by those being appraised and as 'uncomfortable' by subordinate appraisers especially if they are not anonymous.

360-degree appraisal

This multi-dimensional approach includes peers, subordinates, external 'customers' and the manager. The aim is to achieve a rounded perspective of the individual's performance. It can dilute subjectivity and open the way for a more balanced view of the range of activities to be assessed. This option is increasingly used in the public sector and is now a standard element of the performance management system in the higher levels of the British Senior Civil Service.

achievement or feedback on how they are expected to improve. Appraisals can also result in support in facing problems and difficulties.

Appraisals benefit managers as they provide information about the work process and the problems that their staffs are facing. These can be discussed and solutions sought. They can also inform the manager how successfully or not personnel policies and procedures are working, how satisfied staffs are in their jobs and how motivated or de-motivated they are. Managers can discover training needs and staff expectations as well as evaluating performance to determine rewards and to spot talent. The benefits to the organization are that appraisals provide information and are a form of audit in discovering skills shortages and development needs, identifying talent, constructing succession plans and pipeline development and ensuring that the goals and objectives of the organization are transmitted to their staff.

Staff appraisal is therefore a multi-faceted versatile process which can be geared to measurement of performance and linked to pay; used to foster integration and participation of staff in decision making about their training and development and work practices, and a key to ensuring total quality management. It is also a means of integrating staff into contributing to the goals of the department and the organization and embracing the changes in culture and direction that top management has planned. Some see it as a system of managerial control or manipulation, others as a form of staff empowerment. It is today an integrated part of performance management systems and of the reward process where PRP has been adopted. Further, it is a means of identifying training and development needs, management succession planning and career development and is an integral part of Human Resource Development (HRD) systems and Organizational Development (OD) processes.

Criticisms of staff appraisal systems

Staff appraisal does not always achieve the benefits described above and there are many problems associated with it which are at the root of much criticism. These include:

- confusion as to the purpose of appraisals – performance assessment or staff development;
- difficulty in setting objectives;
- lack of confidence in the objectivity of the appraiser especially where they are rating staff and rewards are linked to that rating;
- difficulties in rating staff and differentiating between levels of performance;
- the reluctance of managers to make judgements and to demonstrate a 'central tendency';
- the fact that staff appraisals are very time consuming and therefore costly;
- the difficulty in dealing with poor performance;
- the lack of action or follow up after an appraisal;
- the fact that appraisals are often rituals and therefore not taken seriously.

These criticisms attract responses, and reforms and renewal of staff appraisal systems are continuous. Today, satisfaction surveys of staff appraisal systems, as well as commissioned research, tell us about the range of systems in practice as well as some good practice which can assist organizations and countries in developing their staff appraisal and performance management system (Demmke 2007). The SCS performance appraisal system does appear to have overcome many of the problems identified above and has been cited as an example of good practice (Horton 2011).

Rewarding performance

A system of performance management designed to improve and sustain high performance is inevitably linked to rewards. Expectancy theory suggests these rewards must be extrinsic and valued by the employee (Vroom 1964). On the other hand, goal-setting theory places more stress on the need for acceptance of the organizational goals *per se,* so that rewards are more intrinsic (Locke 1968). For the reasons identified above, in many organizations the formal appraisal process is kept separate from the rewards process because the linkage with pay inhibits employees from being self-reflective and open about training needs or problems they are experiencing with their work. It also interferes with the development objectives of the appraisal process. In practice, however, it is difficult to divorce the formal appraisal process from pay and reward decisions and in the civil service, and many other parts of the public sector in the UK, they are inextricably linked as PRP is used.

Reward

Central to HRM philosophy is that rewards are an integral part of HR strategy to obtain commitment, quality, performance and achievement of organizational goals and objectives. Rewards are seen as a means of changing or reinforcing the organizational culture. The aims of reward systems are:

- to attract and retain staff;
- reward performance;
- motivate people;
- reinforce the organizational culture.

When employees join an organization they enter into a contract, which is partly legal and definite and partly psychological and unwritten. Employees have expectations about the rewards they will receive, which will include money, status, social benefits as well as psychological ones. The employer will also have expectations about effort/performance, attitudes, commitment, remuneration and compensation. It is important that these expectations are met on both sides or people will leave, be de-motivated, and productivity will be low.

Performance Related Pay

Traditional reward systems in the public sector have been based on salary scales related to grade (see Chapter 8). In the 1980s, public employers that wanted to create a performance management culture and were committed to the NPM reforms (in central government, the NHS and some Conservative controlled local authorities) introduced PRP for senior managers (Farnham 1993: 111–12). PRP was extended to the whole of the civil service after 1998 and also to education and other public services. PRP refers to the variable part of pay awarded and it may be awarded to an individual, a team or an organization. It is currently being adopted widely in public services throughout the OECD. The reasons why governments have turned to PRP are listed in an OECD Policy Brief (OECD 2005b) as:

- fostering individual motivation by recognizing effort and achievement and rewarding it;
- to compete effectively with the private sector for the most able and talented employees;
- a way of containing salary costs by reducing automatic progression through salary levels or alternatively as a way of lifting salary ceilings with non-consolidated financial reward;
- PRP enables transparency about public salaries and demonstrates their link to performance.

Although there has been a trend towards the use of PRP there are wide variations amongst the different parts of the public sector and about what is rewarded. This depends on whether the performance appraisal is based on outputs and achievement of targets, interpersonal and management skills, improvement in competencies or on values, disciplines and inputs. A new trend is a movement away from individual PRP systems to more collective approaches with PRP linked to teams and/or departments (Landel 2004).

One of the major differences amongst PRP systems is whether payment is in the form of a bonus, which is unconsolidated and has to be earned each year, or whether it is a merit payment and incorporated in the basic salary. The former tends to be the most common. The size of the merit or bonus payment is generally quite small and no more than 10 per cent of base salary. Although PRP is used throughout the civil service and amongst senior staff in the NHS, in some local authorities and universities there are difficulties in operating it. As we have seen above, there are problems stemming from monitoring and measuring staff performance through the staff appraisals. In the SCS there is a sophisticated and highly formalized rating system but this too has invited criticisms. In particular there is the difficulty in distinguishing average performance from good and good from excellent, no matter how complex the criteria may be. There is also a tendency for people to be rated only as very satisfactory even when they have achieved all the objectives set for them, or to be rated as satisfactory even though they have not performed that well. This is referred to as the 'central tendency'. The explanation is partly because line managers do not want to face the consequences of disillusioned or disaffected staff or because they do not have the skills or the tools to make finer distinctions. The response to this difficulty has been to use simpler rating systems and to force a distribution between good, satisfactory and bad – a three-point scale rather than a five-, seven- or ten-point scale, which was used before and still is, in some cases.

Other problems of PRP relate to its implementation. There is resistance from trade unions, staff and also middle managers. There is also inadequate funding of PRP, which means that the bonuses are small while the transaction costs are high, especially in terms of time because of the work needed to be done to implement PRP and not least because of the lack of preparation by line managers.

Performance, as stated above, is in fact a multi-dimensional construct, which involves behaviours as well as results. It is also affected by a number of factors all of which need to be taken into account when managing, measuring and rewarding performance. These include personal factors (skill, confidence, commitment, motivation); leadership factors (the type of encouragement, guidance and support given by the line manager or team leader); team factors (support or not of colleagues); system factors (facilities, equipment, and so on) and contextual factors such as internal/external environmental pressures. It is important, therefore, to decide what is being assessed: performance outcomes or behaviours or both, and whether the focus is only on the personal factors or whether the above contextual factors are to be taken into consideration.

Setting individual objectives and goals is difficult as they must not be too easy or too hard and they must also be linked to the organizational or departmental goals. It certainly relies on effective management and a relationship of trust between managers and employees if the system is to have the positive effects which are claimed for it. The opposite effects can be de-motivation, alienation, stress and emotional burn-out (Brown and Benson 2003). Even where the difficulties appear to be overcome, does PRP work?

Here there is some evidence to draw upon. Much of it indicates that the majority of civil servants, for example, do not see PRP as an incentive to work better or to raise their performance. Staff surveys, internal reports and academic research in the UK (Marsden and Richardson 1992, 1994; Marsden and French 1998; Makinson 2000; SSRB 2004) have all pointed to the fact that, despite wide support in general for the principle of PRP, only a small percentage of respondents thought that the form of PRP practised in their organization encouraged them to work beyond job requirements and in many cases the majority found it divisive. An interesting article by Marsden (2003) provides a convincing explanation for that phenomenon. Most respondents in non-managerial positions considered that base pay was more important than supplementary pay for performance and that job content and career opportunities and personal development were more likely to motivate them than PRP.

There is, however, some evidence that PRP can motivate but it is actually more important as a vehicle for bringing about organizational change and changes in culture. PRP requires the use of effective performance management processes, including setting down clear goals and objectives and requiring one-to-one contact between managers and employees. Informal contacts tend to replace formal ones and so communication is improved. Also there is a link made between the aims and goals of the organization and the individual, and PRP can be linked to new objectives, to fostering team working, introducing flexible working methods and even as a recruitment incentive (Demmke 2007). The study by the OECD (2005b) led it to identify the following lessons:

- that the design of PRP has to take account of the culture of each organization or country;
- that the performance appraisal process is at the heart of the whole performance management system;
- that implementation problems need to be anticipated;
- that PRP goes hand in hand with delegating HRM;
- that the significance and impact of PRP should not be over-estimated;
- that PRP should only be applied in an environment that maintains and supports a trust-based work relationship;
- that PRP should be used above all as a stimulant for introducing wider management and organizational change.

Debates and issues

If public management is a world of settled institutions designed to allow imperfect people to use flawed procedures to cope with insoluble problems (Wilson 1989), then performance management is even more so. As we have seen in this chapter and Chapter 5 there is a fundamental divide between those politicians and others seeking to improve performance and quality by 'market' means, offering a diversity of provision by different suppliers to citizens and consumers empowered to choose, and those politicians and others wanting the same improvements through a top-down hierarchical managerial approach, with providers required to meet centrally determined performance standards in return for public resources. This signals a real change in approach to public services from before the era of NPM. Improved performance is a goal which seems to be shared across the political spectrum, even if the means to achieve it differ. The result, however, is a mixture of the two as there is always continuity as well as change whenever a new government and administration take over.

Performance management started with the Conservatives during the

1980s. Having a preference for market solutions they transferred public activities to the private sector by privatization, CCT and later market testing but they were confronted with the need to raise the performance, productivity and responsiveness of the remaining public services. First the FMI, followed by agencification and internal markets laid the foundations for the use of an array of techniques to control and direct and manage the state organizations. This strategy was continued and embellished by the Labour governments from 1997 to 2010. The Coalition, faced with a national debt which it argues must be reduced to avoid further financial crises, continued with a top-down hierarchical approach in the short term, if only as a pragmatic response to the situation they inherited. During their first two years in office, however, they removed much of the infrastructure of controls (see Chapter 5), leaving public organizations with mainly financial targets to achieve.

In terms of the achievement of the Labour Government's goals, which were to improve both content and the delivery of public services, the evidence is mixed. There were clearly achievements in health, education and law and order, and official statistics confirm improvements in many of those target areas. The Labour party can certainly claim that, as a result of their reforms, there is more information available to the public and to parliament and more accountability to consumers, citizens and local communities. Public Service Management by numbers, however, has received much criticism (McLean *et al.* 2007; Hood 2006, 2007; Modell 2004), as has the extent and impact of gaming (Bevan and Hood 2006). The Select Committee on Public Administration considered whether there should be a cull of targets and league tables because of the effect on staff motivation and morale, although it decided in the end to reject a cull because of the positive effects in terms of accountability and transparency brought about by performance measurement (PASC 2003b: 29). The cull, however, has now happened but largely under the Coalition Government.

The factors impacting on performance in any organization are multiple and it is difficult to identify which has had the most significant effect. Undoubtedly, the imposition of performance management regimes has focused the attention of civil servants and other public officials on their objectives and processes for delivering the desired outputs and outcomes. Targets set externally by central government have driven changes in culture. This has been reinforced by regulatory and inspection systems which have caused organizations to review their own internal management (see Chapter 9). There is greater accountability and openness and, since the 1990s, attention has been directed to meeting public expectations and providing more information on which the public can make its own decisions. So citizens now have more choice and also have a role in influencing the services offered to them and in holding the public sector management to account, although this should not be overstated. The Coalition Government is no less committed to improving the performance and quality of public services, increasing choice and making government more transparent and more accountable through more local democracy and citizen involvement.

The reforms under previous governments have been at a cost. Although no cost-benefit analysis has been carried out on the new management systems, it is evident that there have been costs, including the creation of parallel bureaucracies to regulate and control the performance of delivery organizations; an increase in the administrative tasks falling especially on front-line workers delivering the services, as government by numbers has taken hold. There have been changes in the working practices and employment status of many public officials, which is reflected in part in evidence of low morale amongst public employees. The constant changes and continuous reform have resulted in both reform exhaustion but also cynicism about their impact. It is possible that the pace of change in the management of public organizations over the next few years will be slower because of the expenditure constraints and the need to get agreement within a Coalition government, but they may be more dramatic. The Coalition Government has embarked upon a cull of quangos, a bonfire of performance indicators, a dramatic reduction in the number of public officials, decentralization to local government and the most radical change in the NHS since its inception in 1948. Time will tell!

Chapter 7

Financial Management and Economic Regulation

Financial management is a crucial component of strategic management, as has become clear following the economic crisis of 2008 and the severe budgetary cutbacks imposed in 2010. Yet, even when the economy and budgets are expanding, it is no longer adequate to raise funds efficiently, allocate them according to the political choices made, and record their expenditure faithfully. Public finances must always be managed actively and intelligently to make the most of what might be available from an array of sources. Nevertheless, many of the innovations described below were made during periods of financial pressure. Having presented the UK's budgetary procedures below, we show how it has become a more strategic and effective process and also more transparent. The Coalition Government was able to profit from and build on this modernized system in tackling the budget deficit as it sought to balance the needs of the public sector with those of the economy. The finances of devolved governments and local governments are heavily dependent on the UK budget as we shall see, but they, like central government, seek new sources of funding in difficult times, which in the past few decades has meant turning to the private sector in a variety of ways we consider below.

The UK budgetary process

Her Majesty's Treasury, under the Chancellor of the Exchequer, is responsible for both financial and economic management (in some countries these two functions are separate). The Chancellor's annual 'budget statement' to parliament, which asks approval for the government's tax and other revenue-raising plans, is a highly political and media-covered occasion. Equally important is the Chancellor's 'financial statement' on how the government is managing the ebb and flow of public funds and how they are being allocated to the various services. This statement must be made annually but it can be made more often and at the same time as the budget, at the choice of the Chancellor. Also obligatory since the early 1970s have been twice-yearly parliamentary statements from the Chancellor on the UK's economic outlook and these can be combined with the budget or financial statement or made separately.

In general, policy making is such a shared experience between ministers, officials and interest groups (see the discussion of 'governance' in Chapter 2) that ministers cannot (or should not) claim personal credit for the decisions taken. However, Chancellors can and do credibly present budgets as 'theirs', because taxation discussions are kept within a tight community, other influential members being the prime minister, the Treasury and HM Revenue & Customs (HMRC) within government, and important financial and business interests outside it. Final decisions are taken within an even smaller group, even the Cabinet normally being given only a day's notice, on the basis that publicity about decisions affecting fuel prices, for example, might lose tax revenue as people stock up in advance.

Spending decisions involve greater negotiation with departments, which have their own networks of interested parties to consult. Depending on the approach of an individual government, the Treasury can be very prescriptive, or leave more to inter-ministerial bargaining or, as has been happening recently, set firm totals for departments with them negotiating the details internally. The Treasury is always the crucial actor, having to reconcile departments' ambitions with the government's revenue-raising options and national economic strategies.

Sources of revenue

The traditional sources of UK public revenue, including funds raised by local authorities and other public bodies, can be illustrated by the budget figures in 2011, shown in Figure 7.1.

More than a quarter of total government revenue is derived from *income tax*, which is a very visible tax and therefore highly political. The government must decide how much income tax to impose overall, and how the burden will be shared between people on different levels of income (the Scottish Government will face the same questions from 2014). A graduated (stepped) income tax is progressive (fairer) because higher earners pay a higher proportion of their income, but it is more expensive to administer and has other debatable effects on the UK economy. A slightly smaller share of revenue comes from *National Insurance Contributions* (NICs), paid by employers and employees, which give rights to job-related welfare benefits but the link is now weak. For employees, it works like income tax but because it is less visible it has been favoured as a source of additional revenue by recent governments of all colours. For employers, it is a staff cost and governments therefore have to weigh the benefits for revenue with the disadvantage for job creation.

The next largest slice of revenue comes from *Value Added Tax* (VAT), an 'indirect' tax on spending, that is only visible when subject to political disputes, as in 2010 between Labour and the Coalition. They argued over the balance between reducing VAT to stimulate consumer spending (as the Brown Government did) or increasing VAT to reduce the debt burden or provide

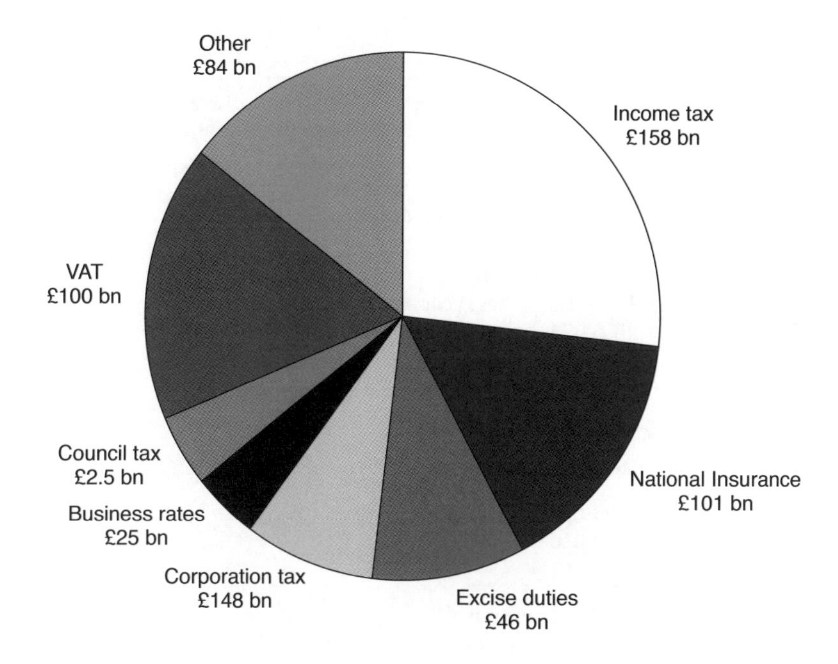

Figure 7.1 ***Budget 2011: sources of government revenue (£589 billion)***

Source: HM Treasury (2011b) *Budget 2011*, HC 836 (TSO), p. 6.

more revenue for public services (as the Coalition did). VAT is generally seen as a regressive tax because the poorest households lose most from a VAT rise if measured as a proportion of income, although they lose slightly less than richer households if measured as a proportion of expenditure (Browne 2010: 6–11). *Excise duty* is an indirect tax like VAT but levied on certain historically imported, luxury goods such as tobacco. *Corporation tax* is paid on UK-registered company profits and confronts the governments with a similar conundrum to NICs of revenue versus business growth. All recent UK governments have kept corporation tax low to compete with other countries (see Northern Ireland below). Council tax and business rates are local government revenue and considered below. 'Others' include a variety of items such as inheritance tax and stamp duty on property transactions, and 'one-offs' such as the bank levy the Coalition announced in 2010.

Table 7.1 shows examples of the 42 new taxation decisions and 15 new spending decisions which were announced in the 2011 budget, although some would not come into force until future years. The way these decisions are presented in the Budget Statement is a good illustration of the incremental nature of budgets, despite talk of 'Zero-Based Budgeting', because it reports only changes from existing arrangements, and, in the end, there is little overall change (down £10 million from 2010) despite some large individual changes (in fuel taxes for example). Comparison between one government

Table 7.1 ***Selected budget policy decisions in 2011***

Objective	Budget policy decision	Tax or spend?	Revenue changes in 2011/12 (£ million)
Growth and enterprise	• Corporation tax: decrease in main rate from 28% to 26% in 2011/12	Tax	–425
	• Bank Levy: first year of 0.075% effective rate	Tax	+630
	• Science facilities: additional investment	Spend	–100
Housing and employment	• Work experience: 80,000 additional places	Spend	–20
Personal taxes	• Personal allowance: increase by £630 in 2012/13	Tax	0
Fuel taxes	• Fuel duty: removal of previously announced increases	Tax	–1,900
	• North Sea: increase in supplementary charge to 30%	Tax	+1,780
Environmental taxes	• Air passenger duty: defer increase for inflation to 2012/13	Tax	-145
Indirect taxes	• Tobacco duty: increase for hand-rolled tobacco	Tax	+80
Net change planned in budget			**–10**

Note: The tax revenue and spending figures are changes to revenue from 'business as usual' (negative if receipts will be lower or spending will be higher than previously planned).
Source: Selected items from HM Treasury (2011b) *Budget 2011*, HC 836, TSO: table 2.1.

and another also shows surprisingly little change in tax strategies. Revenue in 2011 was planned to come only 2 per cent less from businesses and 3 per cent more from citizens than in Labour's last 'normal' budget before the financial crisis (data from HM Treasury 2008a: 11; 2011b: 6).

Total Managed Expenditure

Figure 7.2 shows Total Managed Expenditure (TME), which is the UK government's planned current and capital expenditure throughout the public

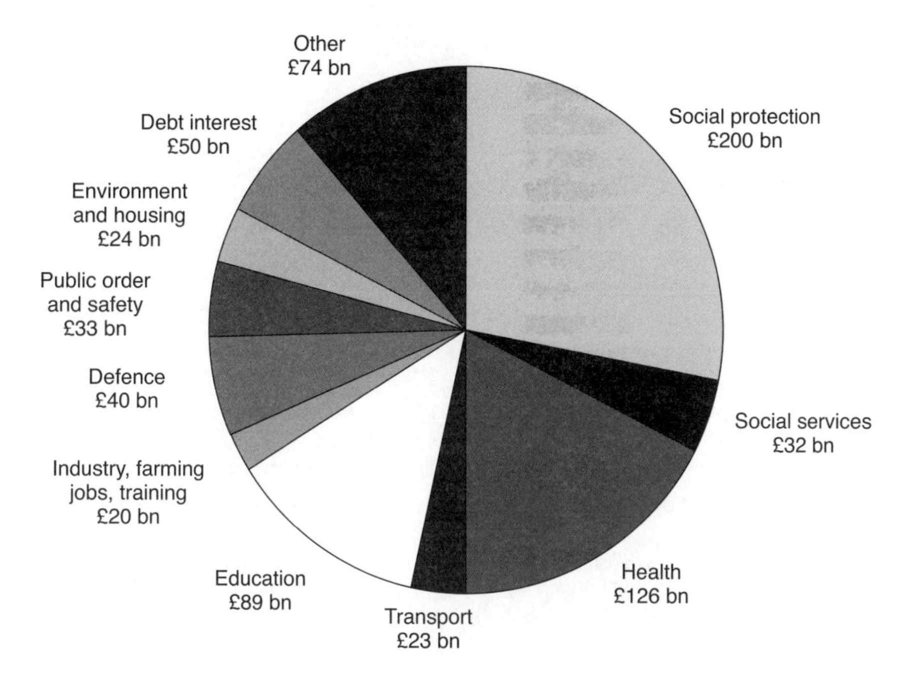

Figure 7.2 ***Budget 2011: Total Managed Expenditure (£710 billion)***

Source: HM Treasury (2011b) *Budget 2011*, HC 836 (TSO), p. 6.

sector (governments, parliaments and NDPBs). Both Labour in 2008 and the Coalition in 2011 planned that half TME would go to health and welfare, though the Coalition allocated a 1 per cent smaller share to welfare benefits (social protection) and a 1 per cent larger share to social services. The Coalition allocated a slightly higher proportion to defence (which Labour had reduced in most years) and a smaller share to industry, farming, jobs, training, environment and housing. Education, public order and safety, and transport were given the same priority in 2011 as in 2008, but the Coalition had to set aside a larger proportion for debt interest (data from HM Treasury 2008a: 11; 2011b: 6).

Tackling the budget deficit

From 1977 to 2010, TME increased every year 'in real terms' (that is, after inflation is taken into account), and from 2003 to 2008 was always in excess of revenue as Labour expanded services, which produced a small 'budget deficit' (see Figure 7.3). In 2008/09 the budget deficit grew dramatically because, first, tax revenue fell as a consequence of the financial crisis and, second, the Brown Government's initial response was to reduce VAT and

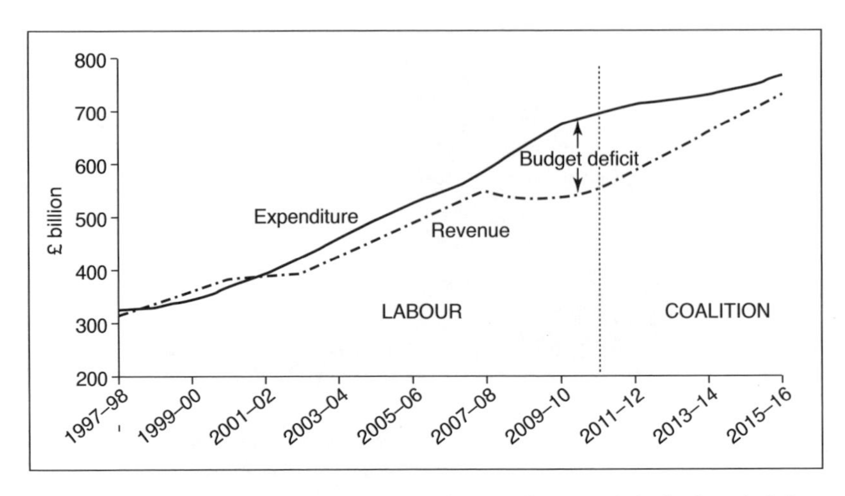

Figure 7.3 ***Government revenue and expenditure and the budget deficit***

Note: The data after 2010–11 are budget forecasts.
Source: Adapted from Office of National Statistics (ONS) data in HM Treasury (2011a) *Public Sector Finances Databank*, 27 May, Table C1.

increase spending, to encourage growth. In contrast, the Coalition argued that reducing the deficit by 2014/15 was a 'necessary precondition for sustained economic growth' (HM Treasury 2010b: 1). It expected to make savings from greater efficiency and cutting pay and pensions, but most reductions would come from job cuts, initially estimated by the Office for Budget Responsibility (OBR) in June 2010 as 490,000 by 2014/15, to which the Coalition responded by cutting welfare instead of some jobs, leading to a revised figure of 330,000 (HM Treasury 2010a: 38; OBR 2010: 6).

The Coalition's financial strategy had four principal components:

- reduce the state's operations to core services, and put pressure on them to do 'better for less';
- save central costs by reducing controls on local bodies, pushing down responsibility for cuts;
- reduce benefits to people of working age and direct the savings towards young children and pensioners;
- cut back contracted goods and services, unless they help economic growth.

The Cameron Government quickly asked departments to conduct a Spending Review, following a planning strategy first adopted by the Major Government during the 1992 crisis and enhanced by the Labour Government (see below). Most departments had to make savings of 25 per cent over four years, but to include 33 per cent savings in administrative costs (running costs, not front line services) meaning that office costs were targeted more than services. Existing health and overseas aid budgets were 'protected': in practice the NHS budget would barely keep pace with inflation, forcing it to find savings to match ever-increasing demand. Education and defence were asked to find 10 per cent cuts. All departments had to consider key questions that mixed market ideology and Cameron's 'Big Society' theme:

- Was the activity essential?
- Did it need to be funded by government?
- Did it provide substantial economic value?
- Could it be targeted towards those who most needed it?
- Could it be provided more cheaply?
- Could it be provided more effectively?
- Could it be provided by non-state providers or citizens?
- Could non-state providers be paid by results?
- Could local bodies rather than central government provide it? (HM Treasury 2010c: 8)

Final decisions on departmental allocations were made at meetings of the traditional leading ministers for financial matters: the prime minister and deputy prime minister, the Chancellor and the chief secretary to the Treasury (two Conservatives, two Liberal Democrats). The Cabinet's Public Expenditure Committee decided capital spending, a small part of overall spending but one that affects the private sector and the UK's engineering skills. The Coalition innovated with a 'zero-based' cross-departmental selection of capital programmes based on their value for economic growth; transport links therefore fared better than prisons (*Financial Times*, 16 October 2010; *Independent*, 21 October 2010). Outside the protected sectors, the reductions amounted to 19 per cent on average in departmental programmes (including 34 per cent in administrative expenditure); and 29 per cent in capital expenditure, all in real terms (HM Treasury 2010a: 5, 11). The most-affected areas were justice, farming and the environment, and local authorities (including police and fire): all had their budgets reduced by about 25 per cent over four years (HM Treasury 2010a: 10).

To put these plans into perspective, overall expenditure by public bodies (including on outsourced services) would in real terms in 2014 be back to just pre-crisis levels, and, as a proportion of GDP, at about the level of 2006, at which point services were substantially better funded than when Labour came to power in 1997 (HM Treasury 2010a: 5; 2011a: Table B3). Nevertheless, the cutbacks were still going to be painful: it is always harder, politically and administratively, to reduce public expenditure than to increase it.

Linking finance and the economy

The budget has evolved from meaning an annual process for allocating expenditure to a macro-economic tool to promote growth and a way of managing the public services for higher performance (Pollitt and Bouckaert 2009: 6–7). At times of economic crisis it is more obvious that governments use fiscal (tax and spend) policy to affect the economy. Budgets have three economic functions:

- *allocation* – between the market and the state, by altering the proportion of the economy that is managed by the government through taxation or buying goods and services;
- *stabilization* – using the effect of taxing and spending decisions to rebalance the economy;
- *distribution* – between sections of society, to achieve goals such as fairness or full employment (usually at the expense of overall economic growth).

There are no 'correct' answers on any of the three functions, only political choices which are based on economic theories that are themselves uncertain. The Keynesian model of allocation and stabilization, which led states to use budget imbalances (especially borrowing) to influence the economy, was widely rejected when it failed to avert the financial crisis of the mid-1970s (Massey and Pyper 2005: 61). There was a general return to liberal economics (see Chapter 2) which preached that governments should leave markets to find their own equilibrium, and that budgets should be fiscally neutral (revenue and expenditure should balance). The Coalition Government's 2010 Emergency Budget, which aimed, as we saw above, to bring the budget back into balance, was met with a Keynesian reaction from some economists, including Labour's shadow Chancellor, who said cutting expenditure would jeopardize recovery (*Financial Times*, 6 June 2011). Economic experts are divided on whether governments should manage markets; with the most detailed international survey to date (Ilzetski, Mendoza and Végh 2010) concluding that the measurable impact of using additional budgetary expenditure to stimulate growth is very small indeed, but more likely to be negative in countries similar to the UK, which have open economies (additional purchasing power is mainly spent on foreign manufacturers' goods) and large central government debts (additional debt further depresses confidence in the economy).

On distribution, comparative research shows that reducing the deficit may increase inequality (OECD 2008). When Finland and Sweden drastically reduced their budget deficits in the 1990s there was a strong increase in income inequality. However, the link is not inevitable if care is taken – the Netherlands adjusted its budgetary balance as fiercely as Sweden without increasing inequality. In the UK, the reduction in inequality under Labour from 2000 had been achieved by focusing its expenditure increases on poorer families, therefore cutbacks could reverse this trend. The Coalition claimed that its austerity budget of June 2010 favoured the poor (HM Treasury 2010b: 67, 76), which seems to be true for the tax changes, including VAT, but not for the cuts to expenditure, because low income families have greater reliance on public services (Browne 2010: 20).

Modernizing financial management

The Coalition Government continued the modernization of financial management already underway in the UK and elsewhere (see Rubin and Kelly 2005). Gordon Brown as Labour's Chancellor 1997–2007 introduced the most radical reforms but credit must also be given to earlier Conservative finance ministers and their advisers (Lipsey 2000; Thain 2002). The changes they all made include the unified budget, fundamental spending reviews, forward planning, resource accounting and performance budgeting, and greater budgetary transparency.

A unified budget

The financial statement on spending was traditionally presented in the autumn, and taxes announced in the following spring's budget. From 1992, the Conservatives presented both in spring as a unified budget, which was helpful to the Chancellor because it compelled ministers to consider the tax (and electoral) consequences of demanding additional expenditure (Lipsey 2000: 122). The second report of the year then merely presented the compulsory economic forecasts. Brown as Labour's Chancellor used the economic forecasts as the occasion for a huge Pre-Budget Report that covered the whole economic and social field, bringing it all within the Treasury's reach. The Coalition originally reverted to a concise spring Budget Report and Financial Statement, with a brief autumn comment on the economic forecasts now produced by the OBR. However, the poor economic outlook predicted by the OBR in November 2011 stimulated a more extensive autumn statement from the Chancellor, leading the government's response.

Spending Reviews

As explained in Chapter 5 – where financial management was discussed as a crucial aspect of strategic management – the annual review and roll forward of spending plans by the Public Expenditure Survey Committee (PESC) was replaced in the 1990s by multi-annual spending reviews and budgetary frameworks. The Major Cabinet inverted the PESC procedure by agreeing the spending total first and asking ministers to defend their departmental share. It later initiated a Fundamental Expenditure Review, in which departments queried the value of every activity – a zero-based approach. The Treasury's own review (see Chapter 4) reduced its double-checking of departmental expenditure. The Labour Government extended the idea of review into a regular multi-annual exercise. Because it had promised to retain the Conservatives' spending plans for two years, but wanted to increase health and education spending, its 1998 Comprehensive Spending Review (CSR) had, as its main objective, the redirecting of existing allocations and under-used assets towards these priorities. However Labour's three-year planning cycle was usually foreshortened to two years because of implementation problems and/or to fit the electoral timetable (Rubin and Kelly 2005: 573; Talbot 2007: 16).

Multi-year spending frameworks

Multi-year planning was facilitated by the Major Government's insight that it was possible to plan a substantial proportion of public expenditure by separating those elements easier to control from the rest. The first group comprises chiefly administrative and programme costs which ministers ought to be able to decide and control. The latter includes welfare provision (which fluctuates with the economy), locally decided revenue (council tax and Scottish business rates) and interest charges, which are not so easily predicted or contained. This distinction enabled departments to be subject to a fixed expenditure total for their 'controllable' activities for some years ahead, while other expenditures would be expected to evolve. The Labour Government's Spending Reviews divided TME between Departmental Expenditure Limits (DELs) for the spending which can be fixed ahead, and Annually Managed Expenditure (AME), which is recalculated twice-yearly. Just over half TME is allocated to departments as DEL, but this proportion varies greatly across departments. A majority of departments have nearly all their spending allocated through DEL with only a small proportion in AME. In contrast, five departments, and notably HMRC and DWP, have a high proportion of spending in AME, because not only tax and benefit payments but also the cost of administering them varies with economic conditions.

For departments, DEL is more secure (but more constraining) than yearly settlements. For the Treasury, it transforms budgetary negotiations from an argument about a department's annual increment to considerations of whether programmes should continue. The Labour Government also allowed departments to carry over some funding into the next year rather than being pushed to 'use it or lose it'. However some departments used End of Year Flexibility to create 'cushions' by deliberate under-spending – the NHS had accumulated a £1.4 billion surplus by 2010 – leading the Coalition to revise this system (*Financial Times* 16 June 2010).

The 2007 CSR refined the system further by making administrative costs a separately controlled item within DEL. As part of the Coalition's campaign on quangos (see Chapter 4), this separate control has now been extended to arm's length bodies (HM Treasury 2010a: 18). The Treasury has gradually reduced the proportion of expenditure in AME, because it is more susceptible to political intervention. The Coalition included AME expenditure on social security, tax credits and public-service pensions in the 2010 Spending Review to see if they could be brought within central government control. Estimated AME totals were allocated to departments for the first time (as separate AME budgets), with the aim of improving the incentives to control AME (HM Treasury 2010a: 18).

Resource accounting and budgeting

The Labour Government changed the procedures for public-sector accounts from the century-old 'cash accounts' to a system modelled on private-sector accounts and already adopted in New Zealand in 1989, followed by the USA and other governments (Lipsey 2000: 204; and see Rubin and Kelly 2005; Scheers *et al.* 2005).

Chan and Xiao (2009: 111) list the technical financial procedures now seen as standard:

- allocation of spending appropriations (money voted by parliament or other authorizing body);
- approval and letting of contracts;
- receipt of goods and services;
- making of payments;
- recording of transactions in the budgetary accounting system in terms of the use of appropriations;
- recording of transactions in the financial accounting system in terms of their effect on assets (financial and other resources), on liabilities (for goods and services ordered) and on revenues and expenditures (increases and decreases in net resources);
- possible consideration of investment management and debt administration.

Until 2001, under the cash accounting system, UK departments recorded purchases when they paid for them, giving them an incentive to delay payments and deterring them from making cheaper bulk purchases; and the accounts did not record liabilities (goods or services ordered but not yet paid). The full cost of a capital project, such as a hospital, was assigned to the year the bill was paid, though its use would spread over decades. Departments had no incentive to sell unused property, because they were not charged for holding capital, even though it could have been invested better elsewhere. Yet there was a strict accounting separation between current expenditure and capital expenditure; it was not easy to purchase capital goods that would save labour with cash allocated for current expenditure. The system was not adapted to performance management because it was difficult to link outcomes and expenditure, or make comparisons with private suppliers which use accruals accounting, in which income is recorded as it is earned (even if payment is not yet received) and expenditure is recorded when liability is incurred (not when the bill is paid). In 1995, the Conservative Government set out a timetable for using accruals accounting throughout the public sector. The Labour Government followed this timetable, starting with departments valuing their existing capital assets, from roads to wine cellars; the reform was fully implemented in 2003.

In the resource accounting and budgeting system, departments record current expenditure against their resource budget (resource section of DEL) when goods have been received or services performed, and reference it to the policy objectives to which they relate. Items bought in bulk (such as medicines in NHS hospitals) are charged to expenditure when they are issued for use, showing how much stock is consumed in any period. Administration costs now include rents and a capital charge for the notional costs of borrowing to fund the department's buildings. Another capital charge is made for the value of programme assets. Depreciation is also charged to the resource budget. Finally, the resource account records future liabilities (expenditure commitments but also bad debts). The capital budget (capital sections of DEL and AMA) records investments, income from capital spending, and loans, and includes an allocation for the capital transactions of NDPBs sponsored by the department. The accounting reform was valuable in itself for providing a more realistic costing of programmes and enhancing budgetary accountability, but it was also a fundamental requirement for Labour's Public Service Agreements (see Chapter 5), and performance budgeting in general.

The Labour Government had said it would publish Whole of Government Accounts from 2005/06 but the Coalition Government was the first to do so. These accrual accounts treat the whole public sector as one unit (see special edition of *Public Money and Management*, 2009). The Coalition published these accounts for 2009/10 to defend its own financial strategy because they revealed the huge future liabilities it had inherited (HM Treasury 2011c; *Financial Times* 11 July 2011).

Accountability, transparency and de-politicization

The Whole of Government initiative was one of several in recent years that have improved accountability by increasing transparency. Many reforms also de-politicized financial decisions by transferring them to independent authorities.

Accounting for propriety and value

The UK government traditionally accounts for its financial management to parliament, especially the Public Accounts Committee (PAC). It is mainly because of PAC that the proportion of departments with professionally qualified finance directors rose from 39 per cent in 2004 to 93 per cent in 2008 (PAC 2008c: Ev2). Aided by the National Audit Office (NAO), whose work is comprehensively explained in Chapter 9, PAC reveals the weaknesses in departments' handling of financial matters. The 40 or so NAO reports which PAC took up with officials and ministers in 2010–11 covered the 'unacceptable' performance of the Student Loans Company (PAC 2010a: 3), the Ministry of Defence's management of its budget and property (PAC 2010b), the Ministry of Justice's financial management (PAC 2011b); and PFI programmes in local authorities and the NHS (PAC 2011c).

PAC is nevertheless examining actions after the event, though officials are sufficiently anxious about appearing before PAC that 'anticipated reaction' drives compliance (Lipsey 2000: 250–3). In extreme cases, when senior responsible officers consider a ministerial decision cannot be defended financially, they write an 'Accounting Officer's Minute' to make their position clear. Despite PAC, the UK parliament is not very effective: 29 of the 36 legislatures examined by Wehner (2006: 777; and see Wehner 2010) had greater capacity for budgetary scrutiny, with real powers to amend budgets and withhold funds.

Transparency and independence

Both Labour and the Coalition took steps to improve confidence in financial policy making. Doubt had grown about Treasury forecasts and the extent of public-sector liabilities (Treasury Committee 2010: 7). Chancellor Brown in 1998 asked the NAO to audit the economic forecasts: the NAO's favourable opinion gave credibility to the Chancellor's Budget and Pre-Budget Statements and to Brown's Golden Rule – to borrow only for investment, as measured over the economic cycle (though there were other problems, such as defining investment and identifying the economic cycle; see Chote 2007: 8). Brown also adopted the NAO's recommendation to report on the forecasts produced by independent institutions (HM Treasury 2006: 193).

The Coalition Government delegated Treasury forecasting to the OBR, one of a set of new independent fiscal councils, some decades after their adoption in the Netherlands, Denmark and the USA (Treasury Committee 2010: 48–9). The Budget Report includes the OBR's judgement of the impact of budget measures and whether the government is likely to meet its fiscal targets. The Chancellor has asked OBR to check other data, such as the government's costing of AME; however, he presented estimates of the Budget's effect on different income groups without an OBR evaluation in 2010 (HM Treasury

2010b: Appendix A). Some scepticism was initially expressed about the OBR's independence and then on its forecasting skills, but it is an advance on previous arrangements, and the Labour leadership has said it would retain the OBR concept (*Financial Times* 1 December 2011).

Making the Bank of England independent

In Brown's first week as Chancellor, in May 1997, he announced that the Bank of England would no longer be subject to directives from the Chancellor on monetary policy, mirroring the position in the US and eurozone countries. The government would set an inflation target and the Bank, advised by a Monetary Policy Committee (MPC), would decide the appropriate interest rate to deliver the target – supplemented after the 2008 crisis by adjusting the money supply ('quantitative easing'). The Bank now reports to parliament's Treasury Committee, and the MPC publishes minutes of its meetings. Yet members of the MPC are nominated by the Chancellor, and Brown ignored the Treasury Committee's opposition to an appointment in 2000 (*Financial Times* 8 July 2011). In 2011, however, similar criticisms by parliamentary committees of people nominated to the Bank's new Financial Policy Committee and to the UK Statistics Authority were accepted by the government and the candidates. It seems a further step has been taken towards improving confidence in the government's operational decisions by delegating such matters to independent authorities (*Financial Times* 6 July 2011; *Independent* 8 July 2011).

Devolved and local governments: sharing the cutbacks

Because devolved and local governments are funded mainly through departments, they too are subject to national government's overall financial management policy, as the spending cuts imposed in 2010 emphasized so dramatically. Devolved and local governments largely follow the UK government's financial management processes, including spending reviews and accruals accounting. They have little financial autonomy, raising only a sixth of their own revenue, smaller than nearly all other OECD countries (Charbit and Michalun 2009: 69). The bulk of their income comes from central grants which relate to the needs and resources of the area. While centralized funding restricts local choice, it reduces the 'post-code lottery' by equalizing service levels across authorities. Local authorities shared the expansion in public expenditure under Labour and are now sharing the returns to previous levels under the Coalition.

Devolving financial powers and responsibility

The devolved governments are funded by a Treasury block grant, based on the 1978 'Barnett formula' which is slowly bringing their high expenditure per capita closer to English levels. The Welsh Assembly would like a new formula, based on social need, but the Brown Government refused to change it (Scotland Office 2009: 10). Cameron has proposed to review it once the economic deficit is under control (*Financial Times* 6 July 2010).

Financial reforms were agreed for Scotland by the Brown and Coalition Governments, to come into force in 2015. The scheme will give the Scottish parliament more power – and responsibility (Calman Commission 2009; and see Chapter 4). Taxpayers in Scotland will pay 10 per cent less to the Treasury and the Treasury will reduce Scotland's grant by the equivalent amount. The Scottish parliament will decide how much of that revenue to replace through a Scottish income tax. Borrowing powers and some smaller taxes will also be transferred. Scotland would then be responsible for raising about 35 per cent of its budget (Scotland Office 2010: 11). The Scottish National Party (SNP) demands 'full fiscal responsibility' (Scottish Government 2010b: Chapter 4), and the SNP Government elected in 2011 has called for a transfer of tax-raising powers, including corporation tax. The Coalition Government had already suggested devolving corporation tax to the Northern Ireland Assembly, which would probably set a rate competitive with the Republic of Ireland. Under EU rules on subsidies, Northern Ireland's grant would be reduced to balance its corporation tax revenue; nevertheless, all main Northern Ireland parties and business groups support the initiative (*Financial Times* 25 March 2011, 11 July 2011).

The devolved parliaments use more transparent budgetary processes than Westminster. Plain language draft spending plans are discussed by parliament and others with ministers some months before final allocations are made, and explanations provided for any subsequent re-allocation (WAG 2011: 1, 4). According to Wales's former top official, the major benefit of devolution was more effective expenditure: deliberation among all Welsh Assembly Members and parties produced outcomes that reflected Welsh needs better than when discussion was mainly confined to Welsh Office ministers and officials (Shortland 2010).

Managing limited local financial autonomy

The Coalition Government, like the Labour Government before it, speaks of 'a new localism'. Yet it seems likely that local authorities will remain strongly constrained by central grants and by rules on borrowing and on funding individual services.

Raising local resources

Though the SNP Government has suggested funding Scottish councils through a local income tax, the whole UK currently operates a distinctive local tax regime based entirely on property (other countries have additional

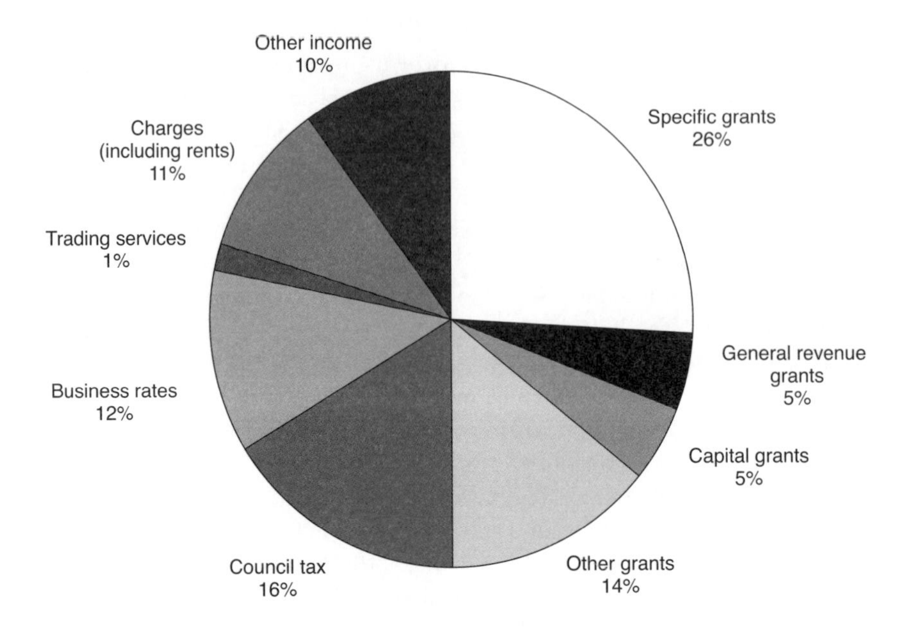

Figure 7.4 ***Sources of local authority income, England, 2009/10***

Source: Adapted from data in DCLG (2011b) *Local Government Financial Statistics England No. 21*, London: DCLG, chart K.1b.

taxes, such as on income, company payrolls or vehicles). Council tax on residential property, and non-domestic ('business') rates on other property, provide about a quarter of local authority income, more in Northern Ireland (see Figure 7.4). However, except in Northern Ireland, the non-domestic rate is decided by national governments. About half local authority income derives from national grants, less in Northern Ireland where local councils do not fund education. Other income derives from charges made from services.

Even *council tax* is not fully within councils' control. After the 1974 financial crisis, both Labour and Conservative central governments tried various means of holding down local spending, of which the most effective was 'rate-capping' (setting a maximum budget increase), and the most opposed was the 'poll tax' – a per capita tax whose failure is charted in Butler *et al.* (1994). Capping remains a reserve power, and authorities feel obliged to conform to central guidelines or risk litigation and new budget-setting negotiations. When the SNP and UK Coalition Governments asked councils to freeze council tax, councils had little choice but to comply. The Localism Act 2011 ostensibly replaces ministerial capping with a local referendum. Residents can veto 'excessive' council tax increases but ministers define what is 'excessive'. If the tax is 'excessive', councils must draw up an alternative, non-excessive, budget and hold a referendum. Councils could argue the case for their 'excessive' budget to voters. In practice, fear of an expensive referendum is likely to constrain their decisions (Sear and Parry 2011: 45). Councils have discretion on changing the criteria for council tax benefit (subsidy) from 2013/14, a Coalition policy which has the potential for influencing social behaviour (the 'nudge' theory) but also creating discord.

Except in Northern Ireland, the *business rate* has, since 1990, been set by national governments and redistributed to councils, originally in proportion to population but now using a needs-based formula. Nationalizing business rates removed local discretion but also a financial incentive for councils to improve the business environment. Two 'public–private partnership' or 'place' schemes typical of New Labour (see Chapter 4) have addressed this problem. First, councils can levy an additional business rate to provide additional services in Business Improvement Districts (BIDs), subject to a ballot of business ratepayers. BIDs are now well established in about a hundred councils, in town centres or commercial and industrial estates. Second, the *Place-shaping* report stimulated the introduction of the Business Rate Supplement to support economic development projects (Lyons 2007; HM Treasury 2007b: 73). It is levied by the Greater London Authority for the Crossrail line with the justification that ratepayers will benefit from increased property values. Conservatives and Liberal Democrats had opposed it because it could be imposed against ratepayers' will: their Localism Act made ballots compulsory. Full re-localization of business rates is unlikely – more councils would lose than would gain, and business interests are opposed (*Financial Times*, 14 March 2011). The government is considering a scheme for councils to keep additional rates revenue above a standard level to encourage them to approve business projects (DCLG 2011c), but its introduction would increase the financial disparities between thriving and deprived areas.

Local authorities' reliance on *government grants* makes them vulnerable to national strategies. In England, the 26 per cent decrease in grants from 2010 to 2014, combined with a standstill in council tax, was forecast to produce an overall drop of 14 per cent in council receipts by 2014/15 (HM Treasury 2010a: 50). In Scotland grants fell by 'only' 2.6 per cent in 2011/12 but in return local authorities had to agree to deliver objectives decided by the Scottish Government (Scottish Government 2010b: Chapter 14).

Grants come in the form of *specific grants* ('ring-fenced'), which finance particular programmes and a formula-based *revenue support grant*, which moderates the differences in financial needs between authorities. The proportion given as specific grant was so large by 2006 that government regrouped the remaining block grant with redistributed business rates as *formula grant*. Some specific grants ('other grants' in Figure 7.4) are transfers over which the council has no discretion (mandatory rent allowances, sixth forms funding). Others are provided by departments for their priorities and repeat the fragmented 'silo' effect of Whitehall. Councils are tempted to distort local priorities to attract this funding. Labour created many small 'pots' to accompany its initiatives (see Chapter 4). By 2009 there were over 100 specific grants for councils to identify, programme, track and report (DCLG 2009: Annex B).

The arguments against specific grants are well-known, and the Scottish and UK governments decided in their 2007 Spending Reviews to simplify the regime. The SNP Government moved all but seven grants into general grant: 'Considerable savings in administrative costs' were achieved on both sides (Scottish Government 2010b: Chapter 14). Gordon Brown adopted a 'place-shaping' approach, creating new Area-Based Grants combining 21 specific grants (HM Treasury 2007b: 156), but more than 100 remained. The Coalition Government brought nearly all within the formula grant for 2011/12. Nevertheless, 10 specific grants were allocated in 2011/12, including a non-ring-fenced Early Intervention Grant for services to young families, such as Sure Start. Area-Based Grants were abandoned but inter-departmental Community Budgets were introduced (HM Treasury 2010a: 50–1). It remains to be seen whether the Coalition will resist pressure for targeted resources (a strong case was made for ring-fencing Sure Start, for example). The lack of administrative resources within Whitehall to track local spending may slow the re-centralizing process down.

Central government rules on councils' *capital resources* have varied. Until 2004, councils were set maximum borrowing levels, partly to control national debt, partly to encourage them to raise capital instead through council house sales. However, until the arrival of the Labour Government, they could reinvest only a small proportion of the receipts. In 2004, Labour allowed local authorities (the Northern Ireland Executive in the case of the province) to borrow, provided they could service the debt according to 'the Prudential Code' developed by CIPFA (Chartered Institute of Public Finance and Accountancy). Capital grants also grew and, in 2009, were the principal source of capital finance, with self-financed borrowing second (data in this section are from DCLG 2011b; Scottish Government 2011; WAG 2010). The 2010 Spending Review cut capital grants but retained 'prudential borrowing' though at the cost of higher rates of interest from the Treasury's Public Works Loan Board.

User charges are the resource over which councils have most discretion. For that reason, they are often the cause of political debate as councillors weigh up rival activities. Authorities make distinctively different decisions on the charges for similar services (swimming pools, home helps, planning applications, inspections, car parks and so on). In the present financial climate, non-mandatory services that cannot be covered by charges will come under the greatest pressure.

Managing local expenditure

Broadly speaking, revenue grants, council tax, business rates and charges

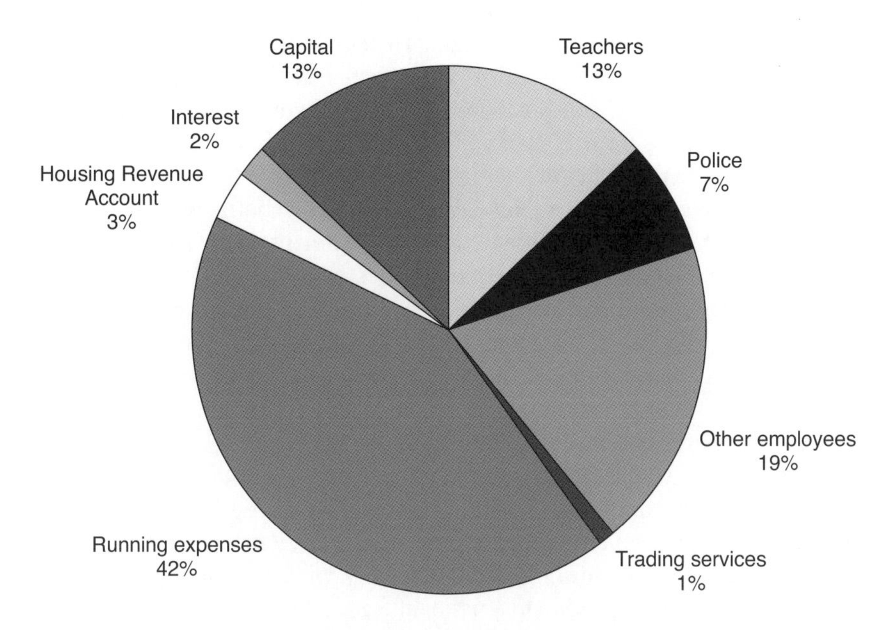

Figure 7.5 ***Local authority expenditure on staff and other costs, England, 2009/10***

Note: Total current and capital expenditure (£168 billion).
Source: Adapted from data in DCLG (2011b) *Local Government Financial Statistics England No. 21*, London: DCLG, chart K.1b and table 3.4a.

fund revenue expenditure, and capital grants, borrowing and capital receipts fund capital expenditure. Figure 7.5 shows that about 40 per cent of expenditure in England (and also in Scotland) goes on *staffing*. Although local authorities are free to set their own pay scales, they are strongly guided by collective negotiations at national level. These arrangements are less influential at chief executive level, where pay is set individually, and seems to have escalated in the last decade (Farnham and White 2011: 36, 40). Nearly half the expenditure on staff, however, relates to schools and police forces which are managed independently. The second largest element is *running costs*: premises, electricity, IT and other procurement. Accounts for council housing and trading services have to be kept separately. In the *Housing Revenue Account* (HRA), expenditure on council housing must be balanced with income from rents and central grants, not subsidized by council tax. Other national rules, such as setting rents in line with market prices, have to be applied. *Trading services* are commercial activities, chiefly industrial estates and investment properties in England, and transport and markets in Scotland. In 2009/10 in England they generated a surplus (transferred to the general account), and in Scotland a loss, mainly on ferry services.

Capital spending by local authorities is mostly on construction and refurbishment. In England and Scotland, councils also make grants and loans to the private or third sector, such as housing associations; in Wales, the grants go mostly to homeowners for renovation. The new 'prudential' borrowing has been exploited by local authorities. However, a large factor in the recent growth in investment was the availability of capital grants, and cuts in central government funding from 2010 will therefore have a large impact. PFI as a programme is discussed below: here we note that local authorities have since 1996, encouraged by departments (PAC 2011c: 5), contracted for housing estates, schools, transport facilities and waste treatment plants which they pay for as they use. Departments issued authorities with PFI credits representing the capital they would part-subsidize: these trigger a stream of annual PFI grant to help pay the contractor. Cutbacks have halted many proposed schemes (though a new programme of centrally procured school projects was announced in 2011) but the main problem of PFI for authorities will be to manage their payments from a diminished overall budget.

Figure 7.6 shows the pattern of *expenditure on services*. Local authorities spend more on education than any other service, but at least 85 per cent must be passed to school governing boards for local management (see Chapter 4), currently according to a formula decided locally but dominated by ministers' criteria (and expected to move to a national formula by 2015). Labour education ministers guaranteed that each school's budget would rise at least in line with costs (and the Coalition that they would not fall by more than 1.5 per cent in 2011/12), meaning that the authority may have to top up school budgets from its own 'inter-school' provision (such as pupil referral units). The real engagement of councils in housing does not show up in revenue accounts or Figure 7.6 because they omit the HRA. To their £17 billion expenditure on

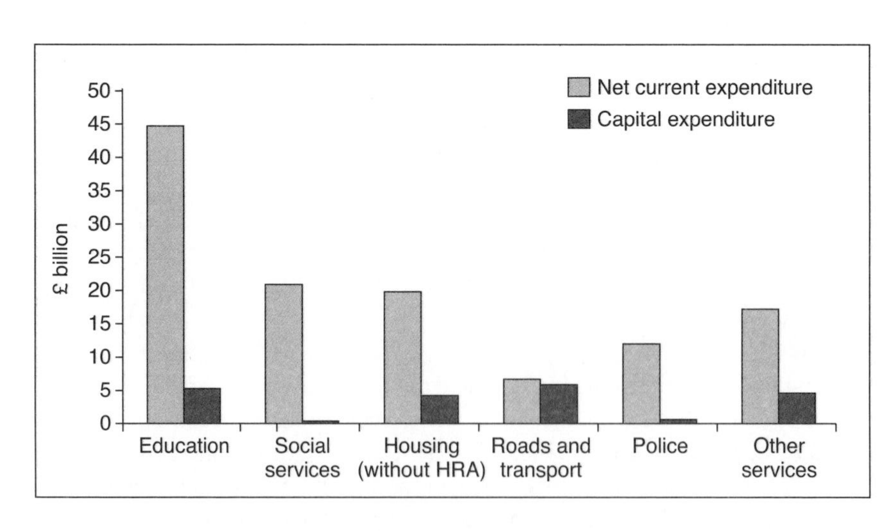

Figure 7.6 ***Local authority expenditure on services, England, 2009/10***

Note: Police services are the responsibility of separate police authorities.
Source: Adapted from data in DCLG (2011b) *Local Government Financial Statistics England No. 21*, London: DCLG, tables 3.2a, 4.2c.

dealing with homelessness and managing housing benefits could be added the £4 billion in the HRA devoted to housing management though, unlike education, it is wholly balanced by user charges. 'Other services' in Figure 7.6 include the fire and waste treatment services managed by joint boards of metropolitan councils. Like police authorities they are financed by precepts (levies), which councils collect on their behalf.

The local government finance system is highly centralized, smoothing out local disadvantage but leaving councils with little room for manoeuvre. Sophisticated financial management skills are needed for a task that is more interesting than keeping prudent accounts but also more frustrating because the need to maximize grant income can lead to decisions that are sub-optimal from the council's perspective. If the Coalition Government avoids creating more specific grants, councils will have more flexibility to work towards objectives that are their own.

Engaging private finance in public services

In the last two decades the UK government has engaged in new financial relationships with the private sector. Public procurement is not new: the novelty is in the supply of whole programmes or in combining supply of services with capital financing. Strategies to bring in private finance do not follow a simple logic, as already illustrated in Chapter 3 by Labour's contrasting choices for London Underground (public-sector operation and private-sector infrastructure), the rail network (private-sector operation and a virtually public infrastructure) and the Channel Tunnel Rail Link (government-guaranteed loans to rescue a private project, followed by the sale of a 30-year concession). The Coalition Government has adopted a fourth strategy for the planned London to Birmingham railway line: publicly procured construction followed by a concession. The more important ways in which public authorities have sought to bring in private finance are described below.

Contracting-out services

Competitive contracting-out was introduced by Conservative governments (see Chapter 4), and further extended by Labour in sectors such as prisons, health and education (Flinders 2005: 219). Governments use the private sector for resources or market-driven efficiency, or both – as in the award of contracts for Birmingham Prison, driven by cuts in the Department for Justice's budget and an official assessment of the publicly run prison as 'failing' (*Financial Times*, 1 April 2011). In 2003, Doncaster and the one other privately managed prison were judged to be in the top six performers along with two PFI prisons and two public prisons (NAO 2003: 8). Doncaster in 2011 became the first to trial 'payment by results'.

Independent Sector Treatment Centres provide an equally controversial example. The government's objective varied over the years: to provide plurality within the NHS; to reduce waiting times; to stimulate innovation; and to save 'spot purchasing' from private hospitals (DH 2000, 2002, 2006). Early Centres were poor financial value: they were paid more than the NHS equivalent to encourage firms to bid (Healthcare Commission 2007: 17), and paid-for capacity was under-used – partly because some NHS staff and GPs were reluctant to offer patients a 'private' service (Audit Commission 2008a: 43–4). The Healthcare Commission (2007: 7) found the Centres provided a service that patients thought highly satisfactory and with apparently good outcomes but data on clinical performance was sometimes lacking and not aligned with NHS data. In 2011, new cross-sector performance measures were agreed; they will help local health commissioners decide whether to renew the contracts now that expansion in health budgets has ceased.

The Private Finance Initiative

PFI was introduced by the Conservative Government in 1992, the principles set out in 1993 (HM Treasury 1993), and further refined under Labour (HM Treasury 2003). The Coalition Government criticized PFI but is continuing to negotiate new projects. Under PFI, contractors finance as well as design, build and maintain or operate a construction project, and are paid over the long term through service charges. The government in 1992 – as now – wanted to relaunch economic growth but without increasing public spending. It argued that projects driven by the profit motive are built more efficiently by companies using borrowed money than those managed by public officials, especially if there are significant risks to project completion. It said that private contractors would design in quality from the start to save on later maintenance ('whole-life costing'), whereas public authorities tend to build at minimum initial cost. Although private contractors pay more to borrow capital, their efficiency savings, the government claimed, outweigh the cheaper borrowing available to public bodies. However, the financial crisis has increased the differential between the costs of public and private borrowing, calling into question this assumption (Treasury Committee 2011: 3).

A defining characteristic of PFI is the transfer of risk (in design, costs of construction or maintenance, loss of payments from late opening or poor performance). The greatest benefit comes from assigning each risk to the party most able to minimize it. The government risks the obligation to pay for 30 years for hospitals and schools, which do not fit current policy requirements, and paying high charges for modifications or risking the financial and political costs of terminating a contract (Treasury Committee 2011: 21). Over-estimated needs and poorly negotiated contracts occur in conventional procurement too – though with less visibility – but the long-term nature of PFI can lock public managers into past delivery patterns. When the crisis

Table 7.2 ***Benefits and problems of the Private Finance Initiative (PFI)***

Feature of PFI	Potential benefits	Potential problems
Ease of financing	Asset can be delivered and enjoyed sooner than feasible through conventional budgetary route	'Pay later' financing may tempt decision makers to ignore poor long-term VfM
Project risks	Allocates risks to those most able to manage and minimize them: more chance of successful result, and overall cost-efficiencies	Public pays for risk transfer in PFI contract but ultimate risk remains with public sector if project cannot be allowed to fail
Commercial risks	Banks financing PFI projects provide additional checks before contracts signed, reducing the commercial risk	Long contract period and high monetary value contracts increase likelihood of commercial failure
Closely specified contracts	Fear of financial penalties encourages contractors to deliver project on time and to price; and/or to provide required service levels	Complexity and importance of PFI contracts adds to time-scales and encourages officials to rely on private sector consultants
Long-term contracts	Specifying output at design and construction stage encourages innovation, quality and productivity	Poor adaptability to changing needs over long pay-back period: contractors likely to charge a high price for modifications

Source: Adapted from National Audit Office (2011a) *Lessons from PFI and Other Projects*, HC 920, TSO, figure 1.

meant that local authorities and NHS trusts had to make economies, PFI payments were sacrosanct, and cutbacks had to be found from other areas (*Financial Times*, 4 June 2011). These and other potential problems – and benefits – of PFI are summed up in Table 7.2.

Some authorities comment that the perceived advantages of PFI are actually a critique of traditional UK procurement (OECD 2005a: 141; Shaoul 2007: 184). The NAO (2011a: 17) has often warned that the UK public sector needs to improve its commercial skills. The Coalition Government created the Major Projects Authority in the Cabinet Office to improve high-level control of projects (not just PFI) and develop contract management skills in the public sector (PAC 2011d: Ev 21–5). Nearly half PFI contracts to date have been signed by schools and hospital trusts, which have a weak bargaining position with the large contractors who manage whole portfolios of PFIs (Webb 2011: 2). Yet some hospital trusts had nobody managing their PFI contract despite opportunities for increasing VfM continuing during the contract's lifetime (PAC 2011d: Ev 33). The Department for Education has started a new programme of PFI schools projects but, this time, it will be based on central procurement and standardized designs. The NAO (2011a: 6) found that most PFI projects were delivering the services expected but that the government had not demonstrated clearly that PFI provided better, or worse, VfM than other forms of procurement. Suspicion remains that its use is driven by motives other than VfM because most PFI debt does not appear in government debt or deficit figures (Treasury Committee 2011: 3). However, although PFI has attracted much attention, the technique is used for only a small part of public investment: 90 per cent of major projects, including major health projects, are conventionally procured, funded and delivered by central government (PAC 2011d: Ev 21).

Varieties of 'public–private partnership'

There are fundamental financial distinctions between different types of 'public-private partnership'. PFI is a procurement tool that produces a liability for long-term annual payments for using an asset which belongs to the contractor. A Public–Private Partnership (PPP) is a shared ownership structure in which the public authority has an equity stake (HM Treasury 2003: 118). PPPs can be defined more widely, to include some PFIs, as 'a risk-sharing relationship between the public and private sectors based upon a shared aspiration to bring about a desired policy outcome' (IPPR 2001: 40). This more political definition emphasizes 'partnership' but omits the profit motive driving PFI. The following examples illustrate the range of possibilities.

Public–Private Partnerships (PPPs)

PPPs, in the Treasury sense of shared ownership, have been used in Europe since the 1920s under the term 'mixed economy company' (Burnham 2001; Bovaird and Tizard 2009). In the UK, the concept of Public Interest Company has emerged (Prabhakar 2006: 88–108), and there are other variants; the SNP Government makes its position plain in the title 'Non Profit Distributing' procurement (NPDs).

National Air Traffic Services (NATS), Glas Cymru and Network Rail are among the best-known mixed economy companies (see Flinders 2005: 219). All three were created after full privatization failed (see Chapter 3). NATS was set up in 2000 by the Labour Government which sold 46 per cent of shares to the Airline Group, with 5 per cent awarded to NATS staff. The government is the largest shareholder, but it does not have a majority of shares and NATS is therefore in the private sector. After initial financial problems, NATS made annual profits and has completed a ten-year investment programme. Its good credit rating led Labour to put it on a list of assets for potential sale (Butcher 2011: 3). The Coalition intends to sell part of its shareholdings, using the 'opportunity costs' argument that, if there is no policy need to hold the assets, the resources could provide better value for money elsewhere (HM Treasury 2011b: 50). The NATS model has been proposed by both Labour and Coalition Governments for the Royal Mail; that is, introducing private capital and employee ownership to help modernization, but a private partner remains to be found.

Glas Cymru was set up by former officials to take over the privatized Dwr Cymru Welsh Water when its owner failed commercially. Glas is owned and controlled by 200 or so members who do not receive dividends: profits are used to reduce debt interest, improve services and reduce charges to customers (Glas Cymru 2011). Glas Cymru is not a shared equity PPP: it is an independent company. However, its constitution and objectives incorporate principles proposed by the Welsh Assembly; its capital investment programme was agreed with the Assembly (Glas Cymru 2000); and it had the support of the First Minister. Under conditions imposed by the water regulator Ofwat, it has to remain a single-purpose company (providing water and sewerage services) and give public commitments to customer benefits and incentive schemes for executive management.

Network Rail is also a single-purpose not-for-dividend private company with an executive responsible to about 100 stakeholders, and a compulsory management incentive scheme. It bought the failed company Railtrack in 2001. Its track charges to train operators are subsidized by government grant; and its debts are guaranteed by the government. To keep the debt off the public balance sheet, Network Rail was organized as a private company, yet it has few private-sector disciplines, and control by the Office of Rail Regulation (ORR) is weak (NAO 2011b: 27–34). This mixture of disputable private status and ineffective public intervention is widely considered unsatisfactory (Transport Committee 2004; Glaister *et al.* 2006: 209–12; Merkert and Nash 2006: 78–80, 91; Shaoul 2006: 156–7; PAC 2011e: 3).

London Underground infrastructure renewal: PPP or PFI?

The 'London Underground PPP' contracts were officially PFI projects (HM Treasury 2003: 119). They had PFI characteristics – asset and risks transferred to contractors; fixed price service payment liabilities; a defined level of service with penalties for poor performance – except that they would be reviewed every seven and a half years and there was no provision for termination of contract (to reassure potential lenders). They were public–private partnerships in being both a deal between the government and private companies and a working relationship between the private infrastructure operators and the public train operator. They seemed to offer 'an improved prospect' over the previous London Underground investment regime (NAO 2004b: 3). Yet private contractors, even if they had performed better, were unlikely to have built a collaborative partnership with the Greater London Authority, which opposed the PPP, and in one way or another wound up the contracts, as seen in Chapter 3 (Glaister *et al.* 2006: 212–17).

Franchising rail services

The franchising of rail services is either a special case of a PPP or 'a privatization too far'. Nearly all passenger services are supplied through area-based franchises for which companies bid competitively. The Department for Transport (DfT) and devolved governments specify a minimum level of service, such as first and last trains, and the DfT regulates some fares. Beyond that, operators try to offer a timetable and fare structure that will maximize their revenues while reducing operating costs through efficient use of staff and trains. The licensing, charging and penalty relationships between the train operators and Network Rail are regulated by ORR, as in the privatized utilities, with the significant exception that ORR does not regulate fare prices.

The Labour Government increased public intervention by substituting Network Rail for Railtrack and giving Network Rail, operators and metropolitan transport authorities very substantial grants (NAO 2008: 9). The DfT took franchising powers back 'in-house' (from a quasi-independent regulator), and has ordered trains to supplement those that operators lease from rolling stock companies. In recent franchise agreements, DfT shared with the operator the financial risk from any future decline in passenger numbers, which produced higher-valued bids (NAO 2008: 6) but – or therefore – did not stop some operators having to abandon their franchise because they could not honour their bid. In these cases, trains run under a management contract from the DfT until a new franchise competition is organized. The question now is whether this complicated and fragmented structure with its disincentives to good financial management can be simplified without further upheavals to rail services (McNulty 2011).

Regulating the public utilities

Rail privatization was not a typical privatization because of franchising but it shared features of the telecommunications, energy and water privatizations: state-owned monopolies were sold to the private sector and constrained in their financial decisions by an independent regulator. The regulator's licensing regime provides assurance on the probity and safety record of companies, but more significantly, enables the regulator to set prices and performance standards, and collect financial and performance data as part of the licence conditions.

The economic arguments for privatizing public enterprises were outlined in Chapter 2; they depend chiefly on market theories that deplore both monopolies and state intervention. However, the government also found financial advantage in offsetting borrowing with privatization receipts, and political advantage in turning voters into shareholders and reducing the power of the public-sector unions (Lawson 1993: 207–8, 227, 238). Traditional economic theory saw the utilities as natural monopolies which should be in public hands to stop consumer exploitation. This theory has been undermined by post-privatization experience. Competition has emerged in apparent monopolies (rival telephone firms, competing electricity retailers, alternative communications systems); just the existence of multiple monopoly suppliers enables comparisons to be made and pressure applied. Public monopolies improve their performance when they become private monopolies: managers focus on the company share price which helps determine whether the firm is taken over and they lose their jobs or whether they make a profit from share option schemes: personal gain has replaced the public-service motivation (Lipsey 2000: 197). The mere threat of a potential rival ('contestable' markets) sharpens incentives for existing operators. The social argument that 'unprofitable' consumers would be ignored has also been countered: partly by conditions imposed in privatization legislation and partly by court rulings.

The regulator is nevertheless crucial to controlling prices while allowing companies to make the profits needed for investment. According to the OECD (2005a: 114): 'The independent regulators play an important role in balancing the public interest in access to utilities at a reasonable cost with the commercial imperatives of the supplier while keeping the whole system at arm's length from political interference'. This 'public interest' model of regulation is contradicted by the 'capture model' which points to 'producer' or 'regulatory' capture, when regulators spend so much time discussing the investment needs of these firms that they begin to see the world through their eyes, not those of consumers (Lipsey 2000: 87). Privatized utilities are also watched by bodies representing consumer interests, but their impact is hard to detect.

The regulated utilities

The UK was a forerunner in the mass privatization of public utilities, though 'not necessarily an exemplar' (Hughes 2003: 103). By 2010, only 18 per cent of UK infrastructure (energy, telecoms, water, waste, transport) was in the hands of public bodies with another 9 per cent owned by not-for-profit companies. About 40 per cent was owned by foreign-owned utilities and investment banks (OFT 2010). Each utility was privatized differently as the government's thinking evolved.

British Telecom (now BT) was the first big utility to be privatized. The government decided that competition law offered insufficient consumer protection and adopted a regulatory system proposed by Stephen Littlechild (1983). Where BT had a monopoly, the maximum annual price rise would be 'the Retail Price Index minus X' (RPI-X) meaning its price in real terms would fall, and profits could be increased only by reducing costs. 'X' would be set by the regulator and reviewed for new efficiencies every few years. This arrangement was expected to serve only until there was credible competition. In the event, the formula not only continued in communications but was applied to other sectors.

The primary duty of the Office of Telecommunications (Oftel) was to ensure that services were supplied wherever reasonable and that operators were able to finance this supply; promotion of competition was only a secondary duty, as it is for its successor, the Office of Communications (Ofcom), which also regulates radio and television and eventually postal services. Ofcom's primary duties, set by Labour, are to ensure that a wide range of services is available throughout the UK and to promote consumers' interests. Nevertheless, all the regulators have driven competition, believing it is the best consumer protection (Thatcher 1998: 129; Ofcom 2010a: 8; 2010b: 3). By 2009, there were enough alternative providers for Ofcom to deregulate the retail part of the fixed-line market. Wholesale prices are still regulated because BT Openreach controls other operators' access to customers, but these prices allow BT 'a fair rate of return' for its investment (Ofcom 2010a: 9–10). Any provider can be fined for poor service, such as TalkTalk in 2011 for charging customers whose accounts it had closed.

British Gas was privatized in 1986 as a monopolistic provider: only the market for large industrial users was opened up. The government therefore gave the Office of Gas Supply a stronger, more complex regulatory role. The formula became RPI–X+Y, where Y was world oil price; the price control regime thus passed fuel purchase costs fully to the consumer on the grounds they were unavoidable. Different elements of costs were controlled separately. Gas (and electricity) privatization legislation specifically made promoting competition a primary duty, although there were also social duties, such as protecting vulnerable users. British Gas proved reluctant to open its infrastructure to fair competition and was referred to the Office of Fair Trading and the Monopolies & Mergers Commission (now Competition Commission). While these regulators proposed new forms of control, ministers chose to rely on competition, and required British Gas to separate transportation (Transco) from trading (Centrica) to make it easier for new traders to emerge. The market was then opened further, including all domestic consumers by 1998 (Simmonds and Bartle 2004: 2–6).

The electricity industry was split up before privatization because of criticisms of gas privatization and because loss-making nuclear power would deter purchasers (Lawson 1993: 236–7). In England and Wales, conventional generation was sold as two companies, and separated from the regional distribution and retail boards; these were monopolies but they had a client–contractor relationship with the generators, unlike in Scotland where Scottish Power and Scottish HydroElectric were privatized as vertically integrated companies; in any case, all generators soon bought distributors. Mergers and acquisitions across the electricity, gas and water sectors have produced a complicated pattern of provision, but not a vigorous market for consumers. Although the Office of Electricity Regulation helped smaller companies by regulatory action, more was achieved by the government – both Conservative and Labour – deciding to open up competition. By 2001, most larger users and a third of domestic consumers had switched supplier at least once (Simmonds 2002: 7).

The Utilities Act 2000 merged the gas and electricity regulators as the Office of Gas and Electricity Markets (Ofgem) and modified the electricity regime to try to increase competition: retail business was detached from distribution, and the licensing regime was altered to let electricity companies operate anywhere in Great Britain (Northern Ireland has separate utility regulation, as we saw in Chapter 3). The legislation gave more weight to the government and its environmental and social aims for energy; the regulator has to take account of the energy minister's guidance on energy efficiency, renewable energy and cross-subsidies that help disadvantaged customers: all these constraints inevitably raise production costs and prices.

Ofgem in 2010 was stimulated by the anger of users at steeply rising prices (and perhaps the question of its own demise as a quango) to conclude that a 'radical overhaul of the retail gas and electricity market' was necessary (Ofgem 2011). Threat of referral to the Competition Commission persuaded the 'big six' energy firms to engage with reforms that would ease entry for new operators. Simplifying the tariff regime would make prices more transparent to users and improve competition. The Coalition's quango review decided to retain Ofgem; at the same time its functions and those of the energy minister were made the subject of a wider exercise with one aim – the clarification of the respective roles of regulator and ministers (DECC 2011).

Privatization of the *water authorities* in England and Wales was helped by the desire of Thames Water to be freed from Treasury control of investment (Lawson 1993: 230). The Office of Water Services (Ofwat) developed 'yardstick' competition between these regional monopolies, setting 'X' for each in relation to the industry average level of efficiency improvement. Ofwat's 2009 rulings for the 2010–14 period set price levels for the worst performers below expected inflation. Some companies complained the rulings overcompensated for the 2005–10 settlement (which had resulted in increased bills and large profits), but did not refer the settlements to the Competition Commission, as they could have done if they had a good case. Ofwat performs a complex balancing act between the impact of the credit crisis on company profits, keeping consumer prices stable, and securing investment in an industry challenged by climate change. Ofwat usually wields the 'stick' of fines on companies, such as for misreporting items in their regulatory accounts, but is now holding out the 'carrot' of deregulation for those companies with consistently good performance. Ofwat's review of future strategy suggests price regulation could be replaced in part by direct competition between water retail suppliers (*Financial Times* 25 October 2010, 25 February 2011, 17 May 2011).

Ultimately, privatization of the state utilities resulted in a change of operator status (not necessarily a change of operator) but little change in government intervention. It is now carried out through 'arm's length' regulatory bodies rather than the traditional directives from ministers quietly mediated by department officials, and it focuses on outcomes (performance and prices) rather than financial support from the government. Relationships are less shadowy. However, the clarity of the 'temporary' regulatory structure has become obscured as both regulators and ministers battle with increasingly complex demands on service providers.

Managing public finances and engaging the private sector

The economic crisis in 2008 drew renewed attention to the crucial place of fiscal policy in the UK's financial management strategy, despite the lack of intellectual or political agreement on the link between budgetary stimulus and economic growth. Yet even the drastic cutbacks in 2010 made little difference to the overall pattern of expenditure between different policy sectors or to the distribution of funding sources – which is not to say that some sections of society and some public authorities were not significantly affected.

The Coalition Government continued the modernization of financial management procedures that the Labour Government had developed, often from ideas conceived by the previous Conservative Government. The process of extending the planning framework was one of evolution but, put together with the unified budget, resource accounting and budgeting, and delegation of some functions to independent experts, the package amounts to radical change.

The devolved parliaments started with more inclusive budgetary arrangements than the UK parliament so far contemplates. Scotland will take on more financial responsibility but Wales and Northern Ireland will be tied to the UK Treasury for longer because they are dependent on financial transfers from England. English local authorities benefited during the Labour administration from a relaxation in central financial controls, though not as much as they had expected – rate-capping and ring-fenced HRAs remain in place, and the Coalition's local referendum on 'excessive' council tax is another tool of the same type. However, local government also experienced a substantial rise in resources under Labour, and is therefore strongly affected by the sudden return to earlier levels of funding.

Councils and hospital trusts that engaged in PFI deals have felt the impact of their payment obligations at a time of cuts. Despite its problems, PFI is too useful to governments to be ignored: the Coalition Government is negotiating further projects, ignoring warnings that they present poor VfM when private borrowing costs are high, and perhaps at other times too. However, PFI is not a large part of procurement despite its political prominence. Other forms of public-private partnership have emerged, some of which bring in the different skills of third sector partners too. This chapter has focused on two groups of private companies that are subject to strong government intervention: those that have failed to be privatized successfully, though they may, as in NATS's case, eventually be so; and the privatized utilities, which were unsuitable for launching into an open market and for that reason were publicly regulated. They remain in an uneasy half-way house between public and private financial management, with neither the transparency and democratic accountability expected of public bodies, nor able to be judged in the market place by the efficiencies, innovations and profits they make.

Chapter 8

Human Resource Management in the Public Sector

The public sector is very labour intensive – around 60 per cent of the budgets of most public organizations are spent on staff. Both public and private organizations now recognize that people are their most important asset and resource, and that human resource management is very important to the success of their organizations. Public organizations want to become employers of choice and to attract people to work in the public sector that have the skills and competencies it needs. The management of human resources has high priority not only because of the high cost of staff but also because human resources are the agents of all government activities. In 2011, some six million people were employed in the UK public sector, 20 per cent of all official employment. There have been significant changes in the way people are managed in the public sector over the last 30 years, which coincides with the introduction of new public management (NPM) and especially performance management but also with changes in the role of the public sector and its relationship with the private and voluntary sectors. As traditional public administration and government has given way to NPM and governance, so traditional personnel management (TPM) has given way to new forms of people management collectively referred to as human resource management (HRM). This chapter examines the reasons for that change and its effect on how public officials are currently organized, recruited, trained, developed, appraised, rewarded and managed in the various public services. Finally, it highlights some of the major issues confronting HRM in the public sector today in the context of public sector contraction and austerity.

The structure of public sector employment in the UK

Public employees are those employed by government bodies throughout the United Kingdom but their status can vary from one part of the public sector to another. Central government employs civil servants who are found throughout the country in government departments and agencies. Until 2010, and the passage of the Constitutional Reform and Governance Act, they were servants of the Crown (Burnham and Pyper 2008) subject to rules and regulations made by ministers using prerogative powers. They now have a statutory basis and the prime minister as Minister for the Civil Service is responsible for managing and regulating the service and reporting annually to parliament. Those functions are usually delegated to a minister in the Cabinet Office. The prime minister approves the appointment of the 'Top 200' civil servants, after taking advice from the Senior Leadership Committee (a committee of senior civil servants). *The Civil Service Management Code* lists the rules and regulations relating to the management of civil servants including the Civil Service Code (now also incorporated in the Constitutional Reform Act 2010) which requires civil servants to be loyal to the government of the day irrespective of its political composition and not to divulge information unless authorized to do so. This code does not apply to political advisers, who have a separate code.

In 2011, there were approximately 500,000 civil servants, or 10 per cent of all public officials (see Chapter 3). The Cabinet Office has overall responsibility for coordinating national human resources policies as well as specific responsibility for the senior civil service (SCS), but departments and agencies have delegated authority to manage their own staff, which covers all HR functions. Northern Ireland is the only devolved government that has its own civil service, dating from 1921, but there is currently a strong move to create a separate civil service in Scotland.

Nearly three million people work in local government in the UK, which includes teachers, social workers, planners, architects, engineers, surveyors, managers and administrators. In contrast to most other European countries, these public sector employees are not civil servants but employees of their respective local authority. This is true throughout the UK. Further, over one million doctors, nurses, paramedics, managers and administrators work in the National Health Service (NHS) in hospital and primary care trusts (until 2013) in England and in Local Health Boards in Wales, Scotland and Northern Ireland. Police officers and civilian staffs are employed by 43 separate police authorities in England and Wales, eight in Scotland and in the Ulster Police Force of Northern Ireland. There are also more than 2,000 non-departmental public bodies (NDPBs) each employing its own staff. This complex of public bodies has no common personnel system – each service has its own policies that are applied within its respective employing bodies, although they are all subject to national human rights, employment, and health and safety legislation, which is a unifying factor.

The number of public officials has waxed and waned since 1980 (see Table 3.2). During the Conservative administrations it fell by 2 million but the civil service had the biggest fall (30 per cent). During the Labour administrations from 1997 to 2010, the civil service, local government and the NHS grew as Labour was committed to improving public services, especially in education and health. The recession and credit crisis from 2008 was beginning to have an impact by 2010 when the government predicted cuts in expenditure and staff. The Coalition Government implemented drastic cuts, which had a significant effect on employment with 67,000 jobs lost in the public sector by the end of 2011.

From personnel management to HRM

The public sector had evolved a distinctive approach to managing people by the middle of the twentieth century, which was characterized by special institutions and practices that were broadly universal (Box 8.1). It was a highly centralized system in which policies on recruitment procedures, pay, conditions of service and all personnel regulations were decided at the top and little discretion was left to line managers or personnel administrators. The style of management was paternalistic and reflected a concern for the welfare of employees and fair treatment. Recruitment was open and competitive using clearly prescribed examinations and tests and there were standard, open-ended contracts with generous pension rights, although some public services, such as the NHS, local government and education, had large numbers of part-time workers whose pay and terms and conditions were not as good. There were national pay structures with long incremental scales and automatic progression each year, with standard holidays, sick leave and pension rights throughout the country. Industrial relations were characterized by voluntary collectivism with pay and conditions determined by collective bargaining and joint regulation. Union membership was very high, ranging from 60 per cent to 90 per cent throughout the public sector. Government was considered to be a 'good' employer setting an example to the private sector as a 'model' employer (Farnham 1999; and see Box 8.2). Central government was generally in advance of both other parts of the public sector and the private sector. It was the first to provide occupational pensions, to reduce working hours and, from the 1950s, introduced equal pay for women. This was not simply altruistic as these practices were aimed primarily at attracting and retaining the best-qualified staff and people with a public service motivation. This remains a major concern today in an increasingly competitive labour market environment.

Until the 1970s there were no professional personnel managers in the public sector (Farnham and Horton 1996b). The personnel administrators (or 'establishment officers') had very limited discretion in the interpretation and application of standardized policies and line managers had few personnel

BOX 8.1 Characteristics of traditional personnel management

- An administrative personnel management function.
- A paternalistic style of management.
- Standardized employment practices.
- Collectivist patterns of industrial relations.
- A model and good practice employer.

Source: Farnham and Horton (1996b: 80).

BOX 8.2 The Good Employer

The Good Employer should ensure that it:

- offers satisfactory rewards – pay, pensions and security;
- provides a worthwhile job and the means to do it so that in the short-term the individual can give of his best and in the long-term can have opportunities for advancement;
- provides a good working environment;
- shows consideration towards staff and respects their aspirations and needs;
- provides security and a sense of common purpose.

Source: Summarized from Civil Service Department (1975) *Civil Servants and Change: Joint Statement by the National Whitley Council and the Wider Issues Review Team* (HMSO), p. 8.

responsibilities. In the civil service, for example, all staff were recruited through centrally organized competitions run by the Civil Service Commission. Pay and conditions of service were determined centrally either through collective bargaining or executive decision for the higher civil service and they were standardized to ensure uniform treatment throughout the country and to facilitate mobility of staff within a uniform and unified structure.

Although there were some variations between local authorities, strong union membership and national collective bargaining resulted in standardized salary structures and terms and conditions accepted by the employers to avoid wage competition for what were limited supplies of specialist labour. From the outset the NHS had uniform structures and pay scales. The industrial parts of the public sector – the newly nationalized industries post-1945 – coal, gas, electricity and railways – had the highest union membership of all and this resulted again in both standardization and close government control through the Boards of each nationalized industry. During the 1970s, these personnel practices began to change due to the influence of the Fulton Report (1968a) in the civil service, the Bains Report (1972) in local government and the pink circular *Development of the Personnel Function* (DHSS 1972) in the NHS. Box 8.3 illustrates the thinking at that time and points to the major changes that followed not only in the NHS but throughout the other public services over the next decade.

The fundamental ideological attack on welfare Keynesianism and 'big government' in the 1980s (Farnham and Horton 1993) saw the public services condemned as overstaffed, inefficient, supplier-led and unresponsive to public needs or demands while the trade unions and professional associations were blamed for the rises in public expenditure. It was also argued that rewards in the public sector were not linked to performance or productivity and public services were devoid of effective management. Throughout the

BOX 8.3 The personnel function of the future

The Personnel Department of the future will differ both in approach and scope from the former Establishments Department. Instead of being mainly regulatory, it will be wider, more comprehensive and more skilled. Whereas the establishment work has been largely concerned with determination and control of complements, pay and grading and management of appointments procedure, personnel work – while including the whole range of establishment work – will also include, for example, advice on recruitment sources and methods; on selection techniques and induction processes; staff appraisal and counselling; training, including the identification of training needs and arrangements to meet them; industrial relations and staff welfare arrangements ... It is important to stress a main guiding principle – that personnel management is a line management function. Departmental heads, including all professional heads, retain final responsibility within the line management structure, for their own staff; though because of the increasing complexity of the work they will wish to look to a Personnel Department for special advice or a specialist service.

Source: Cumin (1978): 1–2.

1980s, the traditional pattern of personnel management was replaced by HRM as successive Conservative governments resorted to managerialism.

Ideas of HRM emerged in the late 1970s in the USA along with ideas of NPM. These were essentially business-oriented approaches to managing people. Successive models of HRM were developed (Beardwell and Holden 1994) and there was a lively debate about the meaning of HRM (Storey 1989, 1992, 1997; Legge 1989, 1995; Blyton and Turnbull 1992) but the core ideas were widely accepted (Box 8.4).

HRM can take the form of a rational, calculative, business-centred approach rooted in managerial concerns for economy and efficiency. Here staff represent a cost to be minimized and controlled, rather than an asset to be valued. In contrast, HRM can also adopt a 'softer' more people-oriented approach seeing human resources as a source of value which must be nurtured to obtain that value. It therefore focuses on people-centred policies such as staff development, training, communication, motivation and leadership. Evidence suggests there is an attempt in UK public services to balance the two, although external environmental factors appear to determine which strategy is foremost at any one time.

The process of change in the public services

The process of change to HRM in the public services has been incremental but since the 1980s a transition has taken place. The policies pursued by successive governments that have had the most impact on people manage-

BOX 8.4 Core ideas common to HRM models

- People are an organization's most important resource and the key to its success.
- People are an asset and investment in 'human capital' is good business. The capital must be maintained and developed to ensure the full exploitation of its potential value.
- Human resources strategy must be integrated with business strategy to ensure the achievement of organizational goals and objectives.
- Employees must be committed to the organization's mission, goals and objectives and to its values to ensure 'business' success.
- Total quality should be the aim of all organizations.
- Organizations and people must be flexible to meet the needs of a constantly changing environment.
- The right to manage is legitimized by the need for the organization to survive in a competitive environment and to achieve its goals and objectives.

ment are the financial management initiatives, the introduction of performance management, agencification, contractorization and the quality movement. Management ideas such as employment flexibility (Farnham and Horton 2000) and competency management (Horton *et al.* 2002) have also transformed employment patterns, staff development and training. Overall, the culture of all public services has been transformed from one emphasizing serving the government and providing national services to one emphasizing service to the customer, the consumer and the client, both internal or external to the organization, and providing choice and more personalized services. E-Government has opened access to government organizations at any time, while freedom of information has also resulted in more 'expert' users of public services who are more challenging of public officials and willing to demand good service. The ICT revolution has had a direct impact on job profiles, competencies and the training that public officials now require.

The old personnel departments headed by second or third level personnel managers/establishment officers have been replaced by HR departments headed by HR Directors, many of whom are members of senior management teams and often on Executive Boards. HR strategies reflect many of the characteristics outlined in the HRM model above – namely integration with business plans, two-way communication to gain the commitment of staff, an emphasis on quality and standards such as Investors in People, using self assessment tools such as the EFQM model and the Balanced Scorecard, and greater flexibility (see Chapter 6). In contrast to the highly centralized, standardized, cost-oriented, ad hoc, pragmatic approach of TPM, which was short term, employee-centred and non-strategic, HRM in the public sector today is more decentralized, 'business'-oriented and now steered from the centre but locally managed. The major personnel role is performed by line managers with specialists in HR departments acting as business partners and advisers. The latter also develop HR processes and systems and monitor their implementation and use by line managers. The fragmented organizations which make up today's public services are more open and diverse, and their HR policies and practices are closer to the private sector on which they have been, and are increasingly, modelled. Finally, the personnel function has been professionalized and incumbents are expected to have professional training and qualifications.

Human resources flexibilities in UK public services

Apart from being committed to reducing the size of the state and transferring services and activities back to the private sector, Governments during the 1980s responded to the need for greater flexibility in their personnel policies and practices to be able to react to an increasingly fast changing environment and also to curb their labour costs. The competitive environment and the changing economic structure towards a knowledge-based economy were major drivers of greater flexibilities including contractual and pay flexibilities, flexibilities in working life and the location of work and task flexibilities (Farnham and Horton 2000: 14–16). To incorporate many of these flexibilities, governments had to increase labour market flexibilities and remove rigidities in the labour market to allow the forces of supply and demand to operate in an unfettered way. This was done by legislating to weaken the trade unions, reducing employment protection by abolishing the wages councils, which established minimum wages in low-pay sectors, and reducing employment protection (Farnham and Pimlott 1995). Another trend was to remove pay from collective bargaining by introducing Pay Review Bodies for nurses, midwives, health visitors and professions allied to medicine (1983) and teachers (1991). There was also more flexibility in organizational design: 'New technologies also gave an impetus to management preferences for operating a flexible workforce unconstrained by multiple grades, skill demarcation lines, payment systems and work patterns' (Horton 2000: 209).

The Mueller Report (1987) recommended a wide range of alternative working patterns including flexible hours, job sharing, term-time working, recurring temporary appointments, on-call arrangements, home-working and career breaks in the civil service and these were gradually introduced. Agencification and the movement to the 'contract state' in the 1980s also offered more flexibility as employment contracts could be time specific, specialist skills could be obtained on a temporary basis and a core/periphery profile of staff could be more easily managed. Many non-core functions throughout the public services were contracted out to the private sector or, if retained in-house, were accompanied by staff reductions and new terms and conditions of employment (Horton 2000). Job sharing, annual hours contracts, working from home and other patterns not only benefited the employer but also employees, especially women. Although flexible working patterns had always existed in local government and the NHS, it was their extension to managerial positions that marked a change. Flexible working patterns undoubtedly contributed to the increased feminization of the public services at all levels.

In addition to the increased flexibility in public organizations the working lives of public sector employees also changed. Career systems and jobs for life have generally given way to what are now called 'position systems' where appointments are to a post and individuals take responsibility for their own career development. Promotion is gained by moving posts and often organizations (although this has long been the practice in local government). This has also been accompanied by a decline in collectivism and a move towards greater individualization. This is reflected in the fall in trade union membership from 13.2 million in 1979 to 7.4 million in 2009 (Certification Office 2010), although public sector membership is still much higher than in the private sector.

Public organizations are now more representative of the publics they serve, and equal opportunity policies and positive action strategies have seen a marked increase in the number of women at all levels and also of people from minority ethnic groups. It is now unlawful to discriminate on grounds of sex, race, ethnicity, religion, marital status, sexual orientation or age. There is also now much more training and positive action to prepare under-represented social groups for advancement. Assertiveness training, women-only management training courses and ethnic minority preparation for entry examinations are common in the civil service and some other public organizations such as the police.

Other significant changes have been increased professionalization of the public professions, such as teaching, nursing, professions allied to medicine, social workers and the police and emergency services; the introduction of a lower level of support workers in all the above professions; and the creation of new professions such as forensic scientists, computer and media systems experts and the social marketing profession. Below we will now trace the major changes in the civil service, local government and the NHS.

The civil service

There have been major changes in the structure, composition, flexibilities and HRM policies of the civil service since 1979. Overall responsibility for HRM rests with the Cabinet Office Capability Group, which has a strategic role, but the function is highly decentralized with all departments and agencies exercising HR responsibilities since 1996. Each has its own HR Director and HR department which determines strategy and monitors its application by line managers, who manage staff on a day to day basis. The specialist HR function has been professionalized and staffs are encouraged to obtain CIPD

(Chartered Institute of Personnel and Development) qualifications. There were 12,500 HR 'professionals' in the civil service in 2008 but in recent years the HR function or elements of it are being contracted out.

A Director General of Leadership and People Strategy was appointed in 2006 from the private sector to head the Capability Group. Her job was to develop the leadership needs of the service, to drive the government's reform programme, ensure that the service has the professional skills needed and the capability to lead, innovate and deliver in the future. This is not easy in such a decentralized system where the centre does not know exactly what the parts are doing. Quarterly meetings of HR Directors are not a very effective coordinating mechanism, which can explain the poor implementation of many government personnel policies. The Coalition Government is seeking to remedy the implementation gap.

Changes in structure

The structures in which civil servants operate and the way their work is carried out have changed. The civil service was originally both socially and organizationally class-based (Drewry and Butcher 1991) and divided both vertically and horizontally like a chequer board. Three horizontal classes, clerical, executive and administrative constituted the backbone of the service and employed the majority of staffs who were generalists. In addition there were hundreds of specialist vertical classes, with a similar horizontal structure to the core but employing engineers, scientists, statisticians, economists and so on. This class structure also mirrored the British educational and social system as those recruited to the lower classes came from lower socio-economic backgrounds and with basic secondary education. The executive classes attracted middle socio-economic groups with A levels or lower grade degrees and those from wealthier backgrounds and elite universities entered the administrative and equivalent specialist classes. Mobility between groups was difficult and the top posts in the civil service were always filled by generalist administrators, predominantly from Oxbridge (Kelsall 1974; Fulton 1968a; Kellner and Crowther Hunt 1980). The specialists were said to be 'always on tap and never on top' (Ridley 1968).

This rigid structure was heavily criticized by the Fulton Report (1968a) that recommended an open more flexible structure to facilitate both vertical and horizontal mobility and ensure the 'best person for the job'. Slowly that has taken place but with major changes since 2000. The terminology has changed too with lower level staffs now called administrative assistants (AA) and administrative officers (AO); executive staffs retain the same titles but the main changes are at the top. Specialists are now called professionals and, since 2007, generalists are also being gradually assigned to professional groups – policy professionals, corporate professionals and operational or delivery professionals (see below).

Departments and agencies determine their own grading systems and there is much structural flexibility. The concept of 'responsibility levels' is used to ensure some degree of comparability. Departmental grades are assigned to levels broadly equivalent (in terms of pay and job content) to the former service-wide grades (see Table 8.1). However classification is not easy to achieve as the types of jobs and levels of responsibility at the same grade vary significantly across different organizations. For example, AOs are employed by the Ministry of Justice to perform clerical work in courts while the Prison Service employs prison officers at broadly the same level; Executive Officers are employed by the Department of Work and Pensions as Benefit Delivery Officers in Job Centres and by the UK Border Agency as Immigration Officers.

The eight main grades today are:

- Senior Civil Service – Board level and senior management positions
- Grades 6 and 7 – Middle management positions
- SEO, HEO and EO – Lower management positions
- AO and AA – Administrative and clerical positions.

Table 8.1 ***Comparison of old and new civil service structures, 2012***

Old title	Grade	New title	Pay band
SCS levels			
Cabinet Secretary and Head of the Civil Service		Cabinet Secretary Head of the Civil Service	Special scale
Permanent Secretary (head of department)	grade 1	Permanent Secretary (head of department)	
Deputy Secretary	grade 2	Director General	3
Under Secretary	grade 3	Director	2
Assistant Secretary	grade 5	Deputy Director	1
Management levels			
Senior Principal	grade 6	Assistant Director	
Principal	grade 7	Team Leader	
Senior Executive Officer	SEO		
Higher Executive Officer	HEO		
Executive Officer	EO		
Administrative grades			
Administrative Officer	AO		
Administrative Assistant	AA		

Note: From 2012, the joint post as Cabinet Secretary and Head of the Civil Service was split between three posts: Cabinet Secretary; Head of the Civil Service (held by a department permanent secretary); and a permanent secretary for the Cabinet Office.

The *professions* of civil servants were recorded for the first time in 2007. These professions now relate to the *post* occupied by the person and are not dependent on any qualifications the individual may have. The range of professions includes the traditional ones of economists, engineering, finance, human resources, legal, librarian, science, tax inspection and so on, but also the new professional categories including operational delivery (delivering front line services) or policy delivery (designing or enhancing services to the public). If a post can be considered operational delivery but also matches one of the specific professions, the person is assigned to the specific profession. As a result of this change, all civil servants are now deemed to be professionals or are expected to be in time.

Who are the civil servants today?

A profile of the civil service in 2009/10 can be found in Table 8.2. It is predominantly female, although this is not reproduced at every level as women constitute only one third of the SCS. They tend to be concentrated in the AA and AO groups and make up the vast majority of part-time workers. The service approximately mirrors the ethnic composition of society although again these ratios are not reflected throughout the rank structure. The number of people with disabilities has increased to 7.1 per cent but this is an unreliable statistic as not all people declare they have a disability and it is a difficult concept to define. Another significant change in recent years has been the work location of civil servants. It is largely due to a policy of de-concentration of government offices to take advantage of local labour markets and avoid the higher costs of employment in the capital and the South East. The Lyons Report (2004) identified scope for major relocations and the Smith Report (2010) identified scope for more.

Table 8.2 ***The civil service in 2009/10***

Feature	Key facts at 31 March 2009
Size	487,000 (full time equivalent); 80% full time and 20% part-time
Gender	53% were women, but women constituted 85% of the part-time workforce
Ethnicity	Almost 9% of civil servants were from minority ethnic groups
Disability	7.1% of civil servants declared themselves to be disabled
Location	Only a quarter of civil servants worked in London and the South East, 9.7% worked in Scotland and 6.9% in Wales. The rest worked in English regions

Source: Office for National Statistics (ONS) *Civil Service Statistics 2009*, available from www.ons.gov.uk.

Recruitment of civil servants

The civil service, once a career system, is now a hybrid: part career and part post. This is partly because people no longer enter the service as a career, as in the past; there is a much higher turnover of staff and people no longer stay in the service 'for life'. It is also because specific jobs are now advertised and people are appointed to a post, often for a specified period of time. The system is also now more open as jobs are advertised both internally and externally and then filled with the 'best person for the job'. Finally, the service has introduced more flexibility to meet the needs of women in particular but also to enable managers to make choices about whether to contract jobs out or retain them in-house.

Recruitment is highly decentralized and civil servants are recruited by departments and agencies, although the recruitment procedures are all bound by the principles of fairness, openness, equal opportunities and selection on the basis of merit. The Civil Service Commission sets out the principles and rules applying to recruitment and monitors the process to ensure conformity. They are especially responsible for the SCS but also give their approval on whether jobs can be filled by outsiders (CSC 2009: 17–20).

Most recruitment is now via the internet as departments have their own websites and post vacancies and application forms for completion electronically (Cabinet Office 2007b; NAO 2009). The aim of the recruitment and selection process is to obtain and retain the best people. The civil service has always been in the forefront in using sophisticated psychometric and competency assessment techniques. These are rigorously evaluated to try to ensure that they are not culturally biased or discriminate against particular groups of applicants. Two problems persist in recruitment: first, the time it takes, resulting in the loss of many suitable candidates to other employers; second, the loss of new recruits within the first year, which raises questions about the effectiveness of recruitment and induction. In 2010 general turnover was running at about 10 per cent for the service overall and was higher amongst external recruits. This is partly because the latter are recruited on fixed contracts but there is also some evidence that SCS appointments from outside stay for shorter periods of time because of a clash of cultures (see below). This high turnover may, however, enable the cutbacks planned by the Coalition Government to be achieved with fewer redundancies.

Recruitment to the SCS has traditionally been through two routes – fast-track direct entry by a competitive examination and internal promotion from the lower ranks. Today the system is far more open although the 'fast stream' has survived. There are currently five fast streams: the graduate, economist, statistician, Government Communication Headquarters (GCHQ) and Technology in Business schemes (see Burnham and Pyper 2008: 198–9 for reports on the fast stream). The fast stream is still a training and development programme and attracts some of the country's most talented graduates. Fast streamers are selected for their potential to become the leaders of the future, and it is anticipated that those with the most talent will reach the highest posts of the SCS.

There were over 14,000 external applicants for the fast streams in 2009, and 629 were recommended for appointment. Comparable figures for the specialist fast tracks were 2,356 and 226. The success ratio is much higher amongst internal candidates, a different route, through which 70 out of 136 were successful. Applications to the fast streams continue to grow and were 20 per cent higher in 2009 than in 2008. Although applicants are drawn from over 60 universities around 30 per cent of successful candidates continue to come from Oxbridge; thus illustrating continuity along with change.

Although numbers of civil servants fell in the last years of the Labour Government the SCS increased by 35 per cent from 2000 to 2009. Many of the posts in the SCS (some 4,200 in 2009) are openly advertised, especially in the highest grades. The majority of SCS positions are still filled from within the service (see Table 8.3), but appointments to the top 200 posts are often filled from outside the service. The appointment of external candidates, especially from the private sector, has always been controversial, partly because they are paid more than internal appointees but also because their turnover is higher. Both the Senior Salaries Review Body (SSRB), and the Civil Service Commissioners (CSC) raised this as an issue (SSRB 2007; CSC 2008: 4). An internal investigation, resulting in the Normington Report (2008), recommended that the Cabinet Office develop a workforce strategy for the SCS and a corresponding pay policy to offset the skills gap and that a case be made for every open competition with stricter enforcement of salary scales. Two years later the Normington proposals had not been acted upon (PASC 2010: 4). However, the Coalition Government intends to achieve a one-third reduction in central government administration by 2014 and their imposition of a salary cap on senior staff indicates further reform.

Table 8.3 ***Composition of new entrants to SCS, as percentage of total SCS entry***

Previous post	2004	2005	2006	2007	2008	2009
Wider public sector and voluntary sector	13	15	13	17	11	8
Private sector	23	21	17	21	18	20
Government departments	64	65	70	62	71	72

Source: Reproduced from Public Administration Select Committee (PASC) (2010b) *Outsiders and Insiders: External Appointments to the Senior Civil Service: Further Report*, HC 500 (TSO), p.14.

Lateral entry

The breaking down of the career system was accelerated by the structural changes introduced after 1988 with the creation of executive agencies headed by chief executives (Horton and Jones 1996; James 2003. Most of the new chief executives were recruited through open competitions and over a third came from outside the service. These chief executives were appointed on fixed term personalized contracts, which have been extended to other posts and to all of the SCS. This is another example of private sector practice and has led to the emerging hybrid nature of the civil service. It has also coincided with the introduction of individualized performance management and performance related pay (see Chapter 6). The short-term contracts, although often renewable, have contributed to the increase in turnover in the civil service. It is another controversial development in the new HRM approach and the arguments for and against a contract and post-based system are identified by Burnham and Pyper (2008: 209). Contracts add to the flexibility of the civil service and are the means of attracting people who may not be willing to become permanent officials, although some brought in on short term contracts decide to stay.

Turnover of staff is, however, a major issue not only because of the high costs and time involved in recruitment but also because of the effect on organizational efficiency and productivity and the loss of expertise. Turnover is highest at the lowest levels (AOs and EOs) where the majority (70 per cent) of civil servants are employed. These posts are usually easier to fill as they recruit mainly from local labour markets. There are, however, some specialist posts that are difficult to fill and departmental human resources teams have been developing workforce plans to assess the capacity and capability of the current workforce and determine the future requirement for staff to fill the gaps. Two strategies are being used: one is to encourage internal staff to obtain professional qualifications in the difficult to fill professions and the other is to try to fill internally or from other government departments, before considering whether to recruit externally. This has become more important under the Coalition as it implements its policy of contraction.

Training and development

The UK is almost unique in its traditional preference for a good general education even for its top civil servants and for 'training on the job' and 'learning from experience'. Specialists have always required a professional training before entering the service although not from specialist institutions as in many countries in continental Europe. (In France, specialists are recruited into the technical corps such as Corps des Ponts et Chaussées, Corps des Mines and Corps des Télécommunications after studying at the Ecole Polytechnique and a further specialist institution. The top administrative corps – Inspection des Finances, Conseil d'Etat, Cour des Comptes and the Corps des Préfets, are recruited from the Ecole Nationale d'Administration, ENA.) The Fulton Report (1968a) was very critical of the UK generalist tradition and recommended that preference be given for relevance in recruitment and that a Civil Service College should be created to train top civil servants along the lines of the French ENA. Preference for relevance was rejected but a College was created in 1970.

The Civil Service College, with its outpost in Edinburgh, was never responsible for all training, which was left to individual departments. It concentrated specifically on training the new entrants to the higher civil service. The training was quite specific in the early years, consisting of block periods of study in economics, statistics and social policy to compensate for the arts and classics backgrounds of most entrants. It also inducted new recruits into the ways of Whitehall. Over the years, that has changed and there is now a menu of courses from which departments could choose to send their new fast streamers, as well as specialist courses in the new professional skills. The old College was succeeded by the National School of Government (NSG) in 2006 which was a self financing non-ministerial department. It continued to offer a menu of courses but many were open to other public and private organizations, particularly its top leadership programmes. Strategic Leadership training was high priority and all new entrants to the SCS were required to undertake staged development (Horton 2009).

Training was fully decentralized in 1996. Many of the larger government departments have their own training organizations but there is a great deal of contracting with private consultancies to run courses. There is also a lot of duplication of training (for example, 250 different leadership courses in 2009) and very little coordination across the service as a whole. It is one of the 'inefficiencies' that the Coalition Government is tackling and reforms are underway to make civil service training more modern, efficient and cost effective. There is a movement away from residential and classroom teaching to work-based and e-learning training; training will focus more on business needs, building priority skills and leadership capability and improving performance management. A new Civil Service Learning operation, established in the Home Office in 2011, will buy in training for the whole civil service replacing the duplication amongst departments. The NSG will close in 2012. It is estimated that this will save about £90 million per year of the £275 million it spent in 2009/10 (Cabinet Office 2011e).

Performance management and staff appraisal

Performance management was introduced into the civil service in the early 1990s as part of the move to a more rational approach to managing government organizations and individual civil servants (see Chapter 6). The system of staff appraisal in place was transformed with the practice of establishing objectives, which staff are expected to achieve each year, and a system of performance related pay (PRP) to enable performance to be linked to rewards. Highly formalized dual appraisal systems are now universal and combine development, performance and reward reviews. This HR function is being continually reviewed and, at the time of writing, the major developments are the use of 360 degree appraisal, electronic processing of information and refining methods of assessing performance.

Competency frameworks

A related development in HR in the civil service has been the use of competency frameworks. These appeared first in the SCS during the 1980s but by the late 1990s most central government organizations were using competency frameworks and many other parts of the public sector were following their example (Farnham and Horton 2000). Competency frameworks form the basis for recruitment, training and development throughout the service and are continually being revised to reflect the changing role of the service and the skills and competencies that it needs. The SCS has a single framework that applies to all members across all government departments and larger agencies. There have been three frameworks since the beginning of the SCS – 1996, 2001 and 2006. The 2001 framework was designed to reflect the modernization agenda of the Labour Government with its emphasis on improvement and delivery of public services. Four years later another competency framework was introduced to remedy the implementation gap, which the Labour Government saw as the result of a lack of appropriate skills within the civil service, particularly in the SCS. The latest framework called Professional Skills for Government introduced in 2006, was one of a series of strategies adopted to ensure the civil service was 'fit for purpose' – to meet the needs of twenty-first century governance. Each government department has a skills strategy driven by the Government Skills Council. The future of this strategy, however, is at risk since government cutbacks under the Coalition Government are likely to affect training.

Industrial relations

Finally, there has been a significant change in industrial relations within the civil service. In 1983, the government de-recognized trade unions at GCHQ and encouraged departments and agencies to do likewise. Very few did, however, although the membership of trade unions has fallen continuously since then. Public sector trade union membership density was 65 per cent in 1979 and is now 56.6 per cent of a much smaller workforce. This is still much higher than the 15.1 per cent density in the private sector (Achur 2010). The relationships between the civil service unions and the civil service management changed during the 1980s and 1990s as a consequence of falling union membership, individualized contracts, PRP and a new approach to communicating with staff (Farnham 1999; Farnham *et al.* 2005). But the major change was in the effects of the decentralization of employment relations, which resulted in the end of the standardized, uniform payment systems and employee relations associated with TPM. There are now some 90 bargaining units and much more variation, as individual organizations are able to develop systems which meet their particular needs. The WERS survey of 2004 (Kersley 2005) indicated that 77 per cent of public sector workplaces still had collective bargaining although there are a smaller number of public sector unions: the three major unions are the First Division Association (FDA), Prospect, and the Public and Commercial Services Union (PCS). The Labour Government's policy on partnerships between public sector unions and employers never entirely realized the hopes of ending adversarial relationships although, at first, there was a decline in the number of industrial disputes. This was not to continue and has increased since 2010 in response to the Coalition's austerity programme and reform of the pensions system (see below).

The major changes in pay determination are the result of delegation of pay arrangements to departments and agencies for all staff below the SCS and the near-universal application of individual performance related pay (IPRP). Each civil service department negotiates pay for its own staff but the 90 separate bargaining units vary widely in size from the QEII Conference Centre (50 staff) to a unit of DWP (about 130,000 staff). Delegation began in the 1990s at the time that PRP was being spread. Each department has to operate within the Civil Service Management Code, which provides a central framework but they then decide, with their unions, their pay, bonus and terms and conditions for their staff. Some departments operate individualized bonus schemes whilst others use team bonuses but most have non-consolidated bonus schemes as well as merit based increments.

The pay of the SCS is examined each year by the Review Body on Senior Salaries which makes recommendations to the government. Its recommendations are usually, but not always, accepted. It advises on the appropriate cost of living and other increases, the amount of the salaries pot to be distributed via PRP, and the maximum and minimum bonuses. The pay of civil servants in general, and of the SCS in particular, has become more controversial because of the need to cut public expenditure and also to ensure that inside appointments are treated no less fairly than outside entrants (SSRB 2010). The Coalition Government in 2010 imposed a 5 per cent cut in top salaries and, in autumn 2011, announced a maximum 1 per cent pay rise over the next two years.

Industrial relations were fairly stable during the early years of the Labour administrations. Civil service salaries rose continuously and as union membership continued to fall there were no prolonged disputes. After 2008, however, the number of disputes rose, first under the Brown Government but more rapidly under the Coalition Government. The root causes of the disputes revolved around pay, redundancies and cutbacks in public services but particularly over pensions. The Coalition's austerity programme and cuts of £6.2 billion in the first year augured a winter of discontent and a return to industrial conflict. Confrontations increased in 2011 over their proposals to abandon final salary pensions, increase pension contributions and raise the retirement age, at which civil servants could draw their state and their occupational pension, to 67. Further strikes are likely as the austerity programme bites.

Local government

Each country that makes up the UK has its own local government system and, not surprisingly, there are variations in the extent to which they have adopted HRM structures and practices although some general trends are evident.

The 500 local authorities found in the UK currently employ around 1.8 million staff in some 600 occupations including teachers, fire-fighters, social workers, planners, surveyors, librarians, leisure centre staff and housing officers. Approximately half of all local government expenditure is on staff. There are also more than 23,000 elected councillors excluding parish councillors. In addition, there were 15 elected mayors in England in 2011, including Boris Johnson the Mayor of London. There will be more mayors following the implementation of the Localism Act 2011 in 2012, as it provides for local communities to opt in favour of mayors by referendum, and the Coalition expects more cities to have mayors by 2013.

All systems of local government have been affected by the developments in NPM and performance and quality management. These national policies have either been imposed on local government or they have been generated by reforming chief executives and senior managers. The regulatory and monitoring systems imposed by central government, including benchmarking, has resulted in a great deal of isomorphism as good practice is promoted and transferred, although there are differences amongst the devolved administrations.

As in central government, local authorities have been involved with re-engineering their structures and processes and this has had implications for personnel. The creation of large directorates comprising related departments has been accompanied by the decentralization of personnel functions with each directorate having its own personnel division responsible for recruitment, training and personnel administration. Education, however, has, in most cases, retained its separateness, partly because of its size in terms of teaching staff but also because it has been more centrally monitored by the various education departments in Whitehall. Each local education department has its own personnel department which has exercised a partnership relationship with individual schools since the 1988 Education Reform Act. Schools now recruit teachers, with the exception of head teachers, determine their own training strategy, although there are seven compulsory in-service training days (INSET days), and conduct their performance reviews but within a nationally imposed framework. They also decide on pay and rewards within the nationally agreed terms and conditions of service and the Pay Review Body salary awards. Scotland, which has always had its own education system, has no performance management agreement, although schools operate a system which makes reference to quality indicators. They also work within a national pay system, which has been determined since 2001 by a Scottish Negotiating Committee for teachers.

Recruitment in local government

From the 1990s, individualized contracts of employment were introduced for senior managers in local government. Some of those senior officials also received fringe benefits, including private health care and company cars as well as PRP. The number of managers in local government has increased disproportionately to other professions, although in line with their increase in both central government and the NHS. Recruitment methods generally reflect the patterns identified in the civil service – with electronic advertising and applications becoming increasingly the norm. Most local authorities use assessment centres for senior staff and find this the most reliable and valid selection method (CIPD 2009). Local authorities generally have rigorous diversity policies.

Training and development

Training and development in local government remains a Cinderella activity, having a relatively low status and typically not operating at a strategic level, although this is not true in education where there is a national policy of promoting continuing professional development (CPD). The major activity in local government remains the provision of 'post-entry training' for new entrants and equipping them with relevant professional qualifications. Beyond that, provision is patchy. Since the 1990s, some authorities are using competence-based NVQ (National Vocational Qualification) models as the vehicle for management development, but in many authorities, especially small ones, little systematic development takes place. Use of appraisal to identify development needs is sporadic but increasing.

Training and development is still only partially professionalized. More staff are entering training through a professional HR or educational route but many are still generalist administrators. Despite some elaborate post-entry training provision, less training is provided to local government employees than to employees in any other major public sector although this is beginning to change as a result of the work of the Skills Councils. There has been a long-standing 'fast stream' accelerated programme for high-flyer entrants in the larger local authorities but these tend to be curtailed during periods of cutbacks. Many in local government are now focusing on management development and using Diplomas in Management Studies and Masters in Business and Public Administration to develop their future middle and strategic managers. The present emphasis however is on leadership (see below).

A Local Government Workforce Strategy was published by the Local Government Association's Improvement and Development Agency in 2007, which acknowledged the importance of people in delivering good public services and set out five strategic priorities:

- Building workforce support for organizational development including new structures and ways of working 'to deliver citizen focused and efficient services, in partnership'.
- Leadership and management development – building visionary and ambitious leadership which makes the best use of both the political and managerial role operating in partnership.
- Skills development in a high performance, multi-agency context.
- Recruitment and retention with partners addressing key future occupational skill shortages, identifying and developing and motivating talent.
- Modernizing pay and rewards to reflect new structures, priorities and ways of working and encouraging a total reward approach.

This is a highly prescriptive agenda but there is little systematic research to establish whether it is being implemented or remains a wish list. The latter is more likely because of the continuing period of austerity.

Industrial relations

The pay and terms and conditions of employment for over 1.4 million local government workers are determined by the National Joint Council for Local Government Services. This body is made up of 12 employers and 58 trade union representatives. The latter are officials of the various trade unions, which are recognized by the employers. In 1997, the NJC agreed a Single Status Agreement which, first of all, sought to remove the different statuses of administrative, technical and manual workers but also gave individual local councils authority to negotiate with employees on their own pay and grading systems.

Pay arrangements for chief executives are determined at the local level but 'there is a voluntary arrangement whereby all but 10 per cent of councils participate in national negotiations with the recognized trade unions via the NJC for Chief Executives and there is a separate NJC for chief officers at the next level down' (Farnham and White 2012). Although the NJCs agree a minimum national pay increase and other terms and conditions, individual local councils decide what pay increase to award. According to the Local Government Association and Local Government Employers in 2009, about two thirds of chief executives are on incremental scales but the rest are on spot salaries, which are reviewed periodically. In addition to their salary, about half of all chief executives receive supplementary payments but only about 6 per cent have PRP. Unlike the private sector, there are still more standardized terms and conditions of service in local government and there is far less difference in leave and pensions between top and lower level officials.

Salaries in local government generally increased slightly above the rate of inflation during the Labour administrations (1997–2010) although generally below the private sector. It has been the salaries of top executives that have received most attention. A survey conducted by the Local Government Employers in 2008 found that the average salary of a local government chief executive was £124,000, although separate research by Income Data Services found that the median average was nearer £141,000 (IDS 2010). This average of course conceals a wide range from less than £80,000 in small districts to £255,000 in a large county council (Farnham and White 2011; Audit Commission 2008b). In addition to the base salary chief executives may receive bonuses (PRP), private health insurance and other benefits.

The National Health Service

The Griffiths Report (1983) was a preface to the managerialization of the NHS, and the replacement of its system of consensus management, by the medical professions, with clear management hierarchies and the appointment of chief executives to run NHS organizations. Griffiths also recommended the introduction of flexible pay systems and, in 1986, PRP was introduced for 800 general managers and linked also to the introduction of performance management (Murlis 1987). The arrival of Len Peach, another outsider, from IBM, in the mid-1980s, signalled major changes in people management, building on the Griffiths proposals. Not only was the structure of the NHS radically changed but also an internal market was introduced with a divide between purchasers and providers. The Labour Party, then in opposition, was very critical of the internal market and, on gaining power in 1997, the new Labour Government abandoned it and replaced it with integrated care. In its White Paper *The New NHS: Modern, Dependable* (DH 1997) the government committed itself to raising the quality of the service, making it more efficient, removing bureaucracy and making it more responsive to the needs of the public. After a further restructuring of the NHS (see Chapter 3), a plan for the NHS was published in 2000.

For ten years, the development of the NHS workforce was informed by the *NHS Plan: A Plan for Investment, a Plan for Reform* (DH 2000), which set out to expand services across the country. This required more staff and the modernization of pay systems, the establishment of national standards and the ending of old-fashioned demarcation between professionals. The NHS was to grow by 50 per cent in cash terms and one third in real terms within five years by building 100 new hospitals and 5,000 drop-in centres by 2010, providing 7,000 extra beds and modernized GP units, re-introducing matrons in hospitals and appointing more consultants, GPs, 20,000 more nurses, 6,500 extra therapists and more child care support for medical staff. There was to be increased decentralization with the opportunity for trusts to earn autonomy. But central control was not relaxed as the Department of Health laid down national standards and introduced regular inspection by new bodies, the Commission for Health Improvement and the National Institute for Clinical Excellence (NICE), now the National Institute for Health and Clinical Excellence. They were designed to ensure that good practice was spread and also to overcome the 'post-code lottery' (regional variations in provision) by specifying the most effective treatment and controlling the use of drugs.

Recruitment

Most of the commitments in the NHS Plan had been delivered by 2010 with over 270,000 more staff, including 42,000 more doctors, 85,000 more nurses and 42,000 scientific and therapeutic staff. The workforce census published in 2009 (IDS 2010) showed that there were 1,368,200 employees, an increase of over 27 per cent since 1997. The biggest increase, however, was in the number of managers. The increase in staff contributed to reductions in waiting times and other performance targets set by the government in the Plan. As in the other public services, recruitment is now computerized and sophisticated selection procedures are used in assessment centres especially for higher level positions. There is more difficulty in filling the top posts in the NHS with posts remaining vacant for longer than six months in 2009 (SSRB 2010: 46). Very high salaries plus up to 40 per cent extra are sometimes paid to get the staff required and/or to retain them.

Training and development

Training and development have been important functions of HRM since the creation of the NHS. Professional bodies have sought to keep their members up to date with medical advances and changing ideas of patient care. But a new Knowledge and Skills Framework (KSF) was introduced in 2008/09. KSF and its associated development review process were at the heart of the career and pay progression strand of the *Agenda for Change* National Agreement. It defined and described the knowledge and skills which NHS staffs need in order to deliver quality services and applied across the whole of the NHS except for doctors, dentists and senior managers, which have their separate arrangements for their development review. KSF fits very well with the HRM approach as it is based on the principles of good people management – how to support effective learning and development of individuals and teams and to promote equality and diversity of all staff.

The NHS invests in the ongoing development of its staff based on a comprehensive system of job evaluation designed to compare all the different jobs in the NHS fairly and based on the principle of equal pay for work of equal value. It is designed to achieve harmonization of terms and conditions. KSF is also designed to support policies and plans for the future development of the NHS in all four countries of the UK. It has been built on an analysis of the competencies that apply to the different staff groups but is less concerned with behaviours than knowledge and skills. The process of job evaluation, which accompanied the introduction of KSF, was extremely difficult as thousands of staff contested the grades they were assigned, especially where it involved demotion or loss of salary. Five years on from the exercise, there were still cases under review. The KSF framework is now used in the annual staff appraisal process and provides the basis for staff improvement and development.

As in other public services, talent and leadership are a major issue in the NHS, but every individual has a responsibility for their own CPD, while trusts are required to create conditions for talent and leadership development. All NHS organizations are responsible for participating in leadership improvement efforts across their region. At the national level there is a National Leadership Council (NLC) whose task is to ensure that NHS organizations have systems and cultures in place to support the development of leaders and leadership for high-quality care. SHAs were supporting leadership development at a regional level through the commissioning and provision of development programmes for senior leaders, while an Appointments Commission was responsible for the recruitment, selection and appointment of the best people, from a diverse range of backgrounds. It currently provides recruitment and selection services to NHS foundation trusts and other health and social care bodies and a year-long induction programme for new non-executives, and it oversees their performance appraisal. The Coalition's plan to abolish these bodies leaves a question mark over what, if anything, will take their place.

The historical structure of the training of nurses, doctors and other professions allied to health (AHP) has been under continuous review since the 1990s. Project 2000 saw a major change in nurse education and training which combined higher education and practical training. Since 2000, the main focus of nurse training has been to raise the minimum standard for the registration of new nurses from diploma to degree and to transform nursing into an all-graduate profession. This has led to many criticisms of the practical capabilities of new nurses coming out of university. There is now a national framework for preceptorship to help the transition from newly registered nurse to fully confident practitioner. Nursing is moving towards comparable status to doctors with nurse consultants and nurse practitioners able to undertake many functions, such as minor surgery and prescribing treatments and drugs, tasks once confined to doctors

Similar developments are taking place in midwifery and many of the professions allied to medicine (AHP) such as radiography, occupational therapy and dentistry. In 2008 the Department of Health and Skills for Health published *Modernising Allied Health Professions (AHP) Careers: A Competence-Based Careers Framework* which provides for a flexible, responsive approach to developing the AHP workforce of the future. The Skills for Health Council is assisting the health and social care system in using AHPs to transform and redesign the health and social care system. Modernizing the health and social care workforce is based on the use of competency frameworks and putting in place the educational levers necessary to build and maintain a flexible and responsive workforce. This requires CPD but the Department of Health in 2010 was also accelerating plans to double its investment in apprenticeships, in order to provide staff who do not have a professional qualification with the opportunity to develop their skills and make progress in their careers, and to provide improved access to NHS careers for those outside the service, including the unemployed and socially excluded. This evolution may slow down as cuts in staff are made and economies sought.

Industrial relations

There is a new form of industrial relations within the NHS which is very different from the past (Burchill and Casey 1996: 43–87). There are still some seventeen unions but there is now much more individual staff engagement and also social partnerships. This reflects the acceptance on the part of management that staff engagement was crucial to the success of the changes inherent in the NHS Plan. A Social Partnership Forum, including representation from SHAs, trades unions, NHS Employers and the Department of Health was formed. The NHS began conducting annual Staff Surveys and set up an Institute for Innovation and Improvement to identify best practice and make it available to all organizations. The future of these institutions is uncertain and awaits the implementation of the Health and Social Care Act 2012.

A NHS Constitution was published in 2009, establishing the principles and values for the NHS in England and setting out the rights of patients, the public and staff. There were four pledges to staff which committed the NHS to provide: well-designed, rewarding jobs; personal development; access to appropriate training and opportunities; and involvement in decisions that affect them. The NHS began to reform pay and pensions policies to ensure that they are 'fit for the twenty-first century'. From 2008, new entrants were put on a scheme with a higher normal pensionable age of 65 and, in 2009, the

1.3 million staff who were members of the old pension scheme were offered the opportunity to move to a new scheme to be implemented over three years, starting with staff aged over 50. The age at which long-serving staff can currently take their pension is 55 but the lump sum has been abolished. Staff can commute part of their pension pot into a lump sum but this means a lower pension. Employers currently contribute 14 per cent of salary but staff on higher salaries will in future contribute more (8.5 per cent instead of 6.5 per cent). The demise of final salary pensions in the NHS is imminent as the Coalition Government policy on pensions is linked to reducing public expenditure.

In 2009 a new structure for pay, terms and conditions for all NHS employees with the exception of doctors, dentists and very senior managers (VSM) was established. VSM salaries are now subject to the Senior Salaries Review Body. This group includes all chief executives and their equivalent in Scotland, Wales and Northern Ireland. VSM salaries are banded from one to five, but also differentiated according to type of organization – PCTs, SHAs and Ambulance Trusts They are also performance related and bonuses can be paid according to which of the four streams they are in – outstanding, exceeds expectations, satisfactory and not satisfactory. Only the first two receive bonuses. As the government intends to abolish SHAs and PCTs the future of this arrangement is very unclear. Industrial relations in the NHS are under considerable pressure as the Coalition's policies on reform are proving very controversial. A broad-based campaign against the Health and Social Bill, the cutbacks in NHS funding and changes in pensions includes some direct action and strikes, pressure on ministers and MPs and the use of a wide range of old and new media to persuade the government to change its mind. They were unsuccessful with the Health and Social Care Act although the government had to accept many amendments and changes to the original bill. It remains to be seen how easy it will be for them to implement the Act!

Current issues

There are a number of current issues common to all the public services in the UK. In fact all western countries are currently faced with these same HR concerns. One is the *ageing of the population and the workforce and the issue of public sector pensions*. Most public services have a skewed labour force with a high percentage in the 50–65 age range. Around 20 per cent of the public sector workforce will be retiring within the next ten years and it is estimated that in 2040 there will be only one person in the workforce for every retired person. The ageing workforce also puts pressure on pensions. The increasing life expectancy of people means they may be drawing pensions for 30 years or more and this burden will rest on the working population, which will be smaller as the dependency ratio increases. Unless productivity or taxation and pension contributions increase significantly there will be a major shortfall. The deflation and fall in share prices and dividends during the recession has also reduced the income from investments, which pension funds rely on, whilst at the same time is reducing the income of a large number of the retired population who rely on income from their savings to supplement their pensions.

The public sector, with its final salary pension schemes and relatively small employee contributions, especially in the civil service, is now facing a crisis. An independent review of public service pensions resulted in the Hutton Report (2011). It made a series of recommendations designed to ensure a system which is sustainable and affordable, and where there is a fair balance between public sector workers and the taxpayer. The government's response was to propose raising the age at which workers could draw their pensions from 60 to 65, except for the uniformed services where it remains at 60, and to raise the retirement age to 67. Second, final salary schemes would be replaced by schemes based on average earnings and third, employee contributions would increase by 50 per cent except for low pay workers, for whom it would remain the same. The government met with strong opposition from the unions who saw the policy as a means of getting the deficit down rather than because of a shortfall in pension funds. Lord Hutton acknowledged that perhaps his proposals had been too optimistic in light of the OBR forecast of a significant fall in GDP over the next five years and the need for immediate reform. It seems that those public sector workers who retain their jobs will have to work longer, pay more and eventually receive smaller pensions.

The ageing population is putting pressure on health and social services as well as pensions, and these expenditures will rise considerably over the next ten to fifteen years as the older population makes the highest demand on these services. The latest proposals are to require people to take out insurance to assist with residential care costs, or that there should be a death tax in addition to inheritance tax which ensures people pay for their care either before or after their death. These problems are international and have stimulated the OECD to undertake research into 'good practices' in managing government employment in the context of an ageing population (OECD 2007). However, more radical solutions are required and governments will need to look to these in changing people's behaviours towards saving for their retirement; families accepting responsibility for caring for parents; people choosing life styles that are healthier and so reducing the burdens on the health service; reviewing issues of euthanasia and the right to choose when and how to die. The latter would involve moral and cultural changes which politicians find difficult to face.

A second issue facing HRM is that of *diversity*. All public services are faced with pressures to examine their diversity strategies to ensure that their public services do not discriminate on the grounds of gender, ethnicity, religion, sexual orientation or age. Diversity, however, is intended to move HR systems away from an emphasis on representation of groups to an emphasis on individual worth and contribution to the organization. The emphasis on diversity is not simply a moral imperative: it is also seen as a business imperative. The civil service already does much better on diversity than the private sector with three times as many women in senior positions and continually improving ratios of ethnic minorities and disabled persons at every level. But diversity is about getting the best people in the right jobs, bringing in and bringing on talented people. By improving diversity the civil service aims to broaden its talent pool and gain a better insight into the society it serves. The civil service set out a ten-point plan in 2005 to deliver diversity (Cabinet Office 2005b) and in 2009 its *Promoting Equality, Valuing Diversity, a Strategy for the Civil Service* (Cabinet Office 2009b) built on that and further mainstreamed equality and diversity. Box 8.5 lists the four major themes of that strategy.

All departments are using impact assessment processes to mainstream equality and diversity into every aspect of business. This means practising equality and valuing diversity when making decisions about recruitment, development and promotion. It also involves role modelling inclusive behaviours and creating an inclusive working environment by creating diverse teams of people and creating opportunities to engage with people from different backgrounds. Permanent Secretaries and Chief Executives are held to account for delivering all the equality and diversity responsibilities and commitments through their performance appraisal discussions with the Head of the Civil Service.

Although diversity is now mainstream and all departments and agencies have diversity objectives, a major concern has been the implications of the Professional Skills for Government programme. A private consultancy firm, Pearn Kandola, conducted an independent assessment of the diversity implications of the programme in 2005. Their report concluded that certain competencies could have a greater potential for adverse impacts, which they

BOX 8.5 The civil service programme for mainstreaming diversity

Four themes:

- Changing behaviour to create a civil service-wide inclusive culture.
- Strengthening leadership down to first-line management level and ensuring clear transparent accountability for delivering diversity.
- Developing a talent management system bringing on people from diverse backgrounds.
- Ensuring a diverse workforce at all levels against set targets.

identified as those with a greater cognitive element and located in the policy delivery areas. They recommended training of all staff involved in assessment and that diversity indicators should be included in all competencies. The government launched a 'Leaders Unlimited' programme which is a corporate diversity development programme aimed at realizing the management potential of women, black and minority ethnic staff, and staff with disabilities.

As early as 1993, the Secretary of State for Health introduced *Ethnic Minorities in the NHS: A Programme for Action* (DH 1993). Its eight goals covered the range of HRM activities but three were specifically focused on education and training. Staff development was to maximize the skills and potential of all personnel in a multi-racial NHS workforce, with particular emphasis on the identifiable needs of people from minority ethnic groups. There was a need to ensure that the time spent in higher specialist training by doctors from minority ethnic groups equates to the time spent by white doctors. Third, was a commitment to increase the proportion of minority ethnic applicants for the NHS Management Training Scheme. This required positive action in recruitment, selection and training (Burchill and Casey 1996). The NHS is also committed to Investors in Diversity which is a national standard against which individual health trusts and organizations can assess themselves or invite assessors to rate them. The impending changes in the NHS with greater autonomy for hospitals and commissioning bodies and the increase in the market may threaten these initiatives.

A third issue is *leadership*. The OECD and its member states now recognize the need for leadership in rapidly changing and modernizing public organizations. They accept that leaders can be developed and trained, and have evolved strategies and policies to raise the profile of leaders and leadership throughout their public services. In the UK, centres of excellence in leadership have been established for all parts of the public sector including local and central government, health, defence, education and police (Horton and Farnham 2007).

The Blair Government set up a Leadership Development Commission to review leadership in local government, recommending the creation of a Leadership Centre for Local Government, which opened in 2004. It is funded by the Department for Communities and Local Government to support and improve leadership development and is uniquely designed for both political leaders and chief executives. Its aim is to improve their skills in commissioning, programme and project management capabilities, procurement, negotiating and contract management capacity, and their delivery, funding and partnering abilities. Similar leadership programmers are expanding throughout the UK and also all OECD countries but, in many cases, quite traditional management training hides behind the new label. Despite the absence of definitive empirical evidence demonstrating the relationship between leadership and performance and the difficulty in measuring that relationship, it has become increasingly accepted that leadership is a key ingredient in the effective performance of individuals, groups, organizations, regions, and even nation states (Bolden 2004).

In the civil service, departments and agencies design their own programmes and invest a great deal of money in both talent spotting and developing leadership potential. Strategic leadership is differentiated from other levels and specific forms of action learning and inter-organizational programmes exist to facilitate networking, and develop the skills of collaborative leadership, now so important in the partnerships which characterize systems of joined-up government and governance. Most public organizations design their own leadership training below the strategic level but the SCS has a long-standing Top Leadership Programme which recruits people from across the public sector and chief executives from top private sector companies. Leadership for the twenty-first century is high on both national and international agendas. The OECD has been investigating and promoting leadership as the key to the transformation of modern states (OECD 2005a), while throughout the public sector in the UK leadership is seen as the key factor in the successful achievement of public sector reform (see Chapter 5). The focus at present, however, is how to lead in a financial crisis and manage contraction and reconstruction. The future of the strategic management programme is uncertain as the rationalization of training in the civil service (see above) takes place and economies are made.

The importance of HRM

HRM is a key area of management. If the HR policies are not right then public organizations will not attract the human resources they need to perform the functions of government and deliver the services that governments have promised the electorate. In our modern system of governance it is not only those employed in public organizations but also people in voluntary and private organizations, in partnerships or contracted to delivery public services that are important. There are clear trends towards convergence of HR practices in private and public organizations both nationally and internationally. However, there are contextual factors that impose limits on the extent of both aspects of convergence (Pollitt and Bouckaert 2004).

The major changes in HRM in the UK public services over the last 20 years have been the changing role of HRM, from service support to business partner, and the decentralization of the HR function within organizations. Further changes have been in employment contracts, flexible working patterns, employment relations and the emphasis on diversity and equal employment rights. Line managers are now primarily responsible for people management and, within the framework of performance management systems, are responsible for controlling, directing and motivating staff, whether in local government, the NHS or the civil service. The fragmentation, which is a consequence of decentralization, has removed much of the standardization and uniformity of the old system and made the public sector more like the private sector with time limited contracts, PRP and self-directed career development. The public sector no longer offers the secure, safe job for life, although there are still people who are public service motivated and choose to work in public services (Perry and Hondeghem 2008; Van Dorpe and Horton 2011). Coordination is difficult within decentralized and fragmented systems but UK governments have used legislation, PSAs and regulatory bodies to rein in public organizations and control over funding to achieve some control of direction, although not always in fine detail. The future for employees in the public services looks bleak, as the Coalition Government has imposed stringent cutbacks in public expenditure, public salaries and pensions whilst raising the retirement age. This policy has an impact on jobs and on the morale of those that retain their jobs as the workload increases but rewards do not. The management of contraction is much more difficult than the management of expansion, albeit they are both subsumed under the rubric of modernization.

Chapter 9

Regulation, Audit and Inspection inside Governance

Regulation, audit and inspection are not new but they have increased dramatically over the last thirty years. The reform of the public sector since 1979 has seen significant changes in its structure and complexity as a result of the demonopolization, marketization and managerialization movements (see Chapter 3). These reforms of public services have fractured the traditional hierarchical forms of accountability and been accompanied by an 'audit explosion' and a proliferation of inspectorates, which has simultaneously led to a blurring of boundaries between audit, inspection, organizational design and consultancy (Clarke 2009: 199). Many writers have claimed that we now live in the age of a new 'regulatory state' (Hood *et al.* 1999; Braithwaite 2000; Scott 2002; Moran 2003; Oliver, Prosser and Rawlings 2010). We need to distinguish, however, between the regulation of those bodies outside of government, which operate within competitive private markets, and those organizations delivering publicly funded or subsidized services which are inside government. Chapter 7 examines the economic regulation of the former nationalized industries and public utilities and those parts of the economy which need to be controlled in the public interest. This chapter examines the growth and proliferation of audit and inspectorate bodies inside government involved in scrutinizing government organizations and those private and third sector bodies delivering public services. It also examines the debates and issues which fuelled the demand for their rationalization and the response of the Coalition Government after 2010.

Types of regulation

Regulation is the oversight of bureaucracies by other public agencies operating at arm's length from the direct line of command, the overseers being endowed with some sort of official authority over their charges (Hood *et al.* 2000). There are three major features of regulators: first, they have an official authority over the bodies they regulate and set down standards for them, which may relate to inputs, procedures, outputs or outcomes; second, there is an organizational separation between the regulator and the regulated; third, regulators monitor performance and may use persuasion or direction to modify the behaviour of the regulated.

There are several types of regulators which include audit bodies, inspectorates, ombudsmen and the regulation by central government departments over local government and the NHS. They use a variety of methods including audit, inspection, adjudication, authorization and certification. There are also different styles of regulation which may be cooperative or confrontational, supportive and advisory or adversarial and punitive. Some regulators operate like management consultants or critical friends, while others are like controllers who police and can name and shame and impose closure. Cope and Goodship (1999) identify a number of models of relationships between regulators and the bodies they regulate: the regulatory control model; the regulatory bargain model; and the regulatory capture model.

The audit explosion

'Regulation has become the modality of choice for state activity in recent years' (Scott 2002: 57) and has displaced earlier modes associated with the post-war welfare state, such as, direct provision of services, public ownership and integrated bureaucracies. Hood and his associates undertook a study of the scale and growth of 'inside' regulation in the UK public sector from 1976 to 1995 and identified no fewer than 134 separate bodies regulating the UK public sector at national government level in 1995 (compared to 110 bodies in 1976), which directly employed over 14,000 staff and cost £766 million to run (Hood *et al.* 1998: 62).They regarded this number as a very conservative estimate and thought there were probably over 200 regulators, 20,000 staff and a budget of £1 billion. Even these figures, however, greatly underestimated the total cost as they excluded the compliance costs, which are the costs incurred by the regulated bodies, including providing information, consulting with the regulators, preparing and organizing visits and inspections. Although difficult to calculate, this figure would probably increase the direct costs estimated by Hood *et al.* to nearer £2 million in the 1990s.

The 'audit explosion' can be traced to the transformation of the state during the Thatcher and Major Governments (1979–97) when many functions were devolved but government retained a regulatory oversight (Power 1994). Regulation inside government grew initially in a very pragmatic and disorganized way, with no rationale or consistent practices, and as a result there was a layering of new practices and regulations upon old ones. This resulted in both complexity and a lack of coordination. There was no joined-up approach to regulation and separate organizations carried out their respective functions in isolation, which resulted in duplication and the potential for conflict (Hood *et al.* 1999; Cope and Goodship 1999; Ashworth, Boyne and Walker 2002). As regulation and regulators increased, their approach began to change and they became more formal, complex, intense and specialized (Hood *et al.* 2000) and also very detailed and prescriptive as more standards were being set down. This had the effect of removing a great deal of discretion from the regulated bodies and appeared to be in conflict with much of successive governments' NPM rhetoric of 'letting managers manage', encouraging flexibility and risk taking, removing red tape and transforming professional bureaucracies into managed businesses.

During the first Blair government, more regulatory bodies were created and central control over the regulatory process increased. For example between 1999 and 2001 five new regulators in the NHS were created:

- National Institute for Clinical Excellence (NICE) which was intended to offer expert guidance on technologies and interventions.
- Commission for Health Improvement, which undertook clinical governance reviews of NHS organizations, monitored the implementation of NICE guidance, and investigated major systems failures.
- Modernisation Agency – designed to support capacity building, leadership, managerial practices and clinical governance.
- National Patient Safety Agency – to monitor adverse events and near misses and issues guidance on patient safety.
- National Clinical Assessment Authority – advice, referrals and targeted assessment of performance of individual doctors.

Other new regulators included the Trading Standards Council, Youth Justice Board, Best Value Inspectorate, Standards Board for England, Commission for Care Standards and the General Teaching Council for England, Wales and Northern Ireland. The scale, scope and intensity of regulation also changed significantly too. Best Value reviews were applied to all public organizations and continuous improvement rather than minimum standards were now required.

This increase in regulation, first under the Conservatives and then under Labour, reflected a loss of confidence in self-regulation by the professional bureaucrats, which had been the norm up to the 1970s. Self-regulation was seen as club regulation (Moran 2003) and the change as one of replacing it with a more independent, objective form of regulation. Cope and Goodship (1999) credited the change in regulation to a combination of NPM, the differentiated polity and the emergence of governance. It is quite evident that decentralization, devolution and the assumption of a steering rather than a rowing role still requires government and the core executive to retain some control over the 'rowers' as, while you can decentralize authority, you cannot abdicate responsibility. As governments were committed to ensure value for money and constant improvement in public services they needed to be able to steer more directly. The aim was to reform and modernize public services through managerialism and to use arm's length agencies and techniques, such as those in the private sector, to ensure compliance. There was an army of private-sector accountants and management consultants willing to assist!

Also arm's length regulation by independent experts separated the regulatory process from bureaucratic or political interference by departments and ministers and ostensibly gave it credibility and authority.

In the latter years under Blair and then Brown there was a change of style with a move back to both 'internal' and 'self-regulation' with external regulators adopting a so called 'light touch'. By 2010, however, a huge public sector regulatory industry had emerged and a parallel set of bureaucracies coexisted alongside the public organizations they were designed to control. Their real cost and effectiveness were not known although there was some evidence that they had contributed to raising standards and increased performance across the public sector. But an emerging issue was the question of who regulated the regulators? The Coalition Government was soon committed to dismantling much of the regulatory framework it inherited in a 'bonfire of the quangos' and moving towards a more 'hands off' approach by central government. Some initial changes were made with the abolition of many performance indicators (PIs) and Public Service Agreements (PSAs) and the promise to abolish the Audit Commission but it remains to be seen what the 'hands off' approach actually means. We will now examine the different types of regulatory bodies, beginning with audits and then inspectorates, before exploring the effects of these multiple regulatory bureaucratic structures and the responses of the Coalition.

National audits

Audit has a long history in the UK (NAO 2012), but it was in the 1860s that the modern system of financial accountability to parliament was introduced. William Gladstone, then Chancellor of the Exchequer, created an Exchequer and Audit Department, responsible for authorizing the issue of money and auditing the accounts of government departments, and appointed a Comptroller and Auditor General (C&AG) to head the department and present reports on the accounts to the Public Accounts Committee (PAC) of the House of Commons, also established in 1861. From 1870, the PAC began to call before it the permanent secretaries of government departments (who are their accounting officers), to answer questions about their accounts. The traditional audit function involved ensuring that departments had spent their money as parliament had allocated it, followed correct procedures and demonstrated probity in the use of public money (Flynn 2007: 170). To begin with, every transaction was examined but as government activity and expenditure grew the Exchequer and Audit Department relied heavily on internal auditing by the departments, who employed their own accountants and auditors, and the Audit Department only sampled the transactions.

Pressure for reform of the national audit system increased as the role of the state changed. The regulatory audit only examined accounts in retrospect, after the money had been spent and was not concerned with whether money was spent efficiently or the taxpayer was getting value for money. Also the C&AG and his department were staffed by civil servants and there was scepticism about its objectivity and independence. In 1983, under the National Audit Act the C&AG formally became an official of the House of Commons with powers to report to parliament, at his or her own discretion, on the efficiency and effectiveness with which departments and other government bodies used public money. The Act also established the National Audit Office (NAO) to replace the Exchequer and Audit Department and to support the C&AG. Its members are not now civil servants.

The change during the 1980s resulted in a movement from regulatory to efficiency, performance and value for money (VfM) audits. This meant that assessments were no longer about whether money had been spent correctly but about how carefully organizations spend money, seek to be economical and to get the best results from any expenditure. VfM audits, which are used at national, regional and local levels, are concerned with the impact of expenditure and the efficiency with which government policies are being implemented, while performance audits provide information for government on whether organizations are meeting government targets and PIs and underpin benchmarking.

We can see, therefore, that the emphasis of central government audits has changed over time. The earliest audits were concerned to see that the money had been spent in the way authorized by parliament and that extra spending had been correctly approved via supplementary estimates. Audit work also concentrated on 'propriety' with the C&AG reporting to parliament on irregular payments and practices by government departments and trying to disclose fraud (Drewry and Butcher 1991: 207–8). During the 1990s performance and VfM audits were introduced. In 2010–11, the Audit Office audited some 470 accounts worth £950 billion (NAO 2011c). The VfM studies, around 600 per year, look at how government projects, programmes and initiatives are implemented and recommend how services could be improved. All these reports are presented to the PAC in the House of Commons.

The audit process

The NAO employs about 800 staff who work in teams and undertake audits of government departments, which include those responsible for UK matters, including the Foreign Office and the Treasury, those responsible for the devolved regions such as the Scotland Office, and all other departments and agencies which cover England. Their role is essentially to save money. They are expected to be generating financial savings to departments at least nine times greater than the cost of the NAO itself and in 2010/11 the NAO (2011c) claimed that £1 billion of financial savings had been achieved. All VfM audit teams follow a prescribed procedure. First, they agree in advance which work of the department will be reviewed and how it will be conducted; second, there is the investigation; third the team produces a draft report which must be agreed word for word with the department; finally all agreed reports are published and presented to the PAC. The PAC considers only about three quarters of them. It calls witnesses but is advised by the C&AG and the NAO on what questions to ask. Its reports are printed and presented to the House of Commons. Some receive wide media coverage (Dunleavy *et al.* 2009: 36–7) but the impact of PAC reports on VfM is continually debated.

Devolved audits

There was only one C&AG and one Audit Office covering England, Wales and Scotland until devolution when Auditors General and Audit Offices were established in Scotland and Wales. The separate Northern Ireland C&AG and Audit Office dates from 1921. All these separate officials and bodies now report to their respective Assemblies. However, unlike in England, the new Audit Offices in the devolved systems cover all public bodies. Audit Scotland carries out financial and performance audits of around 200 bodies including the Scottish Government departments, local councils, the NHS bodies and all further education colleges. In Wales, the Audit Office carries out both financial and performance audits in all devolved public sectors including health and social care, local and central government, fire services, national parks, education, agriculture and community councils. In Northern Ireland, the C&AG and Audit Office is responsible for auditing all government departments and executive agencies, NDPBs, health and personal services but designated local government auditors are responsible for auditing District Councils and other local bodies. (See websites of Audit Scotland, Wales Audit Office and Northern Ireland Audit Office for lists of their audit reports.)

Audit Scotland

As stated above, the scope of Audit Scotland is much broader than that of the UK Audit Office because devolution provided a unique opportunity to think about the basic principles of public audit for the twenty-first century and how to apply them. Robert Black, the first Auditor General for Scotland, wrote:

> Public Audit is not just about signing an opinion on the accounts, important as that always is. It must also look at standards of governance, probity and financial management, and it should also undertake independent and evidence – analysis of value for money and performance – and this should all be done in a way which supports improvement as well as holding to account. (Black 2007: 27)

Most services in Scotland are delivered arm's length from central government – in fact 80 per cent of spending takes place in local authorities, health boards

BOX 9.1 The 2012/13 programme of audit reviews by Audit Scotland

Published in advance:

- learning the lessons of public bodies mergers;
- health inequalities;
- outsourced contracts;
- stroke services;
- reducing re-offending;
- GP prescribing;
- major capital projects in local government;
- NHS annual overview;
- consumer protection services;
- Scottish public finances – workforce planning;
- renewable energy.

The rolling programme:

- commissioning social care;
- intervention in early years;
- mental health follow-up (dementia services);
- Community Justice Authorities;
- integrated health care for stroke patients;
- drug and alcohol follow-up;
- rural development programme;
- young people leaving care;
- call management in emergency services;
- women in custody.

Source: Audit Scotland (2011) 'Our Work Programme for 2012/13', published 14 October, www.audit-scotland.gov.uk, licensed under the Open Government Licence.

and NDPBs. Audit Scotland has an important role, therefore, in reporting to parliament on the use of public money and the performance of the 200 or so public bodies that deliver services. Many of the Audit Scotland reports cut across government and do not belong to one sector. In addition, decisions about what to investigate is more open and a programme of national performance audits is published in advance after formal public consultation (See Box 9.1). The procedure differs markedly from the UK NAO reviews as a project brief is prepared for each audit, including the focus of the work; how it will be carried out; how long it will take; and its anticipated impact. These briefs are made available to the public on the Audit Scotland website. In addition to the fixed programme, there is a rolling programme of potential topics which may be audited at a future date.

Audit reports are not standard but the focus is on VfM, the 3Es, governance and accountability and they all address the following five areas:

- managing reductions in public sector budgeting;
- accountability and specifically at ways of reducing overspending;
- partnership working and value for money;
- user focus and personalization – cost effective ways of delivering services and meeting people's needs;
- environmental auditing – reviewing how Scotland is responding to challenges of reducing carbon emissions.

Audit Scotland can commission other bodies to research and investigate. For example, Ipsos MORI was commissioned to conduct an independent review of the pilot Best Value Audit and inspection of the Scottish Police (Ipsos MORI 2005). Other cross-organization investigations published in 2010 included '*How councils work: an improvement series for councillors' and officers' roles and working relationships: are you getting it right?* (Audit Scotland 2010a) and *Getting it right for children in residential care* (Audit Scotland 2010b). Finally, Audit Scotland has started to look at difficult cross-cutting issues: for example youth justice services, which involve ten budgets and many services, illustrating their joined-up government approach. The fact that Audit Scotland covers the whole of the devolved government has enabled it to undertake performance audits of whole systems and so support improvement as well as holding public bodies to account.

Audit Wales

The pattern of organizations and functions audited by Audit Wales reflect those of Scotland more than the UK system in London. An Auditor General is responsible for the day-to-day running of the Wales Audit Office (WAO), whose mission is to promote improvement so that the people of Wales benefit from accountable and well-managed public services and that they get the best possible VfM. Its role is also to spread good practice. As in Scotland, the Auditor General appoints external auditors for Welsh local authorities but also for police, probation, fire and rescue services and community councils.

There is evidence that the work of the WAO has been very constructive; for example, its report on the Welsh Ambulance Service was implemented almost entirely and resulted in vastly increased performance (Colman 2007). However, the credibility of WAO was undermined in 2010 when it came to light that the accounts of the WAO were not correct and the Auditor General was imprisoned. A new Auditor General took up the post in October 2010 and embarked upon a major restructuring of WAO which led to a new system of governance, and there is now both more transparency and accountability (Wales Audit Office 2010).

Northern Ireland Audit

The Northern Ireland Audit Office (NIAO) provides support to the Northern Ireland Assembly in holding government departments and agencies to account for their use of public money and also for ensuring there is an effective system of local government audit. It also provides support to other public sector bodies in their pursuit of improved financial reporting and VfM. It is headed by the C&AG, whose powers go beyond their counterparts in the rest of the UK and include authorizing the issue of money from the Northern Ireland Consolidated Fund and ensuring there are adequate arrangements for the collection of revenue. The C&AG is also responsible for all external audits of government departments and other authorities (see above) including both financial and VfM audits. They report to the Northern Ireland Assembly and, as with the other national C&AGs, works closely with the Northern Ireland Assembly PAC, presents VfM reports to them and assists in the writing of their reports. All reports are presented to the Assembly, which is required to respond and specify its intended action. The C&AG then follows up the progress of that action. Local Government Auditors are appointed by and report to the Department of the Environment. Examples of VfM and financial reports can be found on the NIAO website (www.niauditoffice.gov.uk) .

The verdict on audit

Although devolution has been accompanied by some divergences in approach to accountability within the UK, the audit agencies have actually been converging as their role has changed since 2000. This is due in part to the work of the Public Audit Forum, which was established in 1998 as a mechanism for collaboration and encouraging good audit practice, and to the development of international accounting standards, which have been adopted by each audit system. But a major reason is that all parts of the UK have engaged in measures to improve public sector performance, ensure value for money and assist in the major structural reforms which have been associated with NPM or modernization (Dowdall 2007).

There are different verdicts on the effectiveness and contribution of audit systems in the UK. In general the devolved systems appear to be operating more effectively than the NAO in Westminster. One critical view is that the NAO/PAC reports are a whitewash. Dunleavy *et al.* (2009) point to NAO's limitations. First, its staff cannot question policy, only the implementation of policy; second, its VfM reports tend to be more financial than managerial and are not sufficiently critical; third it is constrained because of the need for clearance of its reports by the departments and finally, because of its dependence on the PAC and Parliamentary time scales, it is prevented from undertaking in-depth studies. Furthermore, the audit process blunts the NAO's criticisms and often results in bland reports which never name and blame and only lead to action when they are acceptable to the department or agency. Additionally, there is no automatic follow-up to ensure that recommendations have been implemented. It is argued, however, that although it remains difficult to assess the impact of national audits on politicians, civil servants and government departments and agencies or on policy, they produce reports and relevant research, which are available to the public and not least the media and therefore contribute to transparency. Reports that receive close media attention can lead to action and the NAO is now producing reports on its own VfM and how it saves public money. Audit Scotland has attracted less criticism and is, in some respects, a model of good practice as it has more autonomy, is more transparent and can follow up all actions requested by the Scottish parliament.

Local audits

Auditing of sub-national organizations in the past rested originally with district auditors, who were appointed by central government or by local authorities themselves, but all reported to the District Audit Office in central government. The responsibility for auditing local government since 1983 has rested with the Audit Commission for England and Wales, which was established by the Local Government Finance Act 1983. An Accounts Commission responsible for local government audit in Scotland had been appointed under the Local Government (Scotland) Act 1973 but its work has been carried out by Audit Scotland since 2000. In 1990 the NHS was added to the Audit Commission's brief and its name was changed to the Audit Commission for Local Authorities and the NHS. Further extensions to its powers were added to include Best Value inspections (1999), social landlords and comprehensive assessments of local authorities (2003), fire and rescue services (2004) and data-matching services (2007).

The Audit Commission has had a key role in regulating the increasingly dispersed field of public service provision emanating from the many reforms of the Thatcher and Major Governments (Clarke and Newman 1997). Although formally an independent organization, the Audit Commission was set up with the specific political motives of curbing public expenditure and controlling local government (Holloway 1998), but it soon went beyond the focus on economy and control, which was of most interest to the Thatcher government, to write lively reports on how councils – and government departments – could improve the efficiency and effectiveness of local services. From the late 1990s, the core business of the Audit Commission was to deliver VfM in public bodies outside of central government. It appointed and regulated the external auditors to local authorities and subsequently to all the bodies listed above. The majority of appointed auditors were employees of the Audit Commission but some worked for private audit firms, which were experienced in auditing public organizations.

The work of the Audit Commission fell into four main areas: *audit, assessment, research* and *data-matching*. It was the primary *auditor* of local public services and appointed auditors to promote value for taxpayers' money in more than 11,000 public bodies. In 2010/11, it inspected 91 local authorities, police authorities and housing associations and carried out 560 audits (Audit Commission 2011: 6). It also carried out *performance assessments* but, as Flynn points, out it was more 'like a management consultancy, with powers to impose management methods on local authorities as well as assessing and reporting on their performance' (Flynn 2007: 169). For example, in conducting its performance audit of the Bristol Benefits Service, of which it was highly critical (see Box 9.2), the Audit Commission not only inspected and 'scored' the service on its current performance along a number of performance management criteria, but judged its potential performance in the future and made five specific recommendations for improvement strategies, each composed of a number of actions, with the Commission's judgement of their likely effects (Audit Commission 2010: 6–11).

BOX 9.2 An Audit Commission report on Bristol Benefits Service

The Audit Commission's overall conclusion was that Bristol City Council's benefits service was poor and there was no clear prospect of improvement:

- The service was taking too long to process claims. It did not check for errors in a consistent way, leading to overpaid benefits which it found difficult to collect and increased debts for the council. Vulnerable people were at risk.
- Claimants did not find it easy to deal with the benefits service: its letters were sometimes hard to understand and leaflets hard to find. Customer Service Points across the city were good but there were long waits for telephones to be answered at the Customer Service Call Centre, though staff was very supportive of people making claims, knowledgeable and helpful.
- The service had not consulted customers on the service and knew very little about them. It did not try to encourage knowledge of entitlements, though it tackled fraud.
- There was no evidence the service had tried to improve its service to customers, though its overall performance was significantly below the best authorities; it had however reduced the amount it overpaid in benefits because of its own errors.
- Staff development was now more effective but improvement plans were not comprehensive. Improvement targets needed to be put in place to increase effectiveness and value for money.

Source: Summarized from Audit Commission (2010) *Bristol City Council: Benefits Service Inspection* (Audit Commission), p. 4.

In the 1990s, local authorities were required by the government to collect performance indicators in a particular way, which enabled comparisons to be made and benchmarking to take place. After 1997, however, local authorities were required to secure Best Value in the performance of their functions and the Audit Commission carried out *VfM assessments*. It soon became evident that service quality could not be separated from the performance of the local authority as a whole and so, from 2002, the Audit Commission embarked on comprehensive assessments of local authorities or CPAs. There are many claims that CPAs led to great improvements in the performance of local authorities (LGA 2005; Bundred 2007) but CPAs were soon replaced by Comprehensive Area Assessments (CAAs) in 2007 (see Chapter 6). These were subsequently abandoned by the Coalition Government in 2010 when they announced the abolition of the Commission itself (see below).

In addition to its value for money and performance audits, the Audit Commission also carried out *research* for public bodies and central government, providing analysis of complex social problems and best practice in tackling them. It made practical recommendations for policy makers and for people delivering public services. Finally, its work involved *data-matching* where it investigated and detected fraud and errors by comparing sets of data, such as payroll and benefits records. Its National Fraud Initiative identified £215 million of fraud and error, and in addition helped councils identify £100 million in benefit and council tax fraud (Audit Commission 2011: 6).

After 2000 the Commission worked closely and often in partnership with other regulators and inspectorates, including the Commission for Social Care Inspection, the Health Care Commission, Her Majesty's Inspectorate of Constabulary (HMIC), Her Majesty's Inspectors of Prisons and OFSTED and it became difficult to distinguish audit and inspectorate bodies.

In August 2010, Eric Pickles, the new Secretary of State for Communities and Local Government, announced plans to abolish the Audit Commission by 2012/13 and to transfer its responsibilities for overseeing and delivering local audits and inspections and all research activities to the private sector. The rationale for ending the Audit Commission, according to the Secretary of State, was that it 'had, over time, become a creature of Whitehall, rather than a champion of local taxpayers' (Pickles 2011). Instead of focusing on accountability to citizens, the Audit Commission had become an agent of central government reporting *up* to government and judging services in terms of government targets. According to Pickles, the aim of the Coalition Government was to refocus audit on helping local people to hold councils and local public bodies to account for local spending decisions and so they planned to decentralize, pass power down to local people and to replace bureaucratic accountability with democratic accountability. They also hoped to save an estimated £50 million a year in the process.

The plan was for auditors, formerly employed by the Audit Commission, to move into the private sector. Councils would still be audited but they would choose their own auditors from the private sector and there would be a new audit framework for local health bodies. The whole system was to be overseen by the National Audit Office.

The National Audit Offices and the Audit Commission have had an important role in regulating and assessing efficiency, effectiveness and value for money of central government departments, local government, the NHS and other public bodies since the 1980s. The Audit Offices in all four parts of the UK continue to perform their roles as described above, although they are likely to experience further change. The future of the Audit Commission in England, which has produced reports on performance and VfM and had the power to impose management methods and other procedures on local government and other local bodies, is uncertain but at the moment it is continuing to perform the same role.

Inspectorates

Inspectorates also have a long history in the UK and date back to the nineteenth century but inspection has become so important, since the 1980s, as it 'has come to play a pivotal role in the management of hospitals, schools, the police, local government and a host of other services' (Martin and Davis 2008: 7). There are many ways to classify inspectorates (Hood and Scott 1996; Mordaunt 2000) but government policy on their role was set out by the Office of Public Services Reform in 2003). Inspectorates are to provide assurance that quality standards are being met; to provide information to the public; and to generate improvements. The ten principles to guide them are set out in Box 9.3.

Traditionally, inspectorates were service specific and staffed by relevant professionals. In 2005, however, the government rationalized the inspec-

BOX 9.3 Ten principles for inspections

- Pursue the purpose of improvement.
- Focus on outcomes.
- Take a user perspective.
- Be proportionate to risk.
- Encourage self-assessment by managers.
- Use impartial evidence wherever possible.
- Discuss the criteria used for judgement.
- Be open about the processes involved.
- Have regard for value for money including that of the inspection body.
- Continually learn from experience.

Source: Office of Public Services Reform (OPSR) (2003). *The Government's Policy on Inspection of Public Services*, London: Cabinet Office.

torates by merger and reduced them from eleven to four. The four new inspectorates, which became operative in 2007, were: Children's Services, Education and Skills; Adult Services, Social Care and Health; Justice and Community Safety; and Local Services. The staffing of the inspectorates also began to change and they were no longer dominated by professionals. The following section looks at the work of selected inspectorates both before and after the mergers, in England, Scotland and Northern Ireland.

Education

Inspection in education goes back to 1839 (Baker 1976) and its evolution has mirrored the developing system of state education – 'the shift in power between central and local government, the development of the teaching profession and more recent trends towards the participation of parents and learners' (Martin 2008: 52). The present system in schools dates from 1944 when His Majesty's Inspectorate of Schools (HMIS) was created. Its role ranged 'from standard bearer to turbulent priest' (Dunford 1998). At first, most inspections were carried out by inspectors based in Local Education Authorities (LEAs), and HMIs focused on reporting to the Minister for Education about conditions across the country. The government of John Major, concerned about the variable local inspection regimes, decided to introduce a national scheme of inspections through a reconstituted HMIS, which became known as the Office for Standards in Education (OFSTED). It was created as a non-ministerial government department to supervise the inspection of each state-funded school in the country and to publish its reports, instead of reporting to the Secretary of State. Its role was to inspect:

- the quality of education provided in schools;
- the standards achieved in schools;
- the way that financial resources are managed in schools; and
- examine the spiritual, moral, social and cultural development of pupils.

In effect, OFSTED inspects processes, outputs and outcomes and, in particular, the impact of the processes on the educational achievement of the children and the standards reached by the children in SATs (Standard Attainment Tests) and GCSEs (school leaving exams). Before OFSTED, the role of the HMIs was mainly to advise and support the teachers and it had become an increasingly professionalized domain. This prompted a call for more independent and transparent evaluation of schools, especially after the major reforms of the 1980s, which resulted in the local management of schools. Inspection then became more about improving management and raising standards.

OFSTED directly employs HMIs, who are civil servants, but most school inspections are carried out by Additional Inspectors (AIs) employed by external companies known as Regional Inspection Service Providers (RISPs).

There were nearly 2,000 AIs in 2009 and only 443 HMIs. An HMI accompanies an AI in less than 10 per cent of inspections and the reports are produced by the RISPs. They must be checked and signed off by an HMI and reports often require amendments before publication. All new AIs are monitored and approved by an HMI before working independently. The number of RISPs contracted to conduct school inspections was reduced in 2009 from five to three and these cover the North of England, the Midlands and Southern England respectively.

OFSTED carries out regular inspections of each school in England, resulting in a published evaluation of the effectiveness of the school. Before 2005, each school was subjected to a week-long inspection every six years, with two months' notice to prepare for an inspection. This regime was criticized by teachers and school heads as very disruptive of the operation of the school, while others felt the long lead time enabled schools to present an unrealistic picture of their performance during the inspection that did not truly reflect the normal quality of teaching and learning in the school. In 2005, a new system of self-evaluation and short-notice inspections was introduced. Each school now completes a Self-Evaluation Form (SEF) on a continual basis and the new inspections are generally two- or three-day visits every three years, with only two days' notice. Inspectors examine how well the school is managed, what processes are in place to ensure standards of teaching and learning are improving, and how effective school leadership and management are. The SEF serves as the main document when planning the inspection, and is crucial in evaluating the quality of leadership and management and the school's capacity to improve.

All OFSTED reports are posted on its website. In addition to written comments, schools are assessed overall on a four-point scale: 1 (Outstanding), 2 (Good), 3 (Satisfactory) and 4 (Inadequate). Schools rated as Outstanding or Good might not be inspected again for five years but schools judged less favourably tend to be inspected more frequently and may receive little or no notice of subsequent inspection visits. Revised inspection criteria were introduced in 2009 and, in 2010, OFSTED reported that this had resulted in a reduction from 19 per cent to 9 per cent in the number of schools judged to be Outstanding, and an increase from 4 per cent to 10 per cent in the number of schools judged to be Inadequate (OFSTED 2010b).

Under the Labour Government, schools judged to be 'Inadequate' were often placed 'in special measures' as a result of OFSTED stating that they failed to reach appropriate standards against the criteria set down by the Secretary of State. As a result they received support from the LEA, additional funding and resourcing to assist in raising their standards. They were re-appraised frequently until the school was no longer deemed to be failing. The senior managers and teaching staff could be dismissed and the Board of Governors replaced by an appointed Board. Some failing schools were renamed as academies and this policy has been continued under the Coalition (see Chapter 1).

The Labour Government began a review of the performance of national inspectorates in 2003 and an evidence-based report was produced by the Institute of Education and OFSTED in 2004 (Institute of Education/OFSTED 2004). It concluded that OFSTED played an important role as a catalyst for improvement in education, particularly in weaker institutions, and it had also had an impact on the quality of teaching and learning, educational standards, and leadership and management across the whole educational system. It ensured that users were informed about educational services and this had enhanced public confidence in the school system. The report conceded, however, that OFSTED had attracted a lot of criticism, in particular in relation to teachers' workloads and stress and the constant revisions to inspection frameworks, which seemed more intent on reducing inspectors' burden rather than relieving the pressure on the teachers. There was also evidence that there was often less impact of OFSTED reports in schools which fell into the satisfactory category largely because there was no follow up to see if recommendations had been implemented and changes made.

In 2007, the work of OFSTED was increased when it merged with the Adult Learning Inspectorate (ALI) to provide an inspection service covering all post-16 government-funded education (but not Higher Education Institutes and Universities, which are inspected by the Quality Assurance Agency). It also took on responsibility for the registration and inspection of social care services for children, and the welfare inspection of independent and maintained boarding schools from the Commission for Social Care Inspection (CSCI). This made it one of the most wide-ranging of all government inspectorates. Today OFSTED inspects or regulates local services, child-minding, child day care, children's centres, children's social care, state schools, independent schools and teacher training providers, colleges and learning and skills providers in England. It also monitors the work of the Independent Schools Inspectorate. HMIs are empowered and required to provide independent advice to the UK Government and parliament on matters of policy across the range of Children's Services, Skills and Education and to publish an annual report to parliament on the quality of educational provision in England. This breadth of competence has given rise to further criticisms of OFSTED in the light of the Baby P case (see below) which highlighted the unreliability of OFSTED Reviews of Social Service Departments and the superficial nature of their inspections in their new areas of responsibility. See Martin (2008) for a further analysis of the effectiveness of OFSTED in terms of public accountability.

The Education and Training Inspectorate in Northern Ireland, Her Majesty's Inspectorate of Education in Scotland, and Estyn in Wales perform similar functions to OFSTED within their respective education systems (Martin 2008: 54–5).

Social services

The history of the regulation of care services dates back to the Poor Laws of the sixteenth century (Johns and Lock 2008). With the creation of the welfare state and the development of services for children, adults and disabled persons, separate professional inspectorates were created to inspect and monitor standards. After the Seebohm Report (1968) and the creation of local government Social Service Departments, the separate inspectorates were merged into a Social Services Inspectorate in 1985. There were separate inspectorates for England, Wales, Scotland and Northern Ireland and, since devolution, the systems in the separate countries vary.

The role of the SSI initially was to develop, implement and monitor, inspect and review programmes; to collect and analyse evidence about performance and to advise on good practice in social services. The inspectors were mainly social workers. Later, their work was linked to PSAs, Comprehensive Performance Assessments (CPAs) and to local delivery policies, and became more focused on efficiency and VfM. From 2001, the SSI began publishing star ratings and their star ratings contributed to the CPA of local councils (see Chapters 5 and 6). As with OFSTED, excellent ratings entitled councils to a three-year holiday from further inspections, while poor ratings led to interventions and improvement plans.

Evidence of poor standards and a series of scandals in the 1990s led the Labour Government to strengthen the inspectorate (Care Standards Act 2002) and to establish the Commission for Social Care Inspection which was launched in 2004 as a single independent inspectorate for all social services in England. (See Johns and Lock 2008 for examples of scandals and government responses.) It had a much wider remit than the inspectorates it absorbed, and it regulated and inspected residential and nursing homes for adults and children's domiciliary care, fostering and adoption services. This was the first time that all care services had been regulated within a single framework. In 2007, however, OFSTED took over responsibility for regulating children's social services which were transferred from CSCI, including child protection. Shortly after taking on this role, it became evident that the new system was weak, as OFSTED was giving good ratings to local authority social services whose child protection services were seriously flawed. This was highlighted in the case of Baby P in Haringey, three months after Haringey Council had been given a very favourable inspection report (See Box 9.4). Further changes occurred in 2009 when a new single body – the Care Quality Commission – responsible for regulating both social care and health was appointed.

As stated above, there are different approaches in the devolved systems in the UK. In Wales, the Assembly Government's overall policy for health and social care has been to integrate service planning and delivery according to a whole-system approach. It transferred the responsibility of the CSIW (Care

BOX 9.4 The case of 'Baby P'

This case involved Baby P (Peter Connelly) who in his short life (born March 2006 and died August 2007) suffered multiple injuries inflicted by his mother and her partner. The case first came to the notice of a GP in December 2006 and his mother was arrested and Peter was put into the care of a family friend. He was returned home in January 2007 but was admitted to hospital on two occasions and his mother was arrested again. In June 2007, a social worker informed the police and a medical examination concluded that the bruising was due to abuse. On 25 July, Haringey Council's Children & Young People's Service sought legal advice but it was decided that 'the threshold for initiating Care Proceedings... was not met' and Peter was returned to his mother. On 1 August Peter was seen by a locum paediatrician at hospital and injuries were recorded but he was returned home. On 3 August Peter died and the post-mortem revealed horrendous injuries. The police immediately began a murder investigation and Baby P's mother was arrested along with other residents of the house. The court found Peter's mother and her partner and his brother all guilty of child abuse and they were given prison sentences.

Haringey Council initiated a Serious Case Review (SCR) after Peter's death. The *Daily Mail* obtained a copy and revealed details of the catalogue of mistakes, which had led to Peter's (avoidable) death. These included mishandling by officials, missed and delayed meetings, miscommunication among officials, and a failure to follow through with decisions related to the child's safety. Officials had not obtained an 'interim care order' that would have removed Peter from his home when legal grounds had existed for doing so six months before he died. Clearly a range of organizations, in addition to the Social Services Department, were at fault.

The Secretary of State for Children, Schools and Families ordered a nationwide child protection review headed by Lord Laming, who had headed a similar review after the death of Victoria Climbié in 2000, which also involved Haringey Social Services. OFSTED, the Health Commission and the police inspectorate were also ordered to conduct an urgent joint area review (JAR) of safeguarding children in Haringey. The JAR was presented to the minister on 1 December 2008, who exercised his special powers to remove the Head of Children's Services at Haringey Council, and the Deputy Director of Children's Services and two other managers and the key social worker were all dismissed. A new Head of Children's Services was appointed and six monthly reports were submitted to the minister. Staffing was improved although subsequent OFSTED reports have recorded only improvements from a weak position and standards are still only partly satisfactory.

Sources: Compiled principally from Haringey Local Safeguarding Children Board (2010) *Serious Case Review: 'Child A'* [November 2008, March 2009] (Department for Education); and OFSTED/Healthcare Commission/HMIC (2008) *Joint Area Review: Haringey Children's Services Authority Area* (OFSTED).

Standards Inspectorate for Wales) for regulation of independent health care services to the Health Care Inspectorate (2006) and then in 2007 merged CSIW and SSIW (Social Services Inspectorate for Wales) to form the Care and Social Services Inspectorate (CSSIW). This reform was to ensure joint inspection of both health and social care and to ensure a working partnership between local authorities and the voluntary sector as well as the involvement of users. In Scotland recent changes have focused particularly on involving service users in the inspection process and on self-evaluation systems.

The Baby P case and subsequent cases of both child abuse and poor standards of care in homes for the elderly and adults in sheltered accommodation demonstrate that the systems are still not ensuring high standards.

The Police

The first inspectorate of police dates from 1856 in England and 1857 in Scotland. Today, members of Her Majesty's Inspectorate of Constabulary (HMIC) are appointed by the Crown on the advice of the Home Secretary and report to the Chief Inspector of Constabulary who is the Home Secretary's principal professional policing adviser. HMIC is charged with examining and improving the efficiency of the 43 police forces in England and Wales and the Ulster Constabulary in Northern Ireland. HMIC in Scotland is responsible for the inspection of the eight Scottish territorial police forces and other police organizations.

The traditional role of HMIC was as a professional inspectorate offering advice to police officers, police authorities and the government. There was concern about professional capture of HMIC because it included former members of ACPO (Association of Chief Police Officers). There was change in 2009 as a result of the Labour Government's new approach to providing a more public-facing assessment of the service on behalf of the public. The role of HMIC became one of assessing the performance of the forces, drawing attention to under-performance and recommending remedial action. Its role was also to test whether police authorities were exercising effective direction of policing outcomes on behalf of the public and ensuring the efficiency and effectiveness of their forces. The primary functions of HMIC today are listed in Box 9.5.

From 2009, for the first time, police authorities were inspected across all their activities by a joint team from the Audit Commission and HMIC. A new framework was designed to ensure inspections met the government's objectives and these are listed in Box 9.6. In its 2010 report the two bodies jointly published lessons that had been learned from their combined inspections – conducted on Audit Commission lines – on: setting strategic direction and priorities; scrutinizing performance outcomes: achieving results through community engagement and partnerships; and ensuring VfM and productivity (Audit Commission/HMIC 2010: 22–3).

BOX 9.5 The primary functions of HMIC

- Inspection and assessment of all forces in England, Wales and Northern Ireland, British Transport Police, HM Revenue & Customs, and the Serious Organised Crime Agency.
- Inspections on specific themes across forces, working on some with the other criminal justice system inspectorates and other bodies (such as the Haringey Joint Area Review).
- Advisory role within the policing tripartite system (Home Office; police forces; and police authorities). HMIC links forces to the Home Office and advises on appointments to top posts in the police service.

Source: Audit Commission/HMIC (2010) *Learning Lessons: An overview of the first ten joint inspections by HMIC and the Audit Commission* (Audit Commission), p. 2.

Half the inspections of local police authorities had been carried out by mid-2010 when there was a change of government. The proposed abolition of the Audit Commission and the Coalition Government's policy to replace police authorities with elected police and crime commissioners put this strategy into question. But by 2010 there was already evidence of a significant change in the approach of HMIC, away from an inward-looking inspectorate that offered mainly professional advice to chief officers, police authorities and the government, to providing an assessment of the service that judged its activities from the point of view of the public. In particular,

BOX 9.6 Government objectives for police inspections

- Show whether authorities are effective at directing police outcomes.
- Focus on local accountability: how well police authorities are taking account of local views.
- Ensure that police authorities can carry out their duties effectively and are willing to improve where shown to be needed.
- Give authorities clear goals for targeted improvement.
- Provide evidence-based judgements and comparisons against clear standards and performance criteria.
- Give the public accessible information about the comparative performance of their authority.
- Give the Home Secretary a clear picture of police authority performance and persistent or major performance failure.

Note: The responsibilities of police authorities will move to police and crime commissioners following their election in November 2012.

Source: Audit Commission/ HMIC (2009) *Police Authority Inspection: Joint Audit Commission and Her Majesty's Inspectorate of Constabulary Police Authority Inspection Framework* (Audit Commission and HMIC), p. 6.

in its new role, it was drawing attention to persistent under-performance in the area of protecting the public from unacceptable risk and advising police forces and the Home Office on the level of assistance or intervention that might be required. It was also investigating local issues such as anti-social behaviour, threats to public safety, and the protective services provided by the police. It published comprehensive data on VfM, comparing how the 43 police authorities in England and Wales spent their budgets. It also worked with HM Inspectorate of Prisons on a programme of custody visits and with the Audit Commission on a series of inspections of police authorities. At times it also reported on issues raised by particular incidents including the events of the G20 protest in London in April 2009 and the death of Baby P in Haringey (see above). One significant recent development has been HMIC's expansion of its web-based services which enable the public to have access to information and, in particular, the Police Report Card which provides the public with information on the risks where they live, how well the police tackle these risks, and the cost (see HMIC 2011).

The Criminal Justice Agencies

There are five separate service-oriented inspectorates in the criminal justice system of England and Wales, each established by law as independent organizations – these include inspectorates for police (discussed above), probation, prisons, the courts and the prosecution service. A similar set of inspectorates undertake the same functions in Scotland but in Northern Ireland there is a single inspectorate – the Criminal Justice Inspection Northern Ireland. In 2005, the UK Government set out its proposals for reform of the inspection arrangements for criminal justice which proposed a single new Inspectorate for Justice, Community Services and Custody to replace the five existing inspectorates. The Police and Justice Bill was introduced in parliament in 2006 but because of strong opposition it had to be amended and the proposal for the new inspectorate was abandoned (Raine 2008). The government therefore resorted to finding ways to get the existing inspectorates to work more closely together.

All the inspectorates are royal appointments. The first three, Police, Probation and Prisons, are long established, but the Crown Prosecution Service Inspectorate and the Court Administration Inspectorate are relatively new – dating from 2000 and 2003 respectively. The Prosecution Service Inspectorate was created to promote continuous improvement in the efficiency, effectiveness and fairness of the prosecution service. It has had a quite low profile since its creation as it is mainly concerned with the internal management of the prosecution system. Similarly, the courts inspectorate has had little publicity. It covers all the courts of England and Wales but only their administration and not judicial matters, although it is difficult in practice to separate the two. Its main effect has been to raise the standards of the court service across the country and in particular its efficiency and speed.

The Prison Inspectorates for England and Wales (and in Scotland) differ in several ways from the other inspectorates. The origins of the Prison Inspectorate (HMIP) date back to 1835 but it was always inside a government commission or agency and not until 1982 was the fully independent Prison Inspectorate for England and Wales established. Since then only people from outside the prison service have been appointed as chief inspectors and they report today directly to the Justice Secretary, who appoints them. They are supported by prison officers with experience of the service, civil servants and outside experts. The inspector's reports on conditions in the prisons and young offenders' institutions have been influential in changing policy, which an ex-Chief Inspector of Prisons, Judge Stephen Tumim, thinks is because of their independent and more objective status (Raine 2008). Prison inspectors visit each prison annually and their brief is to inspect the conditions of the prisons, their re-offending rates and training and education programmes rather than the management of the prison service *per se*. Because the prison inspectorate gets close media coverage, its chief inspectors tend to have a higher profile than most chief inspectors. The last chief inspector, Anne Owers, was frequently in the news. The public interest in the prison service and the effect of critical reports from the Inspectorate has often led to difficult relationships between the Chief Inspector and the Home Secretary.

Finally, there is the Inspectorate of Probation. The history of this service can be found on www.justice.gov.uk but it changed its role in 2003. It currently independently inspects adult and youth offending work in order to help improve effective practice. It focuses much more on how often practitioners do the right thing than how often they make mistakes. The Inspectorate works closely with other inspectorates and often produces joint reports, for example a Joint Report of the National Audit Office and HMIP on the National Probation Service Information Technology Strategy in 2003.

In spite of the failed attempt to integrate the criminal justice inspectorates, largely because of the concern of the loss of specialist service expertise, significant development in the use of joint inspectorates has gone some way to achieving the Labour Government's aim whilst retaining the different approaches and objectives of the separate inspectorates. Whilst there is evidence of some degree of convergence on style and practice in recent years, they continue to present their own particular styles. Flynn (2007) draws out the contrasts between the prison inspectorate, OFSTED and HMIC, while Stein *et al.* (2010) provide an insight into the work of the Scottish Commission for the Regulation of Care in assessing quality and risk. Downe (2008), in turn, throws light on the inspection of local government services, and Walshe (2008) explains the regulation and inspection of health services.

Evaluating internal regulation

We have seen how the role of audit and inspection has been transformed in recent decades. Audit has moved from a traditional core activity of preventing corruption, fraud and mismanagement to one of reporting on efficiency and value for money and advising organizations on how to improve their management. Auditors are more and more involved with identifying the issues confronting organizations and recommending policy actions whilst identifying risks. Similarly, the role of inspectorates has changed, from professionals monitoring and advising other professionals to ensure professional standards are upheld, to being mixed teams of professionals and lay persons evaluating whether national targets and standards are being met and assessing the effectiveness of the management and leadership of public organizations. In both cases, regulatory bodies have become a means of government control from a distance, rather than independent agencies acting as buffers between government and their delivery organizations to ensure accountability and transparency. They have also become bureaucracies paralleling bureaucracies, adding more to public expenditure than they have possibly saved. Although there is evidence of convergence amongst different audits and inspectorates, the devolved parts of the UK have adopted different regulatory strategies and, in many cases, have succeeded in achieving joined-up government and a more holistic approach to service provision than the central government in Whitehall.

The growth of regulation was an offshoot of the transition of the state after 1979 from public administration to public management and from government to governance. It became a tool used by both Conservative and Labour governments in their reform and modernization strategies allowing decisions to be devolved or decentralized whilst retaining power at the centre, to steer but not row (see Chapters 2 and 4). Supporters in all main political parties point to the positive effect of regulators on performance, accountability and transparency claiming that they have raised standards in schools, improved the efficiency, effectiveness and responsiveness of the NHS and achieved value for money and cost savings in local government. The use of PSAs, national and local performance indicators and targets set by central government has provided a framework within which the Audit Commission and other inspectorates could report on performance and standards and show how to raise both (Bundred and Grace 2008). Davis and Martin (2002) concluded from their study of six Best Value pilots that there was evidence of more demanding targets and service improvements, marginally better responsiveness to the users of the services and some cost savings. Downe and Martin's (2007) study of five local authorities and Best Value inspections found very little evidence that the inspections would lead to significant improvements in service outcomes but they did find evidence that inspections tend to establish a culture in which improvement was more likely and that local government officers and councillors saw inspections as an opportunity to garner support for the changes that the authority wanted. In a wider examination of public service regulation Ashworth *et al.* (2002) again found no positive correlation between specific regulatory instruments and performance although there was definite evidence of improved performance overall, suggesting that regulation did create an improvement culture. Regulation seems to have had an impact, therefore, on the culture of public organizations. The latest trend towards internal self-regulation may look like a return to the norm before the era of NPM and the regulatory state but not only is the context different but so too is the culture of public organizations as they have become managerialized and committed to continuous improvement. Those responsible for internal regulation are now managers and not professional practitioners or administrative bureaucrats. This trend is best described as 'decentred regulation' rather than deregulation.

There are still many critics who challenge these claims made for the regulatory regime. First, there are those who point to the costs of the regulatory bodies, which now number in their hundreds. The costs include not only the direct financial burdens of paying for staff and overheads of the regulators but the indirect financial costs incurred by the regulated bodies. Hood *et al.* (1999), ODPM/Treasury (2005) and LGA (2005) all indicated the scale of these costs. The government estimated that the direct cost of regulation of local government in England was more than £90 million in 2005 and a more recent LGA estimate was in the region of £2 billion per year. The expectation was that audit bodies justified their own costs and demonstrated how it was offset by savings made as a result of their work (see sections on the Audit Office and Audit Commission above). This aim now also applies to inspectorates under the austerity programme of the Coalition. No systematic tally of the costs of individual regulatory bodies appears to have been made but it would certainly amount to billions of pounds.

There are also significant non-financial costs of the unintended consequences of regulation. Some of the hidden costs are the effects of excessive regulation on staff morale, displaced activities and the gaming which distracts staff from activities which may be more important to performance overall and certainly to quality. These costs are almost impossible to quantify but they are real. Furthermore, as Farrell and Morris (1999: 32) indicate, 'while the intention was to reduce paperwork and formality in procedures by undermining hierarchical managerial systems… rather than reducing hierarchies, the need for regulation and control, has, in effect created more hierarchy' – and moreover dual hierarchies because regulators shadow the providers.

Further issues revolve around the question of who regulates the regulators? Kelly (2003) points out that regulators now play an important role in shaping the policy agenda and promoting their own position but how are they controlled? Critics continue to argue that regulation is still dominated by a silo mentality and that institutional fragmentation impedes the attempts at 'joined up' policy and service delivery at local level, with the exception of the devolved systems. However, there is some evidence that criteria are applied consistently and that attempts at coordination and sharing of good practice across regulatory families is increasing. The use of multi-inspectorate teams has resulted in a broader approach with team members coming from different but related backgrounds and, as Mordaunt (2000: 767) predicted, it has brought 'a fresh approach to inspection unhindered by tradition' and there has been a blurring of boundaries between audit, inspections and consultancy.

The Coalition Government is seeking to deconstruct some of the regulatory infrastructure and re-orient the rest. It made commitments in 2010 to have a bonfire of agencies, abolish the Audit Commission, decentralize regulation down to the local level, and encourage the public to assume the regulatory role through local initiatives, referenda and generally the Big Society strategy. Also it plans a return of the auditing role to the market with competition leading to raised standards and greater efficiency. But it remains to be seen exactly what reconstruction will take place as the abolition of the Audit Commission has been delayed until 2014 or 2015 and the other inspectorates are still in place. In particular, there is concern about whether many citizens have the expertise or the interest to scrutinize the barrage of data that councils will have to publish (see the evidence of Professor David Heald and Professor Steve Martin presented to parliament's Communities and Local Government Select Committee in February 2011). The tests of success will be whether the government's claimed saving of £50 million pounds or more materializes; and, even more crucially, whether the auditing standards of the Audit Commission are maintained and local authorities are still subject to robust auditing. Accountability and control of public organizations will always be necessary, while transparency is a basic condition of good governance. We predict that there will be elements of continuity among the changes that will occur within the regulatory regimes but more direct involvement of the public will be a key feature of the future with both positive and unpredictable outcomes.

Chapter 10

Conclusion: Public Management in the UK Today

In a book that seeks to explain 'public management in the UK', Chapter 1 had to start with the UK's unusual territorial arrangements, because it is no longer possible to talk about 'public management in the UK' as a single system. Among the novel aspects of the Blair Government was the decision to allow patterns of public management to vary to fit the ways people in different regions would like public services delivered. The Brown Government agreed to pass even stronger powers to Scotland, which the Coalition Government quickly put into legislation. However, too much should not be made of this diversity. UK government ministers still hold the public purse-strings, particularly significant at a time of recession and cutbacks. They are still in command throughout the UK of high-spending policies such as social welfare (though not of health or education). More generally, the historical development of public services was largely shared across the four territories, and has provided an inheritance of a common UK style of public management.

Recent UK-wide legacies include the turning point in the 1980s from a model in which the state took an interventionist approach to service delivery towards a model based on privatization and marketization, on the basis of neo-liberal economic theories and principles outlined in Chapter 2. This trajectory was not rejected by the Labour Government but redirected towards a renewal of the partnerships with the voluntary and private sectors that have been a traditional feature of public services in the UK. The combined effects of these differing forms of provision can be seen in the current complex institutional framework of public service provision described in Chapter 3. Chapter 4 then identified two sets of processes transferring responsibility for delivery away from the central state: first, an evolving relationship between public, private and voluntary sectors, moving towards a blurring of the boundaries in social enterprises (the Big Society); and second, the devolution, decentralization and delegation of functions, both politically and managerially. In both processes there was an initial emphasis (especially by the Thatcher Government) on individualizing responsibilities at the level of the basic delivery unit (school management body, housing estate, bus company, job centre, career companies, and so on) and then later (especially during the Blair Government) on sharing them (as in Education Action Zones, New Deal for Communities Partnerships, Quality Bus Partnerships, Local Strategic Partnerships, the Connexions Service).

Chapters 5, 6, 7 and 8 explained and analysed four crucial components of public management in the UK today. They showed that strategic planning and management, especially on budgeting and investment, has a longer history in UK central and local government than is often acknowledged, though it often remained somewhat 'theoretical', with the principles not universally translating into practice. There is no doubt that financial management – or the financial element of strategic management – was given a strong boost from the top by the Thatcher and Major Governments, and then performance management – joined to strategic and financial management – became strong themes of the Blair Government. The fourth vital component of public management, dealing with the people who are the agents of all public activities, was examined in Chapter 8. It showed how a transition from traditional public administration to human resource management (HRM) has run alongside, fed into and been driven by, the developments in strategic, performance and financial management of the public sector, but also by newer attitudes in the wider social and economic environment.

One feature of public management that has traditionally distinguished it from private management has been the special requirement for painstaking accounting by officials and political decision makers for their actions. Chapter 9 showed how the privatizing and decentralizing processes described in Chapter 4 were accompanied by an increase in regulation and control by audit offices and inspectors. It detailed the work of the more important institutions, and noted the Coalition's dilemma in seeking to fulfil its Programme commitment to reduce the regulatory burden and to decentralize inspection, while nevertheless ensuring that probity and transparency are assured and that problems with services continue to be identified. Chapter 7 considered a similar dilemma with regard to the economically regulated sector, where the government is uncertain about how much to dictate to private companies and how much to leave to market forces and consumer pressure.

History, culture and place

In discussing the organization of public services, the radical changes naturally come under the spotlight, leaving in the shadows the continuities and the slow evolutions. Reforms have, in recent times, been unusually prominent, currently because of a financial crisis which was bound to stimulate turning points but also because of two successive periods of governments with large parliamentary majorities, which stayed in place over more than a decade, long enough to implement their own ideas for improvements.

Comparative studies point to the importance of the broader constitutional and cultural context for determining whether public management reform takes place and what form the reform takes (Chapter 1). Two factors seem particularly relevant in the UK case. First, there is a centuries-old tendency in

England towards an individualist, 'self-help' stance, which rejects collectivist solutions that might lead to 'big government' or 'the nanny state'. Until the late nineteenth century, the English government left education, health and welfare, prisons, infrastructure and utilities to ad hoc provision by what is now described as the 'third sector', and to private initiative and local authorities. These habits had been given economic and political justification in the late eighteenth century by political philosophers such as Adam Smith, writing on the advantages of market competition and privatized delivery (Chapter 2), or Edmund Burke, the theorist of conservatism, writing on the virtues of keeping 'what works' over designing systems of government from abstract principles. These ideas were not shared by everyone in England, and they did not fit the expectations of universal funded education in Scotland. However, these historical experiences help to explain why market solutions have replaced state provision more easily and widely in the UK than they have in other European countries.

Second, the building of the UK state over centuries had led, by the 1970s, to a four-nation state in which the English element dominated, but the incorporated nations had different organizational structures and policy variations, which were most marked in Northern Ireland and least in Wales. These variations were rarely mentioned in books on public management that, in effect, discussed public management in England – where, after all, more than three-quarters of the UK population live. The devolution or restoration of power in asymmetric ways to three of the four component parts of the UK has markedly increased the differences between the four governmental systems. It is certainly very unlike the conventional pattern of decentralization which gives authorities at the same territorial level the same measure of discretion in the same policy areas. The devolved governments have new possibilities of taking their own paths, diverging further away from the UK government's arrangements for England, as is evident in a number of chapters in this book. In education, Scotland has famously not introduced the fees for university education imposed in England and Wales, while Wales charges a more modest fee and subsidises fees paid by Welsh students in England. Wales has also rejected the systematic testing of pupils (SATs) and the school performance 'league tables' they fed into. Together with differences in the delivery of public utilities, these decisions signify a preference for a more collective provision of public services, and a rejection of the market approach adopted by the UK government, a preference seen too in the maintenance of community comprehensive schools in complete contrast to England's array of quasi-independent 'foundation schools', 'academies' , 'trusts', 'free schools' and so on, in which 'money follows the pupil' (Chapter 4).

During the period that Northern Ireland was run from London, reforms were made to the Northern Ireland Civil Service that mirrored those made to the British civil service but the Northern Ireland Executive's own modernizing reforms adopt and adapt local solutions, as for example, in creating the

Educational and Skills Authority by combining the regional education boards with operational staff in the education department (Chapter 5). In contrast, but also more evidence of divergence, the Welsh Assembly Government and the Scottish Government dismantled quango-like administrative bodies by bringing them into departments (Chapter 3).

Ideas and theories: bureaucracy, markets, communities

Chapter 2 explained the more important economic and political ideas underlying public management strategies. The traditional concept of public service bureaucracies – staffed by impartial permanent officials offering expert advice to political decision makers and giving equal treatment to all citizens – still has many supporters. Though this normative model was never a completely accurate description of the real world, it was deeply ingrained and there remains much scepticism about the new flexibilities, such as the movement of senior staff between sectors: those leaving the public sector for private companies take the knowledge of contracts or policy options they have helped prepare, while those coming from business into government departments often receive higher salaries than internal appointees. Yet such recruitment practices in the civil service have enabled it to become more diverse, more like the community it serves, more aware of the needs of British business, and generally more open to society, as the Fulton Report of 1968 had recommended but with little impact at the time (Chapter 8).

The changes made in the UK, in the 1980s and 1990s, were not primarily driven by the Fulton Report's pragmatic reasoning but by theoretical arguments based on classical liberal economics about the dysfunctional behaviour of public bureaucrats. The New Right rejected the traditional model and accepted public choice theories that public service organizations, and the self-interested individuals who composed them, were inevitably more inefficient and ineffective than private companies, which survived in a competitive market place only if they provided goods that clients wanted, in the right quantities and at the best price. The New Right's solution was to put as much of the public sector as possible into the private sector and manage the parts that had to remain in public hands in ways that were more like those in the market. Nevertheless, there were other economic theories which predicted that the public sector would meet new problems when operating in market-like ways, such as higher transaction costs and regulatory capture (Chapter 7). Traditional permanent bureaucracies often avoid these problems through built-in mechanisms such as trusting relationships, easy communications, coordinating procedures, and a shared ethical culture. Even the prime reference for liberal economics, Adam Smith, had argued that collective provision was more effective for certain public goods, such as education, defence, justice and transport – though where the market could play a useful role it should (Chapter 2).

Governments in many countries were stimulated by the public choice arguments – and by financial constraints and taxpayer pressure – to rethink public management in these terms. While many reform ideas such as performance pay and contracting-out derive directly from public choice analysis, its indirect impact is even wider. The difficulties some UK ministers experienced in the early 1980s in acquiring the information needed to manage their departments (in the basic sense of understanding what resources were being directed towards what objectives and with what results), reinforced the push for business-style management. Enquiries revealed how little attention had been given by top officials and most ministers to the administrative side of government by comparison with policy development, despite the total reliance of policy on execution. Top civil servants were more attuned to looking upwards to ministers in their policy advice role than looking downwards and managing their human and budgetary resources. Breaking up the central bureaucracies into agencies (whether departmental Next Steps Agencies or quangos or Primary Care Trusts) tackled this problem not only by assigning leadership of executive work to senior officials selected specifically for the managerial role, but also by turning them into quasi-autonomous 'businesses' with their own budgets; they could concentrate on delivering a particular range of products towards a particular set of customers, and resources could be managed appropriately towards the objectives set by ministers (Chapter 4). Under the assumption that inefficiencies predicted by public choice theorists applied generally throughout the public sector, governments required an equivalent restructuring in local government services, the NHS and public enterprises, whether through privatization, contracting-out or the recomposition of public bodies into separately managed 'direct service organizations', schools, hospital trusts, and the like.

The fragmentation of institutions, each pursuing its own particular remit in its own way, added a new layer to the 'differentiation' that public policy analysts assert exists between policy areas because of the way that decisions are negotiated and implemented in silo-like networks (linking departments with their partners in local authorities, private companies and the third sector). When the variations between the devolved governments, as discussed above, are combined with this already complex structure, the result is a 'differentiated polity' which presents a challenge for central government to manage as a corporate whole. The alternative 'governance' theory suggested that, as in the Netherlands and other consensus and cooperation-seeking democracies, UK governments should abandon their traditional, unrealistic ambitions to 'command and control' a public sector made up of delegated and devolved and contracted-out components. Instead a more circumspect 'governance' should be adopted, in which political and bureaucratic leaders aim to 'steer' the complexity to achieve more limited outcomes in consultation with those delivering – and receiving – services.

The problems of fragmentation were expressly addressed in just this way by the Blair Government as Labour came back into power, through an avowed emphasis on strategic-level management, collaboration and partnerships. The approach was justified theoretically by a 'Third Way' rejection of both socialist and New Right ideologies – but especially by a rejection of ideologies as a whole, in preference for a 'what matters is what works' pragmatic approach. It was not important whether a public, private or voluntary sector body delivered a service, provided it was delivered well. The idea of governance was translated into practice through, for example, the setting of high-level performance targets for departments (Public Service Agreements, see Chapter 5) that would have to be achieved through collaboration with service delivery partners. However, collaboration frequently transmuted into departmental 'initiatives', top-slicing local authorities' grant funding as incentives for them to introduce particular partnerships or projects that would help achieve the PSAs. Partnerships which, for good reasons, often focused on particularly problematic 'places' or cross-departmental issues, added a new fragmentation (Chapter 4), and in many cases were just another top-down strategy. In developing 'Best Value', English local authorities were required to collaborate in UK government-defined ways with UK government-defined partners for UK government-defined purposes (Chapter 6). Claims of collaboration by UK governments were also seen to be only skin-deep in the requirement for all but the smallest local authorities in England and Wales to choose one of three models of management: in contrast, the Scottish Executive left the choice of management structure to local authorities themselves (Chapter 5).

The Coalition – or more precisely, Cameron for the Conservatives – promised a 'post-bureaucratic' era, to be achieved through 'the Big Society', in which 'state control' was replaced by 'personal, professional, civic and corporate responsibility' (see Chapter 4). In the post-bureaucratic world, Cameron argued, citizens could make and were making their own decisions about public services and could access data that would hold officials directly to account. Citizens are being 'nudged' into being civic-minded (paying tax bills, agreeing to donate organs): behavioural economics has replaced public choice theory. Proposals enacted or under serious consideration in England include local enterprise partnerships set up within locally determined boundaries; 'free' state schools set up by community groups; neighbourhood plans to be approved by local referendums; directly elected police and crime commissioners to hold police forces to account; and referendums in up to twelve large cities (selected by the government) asking citizens if they want directly elected mayors with new powers. The extent to which citizens and localities will welcome and, especially, use the opportunities to take a more direct role in public management remains to be seen: evidence on weak or negative responses to mayoral referendums under Labour's 2000 legislation and on the weak commitment of community groups and individual citizens to Labour's partnerships (Chapters 2 and 4) suggests a degree of pessimism.

Given the widespread adoption of instant communications devices, and easier access to comparative data, communities can feasibly call local public organizations to account and pressure them to tailor provision to local needs but, by the same token, they will be fully aware of different levels of service being provided in other localities, and will be quick to complain of a post-code lottery when inequalities inevitably occur.

Continuity and change in public management

Having recapitulated the theories that fed into recent public management reforms and illustrated the way they have been used by UK governments, the rest of the chapter now sums up their impact in the UK today on the different aspects of public management and indicates the likely direction of travel.

Changing institutional structures and processes

The basic four-part structure of the public organization landscape, as defined by constitutional arrangements – central departments, local authorities, the NHS, public bodies – has remained recognizably the same for 50 years, but each component has undergone considerable change and will continue to do so (Chapter 3). The power of the UK executive to alter institutional arrangements is almost unrivalled among liberal democracies, and most governments use the opportunity, despite the costs in resources and the evidence that changing the structures does not necessarily change the outputs or the outcomes.

The greatest upheavals to UK public institutions occurred over 20 years ago now, under the Thatcher Government. New Labour's contributions tended to be evolutionary modifications, but there was an emphasis on changing relationships, of which devolution and local partnerships were among the most significant. Within departments there was reform in 1988 of almost constitutional significance with their segmentation into executive agencies to which ministers' managerial authority was delegated, although within substantial constraints (Chapter 4). The Labour Government kept the system but tightened the linkage between an agency and its parent department and their joint performance objectives. Its ambitious merging of two agency networks to form Jobcentre Plus was successful in policy and financial terms, but the creation of HM Revenue & Customs from two historic bodies has been notable for its failings with few compensatory benefits. Executive agencies as a concept are now widely accepted and the Coalition has not called them into question, though the government in Scotland has brought some under closer control.

The UK Coalition Government is continuing along the path of devolution, which was the most radical of Labour's reforms, when seen against the background of centuries of centralization. Yet it was a long time in the making:

devolution to Scotland and Wales had nearly occurred in 1979; in Northern Ireland it was the culmination of a long peace process; in all three cases it built on an existing political and administrative distinctiveness (Chapter 1). The Coalition quickly abolished Labour's English regional assemblies, which will struggle to re-emerge. It has picked up and further emphasized Labour's rhetoric of localism and community democracy, but the insistence on working in partnership across sectors that was so much a feature of the Blair years has gone. Rather, communities and social enterprise groups are being invited to promote and deliver their own vision of a local service. Other 'bottom-up' initiatives being encouraged include job-sharing of official posts across councils but the consequences at political level have yet to be tested.

All governments promise 'a cull of quangos' but, as before, the Coalition's review of English national quangos found many were carrying out essential functions that were more effectively performed at arm's length from ministers, either to ensure decisions were seen as independent of politics or because the role was purely technical. Experience suggests that culled quangos will be succeeded by more quangos, at least in England: in Scotland and Wales the historic resentment against London-appointed public bodies obstructs the use of this administrative device. The 'public bodies' category also includes nationalized industries, of which few remain following one of the more spectacular changes of the Thatcher era. New Labour was no longer committed to public ownership and preferred the term 'public–private partnership' (PPP; see Chapter 7). Under financial pressure from 2008, it had started to privatize state-owned assets, and there is no difference in the strategies of Labour and the Coalition for the most prominent remaining public or part-public industries, Royal Mail, NATS and Network Rail.

The Coalition Programme announced an end to the 'top-down' reorganizations of the NHS, yet another restructuring of the NHS in England was soon before parliament, and was more extreme than the Programme had proposed. 'De-bureaucratization' in health services would be achieved through the abolition of the intermediary bodies between the national level and GP commissioning groups. The national level would be reconstituted as an NHS commissioning board. GP commissioning groups were familiar from previous Conservative and Labour reforms but had not before been given this level of budgetary power. The commissioning board had featured strongly in earlier expert reports but had always been rejected by ministers for its weak accountability and lack of local responsiveness. The amendments made under parliamentary and hospital pressure to this organizational streamlining – to add accountability and safeguard a public service – have resulted in a superstructure of oversight that seems unlikely to be workable, even before considering the financial savings that the NHS is required to make in coming years.

Reviewing strategic management and leadership

Strategic management is not a new practice in the UK: wartime strategic planning in the 1940s included economic and social planning and continued after the war (Chapter 5). However, it never took on the comprehensive character seen in some other European countries, being viewed with general scepticism in Whitehall and by a pragmatic society. The Thatcher Government was particularly scornful of planning by officials (there had been serious housing and transport planning failures), arguing that investment decisions should be left to the market. Paradoxically, businesses needed some sense of government direction for their own strategic management; and public organizations, as well, now practise strategic management, identifying and assessing their objectives within the context of the external environment, reviewing performance against the objectives and evaluating the organization and its capacities in a continuous cycle.

Managing change in particular calls for strategic leadership. The Major Government reviewed and proposed structures that could strengthen local government leadership in the new environment of contracting-out and direct service organizations, which had turned specifying requirements, coordinating services and monitoring performance into crucial tasks. Recruitment advertisements for chief executives of local authorities and executive agencies started to include 'leadership', 'strategic management' and 'change management' among the skills being sought.

However, it was the Labour Government which drove from the centre the adoption of strategic management in departments and English local government. The devolved governments, both Labour-dominated and otherwise, have developed their own strategic planning documents, using similar processes and techniques but incorporating the views of a wider range of actors (Chapter 5). The Blair Government started by integrating local and national performance management through PSAs, as seen above, as well as councils' own Local Area Agreements. Civil service leaders conducted a series of Capability Reviews in departments and later developed a Capability Framework in which leadership played an important part. From 1998, the financial planning framework was comprehensively reformed to give departments, and the bodies they funded, greater forward planning capacity over a two- to three-, and later, under the Coalition Government, four- to five-year period (see Chapter 7).

The same imperative for effective strategic management remains at a time of cutbacks. Having removed many of the central controls on local councils, police authorities and NHS bodies, the Coalition Government will be relying on its four-year financial settlements to act as the prime incentive for these organizations to help achieve its own strategic objectives. Following a decade of centrally driven strategic management, most, if not all, public authorities in the UK now recognize that they must act strategically if they are to fulfil their legal and political responsibilities.

Performance management: debates and issues

Cutting across the divide between those who argue for allowing market competition to drive up quality and those who seek improvements through top-down performance management driven by government is a shared concern for improving outcomes. The new emphasis on raising performance levels in public services represents a radical departure from traditional public administration but is replicated in many other countries world-wide and will outlast political changes in the UK government.

Performance management is of concern to all governments that need to show citizens that they are using taxpayers' money effectively but, as just noted, was of particular interest to the Blair Government, especially by the time of the 2001 election, when expenditure on services was increasing and voters had high expectations of Labour. Performance management means managing in a way that achieves more for less, ensuring resources are used efficiently and effectively, being responsive to public needs and demands and, overall, ensuring that quality is put at the centre of an organization's work. It presupposes that performance and quality can be measured and assessed in meaningful ways that will enable an organization using public funds to account to the public sponsor and the relevant accounting body for the results it has achieved from the resources.

The Conservatives initiated performance management during the 1980s to raise the productivity and responsiveness of those services that had not been privatized or contracted-out. The Financial Management Initiative (FMI) sought to link departmental programmes, costs and outputs; and the new Audit Commission invented increasingly sophisticated yardsticks to compare economy, efficiency and effectiveness across 'families' of similar councils. The Labour Governments from 1997 expanded these techniques in local authorities, executive agencies, and whole departments. The Coalition Government has drastically reduced its control of performance, partly to decentralize responsibility, partly to save administrative costs. Lack of resources will hold back the traditional urge of departments to micro-manage other public bodies, and the Treasury will need to rely on financial targets to achieve value for money.

There is good evidence from official statistics that measured performances improved in Labour's target areas of health, education, and law and order; and it seems that performance management has focused public managers' attention on processes for achieving better outcomes. However, it is not easy to demonstrate the exact impact of performance management on performance, since there are multiple factors involved in achieving good performance in any organization and the environmental context is in constant evolution. Undoubtedly, organizations resort to gaming, and political leaders are prone to decide one yardstick and demand performance along a different one when crises erupt. Performance management also has secondary impacts, both positive and negative. On the one hand, targets and regulatory regimes have forced all public organizations to review their internal management and accounting systems (see Chapter 9); and there are real benefits to citizens and customers of public services in terms of transparency, choice and accountability. On the other hand, the impact on working practices and employment status of many officials has contributed to the low morale in many public organizations, perhaps particularly those working in departments and agencies but also in education and more widely; and there has been a huge, though unquantified cost in the creation of inspectorates and regulators, which, in the end, was a strong element in the relaxation, at least temporarily, of the performance regime. The problem remains of how to control the controllers.

Managing public finances and engaging the private sector

In traditional administration, finance was not managed: it was raised, spent and recorded. Accounting standards were stricter than in business but the emphasis was on probity and parsimony. The more active role of managing the finances comes to the fore when budgets are under strong pressure: new finance-raising schemes are created, such as privatization and sell-and-lease-back schemes in the 1980s, the Private Finance Initiative (PFI) in the 1990s, and the PPPs and business rate supplements of New Labour (Chapter 7), all of which continue to be employed by the Coalition Government. Moreover, the national budget takes on the additional role of adjusting the economy. The Coalition's Spending Review, which sought to reduce the budget deficit by substantial cuts to public expenditure, defined its strategy more surely than did the Coalition Programme.

Financial management is a fundamental requirement for strategic management (Chapter 5), performance management (Chapter 6) and an essential component of NPM – indeed the financial crisis of the late 1970s is often seen internationally as a trigger for NPM (Chapter 2). However, despite NPM and FMI, the UK finances were not fully managed until the Blair Government replaced the old cash-recording system with business-like accruals accounting and departmental resource allocations ('resource accounting and budgeting'). Departmental spending was then able, for most departments, to be fixed, matched to programmes and compared with the corresponding outputs. There was more control over future expenditure because commitments were transparently recorded, and there were other efficiency gains, as Chapter 7 explained. Although there were several other elements to New Labour's budgetary reforms (fixing budgetary totals, multi-year planning, unified budgets), most originated under previous Conservative Governments. In contrast, Labour's accounting change was an innovation in the UK (though already in place elsewhere) and a highly significant reform to public management. The Coalition Government has continued the modernization of financial management procedures by extending the financial planning framework both in scope and time, introducing independent verification of budgetary impacts, and publishing the first Whole of Government Accounts, which include the spending of all public bodies including devolved and local governments.

The devolved governments, currently dependent on Treasury grants, almost inevitably adopt similar financial management practices to those of the UK, but they have more inclusive budgetary discussions. The Scottish Parliament will acquire more financial power and responsibility, whether or not it decides to remain in the UK, and Northern Ireland will levy some business taxes, but Northern Ireland and Wales at least will remain tied to the UK budget for the foreseeable future. English local authorities were funded more generously by New Labour than under the Conservative Government but much was in the form of ring-fenced funding, often to be spent in collaboration with other partners, and all within a tight budgetary and performance framework. The Coalition has ceded many controls but at the same time has cut grants substantially.

Chapter 7 considered two groups of private companies that are subject to some degree of public financial management. First are the PPPs created by the Labour Government either to bring private finance into public bodies that needed investment but could not be privatized, or to rescue privatized utilities that provided essential services but whose debts the government did not want on the public balance sheet. The second are public utilities that were privatized by the Conservatives, but which could have used their monopolistic position to exploit customers; their prices and to some extent their investment strategies, are controlled by a government-appointed economic regulator. In both groups there are examples of effective performance, and it seems likely that the Coalition will add to their number with a public–private or mutualized Royal Mail. However, the status of these organizations, which are neither publicly accountable nor subject to the rigours of the market, is widely agreed to be unsatisfactory.

The importance of managing human resources

If financial management is essential to effective public management, the same applies to HRM. Public organizations are labour intensive, with staffing costs often making up half their budgets (Chapter 7), perhaps more if public sector pensions were taken fully into account. They depend on their employees to carry out the functions and deliver the services that are legal obligations and/or have been promised to the local or national electorate. They need to have the right HR policies to be able to attract and retain people with the appropriate skills across the diverse roles. HR practices in the public sector have changed significantly in the last three decades, coming closer to those in the private sector as NPM, performance management and collaboration between the sectors have placed new demands on public bodies, requiring them to act like customer-focused businesses. Just as traditional public administration evolved into NPM and then governance, traditional personnel management has evolved into new methods of people management or HRM (Chapter 8). The place of HR within organizations has undergone considerable structural and cultural transformations, changing from that of service support to business partner, and becoming diffused and decentralized throughout the organization. With the growth of performance management in local and national governments and the NHS, line managers now have the prime responsibility everywhere for managing people, controlling, directing and motivating them.

The main changes in HRM practice have been in the areas of employment contracts, working patterns and employment relations, with an increasing emphasis on diversity and equal employment rights. The creation of separately managed agencies in the civil service, and direct service organizations in local government, and more generally the move to 'the contract state', saw a break from the uniform conditions of service that the traditional model implied, which was neither the most economical way to provide a bureaucracy (since no advantage was taken of variations in local labour markets and living costs across the country), nor was it necessarily appropriate for the many and varied roles that exist within one organization (Chapter 4). Today employment contracts can be made time specific, when particular skills are needed on a temporary basis. Distinctions can be made between permanent staff in core functions, with non-core staff contracted-out or the work retained in-house but at the price of new terms and conditions of employment. These strategies have produced more job-sharing, annualized hours contracts, fixed-term contracts, working from home and other patterns of employment which benefit the public employer and may or may not suit the employee. While these practices were new to the civil service they had long existed in the NHS and local government: what was new everywhere was their extension to managerial positions, assisting the feminization of the public service at this level (Chapter 8).

Employment relations, traditionally characterized in the public services by collective bargaining with a strongly unionized workforce, have been affected directly by these organizational changes and indirectly by the individualization of contracts. Union membership is falling and, in the civil service, bargaining units were further weakened by the decentralization of employment relations, together with the delegation of managerial responsibilities for pay determination to department heads and agency chief executives for all those below senior civil service grades. Pay review bodies have taken teachers and health professionals out of direct collective bargaining over pay although not for other aspects of terms and conditions of employment.

While employment relations improved during the Labour administration from their nadir under the Thatcher Government, they were not particularly good, and the issue of pensions was already problematic. The general problem of retirement pensions in the developed world, created by a demographic imbalance between people living longer and a smaller population of working age, is increased in the public services by relatively generous, inflation-proofed pensions based on final salary and, in some cases, an earlier retirement age. Reductions in pension entitlements (which many officials regard as a contractual obligation and one of the few remaining advantages of public service employment) were therefore proposed by Labour, starting with an increase in civil service retirement age to 65. A further deterioration in conditions, such as an increase in contributions, was suggested by the Coalition Government in the light of the budget deficit. Occasional one day strikes from 2004 had, by 2012, developed into threats of a general strike, with serious long-term consequences for labour relations.

Diversity in HRM terms has, until recently, meant that public service organizations were not to discriminate between employees or potential employees on a lengthening list of grounds, including gender, ethnicity, religion, sexual orientation, age and disability. While the need to monitor performance on these issues placed the stress on a fair representation of the different groups in society, the emphasis is now on the contribution individuals from a variety of backgrounds and experiences can make to a public organization, which must itself respond to the diversity of people it serves.

Evaluating public management in the UK

We concluded this survey of public management in the UK with an assessment of the apparatus that successive governments have put in place to audit, inspect, control and evaluate the performance of the public sector.

Audit offices and inspectorates have been a feature of UK governance for over 150 years, their activities expanding as public expenditure and services grew. However, there has been what some term an 'audit explosion' in the last 30 years, alongside and partly as a consequence of the reforms to the public sector (Chapter 9). As the traditional patterns of accountability and control through hierarchy and 'club government' in Whitehall were disrupted by marketization, managerialism and the delivery of public services through a wider range of providers, so audit, inspection and regulation were amplified to provide reassurance to ministers and departments in an era of 'governance' (Chapters 2 and 4). This movement has created what some term 'the new regulatory state', 'regulation' here meaning 'steering' the organizations within the government domain, rather than the monitoring of regulations for public safety.

Audit and inspection have not only grown but changed their character. Audit has evolved from the traditional administrative activity of preventing corruption, fraud and mismanagement of public funds to identifying problems and risks, and advising on improvements to the organization's cost-effectiveness and performance – significantly, the new Audit Scotland took on all these roles from the start. Similarly, as Chapter 9 illustrated, inspectors are now less likely to be service professionals monitoring and assisting fellow professionals to achieve professionally defined standards, and more likely to be multi-disciplinary teams of management consultants and professionals who evaluate performance relative to government-defined targets and standards, and report on their management and leadership. Indeed 'performance management system' may be as helpful a description as the term 'regulatory state': both are relevant.

Neither the costs nor the benefits of this regulation can be established with certainty. Supporters of the regulatory bodies from all main political parties suggest that performance standards in schools, the NHS and local government have been raised. There is some evidence that the Audit Commission's Comprehensive Performance Assessments of local authorities led to substantial improvements in performance, though less because of any direct impact on service outcomes than because inspection could create a culture in which improvement was more likely, partly because proponents of change within the authority used inspection to gain support. This finding has been supported by other research on regulation across the public sector.

However, auditing local government alone costs about £2 billion, to which must be added the costs of the regulated bodies, including distraction from activities that might add quality (Chapter 9). Audit bodies are expected to demonstrate that their costs are balanced by financial savings, but inspectorates do not have that obligation. A second criticism is that specialized inspection bodies contribute to the silo mentality – except in Scotland, Wales and Northern Ireland, which adopted a more holistic approach. The problem was addressed in England by merging various inspectorates, though the five criminal justice inspectorates remain separate. However, the merger of health, mental health and social care inspection responsibilities within the Care Quality Commission in 2009, combined with funding and staffing problems, overwhelmed the Commission in 2011 when it prioritized the new task of registering GPs and dentists over its core function of inspecting hospitals and care homes and responding to the problems it found.

In other policy areas, the regulatory state is withdrawing: ministers decided the burden of OFSTED's inspection would be lightened; certain categories of schools would be freed from regular OFSTED inspections, allowing effort to focus on poor teaching, though all schools would be subject to unannounced inspection. The Coalition Government's decision in 2010 to withdraw much of the performance control apparatus for local government, and abolish the Audit Commission by the end of the parliament, relies on councils having developed a culture of permanent improvement, and 'de-centres' regulation to council managers. The public will take on new regulatory roles, for example, through the elected police and crime commissioners who will oversee police services. Against the background of steady developments in audit and inspection over the past twenty or more years, the removal of a panoply of centrally imposed audits and performance controls is a radical change. Financial necessity is coinciding with the Cameron Government's political dream of a post-bureaucratic state.

In conclusion, public management in the UK is a continually unfolding story of continuity, change, innovation and reinvention. It cannot be divorced from its political, economic, social and cultural heritage, but it is affected too by its contemporary internal and external environments. There are multiple forces acting on it: it exists within a number of concentric circles of influence such as the European Union, NATO, the OECD, the World Trade Organization, the United Nations and, not least, the global economy. The major forces likely to produce changes to the system analysed in this book include the permanent revolution in technology (and notably, social networking), the crisis in the eurozone and international banking, and the volatile situation in the Middle East and OPEC countries. The future is uncertain but it is bound to be path dependent.

References

Achur, J. (2010) *Trade Union Membership 2009*, London: Department of Business, Innovation and Skills.

Albrow, M. (1970) *Bureaucracy*, London: Macmillan.

Allison, G. ([1979] 1982) 'Public and Private Management: Are They Fundamentally Alike in All Unimportant Respects', reprinted in F. S. Lane (ed.) *Current Issues in Public Administration*, 2nd edn, New York: St Martin's Press, 13–33.

All-Wales Convention (2009) *All-Wales Convention: Summary*, published 18 November, www.allwalesconvention.org.

Anderson, I. (2002) *Foot and Mouth Disease 2001: Lessons to be Learned*, HC 888, London: TSO.

Andrews, R., Boyne, G. and Walker, R. (2006) 'Strategy Content and Organizational Performance', *Public Administration Review*, 66/1, 53–63.

Armstrong, M. (1994) *Performance Management: Key Strategies and Practical Guidelines*, London: Kogan Page.

Ashworth, N., Boyne, G. and Walker, R. (2002) 'Regulatory Problems in the Public Sector: Theories and Cases', *Policy and Politics*, 30/2, 195–211.

Audit Commission (2005a) 'Customer focus: North Dorset District Council', press release, London: Audit Commission.

Audit Commission (2005b) 'Customer focus: North Wiltshire District Council', press release, London: Audit Commission.

Audit Commission (2008a) *Is the Treatment Working?*, London: Audit Commission.

Audit Commission (2008b) *Tougher at the Top? Changes in the Labour Market for Single Tier and County Council Chief Executives: A Discussion Paper*, London: Audit Commission.

Audit Commission (2010) *Bristol City Council: Benefits Service Inspection*, London: Audit Commission.

Audit Commission (2011) *Annual Report and Accounts 2010/11*, London: TSO.

Audit Commission/HMIC (2009) *Police Authority Inspection: Joint Audit Commission and Her Majesty's Inspectorate of Constabulary Police Authority Inspection Framework*, London: Audit Commission and HMIC.

Audit Commission/HMIC (2010) *Learning Lessons: An Overview of the First Ten Joint Inspections by HMIC and the Audit Commission*, London: Audit Commission.

Audit Scotland (2009) *Making an Impact: An Overview of the Audits of Best Value and Community Planning 2004–09*, Edinburgh: Audit Scotland.

Audit Scotland (2010a) *How Councils Work: An Improvement Series for Councillors and Officers Roles and Working Relationships: Are You Getting it Right?*, Edinburgh: Audit Scotland.

Audit Scotland (2010b) *Getting it Right for Children in Residential Care*, Edinburgh: Audit Scotland.

Audit Scotland (2011) 'Our Work Programme for 2012/13', published 14 October, www.audit-scotland.gov.uk.

Bagehot, W. [1867] (1963) *The English Constitution*, London: Fontana.

Bains Report (1972) *The New Local Authorities: Management and Structure*, London: HMSO.

Baker, E. (1976) 'The Role of HM Inspectors', *Education and Training*, 18/2, 50–6.

Barber, M. (2007) *Instruction to Deliver*, London: Methuen.

Bartle, I. and Vass, P. (2007) 'Self-regulation within the Regulatory State', *Public Administration*, 85, 885–905.

Batty, E., Beatty, C., Foden, M., Lawless, P., Pearson, S. and Wilson, I. (2010) *The New Deal for Communities Evaluation: Final Report, 7,* London: Department for Communities and Local Government.

Beardwell, I. and Holden, L. (eds) (1994) *Human Resources Management: A Contemporary Approach*, London: Pitman.

Bellamy, C. (2009) 'Managing ICTs in public sector organizations', in T. Bovaird and E. Löffler (eds) *Public Management and Governance*, 2nd edn, London: Routledge.

Bendell, T., Boulter, L. and Kelly, J. (1994) *Implementing Quality in the Public Sector*, London: Pitman Publishing.

Benington, J. and Moore, M. H. (2010) 'Public Value in Complex and Changing Times', in J. Benington and M. H. Moore (eds) *Public Value: Theory and Practice*, Basingstoke: Palgrave Macmillan.

Bevan, G. and Hood, C. (2006) 'What's Measured is what Matters: Targets and Gaming in the English Public Health Care System', *Public Administration*, 84, 517–38.

Bevir, M. and Richards, D. (2009) 'Decentring Policy Networks: A Theoretical Agenda', *Public Administration*, 87, 3–14.

Black, O., Herbert, R. and Richardson, I. (2004) 'Jobs in the Public Sector mid-2003', *Labour Market Trends*, July, 271–81.

Black, R. W. (2007) 'Lessons from Scotland', in M. Lavender (ed.) *Watchdogs Straining at the Leash*, London: CIPFA.

Blair, T. (1998a) *The Third Way: New Politics for the New Century*, London: Fabian Society.

Blair, T. (1998b) *Leading the Way: New Visions for Local Government*, London: IPPR.

Blyton, P. and Turnbull, P. (eds) (1992) *Reassessing Human Resource Management*, London: Sage.

Bogdanor, V. (ed.) (2005) *Joined-Up Government*, Oxford: Oxford University Press for the British Academy.

Bolden, R. (2004) *What is Leadership? Leadership South West Research Report 1*, Exeter: University of Exeter Centre for Leadership Studies.

Bouckaert, G. and Halligan, J. (2007) *Managing Performance: International Comparisons*, London: Routledge.

Bouckaert, G. and Van Dooren, W. (2009) 'Performance Measurement and Management in Public Organizations', in T. Bovaird and E. Löffler (eds) *Public Management and Governance*, 2nd edn, London: Routledge.

Bovaird, T. (2009) 'Strategic Management in Public Sector Organisations', in T. Bovaird and E. Löffler (eds) *Public Management and Governance*, 2nd edn, London: Routledge.

Bovaird, T. and Löffler, E. (2009a) 'The changing context of public policy', in T.

Bovaird and E. Löffler (eds) *Public Management and Governance*, 2nd edn, London: Routledge.

Bovaird, T. and Löffler, E. (2009b) 'Quality Management in Public Sector Organizations', in T. Bovaird and E. Löffler (eds) *Public Management and Governance*, 2nd edn, London: Routledge.

Bovaird, T. and Russell, K. (2007) 'Civil Service Reform in the UK, 1999-2005: Revolutionary Failure or Evolutionary Success?', *Public Administration*, 85, 301–28.

Bovaird, T. and Tizard, J. (2009) 'Partnership Working in the Public Domain', in T. Bovaird and E. Löffler (eds) *Public Management and Governance*, 2nd edn, London: Routledge.

Bowman, C. (1990) *The Essence of Strategic Management*, Englewood Cliffs, NJ: Prentice-Hall.

Boyne, G. A. (2002) 'Public and Private Management: What's the Difference?', *Journal of Management Studies*, 39, 97–122.

Boyne, G. A. (2003) 'Sources of Public Service Improvement: A Critical Review and Research Agenda', *Journal of Public Administration Research and Theory*, 13, 367–94.

Boyne, G. A., James, O., John, P. and Petrovsky, N. (2010) 'Does Political Change Affect Senior Management Turnover? An Empirical Analysis of Top-Tier Local Authorities in England', *Public Administration*, 88, 136–53.

Braithwaite, J. (2000) 'The New Regulatory State and the Transformation of Criminology', *British Journal of Criminology*, 40, 222–38.

Brereton, M. and Temple, M. (1999) 'The New Public Service Ethos: An Ethical Environment For Governance', *Public Administration*, 77, 455–74.

Brooke, R. (1991) 'The Enabling Authority', *Public Administration*, 69, 525–32.

Brown, M. and Benson, J. (2003) 'Rated to Exhaustion? Reactions to Performance Appraisal Processes', *Industrial Relations Journal*, 34, 67–81.

Browne, J. (2010) *Personal Taxes and Distributional Impact of Budget Measures*, London: Institute for Fiscal Studies, www.ifs.org.uk, accessed 19 July 2011.

Bulmer, S. and Burch, M. (2000) 'The Europeanisation of British Central Government', in R. A. W. Rhodes (ed.) *Transforming British Government, I*, London: Macmillan.

Bulmer, S. and Burch, M. (2005) 'The Europeanization of UK Government: From Quiet Revolution to Explicit Step-change?', *Public Administration*, 83, 861–90.

Bundred, S. (2007) 'New Role for Auditors in Government Performance and Accountability', in M. Lavender (ed.) *Watchdogs Straining at the Leash*, London: CIPFA.

Bundred, S. and Grace, C. (2008) 'Holistic Public Service Inspection', in H. Davis and S. Martin (eds) *Public Services Inspection in the UK*, London: Jessica Kingsley Publishers.

Burchill, F. and Casey, A. (1996) *Human Resource Management: The NHS: A Case Study*, Basingstoke: Macmillan Business.

Burnham, J. (1999) 'France: A Centrally Driven Profession', in D. Farnham (ed.) *Managing Academic Staff in Changing University Systems*, Buckingham: Open University Press.

Burnham, J. (2000) 'Human Resource Flexibilities in France', in D. Farnham and S. Horton (eds) *Human Resource Flexibilities in the Public Services: International Perspectives*, London: Macmillan.

Burnham, J. (2001) 'Local Public–Private Partnerships in France: Rarely Disputed, Scarcely Competitive, Weakly Regulated', *Public Policy and Administration*, 16/4, 47–60.

Burnham, J. (2009) *Politicians, Bureaucrats and Leadership in Organizations: Lessons from French Regional Planning*, Basingstoke: Palgrave Macmillan.

Burnham, J. and Pyper, R. (2008) *Britain's Modernised Civil Service*, Basingstoke: Palgrave Macmillan.

Bushnell, D. S and Halus, M. B (1992) 'TQM in the Public Sector: Strategies for Quality Service', *National Productivity Review*, 11/3, 355–70.

Butcher, L. (2011) 'Aviation: National Air Traffic Services (NATS)', *House of Commons Library Standard Note*, SN/BT/1309.

Butler, D., Adonis, A. and Travers, T. (1994) *Failure in British Government: The Politics of the Poll Tax*, London: Oxford University Press.

Butler, R. (2004) *Review of Intelligence on Weapons of Mass Destruction*, HC 898, London: TSO.

Cabinet Office (1991a) *The Citizen's Charter: Raising the Standard*, Cm 1599, London: HMSO.

Cabinet Office (1991b) *The Citizen's Charter: A Guide*, London: Cabinet Office.

Cabinet Office (1994) *The Civil Service: Continuity and Change*, Cm 2627, London: HMSO.

Cabinet Office (1996) *Citizen's Charter: Five Years On*, Cm 3370, London: HMSO.

Cabinet Office (1998a) *Service First: The New Charter Programme*, London: Cabinet Office.

Cabinet Office (1998b) *Better Quality Services: A Handbook for Creating Public/Private Partnerships through Market Testing and Contracting Out*, London: TSO.

Cabinet Office (1999a) *Modernising Government*, Cm 4310, London: TSO.

Cabinet Office (1999b) *Civil Service Reform: Report to the Prime Minister from Sir Richard Wilson*, London: Cabinet Office.

Cabinet Office (2004) *Civil Service Statistics*, London: Cabinet Office.

Cabinet Office (2005a) *Transformational Government Enabled by Technology*, Cm 6683, London: TSO.

Cabinet Office (2005b) *Delivering a Diverse Civil Service: A 10 Point Plan*, London: Cabinet Office.

Cabinet Office (2006) *Capability Reviews: The Findings of the First Four Reviews*, London: Cabinet Office.

Cabinet Office (2007a) *Staff Transfers in the Public Sector: Statement of Practice* (1st edn, 2000), London: Cabinet Office.

Cabinet Office (2007b) *E-recruitment Projects in the Public Sector*, London: Cabinet Office.

Cabinet Office (2009a) *Capability Reviews: Refreshing the Model of Capability*, London: Cabinet Office.

Cabinet Office (2009b) *Promoting Equality, Valuing Diversity: A Strategy for the Civil Service*, London: Cabinet Office.

Cabinet Office (2010) *The Coalition: Our Programme for Government*, London: Cabinet Office.

Cabinet Office (2011a) *Government Response to the Public Administration Select Committee Report, 'Smaller Government: Shrinking the Quango State'*, Cm 8044, TSO.

Cabinet Office (2011b) *Public Bodies Reform: Proposals For Change*, published 16 March, www.cabinetoffice.gov.uk.

Cabinet Office (2011c) *Public Bodies Reform: Policy*, www.cabinetoffice.gov.uk, accessed 9 January 2012.

Cabinet Office (2011d) *Public Bodies Reform: Quarterly Status Check*, published October, www.cabinetoffice.gov.uk.

Cabinet Office (2011e) 'Shake up of Civil Service Training', press release 13 October, www.cabinetoffice.gov.uk.

Cabinet Office/ DTLR (Department of Transport, Local Government and the Regions) (2002) *Your Region, Your Choice: Revitalising the English Regions*, Cm 5511, London: TSO.

Cabinet Office/ PIU (2001) *Strengthening Leadership in the Public Sector: A Research Study by the Performance and Innovation Unit*, London: Cabinet Office.

Calman Commission (2008) *The Future of Scottish Devolution within the Union: A First Report*, Edinburgh: Commission on Scottish Devolution.

Calman Commission (2009) *Serving Scotland Better: Scotland and the United Kingdom in the 21st Century (Final Report)*, Edinburgh: Commission on Scottish Devolution.

Cameron, D. (2010a) 'From Central Power to People Power', speech to Conference of the Post-Bureaucratic Age, February 22, www.conservatives.com, accessed 10 May 2011.

Cameron, D. (2010b) 'PM's Speech at Civil Service Live', 8 July, number 10.gov.uk, accessed 20 November 2011.

Cameron, Lord (1969) *Disturbances in Northern Ireland*, Cmd 532, Belfast: HMSO.

Campbell, C. and Wilson, G. K. (1995) *The End of Whitehall: Death of a Paradigm?*, Oxford: Blackwell.

Campbell, G. A. (1955) *The Civil Service in Britain*, Harmondsworth: Penguin.

Carmichael, P. (2002) 'The Northern Ireland Civil Service: Characteristics and Trends since 1970', *Public Administration*, 80, 23–49.

Carter, N. and Klein, R. (eds) (1992) *How Organisations Measure Success: The Use of Performance Indicators in Government*, London: Routledge.

Caulfield, J. and Schulz, J. (1989) *Planning for Change: Strategic Planning in Local Government*, Harlow: Longman.

Certification Office (2010) *Certification Officer's Annual Report 2009/10*, London: Certification Office.

Chan, J. L and Xiao, X. (2009) 'Financial Management in Public Sector Organizations', in T. Bovaird and E. Löffler (eds) *Public Management and Governance*, 2nd edn, London: Routledge.

Chapman, R. A. (1997) 'The End of the Civil Service', in P. Barberis (ed.) *The Civil Service in an Era of Change*, Aldershot: Dartmouth.

Charbit, C. and Michalun, M. (2009) 'Mind the Gaps: Managing Mutual Dependence in Relations among Levels of Government', *OECD Working Papers on Public Governance*, 14, Paris: OECD.

Chitty, C. (2009) *Education Policy in Britain*, Basingstoke: Palgrave Macmillan.

Chote, R. (2007) 'Public Finances: the Constraints', in C. Talbot and M. Baker (eds) *The Alternative Comprehensive Spending Review 2007*, Manchester: Manchester University Press.

Christensen, J. (2004) 'Political Responsiveness in a Merit Bureaucracy: Denmark', in B. G. Peters and J. Pierre (eds) *Politicization of the Civil Service in Comparative Perspective: The Quest for Control*, London: Routledge.

CIPD (Chartered Institute of Personnel and Development) (2009) *Meeting the UK People Management Skills Deficit*, London: CIPD.

CIPD (2010) *Leadership: An Overview*, London: CIPD.

Civil Service Department (1975) *Civil Servants and Change: Joint Statement by the National Whitley Council and the Wider Issues Review Team*, London: HMSO.

Clarke, J. (2009) 'Scrutiny, Inspection and Audit in the Public Sector', in T. Bovaird and E. Löffler (eds) *Public Management and Governance*, 2nd edn, London: Routledge.

Clarke, J. and Newman, J. (1997) *The Managerial State*, London: Sage.

Clarke, M. and Stewart, J. (1988) *The Enabling Council: Developing and Managing a New Style of Local Government*, Luton: Local Government Training Board.

Collard, R. (1989) *Total Quality Success through People*, London: IPM.

Colman, J. (2007) 'A Case Study from Wales', in M. Lavender (ed.) *Watchdogs Straining at the Leash*, London: CIPFA.

Conservative Party (2009) *Control Shift: Returning Power to Local Communities*, London: Conservative Party.

Conservative Party (2010a) *Invitation to Join the Government of Britain: The Conservative Manifesto 2010*, London: Conservative Party.

Conservative Party (2010b) *An Invitation to Public Sector Workers*, London: Conservative Party.

Cope, S. and Goodship, J. (1999) 'Regulating Collaborative Government: Towards Joined-up Government?', *Public Policy and Administration*, 14/2, 2–16.

Copus, C. (2006) *Leading the Localities: Executive Mayors in English Local Governance*, Manchester: Manchester University Press.

Crosby, P. (1979) *Quality is Free*, New York: McGraw-Hill.

Crosby, P. (1984) *Quality without Tears*, New York: McGraw-Hill.

CSC (Civil Service Commissioners) (2008) *Civil Service Commissioners Annual Report 2007/08*, London: CSC.

CSC (2009) *Civil Service Commissioners Annual Report 2008/09*, London: CSC.

Cumin, M. (1978) *Personnel Management in the National Health Service*, London: Heinemann.

Cunha Marques, R. and De Witte, K. (2010) 'Towards a Benchmarking Paradigm in European Water Utilities', *Public Money and Management*, 30, 42–8.

Darlow, A., Hawtin, M., Jassi, S., Monro, S., Percy-Smith, J. and Purcell, M. (2008) *Formative Evaluation of Community Strategies 2004–2007: Final Report*, London: Department for Communities and Local Government.

Davies, B. and Davies, B. J. (2009) 'Strategic Leadership', in B. Davies (ed.) *The Essentials of School Leadership*, 2nd edn, London: Sage.

Davies, J. S. (2002) 'The Governance of Urban Regeneration: A Critique of the "Governing without Government" Thesis', *Public Administration*, 80, 301–22.

Davis, H. and Martin, S. (2002) 'Evaluating the Best Value Pilot Programme: Measuring "Success" and "Improvement"', *Local Government Studies*, 28/2, 55–68.

Davis, H. and Martin, S. (eds) (2008) *Public Services Inspection in the UK*, London: Jessica Kingsley Publishers.

Day, P. and Klein, R. (2000) 'The Politics of Managing the National Health Service', in R.A.W. Rhodes (ed.) *Transforming British Government, I*, London: Macmillan.

DCLG (Department for Communities and Local Government) (2006) *Strong and Prosperous Communities: The Local Government White Paper*, Cm 6939, London: TSO.

DCLG (2007a) *Housing Statistics*, London: DCLG.

DCLG (2007b) 'Green Light for Five Flagship Unitary Councils', press release 5 December, www.communities.gov.uk..

DCLG (2008a) *Communities in Control: Real People, Real Power*, Cm 7427, London: TSO.

DCLG (2008b) *Creating Strong, Safe and Prosperous Communities: Statutory Guidance*, London: DCLG.

DCLG (2009) *Local Authority Revenue Expenditure and Financing England: 2009–10 Budget*, published 22 December, www.communities.gov.uk

DCLG (2010a) *Housing and Planning Statistics*, London: DCLG.

DCLG (2010b) *Decentralisation and the Localism Bill: An Essential Guide*, London: DCLG.

DCLG (2011a) *Localism Bill: General Power of Competence for Local Authorities: Impact Assessment*, London: DCLG.

DCLG (2011b) *Local Government Financial Statistics England No. 21*, London: DCLG.

DCLG (2011c) 'Local Government Resource Review: Proposals for Business Rates Retention', 18 July, www.communities.gov.uk.

De Bruijn, H. (2002) *Managing Performance in the Public Sector*, London: Routledge.

DECC (Department of Energy and Climate Change) (2011) *Planning our Electric Future: A White Paper for Secure, Affordable and Low-Carbon Electricity*, CM 80, London: TSO.

Deming, W. (1982) *Out of the Crisis: Quality, Productivity and Competitive Position*, Cambridge, MA: MIT Press.

Demmke, C. (2007) *Performance Assessment in the Public Services of the European Union Member States*, Maastricht: EIPA.

DETR (Department for the Environment, Transport and the Regions) (1998a) *Modernising Local Government: Improving Local Service through Best Value,* London: DETR.

DETR (1998b) *Modern Local Government: In Touch with the People*, Cm 4014, London: TSO.

DETR (2000) *Local Government Financial Statistics England: No. 11: 2000,* London: DETR.

DfE (Department for Education) (2011) 'New Free Schools', press notice, 5 September, www.education.gov.uk.

DfES (Department for Education and Skills) (2005) *Youth Matters*, Cm 6629, London: TSO.

DfT (Department for Transport) (2011) 'Dover Harbour Board Proposed Transfer Scheme', press notice, 30 November, www.dft.gov.uk.

DH (Department of Health) (1993) *Ethnic Minorities in the NHS: A Programme for Action*, London: HMSO.

DH (1997) *The new NHS: Modern, Dependable*, Cm 3807, London: TSO.

DH (1998) *The National Health Service Wales: Putting Patients First*, Cm 3841, London: TSO.

DH (2000) *The NHS Plan: A Plan for Investment, a Plan for Reform*, Cm 4818, London: TSO.
DH (2002) *Delivering the NHS Plan: Next Steps on Investment, Next Steps on Reform*, London: TSO.
DH (2006) *The Government's Response to the Health Committee's Report on Independent Sector Treatment Centres*, Cm 6930, London: TSO.
DH (2010) *Equity and Excellence: Liberating the NHS*, Cm 7881, London: TSO.
DH and Skills for Health (2008) *Modernising Allied Health Professions (AHP) Careers: A Competence-Based Career Framework*, London: Department of Health.
DHSS (Department of Health and Social Security) (1972) *Development of the Personnel Function*, London: HMSO.
Doig, A. (1997) 'People or Positions? Ensuring Standards in the Reformed Public Sector', in P. Barberis (ed.) *The Civil Service in an Era of Change*, Aldershot: Dartmouth.
Donabedian, A. (1980) *Explorations in Quality Assessment and Monitoring I. Definitions of Quality and Approaches to Assessment*, Ann Arbor: Health Administration Press.
Donabedian, A. (1988) 'The Quality of Care: How can it be Assessed?', *Journal of the American Medical Association*, 260, 1743–48.
Dowdall, J. (2007) 'Audit and Accountability in a Devolved Northern Ireland', in M. Lavender (ed.) *Watchdogs Straining at the Leash*, London: CIPFA.
Downe, J. (2008) 'Inspection of Local Government Services', in H. Davis and S. Martin (eds) *Public Services Inspection in the UK*, London: Jessica Kingsley Publishers.
Downe, J. and Martin, S. (2007) 'Regulation inside Government', *Policy and Politics*, 35/2: 215–32.
Drewry, G. and Butcher, T. (1991) *The Civil Service Today*, 2nd edn, Oxford: Basil Blackwell.
Dunford, J. (1998) *Her Majesty's Inspectorate of Schools since 1944: Standard Bearers or Turbulent Priests?*, London: Routledge.
Dunleavy, P., Gilson, C., Bastow, S. and Tinkler, J. (2009) 'The National Audit Office, the Public Accounts Committee and the Risk Landscape in UK Public Policy', report produced for the Risk and Regulatory Advisory Council, http://bis.ecgroup.net/Publications/.
Durose, C., and Richardson, L. (2009) 'Neighbourhood: a Site for Policy Action, Governance … and Empowerment?', in C. Durose, S. Greasley and L. Richardson (eds) *Changing Local Governance, Changing Citizens*, Bristol: Policy Press.
Durose, C., Greasley, S. and Richardson, L. (2009) 'Changing Local Governance, Changing Citizens: Introduction', in C. Durose, S. Greasley and L. Richardson (eds) *Changing Local Governance, Changing Citizens*, Bristol: Policy Press.
Efficiency Unit (1988) *Improving Management in Government: The Next Steps* [Ibbs Report], London: HMSO.
Efficiency Unit (1991) *Making the Most of Next Steps: The Management of Ministers' Departments and their Executive Agencies* [Fraser Report], London: HMSO.
Eliassen, K. A. and Sitter, N. (2008) *Understanding Public Management*, London: Sage.
Ellis, R. and Treasure, G. (2005) *Britain's Prime Ministers*, London: Shepheard-Walwyn.

Erridge, A. (2009) 'Contracting for Public Services', in T. Bovaird and E. Löffler (eds) *Public Management and Governance*, 2nd edn, London: Routledge.

Farnham, D. (1993) 'Human Resources Management and Employee Relations', in D. Farnham and S. Horton (eds) *Managing the New Public Services*, Basingstoke: Macmillan.

Farnham, D. (1999) 'Human Resource Management and Employment Relations', in S. Horton and D. Farnham (eds) *Public Management in Britain*, Basingstoke: Palgrave Macmillan.

Farnham, D. and Horton, S. (eds) (1993) *Managing the New Public Services*, Basingstoke: Macmillan.

Farnham, D. and Horton, S. (eds) (1996a) *Managing the New Public Services*, 2nd edn, Basingstoke: Macmillan.

Farnham, D, and Horton, S. (eds) (1996b) *Managing People in the Public Services*, Basingstoke: Macmillan.

Farnham, D. and Horton, S. (1999) 'Managing Private and Public Organisations', in S. Horton and D. Farnham (eds) *Public Management in Britain*, Basingstoke: Palgrave Macmillan.

Farnham, D. and Horton, S. (2000) 'The Flexibility Debate', in D. Farnham and S. Horton (eds) *Human Resource Flexibilities in the Public Services: International Perspectives*, Basingstoke: Macmillan.

Farnham, D. and Horton, S. (2002) 'HRM Competency Frameworks in the British Civil Service', in S. Horton, D. Farnham and A. Hondeghem (eds) *Competency Management in the Public Sector: European Variations on a Theme*, Amsterdam: IOS.

Farnham, D. and Pimlott, J. (1995) *Understanding Industrial Relations*, London: Cassell.

Farnham, D. and White, G. (2011) 'Rewarding Leaders in the UK Public Services: What's Happening to Executive Pay', *International Journal of Employment Studies*, 19/1, 26–49.

Farnham, D., Hondeghem, A. and Horton, S. (eds) (2005) *Staff Participation in Public Management Reform*, Basingstoke: Palgrave Macmillan.

Farrell, C. and Morris, J. (1999) 'Markets, Bureaucracy and Public Management: Professional Perception of Bureaucratic Change in the Public Sector: GPs, Headteachers and Social Workers', *Public Money and Management*, Oct–Dec, 31–6.

Fawcett, P. and Rhodes, R. A. W. (2007) 'Central Government' in A. Seldon (ed.) *Blair's Britain 1997–2007*, Cambridge: Cambridge University Press.

Finer, S. E. (1958) *Anonymous Empire: A Study of the Lobby Group in Great Britain*, London: Pall Mall.

Fletcher, C. (2001) 'Performance Appraisal and Management: The Developing Research Agenda', *Journal of Occupational and Organizational Psychology*, 74, 473–87.

Fletcher, C. (2002) *Appraisal: An Individual Psychological Perspective*, Wiley: New York.

Flinders. M. (1999) 'Quangos: Why do Governments Love Them?', in M. Flinders and M. Smith (eds) *Quangos, Accountability and Reform*, Basingstoke: Macmillan.

Flinders, M. (2005) 'The Politics of Public–Private Partnerships', *British Journal of Politics & International Relations*, 7, 215–39.
Flynn, N. (2007) *Public Sector Management*, 5th edn, London: Sage.
Flynn, N. and Strehl, F. (1996) *Public Sector Management in Europe*, New York: Prentice-Hall.
Foreign Affairs Committee (2011) *The UK's Foreign Policy towards Afghanistan and Pakistan*, HC 514, Memorandum 17, London: TSO.
Foster, C. D. (2001) 'The Civil Service under Stress: The Fall in Civil Service Power and Authority', *Public Administration*, 79, 725–50.
Foster, C.D. and Plowden, F. J. (1996) *The State under Stress: Can the Hollow State be Good Governance?*, Buckingham: Open University Press.
Fowler, A. (1990) *A Good Start: Effective Employee Induction*, London: IPM.
Friedman, M. and Friedman, R. (1980) *Free to Choose*, Harmondsworth: Penguin.
Fulton Report (1968a) *The Civil Service: Report of a Committee of Inquiry into the Civil Service 1966–68, I*, Cmnd 3638, London, HMSO.
Fulton Report (1968b) *The Civil Service: Report of a Committee of Inquiry into the Civil Service 1966–68, II*, Report of a Management Consultancy Group, Cmnd 3638, London, HMSO.
Gamble, A. (2010) 'The Political Consequences of the Crash', *Political Studies Review*, 8, 3–14.
Garrett, J. (1973) *The Management of Government*, Harmondsworth: Penguin.
Garrett, J. (1980) *Managing the Civil Service*, London: Heinemann.
Geddes, M., Fuller, C. and Geddes, M. (2007) *National Evaluation of Local Strategic Partnerships: Report on the 2006 Survey of all English LSPs*, London: Department for Communities and Local Government.
Gershon, P. (2004) *Releasing Resources to the Front Line*, London: TSO.
Giddens, A. (1998) *The Third Way: The Renewal of Social Democracy*, Cambridge: Polity Press.
Giddens, A. (2007) *Over to you, Mr. Brown*, Cambridge: Polity Press.
Glaister, S., Burnham, J., Stevens, H. and Travers, T. (2006) *Transport Policy in Britain*, 2nd edn, Basingstoke: Palgrave.
Glas Cymru (2000) 'Glas to acquire Welsh Water from WPD', press release, 3 November 2000, Cardiff: Glas Cymru.
Glas Cymru (2011) 'Company information', www.dwrcymru.com, accessed 18 September 2011.
Glass, N. (2005) 'Surely Some Mistake?', *Guardian*, 5 January.
Goldfinch, S. and Wallis, J. (2010) 'Two Myths of Convergence in Public Management Reform', *Public Administration*, 88, 1099–115.
Government of Wales (2011) 'A Single Environment Body for Wales', statement by the Environment Minister, 29 November, www.wales.gov.uk, accessed 27 December 2011.
Greener, I. (2009) *Public Management: A Critical Text*, Basingstoke: Palgrave Macmillan.
Griffiths, R. (1983) *NHS Management Inquiry: Report*, London: DHSS.
Gulick, L. (1937) 'Notes on the Theory of Organization', in L. Gulick and L. Urwick (eds) *Papers on the Science of Administration*, New York: Institute of Public Administration.

Gulick, L. and Urwick, L. (eds) (1937) *Papers on the Science of Administration*, New York: Institute of Public Administration.
Gunn, L. (1988) 'Public Management: A Third Approach?', *Public Money and Management*, 8/1–2, 21–5.
Ham, C. (2009) *Health Policy in Britain*, 6th edn, Basingstoke: Palgrave Macmillan.
Haringey Local Safeguarding Children Board (2010) *Serious Case Review: 'Child A'* [November 2008; March 2009], London: Department for Education.
Hax, A. (1990) 'Redefining the Strategy Concept', *Planning Review*, May/June, 28–31.
Hayek, F. A. (1944) *The Road to Serfdom*, London: Routledge & Kegan Paul.
Healthcare Commission (2007) *Independent Sector Treatment Centres: A Review of the Quality of Care*, London: Commission for Healthcare Audit and Inspection.
Health Development Agency (2004) 'Lessons from Health Action Zones', *HDA Briefing*, 9, available from http://www.nice.org.uk, accessed 17 May 2011.
Heath, G. and Radcliffe, J. (2007) 'Performance Management and the English Ambulance Service', *Public Money and Management*, 27, 223–8.
Heinrich, C. J. (2003) 'Measuring Public Sector Performance and Effectiveness', in B. G. Peters and J. Pierre (eds) *The Handbook of Public Administration*, London: Sage.
Henkel, M. (1991) *Government, Evaluation and Change*, London: Jessica Kingsley.
Heywood, A. (1998) *Political Ideologies*, 2nd edn, Basingstoke: Macmillan.
Hillyard, M. (1999) 'Postal Services Bill: Bill 54 of 1999–2000', *House of Commons Research paper 00/18*, London: House of Commons Library.
HMIC (2011) *Her Majesty's Inspectorate of Constabulary in 2009/10*, London: HMIC.
HM Treasury (1991) *Competing for Quality,* Cm 1730, London: HMSO.
HM Treasury (1993) *Breaking New Ground: The Private Finance Initiative*, London: HM Treasury.
HM Treasury (1994) *Fundamental Review of Running Costs: HM Treasury*, London: HM Treasury.
HM Treasury (1998) *Modern Public Services for Britain: Investing in Reform: Comprehensive Spending Review: New Public Spending Plans 1999–2002*, Cm 4011, London: TSO.
HM Treasury (2001) *Managing Resources: Full Implementation of Resource Accounting and Budgeting*, London: HM Treasury.
HM Treasury (2003) *PFI: Meeting the Investment Challenge*, London: HM Treasury.
HM Treasury (2006) *Pre-Budget Report: Investing in Britain's potential: Building our Long-Term Future*, Cm 6984, London: TSO.
HM Treasury (2007a) *Pre-Budget Report and Comprehensive Spending Review: Meeting the Aspirations of the British People,* Cm 7227, London: TSO.
HM Treasury (2007b) *Budget 2007: Building Britain's Long-term Future: Prosperity and Fairness for Families*, HC 342, London: TSO.
HM Treasury (2008a) *Budget 2008: Stability and Opportunity: Building a Strong, Sustainable Future*, HC 388, London: TSO.
HM Treasury (2008b) *Pre-Budget Report: Supporting People through Difficult Times*, Cm 7484, London: TSO.
HM Treasury (2010a) *Spending Review 2010*, Cm 7492, London: TSO.
HM Treasury (2010b) *Budget 2010*, HC 61, London: TSO

HM Treasury (2010c) *The Spending Review Framework*, Cm 7872, London: TSO.

HM Treasury (2011a) *Public Sector Finances Databank*, 27 May, www.hm-treasury.gov.uk.

HM Treasury (2011b) *Budget 2011*, HC 836, London: TSO.

HM Treasury (2011c) *Whole of Government Accounts: Unaudited Summary Report 2009–10*, 13 July, www.hm-treasury.gov.uk.

Hofstede, G. H. (2001) *Culture's Consequences: Comparing Values, Behaviors, Institutions and Organizations across Nations*, 2nd edn, Thousand Oaks, CA: Sage.

Hogwood, B., Judge, D. and McVicar, M. (2000) 'Agencies and Accountability', in R.A.W. Rhodes (ed.) *Transforming British Government I*, London: Macmillan.

Holliday, I. (2000) 'Is the British State Hollowing Out?', *Political Quarterly*, 71, 167–76.

Holloway, D. G. (1998) 'Accounting for the Audit Commission: An Assessment of the Contribution of the Audit Commission to Educational Change', *Educational Management and Administration*, 26/1, 49–55.

Homburg, V., Pollitt, C. and van Thiel, S. (2007) 'Introduction', in C. Pollitt, S. van Thiel and V. Homburg (eds) *New Public Management in Europe: Adaptation and Alternatives*, Basingstoke: Macmillan.

Home Affairs Committee (2008) *A Surveillance Society?*, HC 58, London: TSO.

Home Office (2011) 'Scrutiny: Police and Crime Panels', www.homeoffice.gov.uk, accessed 28 November 2011.

Hood, C. (1991) 'A Public Management for All Seasons?', *Public Administration*, 69, 3–19.

Hood, C. (2000), 'Paradoxes of Public-sector Managerialism, Old Public Management and Public Service Bargains', *International Public Management Journal*, 3/1, 1–22.

Hood, C. (2005) 'Public Management: the Word, the Movement, the Science', in E. Ferlie, L. E. Lynn and C. Pollitt (eds) *The Oxford Handbook of Public Management*, Oxford: Oxford University Press.

Hood, C. (2006) 'Gaming in Target World', *Public Administration Review*, 66, 515–22.

Hood, C. (2007) 'Public Service Management by Numbers: Why Does it Vary? Where Has it Come From? What are the Gaps and the Puzzles?', *Public Money and Management*, 27, 95–102.

Hood, C. and Lodge, M. (2011) 'The "Post-Bureaucratic Age": Some Analytic Challenges', in Public Administration Select Committee, *Change in Government: The Agenda for Leadership*, HC 714, Ev 56–58, London: TSO.

Hood, C. C. and Margetts, H. Z. (2007) *The Tools Of Government In The Digital Age*, Basingstoke: Palgrave Macmillan.

Hood, C. and Scott, C. (1996) 'Bureaucratic Regulation and New Public Management in the United Kingdom: Mirror Image Development?', *Journal of Law and Society*, 23/3, 321–45.

Hood, C. James, O. and Scott, C. (2000) 'Regulation of Government has it Increased, is it Increasing, should it be Diminished?', *Public Administration*, 78, 283–304.

Hood, C., James, O., Jones, G., Scott, C. and Travers, T. (1998) 'Regulation Inside Government: Where New Public Management Meets the Audit Explosion', *Public Money and Management*, 18/2, 61–8.

Hood, C., Scott, C., James, O., Travers, T., and Jones, G. (1999) *Regulation inside Government*, Oxford: Oxford University Press.

Horton, S. (2000) 'Human Resource Flexibilities in UK Public Services', in D. Farnham and S. Horton, S. (eds) *Human Resource Flexibilities in the Public Services: International Perspectives*, Basingstoke: Macmillan.

Horton, S. (2006) 'The Public Sector Ethos in the British Civil Service: An Historical Institutional Analysis', *Public Policy and Administration*, 21/1, 32–48.

Horton, S. (2009) 'Evaluation of Leadership Development and Training in the UK Senior Civil Service: The Search for the Holy Grail?', in J. Raffel, P. Leisink and A. Middlebrooks (eds) *Leading the Future of the Public Secto*r, Cheltenham: Edward Elgar.

Horton, S. (2011) 'How Management of Competencies and Performance Assessment can Contribute to the Collective Achievement: A Case Study of the United Kingdom', paper presented at a seminar organized by the Lithuanian Institute of Public Administration, Vilnius, Lithuania 12–13 May 2011.

Horton, S. and Farnham, D. (eds) (1999) *Public Management in Britain*, Basingstoke: Palgrave Macmillan.

Horton, S. and Farnham, D. (2007) 'Turning Leadership into Performance Management' in R. Koch and J. Dixon (eds) *Public Governance and Leadership*, Wiesbaden: Deutscher Universitäts-Verlag, 429–55.

Horton, S., Hondeghem, A. and Farnham, D. (eds) (2002) *Competency Management in the Public Sector: European Variations on a Theme*, Amsterdam: IOS.

Horton, S. and Jones, J. (1996) 'Who are the New Public Managers? An Initial Analysis of 'Next Steps' Chief Executives and Their Managerial Role', *Public Policy and Administration,* 11/4, 18–44.

Hughes, O. (2003) *Public Management and Administration: An Introduction,* 3rd edn, Basingstoke: Palgrave Macmillan.

Hughes, O. (2012) *Public Management and Administration,* 4th edn, Basingstoke: Palgrave Macmillan.

Hutton, Lord (2004) *Report of the Inquiry into the Circumstances Surrounding the Death of Dr David Kelly, C.M.G.*, HC 247, London: TSO.

Hutton Report (2011) *Independent Public Service Pensions Commission: Final Report*, London: TSO.

IDS (Income Data Services) (2010) *Pay in the Public Services: Review of 2009; Prospects for 2010*, London: IDS.

Ilzetzki, E., Mendoza, E.G. and Végh, C. A. (2010) 'How Big (Small?) are Fiscal Multipliers?', *CEP Discussion Paper*, 1016, London: LSE/CEP. www.cep.lse.ac.uk

IMF (International Monetary Fund) (2011) 'United Kingdom: 2011 Article IV Consultation: Concluding Statement of the Mission', 6 June, www. imf.org.

Institute of Education/OFSTED (2004) *Improvement through Inspection: An Evaluation of the Impact of OFSTED*, London: Institute of Education.

Institute of Management Services (IMS) (1992) *Total Quality Management: Philosophy, Concepts and Fundamental Processes*, London: IMS.

IPPR (Institute for Public Policy Research) (2001) *Building Better Partnerships*, London: IPPR.

Ipsos MORI (2005) *Management Improvement: A Thematic Inspection of Performance Management in the Scottish Police*, Edinburgh: Scottish Government.

Isaac-Henry, K. (1999) 'Strategic Management in the Public Services', in S. Horton and D. Farnham (eds) *Public Management in Britain*, Basingstoke: Palgrave Macmillan.

James, O. (2003) *The Executive Agency Revolution in Whitehall*, Basingstoke: Palgrave.

Jeffery, C. (2006) 'Devolution and the Lopsided State', in P. Dunleavy, R. Heffernan, P. Cowley and C. Hay (eds) *Developments in British Politics 8*, Basingstoke: Palgrave Macmillan.

Jenkins, R. (1997) *Gladstone*, New York: Random House.

John, P. (2009) 'Citizen governance: where it came from, where it's going', in C. Durose, S. Greasley and L. Richardson (eds) *Changing Local Governance, Changing Citizens*, Bristol: Policy Press.

John, P., Smith, G. and Stoker, G. (2009) 'Nudge Nudge, Think Think: Two Strategies for Changing Citizen Behaviour', *Political Quarterly*, 80, 361–70.

Johns, C. and Lock, D. (2008) 'Inspection of Adult and Children's Social Care', in H. Davis and S. Martin (eds) *Public Services Inspection in the UK*, London: Jessica Kingsley Publishers.

Johnsen, A. (2005) 'What Does 25 years of Experience Tell Us About the State of Performance Measurement in Public Policy and Management?', *Public Money and Management*, 25, 9–17.

Jones, B. (2002) 'Welsh Devolution: Balancing Opportunities and Frustrations', in S. Henig, (ed.) *Modernising Britain: Central, Devolved, Federal?*, London: The Federal Trust.

Jones, K. (2000) *The Making of Social Policy*, London: Athlone Press.

Jordan, A. G. and Richardson, J. J. (1987) *British Politics and the Policy Process: An Arena Approach*, London: George Allen & Unwin.

Joyce, P. (1999) *Strategic Management for the Public Services*, Buckingham: Open University Press.

Joyce, P. (2000) *Strategy in the Public Sector: An Effective Guide to Management Change*, New York: John Wiley.

Joyce, P. (2008) 'The Strategic, Enabling State: A Case Study of the UK, 1997–2007', *International Journal of Leadership in Public Services*, 4/3: 24–36.

Joyce, P. (2012) *Strategic Leadership in the Public Services*, London: Routledge.

Joyce, P. and Woods, A. (1996) *Essential Strategic Management: From Modernism to Pragmatism*, London: Butterworth/Heinemann.

Juran, J. (1951) *Quality Control Handbook*, New York: McGraw-Hill.

Juran, J. (1992) *Juran on Quality by Design*, New York: Free Press.

Kahn, A. E. (1970) *The Economics of Regulation: Principles and Institutions*, 2 vols, New York: Wiley.

Kaplan, R. S. and Norton, D. P. (1996) 'Using the Balanced Scorecard as a Strategic Management System', *Harvard Business Review*, January–February, 75–85.

Kawalek, P. (2007) 'eGovernment: terminology and concepts', in C. Talbot and M. Baker (eds) *The Alternative Comprehensive Spending Review 2007*, Manchester: Manchester University Press.

Keehley, P. and Abercrombie, N. (2008) *Benchmarking in the Public and Nonprofit Sectors*, San Francisco: Jossey-Bass/Wiley.

Kellner, P. and Crowther-Hunt, N. (1980) *The Civil Servants: An Inquiry into Britain's Ruling Class*, London: Macdonald.

Kelly, G., Mulgan, G. and Muers, S. (2002) *Creating Public Value: An Analytical Framework for Public Service Reform*, London: Cabinet Office Strategy Unit.

Kelly, J. (2003) 'The Audit Commission: Guiding, Steering and Regulating Local Government', *Public Administration*, 81, 459–76.

Kelly, S. and Rodden, C. (1998) *From Watchdog to Guidedog? The Evolving Role of the Accounts Commission for Scotland*, Glasgow: Glasgow Caledonian University.

Kelsall, R. (1974) 'Recruitment to the Higher Civil Service: How has the Pattern Changed?', in P. Stanworth and A. Giddens (eds) *Elites and Power in British Society*, Cambridge: Cambridge University Press.

Kersley, B. (2005) *Inside the Workplace: First findings from the 2004 Workplace Employment Relations Survey* [WERS 2004], London: Department of Trade and Industry.

Kickert, W. (1997) 'Public Governance in the Netherlands: An Alternative to Anglo-American "Managerialism"', *Public Administration*, 75, 731–52.

Kickert, W. (2003) 'Beneath Consensual Corporatism: Traditions of Governance in the Netherlands', *Public Administration*, 81, 119–40.

Kickert, W. (2007) 'Public Management Reforms in Countries with a Napoleonic State Model: France, Italy and Spain', in C. Pollitt, S. van Thiel and V. Homburg (eds) *New Public Management in Europe: Adaptation and Alternatives*, Basingstoke: Macmillan.

Kilbrandon Report (1973) *Report of the Royal Commission on the Constitution 1969–73*, Cmnd 5460, London: HMSO.

King's Fund (2011) *Briefing: The Health and Social Care Bill: Second Reading in the House of Lords*, published 11 October, www.kingsfund.org.uk.

Koch, R. and Dixon, J. (eds) (2007) *Public Governance and Leadership*, Wiesbaden: Deutscher Universitäts-Verlag.

Kunkel, S., Rosenquist, U. and Westerling, R. (2007) 'The Structure of Quality Systems is Important to the Process and Outcome: An Empirical Study of 386 Hospital Departments in Sweden', *BMC Health Services Research*, 7, 104, published 9 July 2007, www.biomedcentral.com.

Landel, D. (2004) *Performance-Related Pay Policies for Government Employees: Main Trends in OECD Countries*, Paris: OECD.

Lawson, N. (1993) *The View from No. 11: Memoirs of a Tory Radical*, Ealing: Corgi.

Leach, R. and Percy-Smith, J. (2001) *Local Governance in Britain*, Basingstoke: Palgrave Macmillan.

Leach, S., Stewart, J. and Walsh, K. (1994) *The Changing Organisation and Management of Local Government*, London: Macmillan.

Lee, J. M., Jones, G. W. and Burnham, J. (1998) *At the Centre of Whitehall*, London: Macmillan.

Legge, K. (1989) 'Human Resource Management: A critical analysis', in J. Storey (ed.) *New Perspectives on Human Resources Management*, London: Macmillan.

Legge, K. (1995) *Human Resource Management*, London: Macmillan.

LGA (Local Government Association) (2005) *Inspection: Time Well Spent? A Survey on the Impact of Inspection and Audit Regimes*, London: LGA.

Liberal Democrats (2010) *Liberal Democrat Manifesto 2010: Building a Fairer Britain*, London: Liberal Democrats.

Lipsey, D. (2000) *The Secret Treasury*, London: Viking.

Littlechild, S. (1983) *Regulation of British Telecommunications Profitability: Report to the Secretary of State*, London: Department of Industry.
Local Government Employers (LGE) (2006) *Unblocking the Route to Equal Pay in Local Government*, London: Local Government Employers.
Local Government Employers (2008) 'Equal Pay', *Focus*, 01/08, London: Local Government Employers.
Locke, E. A. (1968) 'Towards a Theory of Task Motivation and Incentives', *Organisational Behavior and Human Performance*, 3, 157–89.
Lodge, M. (2010) 'Public Service Bargains in British Central Government: Multiplication, Diversification even Reassertion?', in M. Painter and B. G. Peters (eds) *Tradition and Public Administration*, Basingstoke: Palgrave Macmillan.
Löffler, E. (2009) 'Public Governance in a Network Society', in T. Bovaird and E. Löffler (eds) *Public Management and Governance*, 2nd edn, London: Routledge.
Lowndes, V. (1992) 'Decentralisation: The Potential and the Pitfalls', *Local Government Policy Making*, 18/4, 53–63.
Lowndes, V., Pratchett, L. and Stoker, G. (2001) 'Trends in Public Participation: I: Local Government Perspectives', *Public Administration*, 79, 205–22.
Lynn, L. E. (2006) *Public Management: Old and New*, New York: Routledge.
Lyons, M. (2004) *Well placed to deliver? Shaping the Pattern of Government Service: Independent Review of Public Sector Relocation*, London: TSO.
Lyons, M. (2007) *Place-shaping: A Shared Ambition for the Future of Local Government*, London: TSO.
Makinson, J. (2000) *Incentives for Change: Rewarding Performance in National Government Networks*, London: HM Treasury.
Mandleson, P. and Liddle, R. (1996) *The Blair Revolution: Can New Labour Deliver*, London: Faber & Faber.
Marsden, D. (2003) 'Renegotiating Performance: The Role of Performance Pay in Renegotiating the Effort Bargain', Discussion Paper 576, Centre for Economic Performance, LSE, http://cep.lse.ac.uk.
Marsden, D. and French, S. (1998) 'What a Performance: Performance-Related Pay in the Public Services', Centre for Economic Performance, LSE, http://cep.lse.ac.uk.
Marsden, D. and Richardson, R. (1992) 'Motivation and Performance-Related Pay in the Public Sector: A Case Study of the Inland Revenue', Discussion Paper 75, Centre for Economic Performance, LSE, http://cep.lse.ac.uk.
Marsden, D. and Richardson, R. (1994) 'Performing for Pay? The Effects of 'Merit Pay' in a Public Service', *British Journal of Industrial Relations*, 32, 243–61.
Martin, J. (2008) 'Inspection of Education and Skills: From Improvement to Accountability', in H. Davis and S. Martin (eds) *Public Services Inspection in the UK*, London: Jessica Kingsley Publishers.
Martin, S. and Davis, H. (2008) 'The Rise of Public Services Inspection', in H. Davis and S. Martin (eds) *Public Services Inspection in the UK*, London: Jessica Kingsley Publishers.
Massey, A. (1999) 'Quality Issues in the Public Sector', *Public Policy and Administration*, 14/3, 1–14.
Massey, A. and Pyper, R. (2005) *Public Management and Modernisation*, Basingstoke: Palgrave Macmillan.
Maud Report (1967) *Committee on the Management of Local Government*, London: HMSO.

Maude, F. (2011) 'Public Bodies Reform', written ministerial statement, 15 December, www.cabinetoffice.gov.uk.
McLean, I., Haubrich, D. and Gutiérrez-Rameira, R. (2007) 'The Perils and Pitfalls of Performance Management: The CPA Regime for Local Authorities in England', *Public Money and Management*, 27, 111–17.
McNulty, R. (2011) *Realising the Potential of GB Rail: Report of the Rail Value for Money Study*, London: Department for Transport.
McVicar, M. (1993) 'Education', in D. Farnham and S. Horton (eds) *Managing the New Public Services*, Basingstoke, Macmillan.
McVicar, M. (1996) 'Education', in D. Farnham and S. Horton (eds) *Managing the New Public Services*, 2nd edn, Basingstoke: Macmillan.
McVicar, M. and Robins, L. (1994) 'Education Policy: Market Force or Market Failure', in S. Savage, R. Atkinson and L. Robins (eds) *Public Policy in Britain*, Basingstoke: Macmillan.
Mellon, E. (2000) 'Executive Agency Chief Executives: Their Leadership Values', in K. Theakston (ed.) *Bureaucrats and Leadership*, Basingstoke: Macmillan.
Merkert, R. and Nash, C. (2006) 'The Restructuring of the Rail System in Britain: An Assessment of Recent Developments', in IEA, *The Railways, the Market and the Government*, London: IEA.
Ministry of Reconstruction (1918) *Report of the Machinery of Government Committee* [Haldane Committee], Cd 9230, London: HMSO.
Minogue, M. (1998) 'Changing the State: Concepts and Practice in the Reform of the Public Sector', in M. Minogue, C. Polidano and D. Hulme (eds) *Beyond the New Public Management*, Cheltenham: Elgar.
Mintzberg, H. (1996) 'Five Ps for Strategy', in H. Mintzberg and J. Quinn (eds) *The Strategy Process*, 3rd edn, Hemel Hempstead: Prentice-Hall.
Mitchell, J. (2003) 'Devolution and the Future of the Union', in J. Fisher, D. Denver and J. Benyon (eds) *Central Debates in British Politics*, Harlow: Pearson Longman.
Mitchell, J. (2009) *Devolution in the UK*, Manchester: Manchester University Press.
Modell, S. (2004) 'Performance Measurement Myths in the Public Sector: A Research Note', *Financial Accountability and Management*, 20/1, 39–55.
Moran, M. (2003) *The British Regulatory State*, Oxford: Oxford University Press.
Mordaunt, E. (2000) 'The Emergence of Multi-Inspectorate Inspections', *Public Administration*, 78, 751–69.
Morgan, C. and Murgatroyd, S. (1994) *Total Quality Management in the Public Sector: An International Perspective*, Buckingham: Open University Press.
Moore, M. H. (1995) *Creating Public Value: Strategic Management in Government*, Cambridge, MA: Harvard University.
Morse, R., Buss, T., and Kinghorn, C. M (2007) *Transforming Public Leadership for the 21st Century*, New York: M.E. Sharpe.
Mueller Report (1987) *Flexible Working Patterns*, London: Cabinet Office.
Mulgan, G. (2005) 'Joined-Up Government: Past, Present, and Future', in V. Bogdanor (ed.) *Joined-Up Government*, Oxford: Oxford University Press for the British Academy.
Mulgan, G. (2010) 'Effective Supply and Demand and the Measurement of Public and Social Value', in J. Benington and M. H. Moore (eds) *Public Value: Theory and Practice*, Basingstoke: Palgrave Macmillan.

Murlis, H. (1987) 'Performance-related pay in the public sector', *Public Money*, March, 6/4, 29–33.

NAO (National Audit Office) (2001) *Education Action Zones: Meeting the Challenge: Executive Summary*, HC 130, London: TSO.

NAO (2002) *Community Legal Service: The Introduction of Contracting*, HC 89, London: TSO.

NAO (2003) *The Operational Performance of PFI Prisons*, HC 700, London: TSO.

NAO (2004a) *Connexions Service: Advice and Guidance for All Young People*, HC 484, London: TSO.

NAO (2004b) *London Underground PPP: Were they Good Deals?*, HC 645, London: TSO.

NAO (2008) *Department for Transport: Letting Rail Franchises 2005–2007*, HC 1047, London: TSO.

NAO (2009) *Recruiting Civil Servants Efficiently*, HC 134, London: TSO.

NAO (2010) *Reorganising Central Government*, HC 452, London: TSO.

NAO (2011a) *Lessons from PFI and Other Projects*, HC 920, London: TSO.

NAO (2011b) *Office of Rail Regulation: Regulating Network Rail's Efficiency*, HC 828, London: TSO.

NAO (2011c) *National Audit Office Annual Report 2011*, London: NAO.

NAO (2012) 'History of the National Audit Office', www.nao.org.uk, accessed 14 January 2012.

Needham, C. (2007) *The Reform of Public Services under New Labour: Narratives of Consumerism*, Basingstoke: Palgrave Macmillan.

Newman, J. (2001) *Modernising Governance*, London: Sage.

New Zealand Treasury (1987) *Government Management*, Wellington: Government Printer.

Niskanen, W. A. (1971) *Bureaucracy and Representative Government*, Chicago: Aldine.

Niskanen, W. A. (1973) *Bureaucracy, Servant or Master?: Lessons from America*, London: Institute of Economic Affairs.

Niskanen, W. A. (1994) *Bureaucracy and Public Economics*, Cheltenham, Edward Elgar.

Normington, D. (2008) *Senior Civil Service Workforce and Reward Strategy: Report of the Steering Group to the Cabinet Secretary*, London: Cabinet Office.

Northcote, S. H. and Trevelyan, C. E. (1854) *Report on the Organisation of the Permanent Civil Service*, London: Eyre & Spottiswoode for HMSO.

Norton, P. (2004) 'The changing constitution', in B. Jones, D. Kavanagh, M. Moran and P. Norton (eds) *Politics UK*, 5th edn, Harlow: Pearson Longman.

Oakland, J. (1993) *Total Quality Management: The Route to Improving Performance*, Abingdon: Hope Services.

OBR (Office for Budgetary Responsibility) (2010) 'Economic and Fiscal Outlook Launch Presentation', 29 November, www.budgetresponsibility.independent.org.uk.

OCPA (Office of the Commissioner for Public Appointments) (2010) *Fifth Report 2009/10*, London: OCPA.

ODPM (Office of the Deputy Prime Minister) (2002) *Council Tax Consultation: Guidelines for Local Authorities: Summary*, London: ODPM.

ODPM (2004) *The Future of Local Government: Developing a 10-year Vision*, London: ODPM.

ODPM/HM Treasury (2005) *Securing Better Outcomes: Developing a New Performance Management Framework*, London: ODPM.
OECD (Organisation for Economic Co-operation and Development) (2001) *Public Sector Leadership for the 21st Century*, Paris: OECD.
OECD (2002) *Distributed Public Governance: Agencies, Authorities and Other Government Bodies*, Paris: OECD.
OECD (2004) *Public Sector Modernisation: Changing Organisational Structures: Policy Brief*, Paris: OECD.
OECD (2005a) *Modernising Government: The Way Forward*, Paris: OECD.
OECD (2005b) *Paying for Performance: Policies for Government Employees*, Policy Brief, Paris: OECD.
OECD (2007) *Ageing and the Public Service: Human Resource Challenges*, Paris: OECD.
OECD (2008) *Growing Unequal: Income Distribution and Poverty in OECD Countries*, Paris: OECD.
OECD (2009a) *Government at a Glance 2009*, Paris: OECD.
OECD (2009b) 'Mind the Gaps: Managing Mutual Dependence in Relations among Levels of Government', *OECD Working Papers on Public Governance*, 14, Paris: OECD.
OECD (2009c) *Measuring Government Activity*, Paris: OECD.
Ofcom (Office of Communications) (2010a) *Annual Report 2009/10*, London: TSO.
Ofcom (2010b) *The Consumer Experience: Telecoms, Internet and Digital Broadcasting*, London: Ofcom.
Ofgem (Office of Gas and Electricity Markets) (2011) 'Ofgem to Press Ahead with Radical Overhaul of the Retail Gas and Electricity Market', press notice, 22 June.
OFSTED (Office for Standards in Education) (2002) *Connexions Partnerships: The First Year 2001–2002*, London: OFSTED
OFSTED (2003) *Excellence in Cities and Education Action Zones: Management and Impact*, HMI 1399, London: OFSTED.
OFSTED (2010a) *Moving through the System: Information, Advice and Guidance*, Manchester: OFSTED.
OFSTED (2010b) *The Annual Report of Her Majesty's Chief Inspector of Education, Children's Services and Skills*, London: OFSTED.
OFSTED/ Healthcare Commission/ HMIC (2008) *Joint Area Review: Haringey Children's Services Authority Area* (OFSTED).
OFT (Office of Fair Trading) (2010) *Infrastructure Ownership and Control Stock-take*, OFT 1290, www.oft.gov.uk, accessed 6 January 2011.
Oliver, D., Prosser, T. and Rawlings, R. (eds) (2010) *The Regulatory State: Constitutional Implications*, Oxford :Oxford University Press.
O'Neill, M. (2004) 'State Building and National Integration' in M. O'Neill (ed.) *Devolution and British Politics*, Harlow: Pearson Longman.
OPSR (Office of Public Services Reform) (2002) *Better Government Services: Executive Agencies in the 21st Century*, London: Cabinet Office.
OPSR (Office of Public Services Reform) (2003) *The Government's Policy on Inspection of Public Services*, London: Cabinet Office.
ORR (Office of Rail Regulation) (2010) *National Rail Trends 2009–10 Yearbook*, London: ORR.
Osborne, D. and Gaebler, T. (1992) *Reinventing Government: How the*

Entrepreneurial Spirit in Transforming the Public Sector, Reading, MA: Addison-Wesley.
Ostrom, V. (1973) *The Intellectual Crisis in American Public Administration*, Tuscaloosa, AL: University of Alabama Press.
O'Toole, B. (1993) 'Permanent Secretaries, Open Competition and the Future of the Civil Service', *Public Policy and Administration*, 8/3: 1–3.
O'Toole, B. (2006) 'The Emergence of a "New" Ethical Framework for Civil Servants', *Public Money and Management*, 26/1: 39–46.
PAC (Public Accounts Committee) (1987) *The Financial Management Initiative*, HC 61, London: HMSO.
PAC (1994) *The Proper Conduct of Public Business*, HC 154, London: HMSO.
PAC (2004) *Connexions Service*, HC 618, London: TSO.
PAC (2008a) *The Roll–out of the Jobcentre Plus Office Network*, HC 532, London: TSO.
PAC (2008b) *Tax Credits and PAYE*, HC 300, London: TSO.
PAC (2008c) *Managing Financial Resources to Deliver Better Public Services*, HC 519, London: TSO.
PAC (2010a) *Customer First Programme: Delivery of Student Finance*, HC 424, London: TSO.
PAC (2010b) *Managing the Defence Budget and Estate*, HC 503, London: TSO.
PAC (2011a) *Departmental Business Planning*, HC 650, London: TSO.
PAC (2011b) *Ministry of Justice Financial Management*, HC 574, London: TSO.
PAC (2011c) *PFI in Housing and Hospitals*, HC 631, London: TSO.
PAC (2011d) *Lessons from PFI and Other Projects*, HC 1201, London: TSO.
PAC (2011e) *Office of Rail Regulation: Regulating Rail's Efficiency*, HC 1036, London: TSO.
Page, E. C. (1997) *People Who Run Europe*, Oxford: Clarendon Press.
Parry, K. (2010) 'Local Democracy, Economic Development and Construction Act 2009: A Summary', *Standard Note SN/PC/05268*, London: House of Commons Library.
Parry, K. (2011) 'Directly-elected Mayors', *Standard Note SN/PC/5000*, London: House of Commons Library.
PASC (Public Administration Select Committee) (2001) *Mapping the Quango State*, HC 367, London: TSO.
PASC (2003a) *Government by Appointment: Opening up the Patronage State*, HC 165, London: TSO.
PASC (2003b) *On Target? Government by Measurement*, HC 62, London: TSO.
PASC (2005) *Choice, Voice and Public Services*, HC 49, London: TSO.
PASC (2007) *Machinery of Government Changes*, HC 672, London: TSO.
PASC (2010a) *Smaller Government: Shrinking the Quango State*, HC 537, London: TSO.
PASC (2010b) *Outsiders and Insiders: External Appointments to the Senior Civil Service: Further Report*, HC 500, London: TSO.
PASC (2011a) *Change in Government: The Agenda for Leadership*, HC 714, London: TSO.
PASC (2011b) *Departmental Business Plans: Oral Evidence*, HC 693, London: TSO.
Perry, J. and Kraemer, K. (eds) (1983) *Public Management: Public and Private Perspectives*, Palo Alto, CA: Mayfield.

Perry, J. and Hondeghem, A. (eds) (2008) *Motivation in Public Management*, Oxford: Oxford University Press.
Peters, B. G. (2000) 'Is Democracy a Substitute for Ethics? Administrative Reform and Accountability', in R. A. Chapman (ed.) *Ethics in Public Service for the New Millennium*, Aldershot: Ashgate.
Peters, B. G. and Pierre, J. (2004) 'Politicization of the Civil Service: Concepts, Causes, Consequences', in B. G. Peters and J. Pierre (eds) *Politicization of the Civil Service in Comparative Perspective: the Quest for Control*, London: Routledge.
Peters, T. and Waterman, L. (1982) *In Search of Excellence*, New York: Harper & Row.
Pickles, E. (2010) 'Regional Government', ministerial statement, 22 July, www.communities. gov.uk.
Pickles, E. (2011) Speech at Chartered Institute of Public Finance and Accountancy Annual Conference 2011, 7 July, www.communities,gov.uk.
Pierre, J. (2004) 'Politicization of the Swedish Civil Service: A Necessary Evil – or Just Evil?', in B. G. Peters and J. Pierre (eds) *Politicization of the Civil Service in Comparative Perspective: the Quest for Control,* London: Routledge.
Plowden Report (1961) *Control of Public Expenditure*, Cm 1432, London: HMSO.
Pollitt, C. (1974) 'CPRS 1970–74', *Public Administration*, 52, 375–402.
Pollitt, C. (1977) 'The Public Expenditure Survey 1961–72', *Public Administration*, 55, 127–42.
Pollitt, C. (1990) *Managerialism in the Public Sector*, Oxford: Blackwell.
Pollitt, C. (2001) 'Convergence: The Useful Myth?', *Public Administration*, 79, 933–47.
Pollitt, C. (2007a) 'Convergence or Divergence: What has been happening in Europe?', in C. Pollitt, S. van Thiel and V. Homburg (eds) *New Public Management in Europe: Adaptation and Alternatives*, Basingstoke: Macmillan.
Pollitt, C. (2007b) 'New Labour's Redisorganization: Hyper-modernism and the Costs of Reform – A Cautionary Tale', *Public Management Review*, 9, 529–43.
Pollitt, C. and Bouckaert, G. (2000) *Public Management Reform: A Comparative Analysis*, Oxford: Oxford University Press.
Pollitt, C. and Bouckaert, G. (2004) *Public Management Reform: A Comparative Analysis*, 2nd edn, Oxford: Oxford University Press.
Pollitt, C. and Bouckaert, G. (2009) *Continuity and Change in Public Policy and Management*, Cheltenham: Edward Elgar.
Pollitt, C., Harrison, S., Dowswell, G., Jerak-Zvidevent, S. and Bal, R. (2010) 'Performance Regimes in Health Care: Institutions, Critical Junctures and the Logic of Escalation in England and the Netherlands', *Evaluation*, 16/1, 13–29.
Porter, M.E. (1980) *Competitive Strategy: Techniques for Analyzing Industries and Competitors*, London: Collier Macmillan.
Power, M. (1994) *Evaluating the Audit Explosion*, London: Demos.
Prabhakar, R. (2006) *Rethinking Public Services*, Basingstoke: Palgrave Macmillan.
Pratchett, L. (2004) 'Electronic Government in Britain', in M. Eifert and J. O. Püschel (eds) *National Electronic Government; Comparing Governance Structures in Multi-Layer Administrations*, London: Routledge.
Pratchett, L., Durose, C., Lowndes, V., Smith, G., Stoker, G. and Wales, C. (2009) *Empowering Communities to Influence Local Decision Making: Evidence-based*

Lessons for Policy Makers and Practitioners, London: Department for Communities and Local Government.

Premfors, R. (1998) 'Reshaping the Democratic State: Swedish Experiences in a Comparative Perspective', *Public Administration*, 76, 141–59.

Proeller, I. and Siegel, J. (2009) 'Strategic Management in Central Government: A Comparison of International Aspects'. Paper presented at EGPA Conference, Malta 2009, to the group Strategic Management in Government www.egpa.be

Public Money and Management (2009) 'Whole of Government Accounting: International Trends', special edition, 29/4, July.

Purvis, M. (2011) 'Health and Social Care Bill (HL Bill 92 of 2010–12)', *House of Lords Library Note*, LLN 2011/029, London: House of Lords.

Pyper, R. (1995a) *The British Civil Service*, London: Prentice-Hall/Harvester Wheatsheaf.

Pyper, R. (1995b) 'Ministerial Responsibility and Next Steps Agencies', in P. Giddings (ed.) *Parliamentary Accountability: A Study of Parliament and Executive Agencies*, London: Macmillan.

Quinn, J. (1995) 'Strategy for Change' in H. Mintzberg, and J. Quinn (eds) *The Strategy Process*, Hemel Hempstead: Prentice-Hall.

Quirk, B. (1997) 'Accountable to Everyone: Postmodern Pressures on Public Managers', *Public Administration*, 75, 569–86.

Quirk, B. (2011) *Re-imagining Government: Public Leadership and Management in Challenging Times*, Basingstoke: Palgrave Macmillan.

Raffel, J., Leisink, P. and Middlebrooks, A. (eds) (2009) *Public Sector Leadership: International Challenges and Perspectives*, Cheltenham: Edward Elgar.

Raine, J. W. (2008) 'Inspection and the Criminal Justice Agencies', in H. Davis and S. Martin (eds) *Public Services Inspection in the UK*, London: Jessica Kingsley Publishers.

Rainey, H. G. and Chun, Y. H. (2005) 'Public and Private Management Compared', in E. Ferlie, L. E. Lynn and C. Pollitt (eds) *The Oxford Handbook of Public Management*, Oxford: Oxford University Press.

Ramsden (2002) 'National Insurance Act, 1911', in J. Ramsden (ed.) *The Oxford Companion to Twentieth-Century British Politics*, Oxford: Oxford University Press, 459–60.

Randall, G. (1974) *Staff Appraisal*, London: IPM.

Rawlinson, D. and Tanner, B. (1990) *Financial Management in the 1990s*, London: Longman.

Rees, M. and Lowman, M. (2009) 'Performance Management: Motivation and Reward', in C. Rayner and Adam-Smith, D. (eds) *Managing and Leading People*, London: CIPD.

Rhodes, R. A. W. (1997) *Understanding Governance: Policy Networks, Governance, Reflexivity and Accountability*, Buckingham: Open University Press.

Rhodes, R. A. W. (2000) 'The Governance Narrative: Key Findings and Lessons from the ESRC's Whitehall Programme', *Public Administration*, 78, 345–63.

Rhodes, R.A.W., Carmichael, P., McMillan, J. and Massey, A. (2003) *Decentralizing the Civil Service: From Unitary State to Differentiated Polity in the United Kingdom*, Buckingham: Open University Press.

Rhodes, R. A. W, and Wanna, J. (2007) 'The Limits to Public Value, or Rescuing

Responsible Government from the Platonic Guardians', *Australian Journal of Public Administration*, 66, 406–21.
Rhodes, R. A. W, and Wanna, J. (2008) 'Stairways to Heaven: A Reply to Alford', *Australian Journal of Public Administration*, 67, 367–70.
Richard, I. (2004) *Report of the Commission on the Powers and Electoral Arrangements of the National Assembly of Wales*, London: TSO.
Richards, D. and Smith, M. (2002) *Governance and Public Policy in the UK*, Oxford: Oxford University Press.
Richardson, J. J. and Jordan, A G. (1979) *Governing under Pressure: The Policy Process in a Post-Parliamentary Democracy*, Oxford: Martin Robertson.
Ridley, F. (1968) *Specialists and Generalists*, London: Allen and Unwin
Ridley, N. (1988) *The Local Right: Enabling not Providing*, London: Centre for Policy Studies.
Rouban, L. (1998) *La Fin des Technocrates?*, Paris: Presses de Sciences Po.
Rouban, L. (1999) 'Introduction: Citizens and the New Governance' in L. Rouban (ed.) *Citizens and the New Governance: Beyond Public Management*, Amsterdam: IOS Press.
Rouse, J. (1999) 'Performance Management, Quality and Contracts', in S. Horton and D. Farnham (eds) *Public Management in Britain*, Basingstoke: Palgrave Macmillan.
Rubin, I.S. and Kelly, J. (2005) 'Budget and Accounting Reforms', in E. Ferlie, L.E. Lynn and C. Pollitt (eds) *The Oxford Handbook of Public Management*, Oxford: OUP.
Samuels, M. (1998) *Towards Best Practice: An Evaluation of the First Two Years of the Public Sector Benchmark Project 1996–98*, London: Cabinet Office.
Sandford, M. (2002) *A Commentary on the Regional Government White Paper, Your Region, Your Choice: Revitalising the English Regions, Cm 5511*, London: Constitution Unit.
Scheers, B., Sterck, M. and Bouckaert, G. (2005) 'Lessons from Australian and British Reforms in Results Oriented Financial Management', *OECD Journal on Budgeting*, 5/2, 133–62.
Scotland Office (2009) *Scotland's Future in the United Kingdom*, Cm 7738, London: TSO.
Scotland Office (2010) *Strengthening Scotland's Future*, Cm 7973, London: TSO.
Scott, C. (2002) 'Private Regulation of the Public Sector: A Neglected Facet of Contemporary Governance', *Journal of Law and Society*, 29/1, 56–76.
Scott, D. (2009) 'Government beyond the Centre', in P. Cairney (ed.) *Scotland Devolution Monitoring Report: May 2009*, London: UCL Constitution Unit.
Scott, R. (1996) *Report of the Inquiry into the Export of Defence Equipment and Dual-Use Goods to Iraq and Related Prosecutions*, HC 115, London: HMSO.
Scottish Executive (2005) *The Government's Economic Strategy*, Edinburgh: Scottish Executive.
Scottish Government (2007) *The Government Economic Strategy*, Edinburgh: Scottish Government.
Scottish Government (2009) *Your Scotland, Your Voice: A National Conversation*, Edinburgh: Scottish Government.
Scottish Government (2010a) *Shaping Up: Core Review Report*, Edinburgh: Scottish Government.

Scottish Government (2010b) *Scotland's Spending Plans and Draft Budget 2011–12*, www.scotland.gov.uk, accessed 16 August 2010.

Scottish Government (2011) *Scottish Local Government Finance Statistics 2009–10*, Edinburgh: Scottish Government.

Sear, C. and Parry, K. (2011) 'Localism Bill: Local Government and Community Empowerment', *Research Paper 11/02*, London: House of Commons Library.

Seddon, J. (2008) *Systems Thinking in the Public Sector*, Axminster: Triachy Press.

Seebohm, F. (1968) *Report of the Committee on Local Authority and Allied Personal Social Services*, Cmnd 3703, London: HMSO.

Seely, A. (2004) 'Commissioners for Revenue and Customs Bill', *House of Commons Research Paper 04/90*, London: House of Commons Library.

Self, P. (1993) *Government by the Market? The Politics of Public Choice*, Basingstoke: Macmillan.

Shaoul, J. (2006) 'The Cost of Operating Britain's Privatized Railways', *Public Money and Management*, 26, 151–8.

Shaoul, J. (2007) 'Using the Private Sector to Finance Capital Expenditure: The Evidence', in C. Talbot and M. Baker (eds) *The Alternative Comprehensive Spending Review 2007*, Manchester: Manchester University Press.

Sheaff, R., Pickard, S. and Smith, K. (2002) 'Public Service Responsiveness to Users' Demands and Needs', *Public Administration*, 80, 435–52.

Shortland, J. (2010) 'New Development: The Evolution of Welsh Devolution', *Public Money and Management*, 30/2, 87–90.

Simmonds, G. (2002) *Regulation of the UK Electricity Industry*, Bath: Centre for Regulated Industries.

Simmonds, G. and Bartle, I. (2004) *The UK Gas Industry 2003/2004*, Bath: Centre for Regulated Industries.

Smith, A. ([1776] 1904) *An Inquiry into the Nature and Causes of the Wealth of Nations*, 5th edn, edited E. Cannan, London: Methuen.

Smith, I. R (2010) *Relocation: Transforming Where and How Government Works*, London: HM Treasury.

Smout, T. C. (1986) *A Century of the Scottish People 1830–1950*, London: Collins.

SSRB (Senior Salaries Review Board) (2004) *Twenty-Sixth Report on Senior Salaries*, London: TSO.

SSRB (2007) *Twenty-Ninth Report on Senior Salaries 2007*, London: TSO.

SSRB (2008) *Thirtieth Report on Senior Salaries 2008*, London: TSO.

SSRB (2010) *Thirty-Second Report on Senior Salaries 2010*, London: TSO.

Stein, W., Asenova, D., McCann, C. and Marshall, A. (2010) 'Modern Concepts of Quality and Risk: Challenges for the Regulation of Care of Older People in Scotland', *Public Policy and Administration*, 25/3, 305–26.

Stoker, G. (ed.) (1991) 'Reflections on Neighbourhood Decentralization in Tower Hamlets', *Public Administration*, 69, 373–84.

Stoker, G. (ed.) (1999) *The New Management of British Local Governance*, Basingstoke, Macmillan.

Stoker, G. (ed.) (2000) *The New Politics of British Local Governance*, Basingstoke, Macmillan.

Stoker, G. (2004) *Transforming :ocal Governance: From Thatcherism to New Labour*, Basingstoke, Palgrave Macmillan.

Stoker, G. (2011) 'Was Local Governance Such a Good Idea? A Global Comparative Perspective', *Public Administration*, 89, 15–31.
Storey, J. (1989) *New Perspectives in Human Resource Management*, London: Routledge.
Storey, J. (1992) *Developments in the Management of Human Resources*, Oxford: Blackwell.
Storey, J. (ed.) (1997) *Human Resource Management: a critical text*, London: Routledge.
Surveillance Studies Network (2006) *A Report on the Surveillance Society*, Wilmslow: Information Commissioner's Office.
Talbot, C. (1996) 'The Prisons Service: A Framework of Irresponsibility?', *Public Money and Management*, 16/1, 5–7.
Talbot, C. (1999) 'Public Performance: Towards a New Model?', *Public Policy and Administration*, 14/3, 15–34.
Talbot, C. (2007) 'Spending Reviews and Public Service Agreements', in C. Talbot and M. Baker (eds) *The Alternative Comprehensive Spending Review 2007*, Manchester: Manchester University Press.
Taylor, A. (2000) 'Hollowing out or Filling in? Taskforces and the Management of Cross-cutting Issues in British government', *British Journal of Politics and International Relations*, 2, 46–71.
Taylor, F. W. (1911) *Principles and Methods of Scientific Management*, New York: Harper.
Taylor, M. (2011) *Public Policy in the Community*, 2nd edn, Basingstoke: Palgrave.
Thain, C. (2002) 'Economic Policy', in P. Dunleavy, A. Gamble, R. Heffernan, I. Holliday and G. Peele (eds) *Developments in British Politics 6*, revd edn, Basingstoke: Palgrave.
Thatcher, Margaret (1987) Interview for *Woman's Own*, September 1987, Margaret Thatcher Foundation, www.margaretthatcher.org/document/106689, accessed 30 November 2011.
Thatcher, Mark (1998) 'Institutions, Regulation and Change: New Regulatory Agencies in British Privatised Utilities', *West European Politics*, 21/1, 120–47.
Theakston, K. (1995) *The Civil Service since 1945*, Oxford: Basil Blackwell.
Thompson, J. (1997) *Strategic Management: Awareness and Change*, 3rd edn, London: International Thomson Business.
Transport Committee (2004) *The Future of the Railway*, HC 145, London: TSO.
Travers, T., Jones, G. and Burnham, J. (1993) *The Impact of Population Size on Local Authority Costs and Effectiveness*, York: Joseph Rowntree Foundation.
Travers, T., Jones, G. and Burnham, J. (1997) *The Role of the Local Authority Chief Executive in Local Governance*, York: Joseph Rowntree Foundation.
Treasury Committee (2007) *The Efficiency Programme in the Chancellor's Departments*, HC 483, London: TSO.
Treasury Committee (2009) *Administration and Expenditure of the Chancellor's Departments, 2007–08*, HC 35, London: TSO.
Treasury Committee (2010) *Office for Budgetary Responsibility*, HC 385, London: TSO.
Treasury Committee (2011) *Private Finance Initiative*, HC 1146, London: TSO.
Trosa, S. (1994) *Next Steps: Moving On*, London: Office of Public Service and Science.

Van der Meer, F. (2004) 'Dutch Government Reform and the Quest for Political Control', in B. G. Peters and J. Pierre (eds) *Politicization of the Civil Service in Comparative Perspective: the quest for control*, London: Routledge.
Van Dooren, W., Bouckaert, G. and Halligan, J. (2010) *Performance Management in the Public Sector*, Abingdon: Routledge.
Van Dorpe, C. and Horton, S. (2011) 'The Public Service Bargain in the United Kingdom: The Whitehall Paradigm in Decline?', *Public Policy and Administration*, 26, 235–52.
Vroom, V. (1964) *Work and Motivation*, New York: Wiley and Sons.
WAG (Welsh Assembly Government) (2010) *Welsh Local Government Financial Statistics 2010*, Cardiff: WAG.
WAG (2011) *Final Budget 2011–2012*, Cardiff: WAG.
Wales Audit Office (2010) *International Peer Review of the Wales Audit Office: Update to the Public Accounts Committee*, Cardiff: Wales Audit Office.
Walshe, K. (2008) 'Regulation and Inspection of Health Services', in H. Davis and S. Martin (eds) *Public Services Inspection in the UK*, London: Jessica Kingsley Publishers.
Wanless, D. (2002) *Securing our Long-Term Health: Taking a Long Term View*, London: HM Treasury.
Webb, D. (2011) 'Recent PFI Developments', *Standard Note: SN/EP/06007*, London: House of Commons Library.
Weber, M. ([1921] 1947) 'Legal Authority with a Bureaucratic Administrative Staff', in *The Theory of Social and Economic Organization*, trans. A. M. Henderson and T. Parsons, New York: Free Press, 329–41.
Wehner, J. (2006) 'Assessing the Power of the Purse: An Index of Legislative Budget Institutions', *Political Studies*, 54, 767–85.
Wehner, J. (2010) *Legislatures and the Budget Process: The Myth of Fiscal Control*, Basingstoke: Palgrave Macmillan.
Weir, S. and Hall, W. (eds) (1994) *EGO Trip: Extra-Governmental Organisations in the United Kingdom and their Accountability*, Colchester: University of Essex: Democratic Audit/Scarman Trust.
Weller, P., Bakvis, H. and Rhodes, R.A.W. (eds) (1997) *The Hollow Crown: Countervailing Trends in Core Executives*, Basingstoke: Macmillan.
West Midlands Regional Assembly (2008) *Transforming Transport: Strategic Review 2000–2008: Consultation Draft*, Birmingham: West Midlands Regional Assembly.
White, G. and Drucker, J. (eds) (2009) *Reward Management*, London: Routledge.
Whitehead, C. (1988) 'Introduction: Theory and Practice', in C. Whitehead (ed.) *Reshaping the Nationalised Industries*, Oxford: Policy Journals.
Williams, R. (1998) *Performance Management: Perspectives on Employee Performance*, London: Thompson.
Williamson, O. (1975) *Markets and Hierarchies*, New York: The Free Press.
Wilson, D. (2003) 'Regulating Society: Quangos', in J. Fisher, D. Denver and J. Benyon (eds) *Central Debates in British Politics*, Harlow: Pearson.
Wilson, D. and Game, C. (2011) *Local Government in the United Kingdom*, 5th edn, Basingstoke: Palgrave Macmillan.
Wilson, J. Q. (1989) *Bureaucracy: What Government Agencies Do and Why They Do It*, New York: Basic Books.

Wilson, W. (1887) 'The Study of Administration', *Political Science Quarterly*, 2, June, 192–222.

Work and Pensions Committee (2006) *The Efficiency Savings Programme in Jobcentre Plus*, HC 834, London: TSO.

Yukl, G. (2002) *Leadership in Organizations*, London: Prentice-Hall.

Index